1-2-3 for the Macintosh Made Easy

1-2-3 for the Macintosh Made Easy

Mary Campbell

Osborne **McGraw-Hill**

Berkeley New York St. Louis San Francisco
Auckland Bogotá Hamburg London Madrid
Mexico City Milan Montreal New Delhi Panama City
Paris São Paulo Singapore Sydney
Tokyo Toronto

Osborne **McGraw-Hill**
2600 Tenth Street
Berkeley, California 94710
U.S.A.

For information on translations or book distributors outside of the U.S.A., please write to Osborne **McGraw-Hill** at the above address.

1-2-3 for the Macintosh Made Easy

1234567890 DOC 998765432

ISBN 0-07-881774-9

Publisher

Kenna S. Wood

Acquisitions Editor

Elizabeth Fisher

Associate Editor

Scott Rogers

Project Editor

Kathy Krause

Technical Editor

Sandra Horwich

Copy Editor

Paul Medoff

Proofing Coordinator

Nancy Pechonis

Proofreaders

Jeffrey Barash
Valerie Haynes Perry
Louise Sellers

Indexer

Richard Shrout

Director of Electronic Publishing

Deborah Wilson

Production Supervisor

Barry Bergin

Production Assistant

George Anderson

Computer Designer

Marcela V. Hancik

Illustrators

Lance Ravella
Fred Lass

Typesetters

Jani Beckwith
Helena Charm
J. E. Christgau
Peter Hancik
Susie Kim

Word Processor

Lynda Higham

Cover Design

Mason Fong

Contents at a Glance

Contents

Acknowledgments

This book is the result of the efforts of many individuals. I would like to extend my special thanks to the following individuals:

Gabrielle Lawrence, who helped with every phase of the book.

Liz Fisher, who worked with Lotus on the content needed for this book and managed the entire project.

Scott Rogers, who prepared all of our chapters for production.

Kathy Krause, who did a fine job as project editor.

Everyone in the production department at Osborne, who did their usual wonderful job with the production of this book.

John Ford at Apple, for loaning me a high-powered Mac and high resolution monitor to supplement my more basic Macintosh hardware.

Sandra Horwich, for her thorough technical review.

All of those at Lotus who were such an immense help through the beta process for 1-2-3 for the Macintosh.

Introduction

1-2-3 for the Macintosh is the long-awaited new release of 1-2-3 designed to utilize all of the Apple Macintosh features. A full-powered release of 1-2-3 that utilizes the Macintosh's unique graphical interface, the package is an advanced spreadsheet product that offers a familiar Macintosh environment and provides spreadsheet publishing, sophisticated presentation features, and macros for automating tasks.

1-2-3 for the Macintosh Made Easy is an introduction to Macintosh essentials as well as the features of 1-2-3 for the Macintosh. You will find that it will get you started quickly, whether you are new to 1-2-3 or just to the Macintosh version of the product.

About This Book

This book is designed to present 1-2-3's features in an easy-to-learn format. You will use these new features as you create practical application examples. Because you are introduced to the commands in the context of application examples, you will not only see the keystrokes used to make things happen, but will also learn what capabilities these features offer. Special application paragraphs, set off with apple icons, highlight additional ideas for putting specific features to work for you.

The exercises within the book are presented in a step-by-step tutorial format to guarantee your success. Knowing when to use a command is not left to chance, since you are offered detailed instructions throughout.

How This Book Is Organized

This book is divided into 14 chapters and two appendixes. Each chapter is designed to contain just the right number of new features to cover in a single session. The first few chapters provide the building blocks for your first 1-2-3 document. After you have mastered these topics, you will probably want to progress through the remaining topics sequentially, leading gradually to more advanced topics. If you are already familiar with 1-2-3, you may want to move directly to the more advanced examples. Because the models in the later chapters are self-contained, you can also work with them without first becoming familiar with the examples in earlier chapters. The building block approach presented in this book will help you increase your 1-2-3 skills rapidly as you move from chapter to chapter.

Chapter 1, "Worksheet Basics," will get you started with 1-2-3 for the Macintosh. It explains how to start the software and how to use the mouse and the keyboard to select cells. It also details the important features of the 1-2-3 workspace.

Chapter 2, "Entering Text and Numbers," provides techniques for entering text and numbers on the worksheet. It introduces error correction and the Undo feature as well as access to 1-2-3's help features.

Chapter 3, "Defining Your Calculations," provides an introduction to the use of formulas in the worksheet. You will learn how to use formulas to add "what-if" capabilities, which make your worksheet a powerful tool.

Chapter 4, "@Functions and Other Formula Options," provides the information that you will need to use @functions in the models that you build. In this chapter, you will also learn how to reference data from other spreadsheets.

Chapter 5, "Menus, Dialog Boxes, and Palettes," focuses on the use of these essential elements. You will find that the Macintosh environment makes it easy to select what you need to complete 1-2-3 tasks quickly.

Chapter 6, "Changing the Appearance of Worksheet Entries," provides information on tailoring the format of your entries to your needs. You will learn how to work with groups of cells, called ranges, and with multiple ranges, called collections. You will learn how to select currency, fixed, percent, scientific notation, date, or other cell formats on the worksheet. You will also learn about using fonts, colors, and borders for controlling the appearance of your entries.

Chapter 7, "Changing Row and Column Options," shows you how to alter attributes of one or more columns or rows. You will learn how to change the width of columns and the height of rows. You will also learn how to hide and redisplay columns.

Chapter 8, "Managing Documents and Sheets," shows you how to protect your investment in information through the use of files that can be stored permanently on your disk. You will learn about using multiple files simultaneously, as well as how to use multiple documents within one file.

Chapter 9, "Making 1-2-3 Do Your Work," describes the many functions 1-2-3 provides to help you save time while accomplishing your spreadsheet goals. For example, you can copy entries that you have already made to other locations on the worksheet, or rearrange worksheet data to change 1-2-3 documents. You will also learn to use 1-2-3's search feature to locate cell entries quickly.

Chapter 10, "Printing Your Worksheet," provides explanations and examples of 1-2-3's print features. You will learn how to do everything from printing a draft of your worksheet to adding headers and other sophisticated options.

Chapter 11, "Creating Graphs," introduces 1-2-3's graphing features, which provide tools for presenting numeric data in an understandable fashion. You will learn how to print a graph along with your other worksheet entries.

Chapter 12, "Data-Management Basics," covers the data-management features of the package. You can use these to create a simple database. You will also find examples that show you how to sort information in the database and selectively copy information to create a quick report.

Chapter 13, "Advanced Techniques," introduces the powerful problem-solving capabilities of Backsolve. The chapter also introduces you to features for adding drawings to the worksheet. You will also learn how to extract data from your current 1-2-3 document for use in other documents.

Chapter 14, "Macros," examines the basics of 1-2-3 macros, including the 1-2-3 Macro Transcript window, which makes macro creation easy. You will learn how to record keystrokes so that you can execute commands at a later time.

The appendixes provide detailed installation instructions and a reference containing essential Macintosh features.

Conventions Used in This Book

Throughout this book you will be instructed to make entries in 1-2-3 documents. The entries you are to type will be shown in boldface. If you are already somewhat familiar with the technique being presented, you can scan the instructions quickly and enter only the information in boldface to perform the exercise.

In each instruction requiring a menu selection, the full menu command is shown. You can choose to type the highlighted letter of each menu option, highlight the desired option and press (enter), or select the desired option with a mouse.

1

Worksheet Basics

You are about to enter the world of 1-2-3 for the Macintosh. This journey will give you a new way of working with everyday business problems—a way that is both efficient and flexible. Traditionally, accountants and business managers have worked out business problems and evaluated financial decisions using green-bar columnar pads. 1-2-3 replaces the paper versions of these worksheets by turning your computer into a larger, electronic version of this columnar pad.

You will learn to use 1-2-3's worksheet features to handle the same types of problems previously solved on columnar pads. Applications such as budgeting, financial planning, project cost projections, break-even analysis, and cost planning are some of the applications you might consider. You will also learn to pattern calculations after real-world situations and lay out worksheets representing the problem to be solved. Since you will be working with the Macintosh, you will learn how to use all of 1-2-3's features to take advantage of the Macintosh's graphical interface, including on-sheet graphs and drawing.

The electronic worksheet that 1-2-3 places into your computer's memory has a structure organized to help you construct these worksheets. The electronic worksheet is arranged into rows, columns, and sheets that you can use to better organize your data. This structure allows you to enter numbers, text, and computations in many locations. Making entries on 1-2-3's worksheet offers significant advantages over making them on paper. For example, on a paper worksheet, you must update calculations every time you change a number; however, because 1-2-3 remembers calculations, it recalculates the worksheet automatically when you update a number.

In this chapter, you look at beginning and ending a 1-2-3 session and at worksheet organization. It is in this chapter that you will gain the understanding you need to use 1-2-3's features effectively.

Although you probably are eager to start using 1-2-3's features right away, you may have to complete some preliminary work first. Before you begin, 1-2-3 must be installed on your hard disk. Appendix A, "Installing 1-2-3 for the Macintosh," provides instructions for installing 1-2-3. If you are not familiar with the Macintosh, you may want to read Appendix B, "Using the Macintosh," to familiarize yourself with the basic Macintosh features you may use in 1-2-3.

Starting and Quitting 1-2-3

To use 1-2-3, you must be able to open and close 1-2-3. As with other Macintosh applications, opening an application makes it available to be used. Starting 1-2-3 is easy. All you need to do is open the folder with the Lotus 1-2-3 application document. Next, double-click the Lotus 1-2-3 icon. (A *double-click* is two presses of the mouse button in rapid succession with the pointer on a name or icon.) 1-2-3 is opened and a blank untitled worksheet is opened automatically.

When you have finished all of your 1-2-3 tasks for the day, you will want to leave 1-2-3. Choose Quit from the File menu to end your session. To make this selection, move the pointer to File and *drag* it (move the mouse while holding the button) downward until Quit is highlighted. Quit displays ⌘-Q next to it, telling you that you can also choose this command by holding down the ⌘ key while you press Q.

Once you tell 1-2-3 that you want to quit, 1-2-3 displays a prompt for saving each open worksheet that you have changed and have not saved. You can select Yes to save a worksheet under its current name, select No to close a worksheet without saving it, select Save As and supply a new name for the worksheet, or select Cancel to remain in 1-2-3. When you leave 1-2-3, you are returned to the Macintosh desktop.

Worksheet Organization and the 1-2-3 Window

When you open 1-2-3, you see the 1-2-3 workspace. Your screen should look similar to the one shown in Figure 1-1. Due to different monitors, your screen may look different. For example, W'Sheet may be spelled out as Worksheet, and more columns and rows may appear on the worksheet. In addition to the worksheet, there are other elements on the screen that will be discussed later in this chapter. These special elements are marked in Figure 1-1.

This initial display lets you see only a few columns and rows (the upper-left corner) of the first sheet in the worksheet. The sheet is actually much larger than it first appears. A sheet has 256 columns, named A to IV, and 8192 rows, numbered from 1 to 8192. Columns use single letters first, then AA to AZ, BA to BZ, and so on.

1-2-3 lets you insert extra *sheets* into a worksheet just as you might add extra sheets to a folder or notebook. Although a new worksheet has only one sheet, sheet A, you can add as many as 255 additional sheets for a total of 256 sheets in a worksheet. Sheets are named like columns, with single letters used first and then double-letter combinations beginning with AA and ending with IV. The first sheet is A, and the last is IV. You do not need to concern yourself with additional sheets just yet. You will want to explore many of 1-2-3's possibilities with one sheet before adding sheets. Figure 1-2 shows a diagram of a worksheet, which you can compare to the small portion that is visible when you first open 1-2-3.

Cells and the Pointer

Each location on the worksheet is referred to as a *cell.* Each cell is uniquely identified by its *sheet location*, its *column location,* and its *row location.* When

Figure 1-1. *Initial 1-2-3 display*

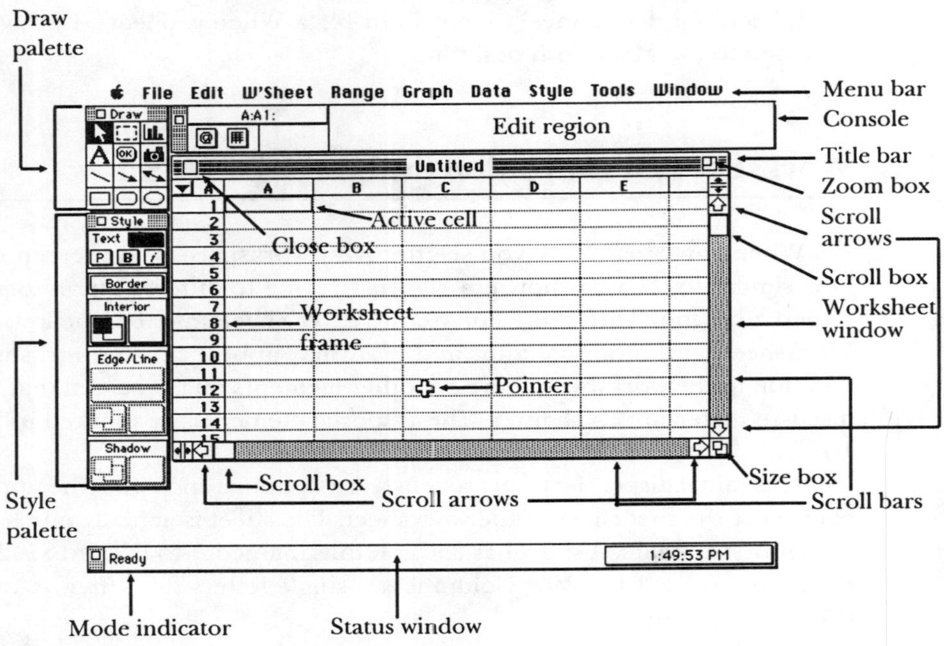

you combine these three pieces of information, you have a *cell address.* Giving 1-2-3 a cell address is like giving someone an address, providing the city, street name, and street number to indicate the correct location. If you do not provide a sheet in a cell address (which is comparable to indicating which page of a notepad to use), 1-2-3 assumes you are referring to the current sheet, just as you might give someone a street name and number with the assumption that the address is in the current city.

Since you will work initially only with sheet A, when you do not specify a sheet, 1-2-3 automatically assumes you want to use sheet A. When you do specify a sheet, follow the sheet letter with a colon to indicate to 1-2-3 that it is a sheet letter. The column letter and the row number are next. For example, you can indicate locations such as A:A1, A:C10, D:IV8192, A:Z1025, and

Figure 1-2. *Structure of a 1-2-3 worksheet*

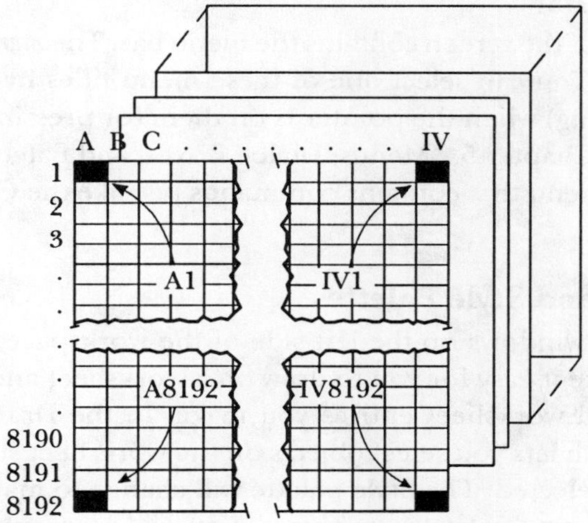

IJ850. 1-2-3 displays the sheet letters, column letters, and row numbers in a *worksheet frame,* which is the top and left border of the worksheet window in Figure 1-1.

Your worksheet always has an active cell. The *active cell* is important since it is the cell where you will record an entry. To change the cell where you make an entry, you must select another cell to be the active cell. You can distinguish this cell from others by the frame around its borders. You can also look at the console near the top of the screen to see its cell address displayed.

The 1-2-3 Workspace

The 1-2-3 workspace has several components. They are identified in Figure 1-1. This workspace includes a menu bar and five windows: the Draw palette, the Style palette, the console, the worksheet window, and the status window. Each window includes a close box and a bar at the top or left that you can use to move the window to a new location.

The Menu Bar

The top of the screen contains the menu bar. The *menu bar* displays 1-2-3's menu titles. You can select one of these menu titles by pressing the mouse button (*clicking*) when the pointer is on them (or pressing (option)-(/)). As you will learn in Chapter 5, "Menus, Dialog Boxes, and Palettes," each menu title has its own menu that contains commands just like the Quit command in the File menu.

The Draw and Style Palettes

The two windows on the left side of the workspace, the Draw and Style palettes, make it easy for you to draw on a worksheet and to add styles to the drawings and worksheet entries you make. In the Draw palette, the arrow pointer, which lets you select objects on the worksheet such as the active cell, is normally selected. The Style palette will change to match the types of style changes you can make to an object. You will learn more about the Draw palette in Chapter 11, "Creating Graphs," and Chapter 13, "Advanced Techniques." You will learn more about the Style palette in Chapter 6, "Changing the Appearance of Worksheet Entries." If you do not see the Draw palette, you can show it by pressing (⌘)-(D).(You can also select the Draw command from the Tools menu.) If you do not see the Style palette, you can show it by pressing (⌘)-(Y) (the keyboard shortcut of the Show|Hide Palette command in the Style menu).

The Console

Just below the menu bar is the console. The *console* displays the address of the active cell on the upper-left side, and the contents of the cell on the right side, the *edit region*. As you make an entry, 1-2-3 also displays *confirm* and *cancel buttons* below the address. These look like a green check mark and a red X, respectively, which you can select to accept or cancel your entry. The console also includes the Function pop-up and Range pop-up menus, which look like the @ sign and the grid, below the address. If you do not see the console, you can show it by choosing Floaters from the Window menu (drag the pointer from Window to Floaters) and then choosing Show Console (drag the pointer from Floaters to the right or left to highlight Show Console).

The Status Window

The *Status window* provides information about the current 1-2-3 session. It tells you what mode 1-2-3 is in so you know what type of information 1-2-3 expects from you. The Status window also displays various indicators that display the status of various 1-2-3 features. Finally, the status window contains the time, but it can also contain the date or the remaining memory. If you do not see the status window, you can show it by choosing Floaters from the Window menu (drag the pointer from Window to Floaters) and then choosing Show Status (drag the pointer from Floaters to the right or left to highlight Show Status).

Most of the time, the *mode indicator* is Ready, indicating that 1-2-3 is ready to respond to whatever you enter. The mode indicator can tell you either that 1-2-3 is busy with your previous request or that it is ready to do something new. It can also tell you to correct an error, point to a worksheet location, or select a menu choice. Once 1-2-3's mode indicator changes from Ready to another mode, you must either follow along with 1-2-3 or find a way to change the indicator. Many new users become frustrated at this point, but you can avoid difficulties by watching the mode indicator and staying in sync with the current mode. Table 1-1 lists all the modes you will encounter, along with their meanings. They will also be pointed out in later chapters as new activities cause mode changes.

The *status indicators* inform you that you have pressed a key combination, have a feature turned on, or that you need to know something about your session–perhaps that you are low in memory. For example, if you press the (end) key on an extended keyboard, you will see End in the status window. Other status indicators–Calc, Circ, Cmd, File, Group, Mem, RO, SST, and Step–monitor advanced features and have broader meanings. They will be discussed as they occur later in the book.

The Worksheet Window

The remaining area of your 1-2-3 workspace is for *worksheet windows.* Initially, 1-2-3 puts an empty worksheet named Untitled in a worksheet window. A worksheet window has a title bar that includes a close box, a

Table 1-1. *Mode Indicators*

Indicator	Meaning
Edit	You are editing an entry. The entry can be in a cell or in response to a command. 1-2-3 switches to Edit mode when you try finalizing a cell entry that contains an error.
Error	1-2-3 has encountered an error.
Files	1-2-3 is listing files in its Classic menu.
Find	The Data Query command is highlighting database records that you have told it to find.
Label	1-2-3 has decided that you are entering text.
Menu	1-2-3 is waiting for you to make a selection from the menu.
Point	1-2-3 is waiting for you to point to a cell or range.
Ready	1-2-3 is waiting for you to make a new request.
Value	1-2-3 has decided that you are entering a value.
Wait	1-2-3 is busy processing your last command or entry. The pointer will appear as a watch while this indicator is displayed.

document title, and a zoom box that let you close and move the 1-2-3 window, as described in Appendix B, "Using the Macintosh." You can drag anywhere on the *title bar,* the striped bar at the top of the window with a name in the center, to move the window to a new location. You can click the *close box,* at the left of the title bar, to close the worksheet window. You can click the *zoom box,* at the right of the title bar, to enlarge the worksheet window to fill the area not used by the other windows or click it a second time to return the window to its previous size. You can drag the *size box,* in the lower-right corner of the window, to change the location of the lower-right window corner.

Moving Around the Worksheet

Now you are ready to learn about navigating 1-2-3's worksheet. This will prepare you for constructing worksheets. You will look at the basic features as well as the more advanced options that let you travel long distances quickly.

Before you can make an entry into a cell, you must select the cell, making it the *active cell.* You can select a cell with the mouse or the keyboard and the results will be the same.

Selecting Cells with the Mouse

1-2-3's basic cell selections are accomplished with the mouse. 1-2-3 for the Macintosh, like other Macintosh applications, is designed to be used with a mouse. Using a mouse lets you make selections by pointing to what you want and pressing the button on the mouse. Pressing the button once is called *clicking.* Pressing the button twice quickly is called *double-clicking. Dragging* means that you hold down the button as you move the mouse to a new position. For example, to select a command from a menu, point to the menu (File, for example) and drag the mouse down to choose the command you want (such as Quit).

The mouse's position on the screen is usually indicated by a *pointer* that looks like a cross or arrow, but it can change to other shapes. For example, when you first start 1-2-3, the pointer looks like a watch; 1-2-3 is telling you to wait until 1-2-3 is ready. You will be introduced to other pointer appearances with the features that use them.

When you want to select a cell with a mouse, click the cell you want. If the cell you want is off the screen, you can change the part of the worksheet that displays in the window by using the scroll bars. The *scroll bars* are the bars on the right and at the bottom of the worksheet window. Each scroll bar has a scroll box. These *scroll boxes* represent your horizontal and vertical positions in the worksheet. By clicking the scroll bar on either side of the scroll box, you can display the previous or next section of worksheet columns or rows. You can also drag the scroll box to a new position on the scroll bar, which changes the displayed worksheet to match the scroll box's new location. If you want to shift the display one row or column at a time, click the arrows at the end of the scroll bars. If you want a cell on another sheet, use the sheet pop-up menu in the upper-left corner of the worksheet frame, as you will learn about in Chapter 8, "Managing Documents and Sheets."

Selecting Cells with the Keyboard

You can also select cells using the keyboard. As you press keys on the keyboard that change the active cell, the border around the active cell moves, and the active cell's contents are displayed in the console. The four basic keys available for any keyboard are the four arrow keys, which each select the next cell in the given direction. You can also use tab or shift-tab in place of → and ← and use return or shift-return in place of ↓ and ↑. Figure 1-3 shows an Apple keyboard and an extended keyboard with many of the keys that you will use to select cells. The extended Apple keyboard contains other keys that you can use in addition to the arrow keys, shift, tab and return.

Note: *On the extended keyboard there are two keys that perform delete functions; they are marked* delete *and* del*. The* delete *key corresponds to the* backspace *key on earlier keyboards, and when pressed it will delete the character to the left of the insertion point. The* del *key, also marked with a* ⌦*, is found only on the extended keyboards. When it is pressed,* del *will delete the character to the right of the insertion point. For purposes of clarity, in this book the* delete *key is called* delete/backspace*, and the* del *key is called the* del *key.*

Even if your keyboard is slightly different, you should find it relatively easy to locate the arrow keys and any other keys your keyboard provides. The keys that you might use to select a cell are listed in Table 1-2. In addition, you can press *key combinations*, for example control-←, which means you hold down the control key while pressing ←.

Figure 1-3. *Apple and Apple extended keyboards*

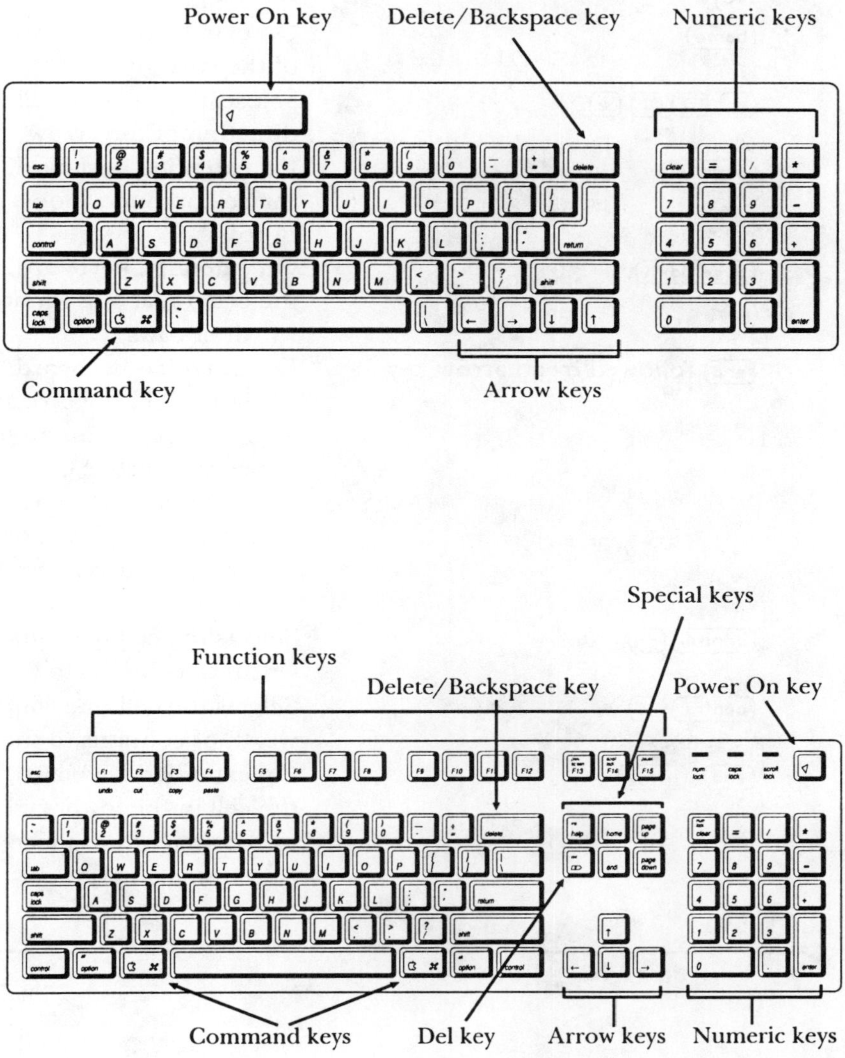

Table 1-2. Worksheet Selection Keys

Keys	Action
home	On extended keyboard selects A1 of the current sheet
← → ↑ ↓	Selects the cell one cell in the direction of the arrow
page up	On extended keyboard, selects the cell up one window's worth of rows
page down	On extended keyboard, selects the cell down one window's worth of rows
end followed by an arrow key	On extended keyboard, selects the last cell in the direction of the arrow that contains an entry, if the current active cell contains an entry; or selects the next cell with an entry in the direction of the arrow if the current active cell is empty
control-→	Selects the cell one window's worth of columns to the right
control-←	Selects the cell one window's worth of columns to the left
end home	On extended keyboard, selects the cell in the lower-right corner of the area of the sheet containing entries

Review

In this chapter you learned how 1-2-3 organizes data and how you can select a cell on the worksheet. You also learned how you can use the console and the status window to provide more information about your 1-2-3 session.

- To start 1-2-3 for the Macintosh, first open the folder containing the Lotus 1-2-3 application document. Next, double-click Lotus 1-2-3. You can leave 1-2-3 for the Macintosh by choosing the Quit command from the File menu, or by pressing ⌘-Q.
- The cell that you can make your entry into is the active cell. You can change which cell you will make an entry into by changing the active cell. Use the mouse or the keys in the following section, "Keys and Commands," to change which cell is active. With a mouse, click the cell you want and use the scroll bars to change the portion of the worksheet displayed in the worksheet window.
- The 1-2-3 workspace is divided into a menu bar and five windows: the Style palette, the Draw palette, the console, the worksheet window, and the status window. The console and the status window provide valuable information about 1-2-3 including the active cell, its contents, the mode indicator, and any status indicators.

Keys and Commands

In this chapter you learned about the 1-2-3 for the Macintosh user interface. You also learned what keys to press to move through the worksheet. Those keys and their descriptions are listed in the following table. Commands and their descriptions are also listed. For example, File Quit in the following table means the Quit command in the File menu.

Entry	Action
⌘-D	Displays or hides the Draw palette window
⌘-Y	Displays or hides the Style palette window
control-←	Selects the cell one window's worth of columns to the left

control-→	Selects the cell one window's worth of columns to the right
↓ or return	Selects the next cell down
end followed by an arrow	On extended keyboard, selects the next cell after a series of cells with entries, or empty cells in the direction of the next arrow key
end home	On extended keyboard, selects the cell in the last column and the last row containing entries
File Quit (⌘-Q)	Leaves 1-2-3 and closes any worksheet
home	On extended keyboard, selects cell A1
← or shift-tab	Selects the next cell to the left
page down	On extended keyboard, selects the cell one screenful of rows down
page up	On extended keyboard, selects the cell one screenful of rows up
→ or tab	Selects the next cell to the right
↑ or shift-return	Selects the next cell up
Window Floaters	Shows or hides the console or status window from the 1-2-3 workspace

2

Entering Text and Numbers

The worksheets you create represent business problems and calculations that you need to solve repeatedly. To create these worksheets with 1-2-3, you will make entries in worksheet cells. No matter how sophisticated a worksheet you create, it will be composed of text and value entries. Text entries describe the values on the worksheet and represent data that is not numeric. Value entries can consist of numeric constants and a variety of different types of formulas. Typically, you start creating a worksheet by entering text and numbers and then move on to the more difficult task of formula creation.

In this chapter, you'll look at entering numbers and text on the worksheet, correcting data-entry errors, using the Undo feature, and accessing 1-2-3's Help feature. Since this chapter covers some of the basic building blocks of worksheet construction, you will want to master it completely before progressing to more advanced topics.

Types of Worksheet Entries

1-2-3 has two basic types of entries for worksheet cells: text entries and value entries. *Text entries* are characters that describe numeric data in the worksheet or store character information such as a name. Text entries are not used in arithmetic calculations, even if the text contains numbers. *Values,* on the other hand, consist of either numbers or formulas. *Formulas* result in numbers but are entered as a series of calculations to perform. 1-2-3 allows only specific entries for values.

1-2-3 determines whether you are entering a value or text based on the first character you type. If this first character is not one of the characters that 1-2-3 considers the start of a value entry, it is treated as text.

Applications: *Although most people think of using 1-2-3 for calculations, you can create many applications with simple text and number entries. You might maintain a list of customers along with their addresses and phone numbers and use nothing more than text entries to record the data. Other application ideas using only text entries and numbers are a price list, a schedule of shipping costs, and a list of suppliers.*

Entering Text

Entering text is as simple as typing the characters you want to appear in the cell. If you type **Sales**, 1-2-3 treats the entry as text because the first character in the entry is an alphabetic character. As soon as you type the **S**, 1-2-3 changes the Ready mode indicator to Label. Since 1-2-3 always makes its determination from the first character, entering **15 Johnson St.** causes 1-2-3 to reject your entry when you attempt to finalize it. The first character is numeric, and 1-2-3 attempts to treat the entire entry as a value. 1-2-3 is very stubborn once it determines the type of entry it thinks you planned for a cell. The only way you can change its mind is by editing the entry, clicking the Cancel button, or pressing ⌘-. (period) or esc to start over. After a little practice with entering text, however, you will know all the tricks to put you in command of how your entries are interpreted.

Text entries in 1-2-3 start with alignment prefixes. *Alignment prefixes* indicate both that an entry is text and how the text is aligned within a cell. Most of your entries will use one of three alignment prefixes—an apostrophe

('), a quotation mark ("), or a caret (^). The difference between these three alignment prefixes is how 1-2-3 aligns the contents of the cell. The ' is the default and left aligns the text entry in the cell. This is the alignment prefix 1-2-3 generates for you if you do not enter one. Using " right aligns the text in the cell, and using ^ centers the text. If you choose right or center alignment, first type " or ^, and then type the text that the cell will contain. If you want to enter text that begins with a character that 1-2-3 considers to be a value, you can start your entry with one of the three alignment prefixes to trick 1-2-3 into treating it as text. To start a worksheet that contains several text entries, try the following exercise:

1. Select A1 so that it is the active cell.
2. Type **Profit Report** and, to finalize the entry, click the Confirm button (the button with the check) in the console region of the screen or press (enter) (it's on the numeric keypad on the right).

As soon as you type the **P**, the mode indicator changes from Ready to Label. If you make a mistake, press (delete)/(backspace) to remove the incorrect characters. You also will see a small bar that moves along in the cell as you make your entry. This is the *insertion point,* since it indicates where the characters you type are inserted. When you finalize the entry, 1-2-3 adds an apostrophe as an alignment prefix to the entry in the console, since that is the default alignment prefix and you did not type one. This apostrophe will not appear in the cell itself.

3. Click A2 or press (↓), type **Prepared by Accounting**, and click A3 or press (return).

In addition to finalizing entries with the Confirm button or (enter) to keep the same cell selected, you have many other options. You can press (return) to finalize the entry and select the cell below your entry. You can press (tab) to finalize the entry and select the cell to the right of your entry. You can also finalize an entry by clicking another cell to select it or by using an arrow key. The results are the same, although moving to another cell to finalize an entry saves you the time it takes to finalize your entry and move to another cell with two different mouse selections or keystrokes.

4. Move to C4.

Whether you use the mouse or keyboard to move to a cell makes no difference to 1-2-3. When the steps tell you to move to a cell, use the keyboard or mouse—whichever is more convenient for you. You can use any combination of keys that moves to the cell you want.

5. Type **^Smith Co,** and press (return) or click C5.

This entry is centered within the cell because you typed ^ as the alignment prefix.

6. Type **^Division A** and click the Confirm button or press (return).
7. Move to B7, type **"Q1**, and click C7 or press (tab).

This entry is right aligned within the cell because you typed " as the alignment prefix.

8. Type **"Q2** and click D7 or press (tab).
9. Type **"Q3** and click E7 or press (tab).
10. Type **"Q4** and click the Confirm button or press (return).
11. Move to A8, type **1991 Profit**, and click the Confirm button or press (return).

1-2-3 beeps and changes "Value" in the status window that appeared during your entry to "Edit" because this entry contains an error. When you typed the **1**, 1-2-3 assumed that you were entering a value. You may have noticed that 1-2-3 displayed the Value mode indicator. Since "Profit" is not part of a value entry, 1-2-3 did not accept the entry. To fix this entry, you need to tell 1-2-3 that you want to treat the entry as text.

12. Click the first 1 in 1991, or press (home) (if you have an extended keyboard) once, or the (←) repeatedly, to move the insertion point to the beginning of the entry; type ', and click the Confirm button or press (return).

1-2-3 now treats this as text because an alignment prefix is the first character of the entry. Like other alignment prefixes that you or 1-2-3 put as the first character, the alignment prefix does not display in the cell on the worksheet.

13. Type **'1992 Profit** and click the Confirm button or press (enter).

This entry is automatically treated as text, because typing the ' causes 1-2-3 to change the mode indicator from Ready to Label. At this point, your text entries look like those shown in Figure 2-1.

Entering Numbers

Numbers are one of the two types of 1-2-3 value entries. As value entries, numbers follow much more rigid rules than do text entries. Like text entries, numbers are constant; they do not change as the result of arithmetic calculations. They do not change unless you take some direct action to change them. Numbers can contain any of the numeric digits from 0 to 9. The other acceptable characters for beginning value entries are the period (.), the plus

Figure 2-1. *Worksheet with text and numbers entered*

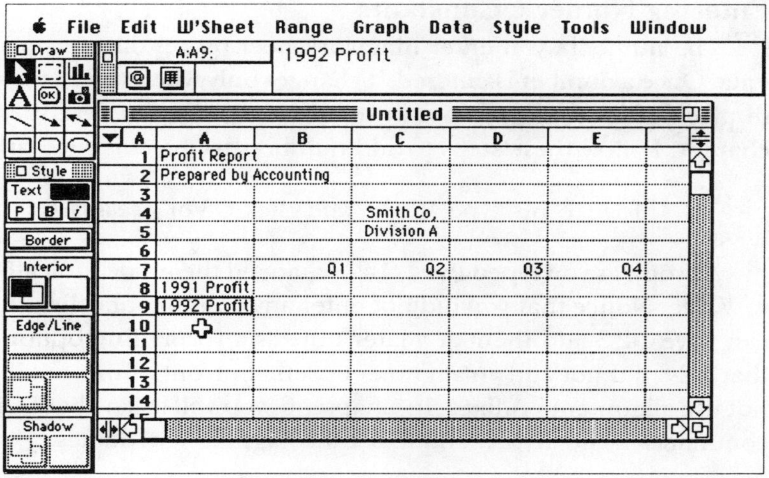

sign (+), the equal sign (=), a left parenthesis ((), the dollar sign ($), the @ sign, and the minus sign (–). The . indicates a decimal point, the + indicates a positive number, and the – indicates a negative number.

Several other characters can be part of a numeric entry in special situations. A percent sign (%) at the end of a numeric entry indicates a percentage, but it is not allowed in other positions within the entry. Spaces cannot be added to numeric entries. Commas, dollar signs, and other formatting characters should be added with formatting, discussed in Chapter 6, "Changing the Appearance of Worksheet Entries." The only letter numeric entries may use is the letter E or e to represent numbers in powers of 10 (referred to as *scientific notation*). For example, 3.86E–5 is .0000386. This number can also be represented as $3.86*10^{-5}$ or 3.86 times .00001.

1-2-3 for the Macintosh also supports the entry of special numbers that represent dates and times. These numbers are called *date and time numbers* and uniquely represent any date and time.

Applications: *Numbers are the basis for your calculations. The types of numbers you enter vary by location. For example, in a checking account register, you would enter check numbers, deposits and withdrawals as numbers. In a product listing, you would enter the product quantities and prices as numbers. Some information, like product numbers, might be entered as text, since these numbers may also contain non-numeric characters, like letters.*

Entering Numeric Constants

The numbers you enter in a worksheet represent the constant numeric data. Once a number is entered, it changes only when you enter a new number in place of it or when you edit the existing entry as described later in this chapter. Follow these steps to add numbers to the current worksheet:

1. Move to B8, type **40000**, and click C8 or press tab.

As soon as you typed the **4**, 1-2-3 changed the mode indicator from Ready to Value. Notice that you did not enter any commas or other characters. You can have 1-2-3 add them at a later time as a formatting option. Also, notice that 1-2-3 did not add an alignment prefix in front of this number. Values do not use alignment prefixes. In Chapter 6, you will learn about using the Align command in the Style menu to set the alignment of values.

2. Type **80000** and click D8 or press (tab).
3. Type **20000** and click E8 or press (tab).
4. Type **–10000** and click the Confirm button or press (return).

Since the first character is a –, 1-2-3 treats the entry as a value and the number that you subsequently enter as a negative number.

5. Complete the entries for the 1991 profit by entering the following numbers in the indicated cells:

B9:	**–30000**
C9:	**–20000**
D9:	**15000**
E9:	**45000**

Figure 2-2 shows the result of entering each number. Remember that it is easy to change any of the entries by simply typing a new number or editing a cell.

Since this is the last entry you will make in the worksheet, save a copy of the worksheet to disk. The commands that handle documents are covered in detail in Chapter 8, "Managing Documents and Sheets." For now, all you need to know is the menu command for saving a document. You can use either the mouse or the keyboard to make your selections. To use the mouse, move the pointer to the File menu, drag down the pull-down menu until Save is highlighted, and release the mouse button to choose Save. With the keyboard, press (⌘)-(S). 1-2-3 displays a dialog box for entering information about saving your current document. You will learn more about dialog boxes in Chapter 5, "Menus, Dialog Boxes, and Palettes."

At this point, tell 1-2-3 the document name you want to use for the worksheet by typing **Profits** (the document name may contain up to thirty characters, including spaces, if you wish, with no colons (:) or backslashes (\). Then press (return) or click the button labeled Save. To remove this document from the screen, click the close box in the upper-left corner of the document or press (⌘)-(W). You can also choose Close from the File menu. 1-2-3 closes the Profits document.

You must open a document before making any additional entries. You can use the New command in the File menu to open a new document or the

Figure 2-2. *Worksheet created with text and values*

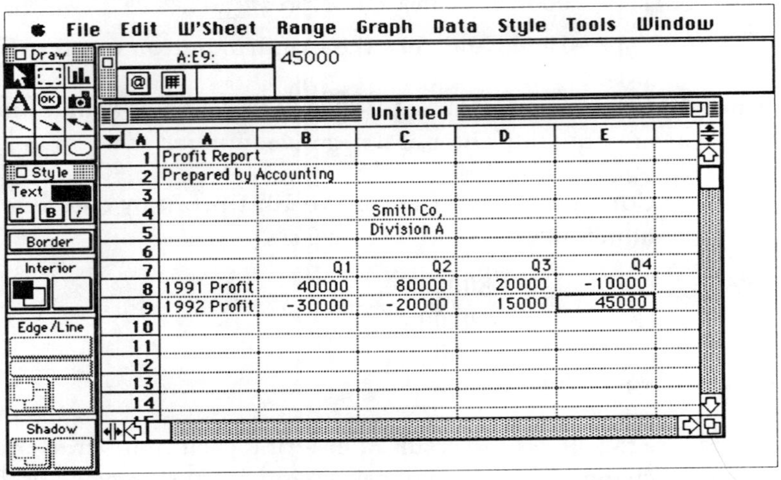

Open command in the File menu to open a document you created earlier. Since you will want a new document to practice correcting errors later in the chapter, choose New from the File menu or press ⌘-N.

Entering Dates and Times

Dates and times can be stored as numbers or text in 1-2-3. You will want to store your dates and times as numbers if you ever want to use them in calculations. To enter a date as text, use an alignment prefix. To enter a date as a number, simply type the date or time in any of the valid formats mentioned later in this section.

Each date and time is assigned a unique number that allows you to use this entry in calculations at a later time. Since it is actually quicker to enter dates or times as values, you will want to enter them as numbers to allow yourself maximum flexibility later.

1-2-3 supports date entries between January 1, 1900 and December 31, 2099. 1-2-3 assigns a date number of 1 to January 1, 1900, and a date number of 73050 to December 31, 2099. Each date between the first and last date is assigned the next sequential number. It is never necessary for you to know the date number to record a date, since you can use an entry that looks like a date to have 1-2-3 record your entry as a date number. To enter a date, you can use either of these formats:

31-Dec-91
12/31/91

If you enter **12/31/91** in a cell, your entry displays as the date number 33603. In Chapter 6, "Changing the Appearance of Worksheet Entries," you will learn how to format these entries to make them appear as dates on the worksheet while they continue to show as date numbers in the edit region.

You can enter a time for any hour, minute, and second in a day. 1-2-3 assigns a unique time number for each second in a day. This number is a decimal fraction ranging from .0 for midnight to .9999884259259 26925 for 11:59:59 p.m. You can use any of these time formats for your entry:

12:59:59
12:59
12:59:59 PM
12:59 PM

You can use these dates and times in calculations. For example, you can subtract two date numbers to determine the number of elapsed days between them.

You cannot enter a date and a time in the same cell, as in **31-Dec-91 6:00 PM**. 1-2-3 *can* store dates and times in the same cell, for instance when a cell contains 33603.75 for 31-Dec-91 6:00 P.M., but this combined date and time is the result of entering the time and date *number* in the cell rather than 31-Dec-91 6:00 PM. (It could also be the result of a calculation.) When you learn in Chapter 6 how to make date and time numbers appear as the date and time they represent, you can have a date and time number appear as a date or a time but not both.

Applications: *Some of the dates you will use in your own applications could include an employee's hire date and the ship dates of invoiced goods.*

Correcting Errors

Everyone makes at least a few mistakes, and it is impossible to predict when you will make your first one, so it is best to be prepared to fix your mistakes. 1-2-3 offers several error-correction methods. The one you use depends on whether you are still entering an incorrect entry or have already finalized the entry.

Fixing an Entry Before It Is Finalized

To make a correction while making an entry in a cell, you can press (delete)/(backspace) to delete the last character you entered. Suppose that you intend to enter **SALES** but that you leave out the E. To try this correction method, follow these steps:

1. Type **SALS** in A1.
2. Press the (delete)/(backspace) key to delete the last S.
3. Type **ES**.

Clicking the Cancel button (the button with an X) in the console or pressing (⌘)-(.) or (esc) is a more dramatic way to eliminate characters. These methods eliminate all the characters you have typed in a cell, as long as you have not finalized the entry.

4. Click the Cancel button or press (⌘)-(.) or (esc).

The entire SALES entry disappears, and 1-2-3 is ready to accept a new entry.

Fixing a Finalized Entry

Once the entry is finalized, you must use other methods for correcting mistakes. The correction methods for finalized entries include retyping entries and using 1-2-3's Edit mode.

2

Retyping Entries

One way to change a finalized cell entry is to retype it. Follow these steps to create and correct a finalized entry:

1. Type **SALS** and click the Confirm button or press (enter).

At this point, you cannot add or remove characters from the entry.

2. With the same cell as the active cell, type **SALES** and press (enter) or click the Confirm button to make the correction.

SALES replaces SALS. This method gets the job done, but requires some unnecessary typing.

Editing a Finalized Entry

A better error-correction method, especially for longer entries, is to edit the entry and change only the mistakes. You must be in Edit mode to make this type of change. To place yourself in Edit mode, you can either click the cell entry in the edit region at the top of the screen, double-click the entry in the cell, or press (⌘)-(E). This is the same Edit mode 1-2-3 automatically places you in if you make an entry it cannot accept. Regardless of how you get there, once you are in Edit mode, you can change the entry to make any correction you want.

When you click the entry in the edit region or double-click the entry in the cell, you can select where the insertion point is placed. When you press (⌘)-(E), the insertion point is placed at the end of the entry in the cell. When you double-click the entry in the cell, 1-2-3 displays the entry beyond the limits of the cell. The edits you make are performed at the cell's location, although the entry is also updated in the edit region. If you start Edit mode by clicking the entry in the edit region, the edit is performed in the edit region but is updated in the cell. You can switch between these two areas by clicking either area. With longer entries, you may find it useful to edit entries in the edit region. You can also change the insertion point's position by clicking another location in the cell's entry. You can select multiple characters in an entry by dragging the mouse over the characters.

Within Edit mode, the keys that you use to select cells function differently. You can press the four arrow keys to move one character or line in that direction (↑ and ↓ only work when you are editing a long entry in the edit region that 1-2-3 has wrapped to use multiple lines). The home key on an extended keyboard also takes on a new function within Edit mode: it moves you to the beginning of the entry. The end key on an extended keyboard moves in the opposite direction; it moves the insertion point to the end of the entry. You can select a group of characters in an entry by holding down the shift key as you move the insertion point to a new location. You can press the delete/backspace key to delete the selected characters or, if no characters are selected, the character to the left of the insertion point, and you can press the del key on the extended keyboard to delete the character to the right of the insertion point. Let's try an example of editing a cell by following these steps:

1. Type **SELRS** and click the Confirm button or press enter.
2. With the same cell selected, double-click the end of SELRS in the cell or press ⌘-E.

1-2-3 displays the entry in the cell and the edit region, like this:

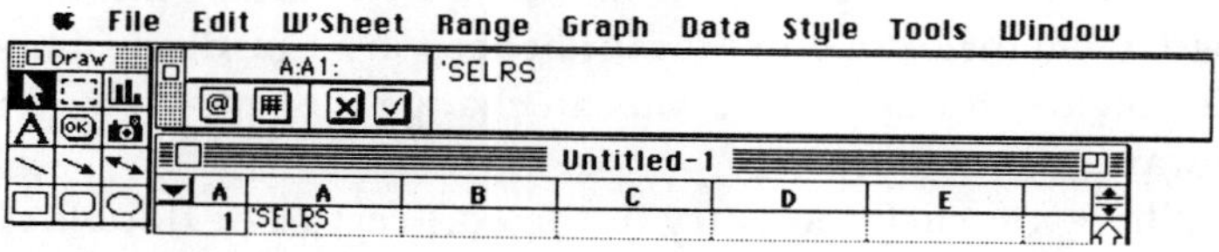

3. Move the insertion point to the end, press delete/backspace to delete the last S, and type **Y**.
4. Click between the L and the R or press the ← twice, and then type **A** to add A to the left of the R.
5. Click between the E and the L or press home and the → three times (if you have an extended keyboard), and then press delete/backspace to remove the E. Type **A** so the entry and edit region looks like this:

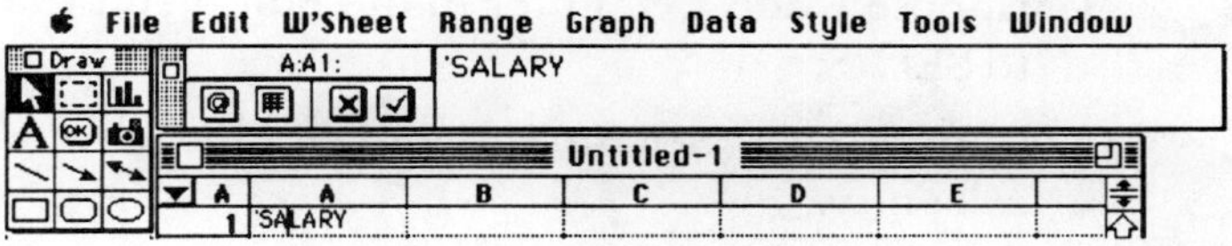

6. Click the Confirm button or press (enter) to finalize the corrected entry.

The Undo Feature

1-2-3 has an Undo feature that reverses the effect of the last entry or menu command you made. The secret to using Undo effectively is to make sure that you invoke it before taking any other action, since it changes only the last action performed.

The actual effect of Undo is to reverse the effect of the actions taken since the last time 1-2-3 was in Ready mode. If you have just made an entry in a cell, using Undo will remove this entry and restore any previous entry in the cell. If you just performed an action requiring multiple steps and 1-2-3 did not return to Ready mode between steps, using Undo would reverse all the steps. The text that follows Undo in the menu tells you exactly what action you will be undoing if you choose the command. Once you undo the last action, Undo in the Edit menu changes to Redo so you can choose it to reperform the action you have just undone.

In Chapter 5, "Menus, Dialog Boxes, and Palettes" you will learn about using Undo to reverse menu commands. For now, you can use Undo to eliminate your last cell entry. All that is required is choosing Undo from the Edit menu or pressing (⌘)-(Z). If your keyboard has function keys, you can also undo the last action by pressing (F1) (Undo). When you display the Edit menu, 1-2-3 displays a description of the action it will undo after Undo. For example, after you edit a cell, 1-2-3 displays Cell Enter after Undo. Try these steps:

1. Choose Undo Cell Enter in the Edit menu to return the cell entry to SELRS.
2. Choose Redo Cell Enter in the Edit menu to restore the edit to the cell entry.
3. Click the close box or press ⌘-W to choose Close from the File menu.
4. Click the No button or type an **N** to omit saving the worksheet.
5. Choose New from the File menu or press ⌘-N to open a new worksheet.

If nothing happens when you attempt to use Undo, Undo may be disabled. To enable the Undo feature, choose the User Setup command from the Tools menu and choose Preferences. Next, check that the Enable Undo box contains an X. If there is no X in the box, click it or press ⌘-E. Click the button labeled Update, press ⌘-U and click OK, or press return to finalize your selections.

You can reverse the effect of Undo if you wish. You can either choose Redo from the Edit menu, press ⌘-Z, or press F1 (Undo). Just as with Undo, Redo tells you what the effect of your selection will be.

Getting Help

Navigating your way around the worksheet and entering numbers and text in worksheet cells probably has seemed quite simple. That is because you have taken everything a step at a time. As you add more skills to your 1-2-3 toolkit, you may find that you need a quick refresher on an earlier topic. Although you can always reread the particular chapter in this book or your 1-2-3 manual, 1-2-3's *help cards* often provide just the hints you need to complete your planned task. Opening a help card is as easy as pressing ⌘-?. You can access help even if you are in the middle of a task, such as entering text in a cell. 1-2-3 opens a help card without disrupting the task in progress; instead, it opens a 1-2-3 help card separate from the 1-2-3 document and makes the help-card window current. You can move this card like other objects on your desktop. If you are not in the middle of a dialog box or

Figure 2-3. *Sample help card*

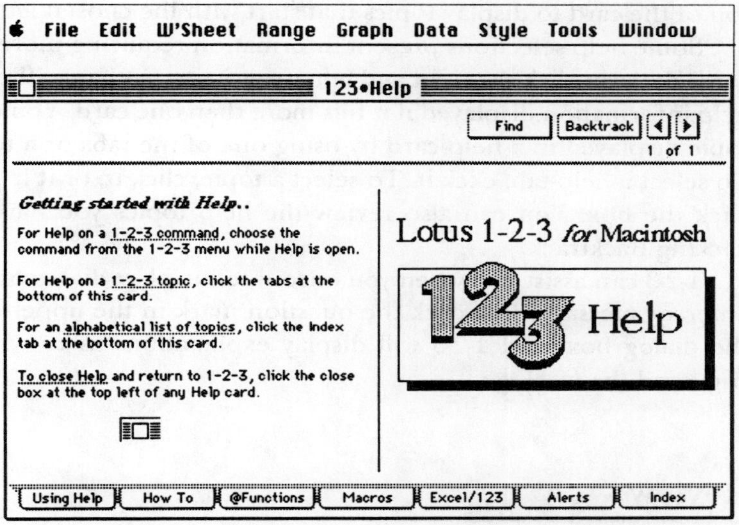

command, 1-2-3 displays a help-card window like the one in Figure 2-3. If you are in the middle of performing a command, the help card will contain information about the command you are performing. Try this now: press (⌘)-(?) to see a help card like the one in Figure 2-3.

Another option for accessing help is selecting 1-2-3 Help from the menu. (With System 7, you choose 1-2-3 Help from the Help menu that has the question mark.) If you have an extended keyboard, you can also access help by pressing the (help) key. If you are in the middle of a command, you can access help by clicking the question mark in the upper corner of the command's dialog box. When you want to leave help and return to your worksheet, click the close box in the upper-left corner of the card.

The *topic tabs,* the labeled rectangular buttons at the bottom of the help card, allow you to choose from the topics Using Help, How To, @Functions, Macros, Excel/123, Alerts, and Index. Each of these topics provides many choices in the next level of selections. After you click a tab, 1-2-3 displays a help card for the selected topic displayed. If you select Alerts or Index, you can select the topic within the Alert or Index list by clicking it to display information on the chosen topic. You can click any of the letters across the top of the card to display topics that start with the chosen letter.

Some help selections present information requiring more than one help card. You can click the right and left arrow icons to change the portion of the help information displayed if it fills more than one card. You can change the topic displayed in a help card by using one of the tabs or a topic on a card. To select a help tab, click it. To select a topic, click it, or if it contains a box, click the box. You can also review the help topics you have looked at by clicking Backtrack.

1-2-3 can assist you when you encounter an alert dialog box that displays an error message. Just click the question mark in the upper-right corner of the dialog box, and 1-2-3 will display explanations as to what might have triggered the message.

Review

In this chapter you have learned how to make simple entries such as text and numbers. More specifically, you have learned the following:

- Cells can be empty or contain text entries or values. Text entries are treated as characters by 1-2-3. Depending on the alignment prefix, text entries may be left aligned ('), right aligned ("), or centered (^). One type of value is a number. Numbers use the digits 0 through 9 and special symbols like ., +, and –. Dates and times are special types of values; you can enter them in one of the acceptable formats and 1-2-3 converts them into date and time numbers which you can use in calculations.
- The method for correcting worksheet entries depends on whether they are finalized. One set of techniques works for entries you are entering and another set works for finalized entries. The Undo feature can eliminate an entry just finalized or reverse the result of the last 1-2-3 command. Just choose Undo from the Edit menu or press ⌘-Z.

- To save the current worksheet, choose Save from the File menu or press ⌘-S, type a name for the worksheet document, and click the Save button or press RETURN. To close a worksheet, click the close box in the upper-right corner of the worksheet, choose Close in the File menu, or press ⌘-W. To open a new empty worksheet, select New from the File menu or press ⌘-N.

Keys and Commands

The keys you have learned how to use in this chapter help you make and correct entries. You have also learned commands that let you save your work and finish a worksheet. These keys, as well as the commands (preceded by the menu from which the commands are issued) are listed in the following table.

Entry	Action
1-2-3 Help or Help 1-2-3 Help or ⌘-?	Displays 1-2-3 help cards.
' ^ or "	Starts a text entry that is left aligned, centered, or right aligned, respectively.
⌘-. or ESC	Eliminates an entry that is not finalized.
⌘-E	Places you in Edit mode for the current cell's contents so you can change the cell's contents without retyping. In Edit mode many of the keys behave differently.
Edit Undo or Redo or F1 or ⌘-Z	Undoes the effect of the last command.
ENTER	Finalizes an entry and keeps the same cell selected.
File Close or ⌘-W	Closes the worksheet.
File New or ⌘-N	Opens a new worksheet document.
File Save or ⌘-S	Saves a document with a name you provide.

return	**Finalizes an entry and moves to the cell below.**
tab	**Finalizes an entry and moves to the cell to the right.**
Tools User Setup Preferences	**Selecting the Enable Undo check box turns the Undo feature on or off.**

3

Defining Your Calculations

Calculations are an important part of many of the business tasks that you perform. Some computations, such as a 10 percent purchase discount, are easy to compute. However, not all calculations are simple. If you want to determine a yearly salary for an employee who receives a raise in the middle of the year, you need to perform a much more complex computation. Complex calculations are difficult to perform unless you write them down. Even when you write down a calculation, it is easy to make mistakes. And if conditions change even slightly, the numbers in your calculations are likely to change. You could find yourself spending a considerable amount of time redoing calculations.

1-2-3 for Macintosh provides many features to make your computations easier than the paper and pencil method of the past. You define the steps in the computational process to 1-2-3, and it performs all the calculations for you. Your instructions to 1-2-3 are called *formulas.* Once these formulas are entered, 1-2-3 handles all the work for you.

This chapter provides easy-to-follow instructions for entering many of the formula types that 1-2-3 supports. You learn how to use references to cells in your formula building. This powerful feature allows you to reuse applications by changing the data in cells that the formulas reference. You explore basic numeric formulas, as well as logical formulas and string formulas. @functions and formulas that link to other worksheet documents are covered in Chapter 4, "@Functions and Other Formula Options."

Formula Basics

Formulas, like the numbers you entered in Chapter 2, "Entering Text and Numbers," are value entries. Unlike numbers, however, they produce results that vary, depending on the current values they reference. This variability makes formulas the backbone of worksheet features. It allows you to make *what-if projections* based on changing the entries on your worksheet. You can update the formula results without changing the formula. The only requirement is that you supply new entries for the variables referenced by the formulas, which are stored in other cells.

Entry Rules

To enter a formula in a cell, you must define for 1-2-3 the location of the variables involved and the operations you wish performed on them. 1-2-3 supports three types of formulas: numeric formulas, logical formulas, and string formulas. A few general rules apply to all formulas, and some special conventions must be observed for special types of formulas. The special rules are explained when each type of formula is discussed, but the general guidelines are given here.

- The first and perhaps most important rule is that the first character in a formula must be a number from 0 through 9 or an entry from the following list:

  + = - (@ $ # .
- The second rule is that extraneous spaces are not allowed except in text within a string formula or a range name.
- The third and last rule pertains to the length limitation for a formula. As with other cell entries, formulas cannot exceed 512 characters.

Numeric Formulas

Numeric formulas are nothing more than instructions for certain operations: addition (+); subtraction (−); multiplication (*); division (/); and exponentiation (^), which represents raising a number to a specific power such as 3 squared or 2 cubed. These operations are the same ones that you can perform with a calculator. When you record a numeric formula on the worksheet, you can build it with arithmetic operators and references to the numbers contained in other cells. The results of the calculation are determined by the current values of the cells referenced. You will see the advantage of formulas more clearly when you change the value of a referenced cell and the formula result is automatically recomputed. Anytime you wish to repeat a set of calculations on new data, you can enter the data without reentering the formulas. The sequence of required computations is stored in the cell containing the formula, and a new result is computed based on the value of the new entry.

Entering Simple Numeric Formulas

You can enter 1-2-3's formulas with numeric constants, as in 4*5 or 3+2. However, numeric constants within formulas are limiting; you have to change the formulas as conditions change. A better method is to store the constants in cells. When you wish to use a value stored in a cell in a formula, you can use its cell address within the formula. Then, if the value changes, you need only enter a new number where it is stored; the formula will use it automatically. Using cell addresses, or *references,* in formulas requires an additional rule. Since cell addresses begin with nonnumeric characters, an entry's initial alphabetic character (as in A2+B3) causes it to be treated like a text entry. Thus, the entry appears in the cell just as you typed it, rather than appearing as a result of calculations. So references in formulas must start with an arithmetic operator, such as + or =.

You might use formulas to calculate a purchase total and its discount. To enter the formulas, follow these steps:

1. Type the following entries in the cells specified:

A2:	**Product 1**	C2:	**4**
B1:	**"Units**	D1:	**"Cost**
B2:	**6**	E1:	**"Discount**
C1:	**"Unit Cost**	F1:	**"Net Cost**

Notice that the " alignment prefix is the first character of some of the text entries. As you will recall from Chapter 2, "Entering Text and Numbers," this causes 1-2-3 to right align the text entry in the cell so the text entries will line up with the values underneath.

2. Move to D2.

Note: *Now that you are familiar with moving around in the worksheet, you will be given only the cell address to move to. Remember, you can move to cells by using the mouse or with arrow keys and other special keys such as* (home) *and* (page down) *if your keyboard has them. It does not matter how you move to a cell–use whatever method you prefer.*

One of several arithmetic operators can begin a formula. The + or = are logical choices to add to the front of the formula; they require only one keystroke and do not affect the contents of B2, the cell containing the number of units purchased. Try it now to see the results.

3. Type **=B2*C2**.
4. Click the confirm button or press (enter) so your formula looks like this:

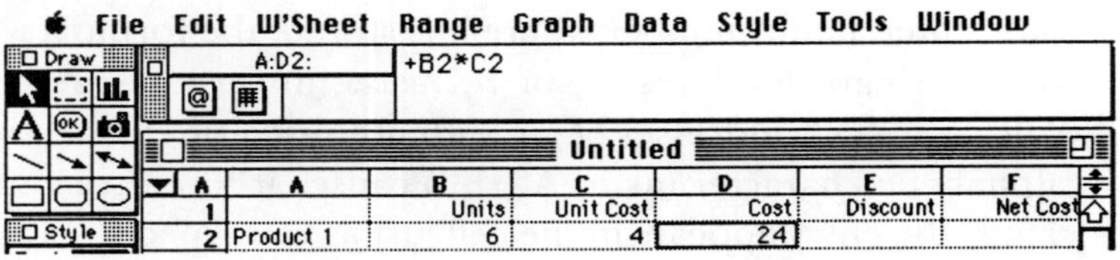

1-2-3 converts the = into a +. When D2 is the active cell, you still see the formula in the console, yet you see the result in the cell. If you decided to change B2 to 10 later on, the result displayed in D2 would change to 40 as evidence that the formula was still doing its assigned task.

When you enter a formula by using references, 1-2-3 is not fussy; it will accept either upper- or lowercase characters. The formula +B2*C2 is equivalent to +b2*c2 or +b2*C2 and computes the same results. Notice that 1-2-3 automatically assumes that the formula uses values from cells on the current sheet because the cell addresses do not include sheet letters. Using values from other sheets will be discussed in Chapter 8, "Managing Documents and Sheets."

You can add two more formulas to compute a discount and the net amount. To compute the discount, move to E2, and then type **+D2*.075** to compute a 7.5 percent discount. To compute the net amount, move to F2, and then type **+D2–E2** and press (enter) or click the confirm button.

If you make a mistake when you enter a formula, you can either edit it to get the results you want or you can reenter it. You learned about editing entries in Chapter 2, "Entering Text and Numbers." To reenter the formula, retype it if you have finalized the incorrect one, or click the Cancel button or press ⌘-. to remove the unfinalized one so you can type the new one.

Applications: *Formulas make it possible to have 1-2-3 do much of your repetitive work. When you are trying to record formulas for a new application, think about how you would instruct a new employee to handle the computations and then define the same steps to 1-2-3.*

Adding Notes to Formulas

1-2-3 allows you to document a formula as you enter it. Although the formula is likely to be perfectly clear to you on the day that you enter it, when you want to change the formula after a period of time has elapsed, it can be difficult to remember the logic behind your entries.

You can place the note in the same entry as the formula calculation by entering a semicolon after the formula and then the text of the note. The combined length of the entry may not exceed 1-2-3's 512-character limit. You can enter any text you want after the semicolon since the note is not part of the calculation and does not need to conform to 1-2-3's rules for value entries. You can also use 1-2-3's editing features to add notes at the end of existing formula entries. Complete the following steps to add a note at the end of a formula in the purchase discount example:

1. Move to D2, and then double-click the cell or press ⌘-E to edit the contents of the cell.

2. Type **;Computes the total cost before discount** at the end of the formula, and click the confirm button or press (enter).

Your note displays in the console when the cell with the note is the active cell, as shown here:

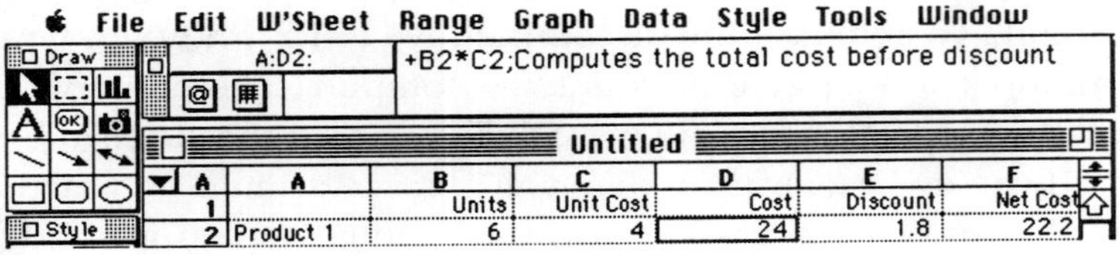

You can perform the same procedure for the formulas in cells E2 and F2, by entering **Computes a 7.5% discount** and **Computes the net amount** as the notes (after entering ;).

You can save this worksheet by choosing Save from the File menu (by dragging the mouse from File down the File menu to Save and releasing the mouse) or pressing (⌘)-(S). Next, type **Discount** in the box under Save As and click the Save button or press (return). You can click the close box or press (⌘)-(W) to close the worksheet. Next, choose New from the File menu or press (⌘)-(N) to open a new worksheet.

Applications: *Notes can be used to explain a formula, define the source of a particular computation, or to indicate when a new formula should be used, for example.*

Building Formulas with the Pointing Method

1-2-3 provides a second method of formula entry that can reduce the error rate. With this method, you type only the arithmetic operators and select the references by pointing to the cells you wish to reference using 1-2-3's Point mode. You will switch to Point mode when you point to a cell by clicking a cell or pressing the arrow keys while you are entering a formula. 1-2-3 adds the cell address to the formula. The pointing method provides visual verification that you are selecting the correct cell and eliminates the problems of typing mistakes.

You can try pointing to build formulas by creating a worksheet that computes an employee's gross pay, given an hourly rate of pay and regular and overtime hours worked. Use a multiplication process to calculate regular pay, and then use another multiplication process to calculate overtime pay before adding the results of the two multiplication operations. 1-2-3 automatically does the multiplication before the addition. Later you will learn more about the order in which 1-2-3 performs calculations and how you can change this order. Keep this worksheet simple for now; enter just the basic information for one employee, following these steps:

1. Type these entries in the cells specified.

A1:	**Employee**	A2:	**J. Smith**
B1:	**"Hours**	B2:	**40**
C1:	**"Rate**	C2:	**3.75**
D1:	**"Overtime**	D2:	**10**
E1:	**"Gross Pay**		

Your entries should look like this:

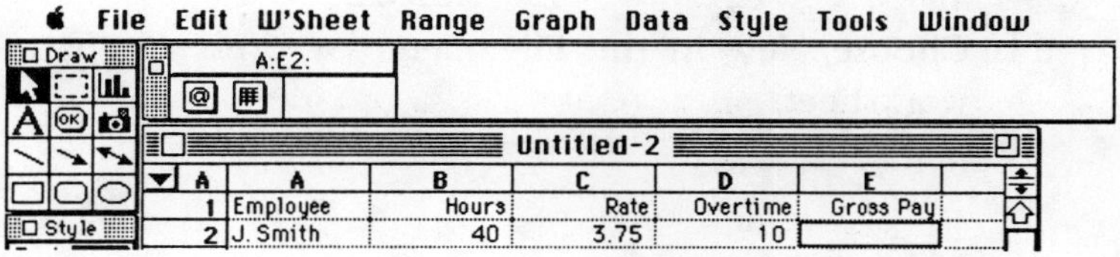

The formula for E2 must calculate gross pay by multiplying regular hours by the rate of pay and then multiplying overtime hours by 1.5 times the rate of pay. The result of these two multiplication operations will be added to obtain the gross pay. This sounds complicated but can be represented succinctly in the formula that you will build with the pointing method.

2. Type + in E2.
3. Click B2 or press the (←) three times.

The reference A:B2 is added to the formula.

4. Type *.

The cell outline returns to E2, where you are entering the formula.

5. Click C2 or press the ← twice.
6. Type +.
7. Click D2 or press the ←.
8. Type ***1.5***.
9. Click C2 or press the ← twice.
10. Click the Confirm button or press enter to finalize the formula with the result of 206.25.

1-2-3 removes the sheet indicators from the references in the formula because they are on the same sheet as the formula. You could add still more employees to this worksheet, but for now, you will save it as Pay.

11. Choose Save in the File menu or press ⌘-S.
12. Type **Pay** and click the Save button or press return to store the 1-2-3 document as Pay.
13. Click the close box or press ⌘-W to close the worksheet.
14. Choose New in the File menu or press ⌘-N to open a new worksheet.

Logical Formulas

Logical formulas compare two or more values. 1-2-3 uses the *logical operators* = for equal, <> for not equal, > for greater than, >= for greater than or equal to, < for less than, and <= for less than or equal to. You can enter logical formulas with the same methods used for numeric formulas but, unlike numeric formulas, they do not calculate numeric results. Instead, a logical formula produces a result of either a 1 or a 0, depending on whether the condition that it evaluates is true or false. If the condition is true, 1 is returned; if the condition is false, 0 is returned. For example, if D4 contains a 5, the logical formula +D4<3 returns 0, since the condition is false. This capability can evaluate a series of complex decisions or influence results in other parts of the worksheet.

If a formula contains both logical operators and arithmetic operators, the expression containing the arithmetic operators is evaluated first. For example, 1-2-3 evaluates the logical formula +D4*2>50 by first multiplying the current value in D4 by 2 and then performing the comparison.

Applications: *Logical formulas allow you to effectively perform two different calculations for a cell depending on whether the result of the logical formula is true or false. You might use logical formulas to determine if a distance is great enough to warrant an added shipping charge, to determine whether the social security maximum tax has been met, or to determine whether to add a sales tax to a purchase.*

Creating a Worksheet to Calculate Commissions

One application of logical operators in a worksheet is the calculation of a commission bonus. In this example, sales personnel are paid a quarterly bonus, which includes a regular sales commission and a bonus paid for meeting sales quotas. The regular commission is computed as 10 percent of total sales. The bonus is calculated by product. A bonus of $1000 is paid for each product for which the sales quota is met. A salesperson could thus gain $3000 by meeting quotas for three products.

Look at the steps required to build the commission worksheet shown in Figure 3-1. First, follow these directions to add the text and numbers that are required:

1. Type the following entries in these cells:

C1:	**Commission Calculation**	A10:	**Bonus:**
A3:	**Employee:**	A13:	**Total Commission Plus Bonus:**
A4:	**Sales Product 1:**	D3:	**John Smith**
A5:	**Sales Product 2:**	D4:	**66000**
A6:	**Sales Product 3:**	D5:	**35000**
A7:	**Total Sales:**	D6:	**9000**
A9:	**Commission:**	F3:	**"Quotas Met**

Figure 3-1. *Commission calculations*

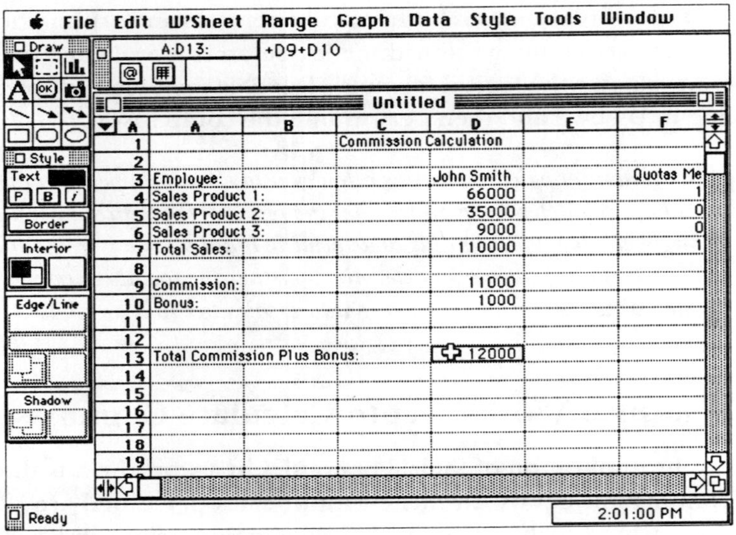

2. Move to F4.

Your worksheet now looks like Figure 3-2.

Adding Formulas to the Commission Worksheet

The number and text entries for this worksheet are now complete. At this point, you are ready to add formulas for calculating the regular and bonus commission. For computing the bonus, assume that the quota is $50,000 per product. Use the following steps to enter the logical formulas for determining whether the sales quota in each category was met:

1. Type **+D4>50000**, in F4 and click F5 or press (return).

This formula produces 1 if the Product 1 quota is met and 0 if it is not.

2. Type **+D5>50000**, and click F6 or press (return).
3. Type **+D6>50000**, and click F7 or press (return).

Figure 3-2. *Numbers and text for the commission worksheet*

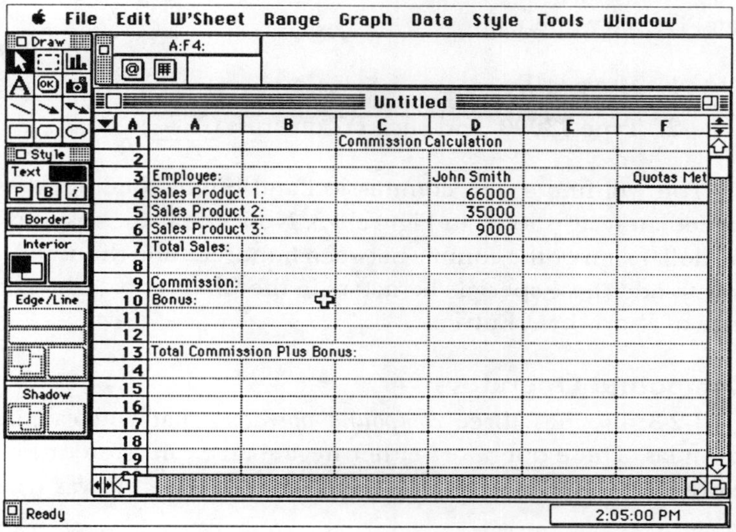

4. Total the number of quotas met by adding the result of each of the logical formulas: type **+F4+F5+F6** in F7, and click the Confirm button or press (enter).

In Chapter 4, "@Functions and Other Formula Options," you will learn a shortcut method for summing entries, but for now you can use simple addition.

5. Total the sales of all three products in the same fashion: move to D7, type **+D4+D5+D6**, and click D9 or press (return) twice.
6. Type **+D7*.1** to enter the commission formula, and click D10 or press (return).
7. Type **+F7*1000** to calculate the bonus commission by multiplying the number of quotas met by 1000, and click D13 or press (return) three times.
8. Type **+D9+D10** in D13, and click the Confirm button or press (enter).

Your completed worksheet should now match the one shown in Figure 3-1. The logical formulas it contains will respond to changes in the worksheet's data. Let's try one:

1. Move to D6.
2. Type **73000**, and click D7 or press (return).

You will find a new commission and bonus totaling $19,400 calculated immediately, as shown in Figure 3-3. Notice that the result does not display the dollar sign or the comma between hundreds and thousands. You will learn how to add these special characters in the Chapter 6, "Changing the Appearance of Worksheet Entries."

Compound Operators

1-2-3 also has three *compound operators* that you can use with logical formulas. These operators either negate an expression or join two different expressions. Negating an expression means that if it was true, negating the

Figure 3-3. *Recomputing the commission*

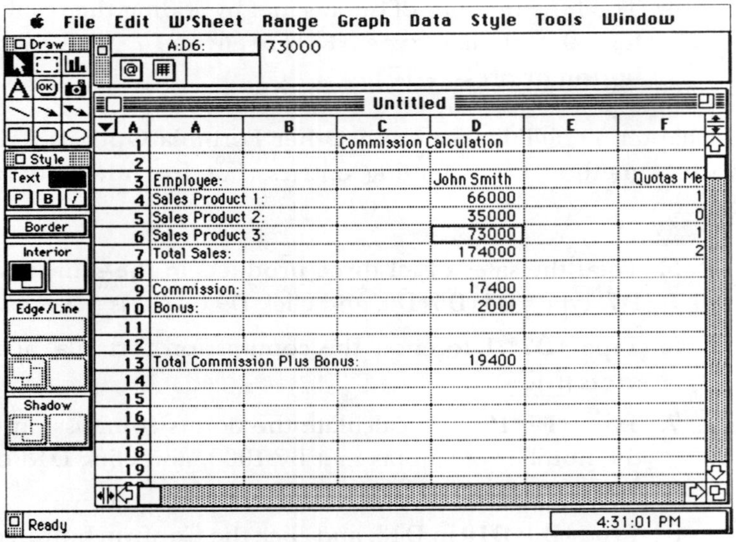

expression makes it false and if it was false, negating the expression makes it true. The negation operator #NOT# has precedence over the two compound operators #AND# and #OR#. When the compound operator #AND# joins two logical expressions, *both* expressions must be true for the compound formula to return a true value. If the two expressions are joined by #OR#, *either* one can be true for the condition to return a true value. For example, the result of joining the logical formulas 5>3 and 4>7 with the #AND# operator, as in 5>3#AND#4>7, is false because 4 is not greater than 7, and the #AND# operator requires both logical expressions to be true for the entire formula to be true. On the other hand, if you used the formula, 5>3#OR#4>7, this formula is true because 5 is greater than 3, and the #OR# operator requires only one of the logical expressions to be true for the entire formula to be true.

You can add a second condition to your commission calculation by using the compound operators. Let's say that bonus commissions require a minimum of six months of service in addition to the minimum sales level for a product. Revise the worksheet to allow for this new condition by following these steps:

1. Move to A11, type **Months in Job:**, and move to D11.
2. Type **4** and move to F4.
3. Edit the cell by double-clicking it or pressing (⌘)-(E), type **#AND#D11>6** at the end of the formula, and then click the confirm button or press (return).
4. Repeat step 3 for the formulas in F5 and F6.

You will find that the bonus commission in Figure 3-4 is now 0, since the employee has been on the job fewer than six months.

5. Move to D11 and type **8**, and click the Confirm button or press (enter) to see the bonus commission calculated again.
6. Choose Save from the File menu or press (⌘)-(S), type **Commission**, and click the Save button or press (return) to save this worksheet.
7. Click the close box or press (⌘)-(W) to close the worksheet window.
8. Choose New in the File menu or press (⌘)-(N) to open a new worksheet.

Figure 3-4. *Using compound operators*

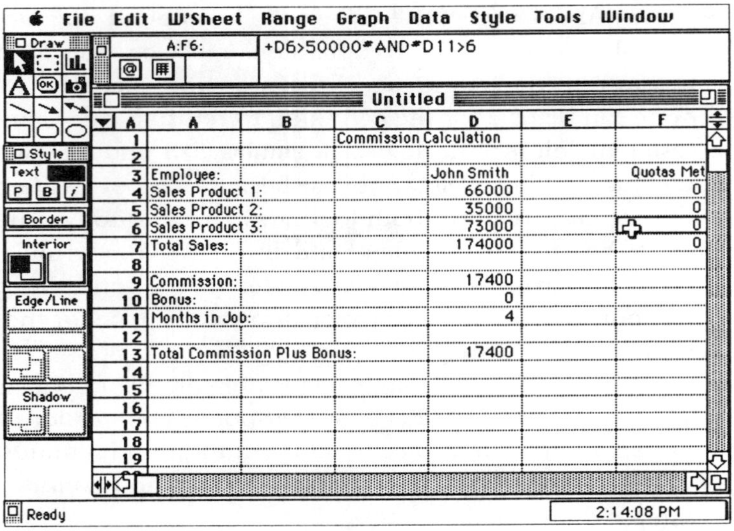

String Formulas

String formulas do not perform formula calculations as numeric formulas do; they let you join character strings to create headings or other data elements for the worksheet. String formulas use only one operator, the ampersand (&), which joins variables containing character strings or string constants. For example, +"John"&"Smith" results in JohnSmith, the formula +"John"&" "&"Smith" results in John Smith, and +A1&A2&A3 results in abc if A1 contains a, A2 contains b, and A3 contains c. The quotes enclose text to distinguish it from cell addresses. As with the other types of formulas, with string formulas you can either type the complete formula or point to the cell addresses and have 1-2-3 place them in the formula for you.

Applications: *Keep string formulas in mind when you need to correct data entry errors. For example, you may want to join text entries into a single one with a string formula such as joining the first and last name of a customer. In Chapter 9, "Making*

1-2-3 Do Your Work," you will learn about a command that you can use to replace the results of the string formula in place of the original text entries.

Let's use a string formula to build a part number for All Parts, Incorporated. The warehouse location, bin number, product type, and vendor are all combined to create a part number. Follow these steps to enter the data for the worksheet:

1. Move to B1, type **All Parts, Inc. Inventory Listing**, and move to A3.
2. Type the following entries in the cells specified:

A3:	**Location**	A4:	**'5**
B3:	**Bin**	B4:	**'12**
C3:	**Type**	C4:	**AX**
D3:	**Vendor**	D4:	**CN**
E3:	**Part No**		

The apostrophe is required for the entries in A4 and B4 because 1-2-3 cannot join text entries with value entries. The apostrophe ensures that the numbers are stored as text entries.

3. Type **+C4&"-"&D4&A4&B4** in E4, and click the Confirm button or press (enter).

The part number for the first item appears as shown here:

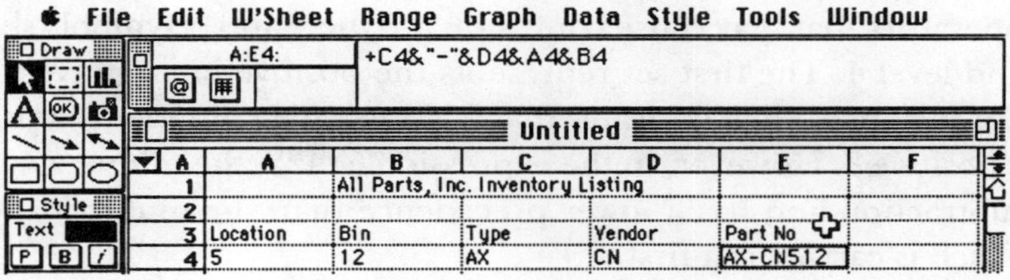

For practice, you may wish to enter the data and the string formula required to build several additional part numbers. Like the other formula types, changing the values for any of the variables immediately changes the results produced by the string formula. Once you have finished with your entries, you can save the worksheet. Choose Save in the File menu or press (⌘)-(S). Next, type **Part Number**, and click the Save button or press (return). To close the window, click the close box or press ⌘-W. Finally, choose New in the File menu or press ⌘-N to open a new worksheet window.

The part-number display in the last example is useful if the worksheet contains additional information to the right that is also important to see. After using the string formula to build the part number, you can move to cells further to the right and view the other data without losing track of the part number.

Performing More Complex Calculations

When 1-2-3 encounters more than one operator in a formula, it does not use a left-to-right order to compute the result. Instead, it evaluates the formula based on a set precedence order for each of the operators. As you begin to build more complex formulas, you will see how important it is to understand 1-2-3's priorities in order to achieve the desired results.

When more than one operator is used in a formula, it is important to know which operation 1-2-3 performs first. Table 3-1 shows the order of precedence for each of the operators, from highest to lowest. The higher the precedence, the sooner the operation is performed. If more than one operator has the same precedence, they are evaluated from left to right.

Notice that parentheses are at the top of the list in Table 3-1. This indicates that any expression enclosed within them is evaluated first. The other operators that may cause confusion are the + and − symbols shown in level 6 and level 4. The first set represents the positive or negative sign of a value. For instance, −5*3 indicates that 5 is a negative number that is multiplied by a positive 3. However, in the expression 5−4*2, the minus symbol represents subtraction and has a lower precedence than the multiplication operation, which is carried out first.

A short example will demonstrate the use of parentheses clearly. Suppose you wish to add the total number of pounds of printed matter in a shipment by combining the 10-pound weight of the books ordered with 3 pounds of stationery items and then multiplying the total weight by the per-pound shipping rate of 25 cents. You will not get the correct result if you enter **10+3*.25**, since 1-2-3 will perform the multiplication first and then add 10 and 0.75, totaling 10.75 rather than the 3.25 you expected. To make 1-2-3 perform

Table 3-1. *Operation Priorities*

Precedence	Operator	Operation Performed
8	()	Parentheses to override priorities
7	^	Exponentiation
6	+ –	Positive/negative indicators
5	/ *	Division and multiplication
4	+ –	Addition and subtraction
3	= <>	Logical operators
	< <=	
	> >=	
2	#NOT#	Compound NOT indicator
1	#AND#	Compound AND, OR, and the string operator
	#OR#	
	&	

the calculation your way, you need to enter the formula as **(10+3)*.25**. 1-2-3 will evaluate the expression within the parentheses first and carry out the multiplication second, resulting in the desired answer of 3.25.

Let's look at another salary worksheet to demonstrate the importance of the precedence and of controlling precedence with parentheses. This worksheet projects a single employee's salary based on his or her current salary, the percentage of increase, and the month of the increase. Since a lengthy formula is required, you will perform only the computation for one employee. To enter the data for the salary computation worksheet, follow these steps:

1. Type the entries for the column headings in the cells specified:

A2:	**"Name**	D1:	**"Increase**
B1:	**"1991**	D2:	**"Percent**
B2:	**"Salary**	E1:	**"1992**
C1:	**"Increase**	E2:	**"Salary**
C2:	**"Month**		

2. Type the entries for the first employee in the cells specified:

   A3: **J. Brown**
   B3: **35900**
   C3: **5**
   D3: **.06**

3. Move to E3 so your text and numbers look like this:

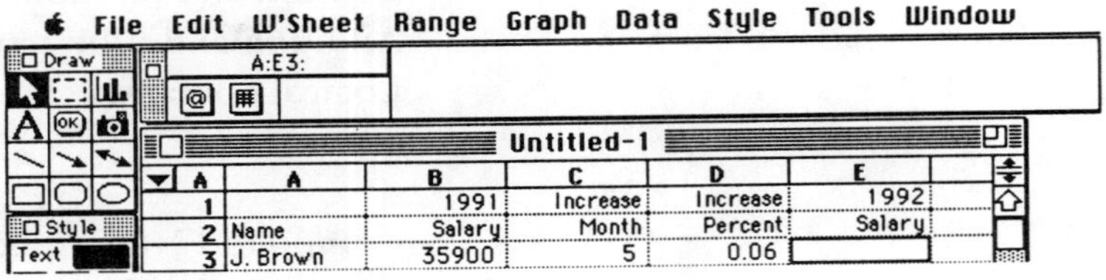

The last step is the most complicated. The formula must compute the current monthly salary and multiply it by the number of months that the individual will continue to receive this salary. The result of this first computation is then added to the figure computed for the amount paid at the new salary level. The total dollars paid at the new salary level are computed by multiplying the current monthly salary by 100 percent plus the increase percentage by the number of months that the individual will receive the increased salary. Predictably, the formula is quite long. The parts of the formula are as follows.

(B3/12)	The annual salary divided by 12 to compute the monthly salary
(C3−1)	The month of the increase minus 1 or the number of months the employee receives his or her current salary
(1+3)	Indicates that the employee will receive 100% of his or her existing salary plus an increase represented by a decimal fraction in D3
12−(C3−1)	The number of months that the employee receives the increased salary amount

4. Combining all these, enter the following formula in E3:

   ((B3/12)*(C3−1))+((B3/12)*(1+D3)*(12−(C3−1)))

Type carefully and give yourself a pat on the back if you manage to complete the entire entry successfully on your first attempt. If you do make a few mistakes, you can always edit your entry to make the necessary corrections. If your mistakes are serious enough, 1-2-3 will place you in Edit mode.

5. Click the Confirm button or press (enter) to finalize your formula, which looks like this:

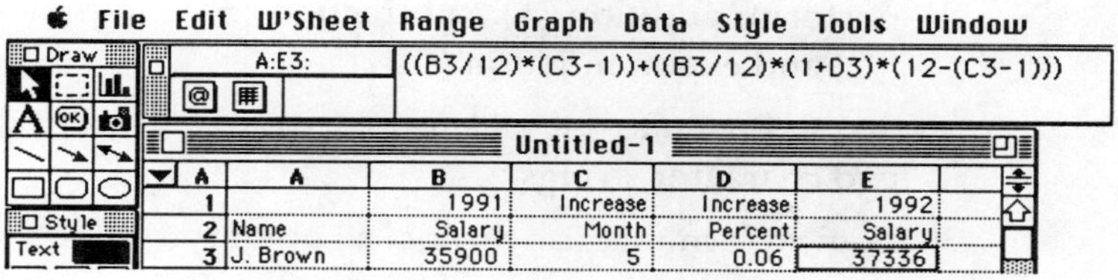

A few extra parentheses have been added to the formula expression to make it more readable. For example, the result would be the same if the parentheses were omitted from (B3/12), since multiplication and division have the same precedence. Using an extra pair of parentheses does not change the value of the expression as long as the parentheses do not change the order of operations. Feel free to add parentheses in this manner whenever they improve the readability of the formula without altering it. In this example, you have entered the data for only one employee, but this worksheet could be expanded easily. To save this worksheet, choose Save in the File menu or press (⌘)-(S). Next, type **Salary**, and click the Save button or press (return).

Review

In this chapter you learned the basics of creating formulas, which is the backbone of 1-2-3's features. More specifically, you learned the following:

- Formulas allow you to define computations that you want 1-2-3 to perform with the contents of cells.

- Formulas must start with a value character and cannot exceed 512 characters.
- You can document a formula by adding a note at the end. Type a semicolon (;) and then type your note.
- Numeric formulas are the most popular type of 1-2-3 formula because they support typical business calculations, such as purchase discounts, sales projections, and invoice extensions.
- You use operators to represent the type of calculation you wish to perform: addition (+), subtraction (−), multiplication (*), division (/), and exponentiation (^).
- String formulas use only one operator, the ampersand (&), to join two character strings.
- Logical formulas use the logical operators to perform a comparison: equal to (=), not equal to (<>), less than (<), less than or equal to (<=), greater than (>), or greater than or equal to (>=).
- Compound operators #NOT#, #AND#, and #OR# can be used to negate an expression or join two expressions together.
- All formula operators do not have the same order of precedence. You can use parentheses to raise the precedence of an operation. 1-2-3 evaluates entries in parentheses first. Table 3-1 lists the order of precedence for operators.

Keys and Commands

You have learned how to enter formulas. Some of the keys you have used for this purpose are

Entry	Action
+ or =	Starts a formula without affecting its value

4

@Functions and Other Formula Options

You already know quite a bit about formulas after reading Chapter 3, "Defining Your Calculations," but 1-2-3 for the Macintosh has many additional formula options. You can name cells and use the names as references in your formulas rather than the cell addresses. You can also reference data in other worksheet documents to access consistent data or to consolidate data from many worksheets into a summary sheet. Another advanced option is the ability to use 1-2-3's @functions to perform computations with formulas that are already part of the package. With the techniques covered in this chapter, you will have all the skills you need to create sophisticated 1-2-3 applications. The step-by-step presentation methods make it easy to master these new skills.

Using Names in Formulas

Using references is better than using constants in formulas. A formula is automatically updated when the contents of the cells referenced change, so you don't need to edit the formula. With many entries on a worksheet, it can be difficult to remember what each cell contains. You will find that cell addresses quickly become meaningless, since you are not certain of the data that a cell address represents.

You can assign a name to a range of contiguous cells. Since this range can be as small as a single cell, you can conceivably assign a unique name to each entry that you place on the worksheet. You can build new formulas by using either the cell address or the range name. Before learning how to assign names to your data, you need to learn about 1-2-3 ranges.

Range Basics

In 1-2-3, a *range* is a group of one or more cells that form a contiguous rectangle. You can use ranges to tell 1-2-3 to take the same action on each of the cells in the group. When used in this way, ranges can save a substantial amount of time over making a separate request to change each cell in the group. You will see more in Chapter 6, "Changing the Appearance of Worksheet Entries," about using ranges this way. For now, you will use ranges to assign names to individual cells.

Since a range can include a rectangular area of cells, you always express a range address as two separate cell addresses separated by one or two periods (1-2-3 will convert one period into two). The standard method of describing a range address is the upper-left cell in the range, one or two periods as a separator, and then the lower-right cell in the range, as in A1.B10 or C3..G20. When you point to a range, 1-2-3 automatically includes the sheet reference, as in A:A1..A:G2 but removes the sheet references when you finalize the entry and the references are in the same sheet as the formula. In Chapter 8, "Managing Documents and Sheets," you will learn to use multiple sheets in a worksheet and how to create ranges that span sheets. You can assign a name to any range so that you can refer to the range by the name rather than by its cell addresses.

In Chapter 12, "Data-Management Basics," and Chapter 13, "Advanced Techniques," you will look at ways of applying names to ranges that include more than one cell. For now, you will assign range names only to individual cells since the formulas you have used so far operate on only one cell at a time.

Naming a Range

To name a range, you need to 1-2-3's Range menu. You will learn more about 1-2-3's Range menu in Chapter 5, "Menus, Dialog Boxes, and Palettes," but as you learned in Chapter 2, "Entering Text and Numbers," you can invoke the menu by dragging the mouse over the menu and menu items you want and releasing the mouse when the selection you want is highlighted. The complicated salary formula you entered in the Salary worksheet in Chapter 3, "Defining Your Calculations," is a good place to try out the benefits of range names.

As you name ranges in the worksheet, you are limited to 15 characters for the range name. Each range name must be unique regardless of case. For example, you cannot have two ranges named Sales and SALES.

To name the three cells used in computing the 1992 salary figure for J. Brown, follow these steps:

1. Choose Open in the File menu (by dragging the mouse from File down the File menu to Open and releasing the mouse) or press ⌘-O. Double-click Salary or press the ↓ until Salary is highlighted and then press return. If you do not have the worksheet available, make the following entries in an empty worksheet:

A2:	**Name**	E1:	**"1992**
B1:	**"991**	E2:	**"Salary**
B2:	**"Salary**	A3:	**J. Brown**
C1:	**"Increase**	B3:	**35900**
C2:	**"Month**	C3:	**5**
D1:	**"Increase**	D3:	**.06**
D2:	**"Percent**	E3:	**((B3/12)*(C3-1))+((B3/12) *(1+-3)*(12-(C3-1)))**

Your worksheet now looks like this:

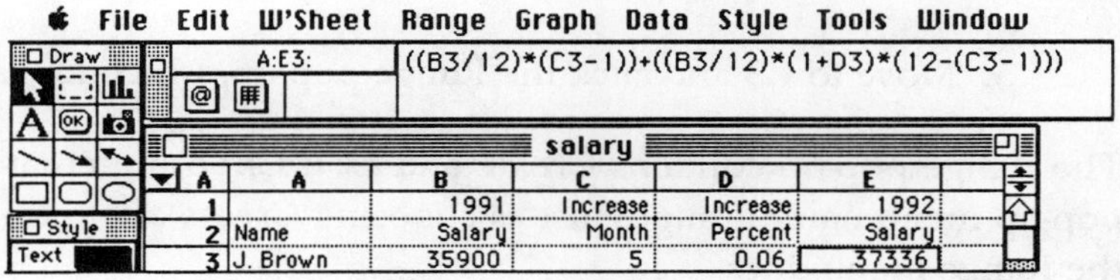

4

2. Move to B3.
3. Choose Name in the Range menu and then choose Create (To choose Create, drag the mouse to the right after choosing Name) or press its keyboard shortcut, (⌘)-(R). 1-2-3 displays a dialog box that looks like this:

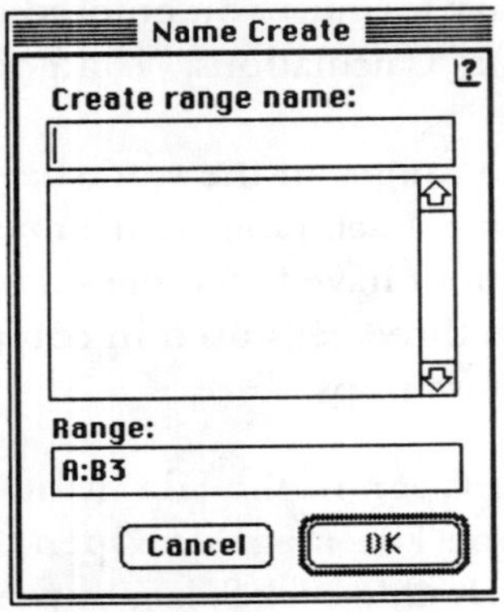

Notice that 1-2-3 is all set to use the active cell for this command. If you forget to select a cell or range before choosing Name in the Range menu and Create, you can select a different range by entering a cell or range address in the box under Range. To do this, click the box; or press (tab), and then point to the range with the mouse or type the cell or range address.

4. Type **Salary_91** and click OK or press (return).

A range name may contain up to 15 characters. You should avoid characters that may confuse 1-2-3 in a formula. That is why Salary_91 uses an underscore instead of a space.

5. Move to C3 and click the Range pop-up, which looks like ▦.

The Range pop-up contains Create and List. Choosing create in the Range pop-up menu names ranges just as choosing Create after choosing Name in the Range menu does.

6. Choose Create or press ⌘-R. Type **INC_MO** and click OK or press return.
7. Move to D3 and then choose Create in the Range pop-up menu, or press ⌘-R. Type **INC_%** and click OK or press return.
8. Move to E3 to see this formula:

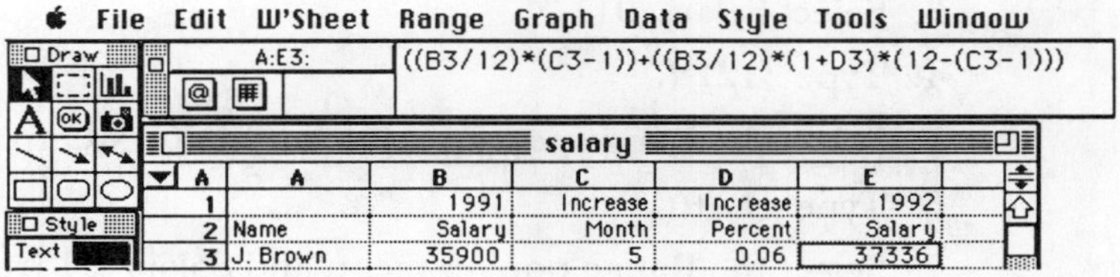

Your formula does not show the range names you have given to the cells the formula uses. This is because in the original formula, you entered cell addresses like D3 rather than range addresses like D3..D3. At this point, retyping the formula with range references would still not convert the cell addresses in the formula to range names. 1-2-3 converts a range address to a range name in existing formulas only at the time you name the range. 1-2-3 does not convert a range address to a range name in formulas you enter *after* naming the range. The solution is to rebuild the formula.

Applications: *You can name the cells in your own applications that contain values you use in many formulas. For example, in a sales projection report, you might name the cells containing the growth percentage or the current year's sales, since these values are used frequently. You may also want to name cells that are out of view from the formulas that use them. For example, in an investment listing, if the minimum required return on investments is in G110 and it is used in formulas in A1..H100, naming the cell means you do not have to remember the cell address as you create the formulas.*

Using Range Names When Building Formulas

The last example showed you that cell addresses in a formula do not change to range names once the cells are named. You must assign names to a range before you reference the range name in a formula. This allows you to specify the name with the Range pop-up menu when you build a formula. Try it now by reentering the formula in E3 with these steps:

1. With E3 still the active cell, type **((**.
2. Select the Range pop-up menu, which now displays the three range names in addition to Create and List.
3. Select Salary_91.
4. Type **/12)*(**.
5. Select the Range pop-up menu and INC_MO from the menu.
6. Type **–1))+((**.
7. Select the Range pop-up menu and Salary_91 from the menu.
8. Type **/12)*(1+**.
9. Select the Range pop-up menu and INC_% from the menu.
10. Type **)*(12–(**.
11. Select the Range pop-up menu and INC_MO from the menu.
12. Type **–1)))** and click the confirm button or press (enter) to display this formula:

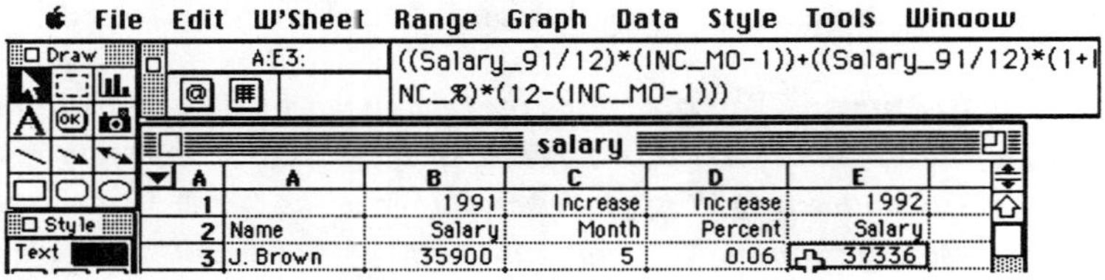

Now instead of the formula using references such as B3, C3, and D3, which do not tell you the data these cells contain, the formula references use the range names Salary_91, INC_MO, and INC_%. The range names let you know the data the formula is using. Although this is still a complex formula, it is a little easier to understand since you do not need to make the mental comparison between cell address and cell contents for each entry in the formula. When you edit a formula that contains range names, the entry includes the range names rather than the addresses they represent.

Applications: *Consider using range names when you have many unique formulas that are complex. Your formulas will be able to be easily read and understood despite the complexity of the calculations.*

Range names are not a good solution in all worksheets. If you expand this worksheet to show the salary computations for a department of 100 individuals, with each individual shown on a different row, range names would be impractical—you would need to assign a unique range name to each of the entries in each of the rows. In such a situation, it is best to continue to use cell addresses in your formulas. However, a worksheet containing a financial statement that is used to prepare ratios is a good application for the assignment of range names because similar data items would not be repeated and range names would make the formulas much more readable.

Follow these steps to build a new formula using range names.

1. With E3 the active cell, choose Name in the Range menu, and choose Create or press ⌘-R. Type **Salary_92**, and click OK or press (return).
2. Move to A4, type **Salary Increase**, and move to E4.
3. Move to E4 and type +.
4. Select the Range pop-up menu and Salary_92 from the menu.
5. Type –.
6. Select the Range pop-up menu and Salary_91 from the menu.
7. Click the confirm button or press (enter) to finalize and display this formula:

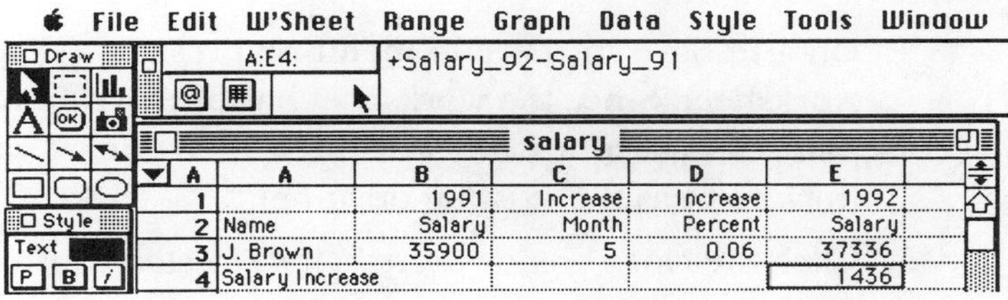

You can also use the Range pop-up menu to quickly move to a named range.

8. Select the Range pop-up menu and Salary_91 from the menu.

1-2-3 moves you to B3, which is the cell named Salary_91.

Deleting Range Names

You can delete range names that you no longer need. To delete a range name, choose Name in the Range menu, and then choose Delete. When you delete a range name, you do not eliminate the worksheet data with the name. The formulas with references to the range names that you delete will revert to displaying cell and range addresses, rather than the range names.

To delete the range name INC_MO from the current worksheet, follow these steps:

1. Choose Name from the Range menu and choose Delete.
2. Double-click INC_MO from the list of range names or press ↓ twice and return once.
3. Move to E3 to display this formula:

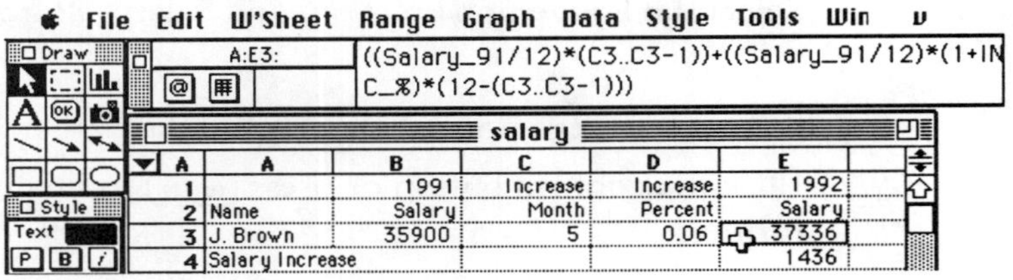

4. Choose Save in the File menu or press ⌘-S to save the altered worksheet. Since the worksheet has been saved once and is already named, Save does not ask for a filename; it saves the modified document as the existing document.
5. Click the close box or press ⌘-W to close this worksheet.
6. Choose New in the File menu or press ⌘-N to open a new worksheet.

Applications: *Delete all unused range names to minimize the length of the list of range names and to find the ones that you want more quickly.*

Creating Linking Formulas

All of the formulas that you have entered have referenced the current worksheet. You can also create formulas in 1-2-3 for the Macintosh that access data in other worksheet documents. This allows you to access important data from other documents so you can use the current worksheet to create a consolidated view of data from many other worksheets. You can use as many references to data in other worksheets as you need within a formula as long as your formula does not exceed 512 characters.

As an example, you might show the budget expenses for three different regions of the company in documents called Region 1, Region 2, and Region 3. To show the total of these three regions on the current sheet, you can create a *link formula* to link these documents and obtain the correct data. This eliminates the extra work and possibility for error that would exist if you had to reenter the region data on the current worksheet.

Applications: *You can use link formulas in your own applications to combine data from another worksheet into the current one. You can use link formulas to total sales and combine budget projections from each segment's worksheet.*

The Syntax of a Link Formula

To reference data in another document, you need to tell 1-2-3 where the data is located. First, you enter the document name enclosed in double angle brackets (<< >>). If you specify only a document name in the angle brackets, as in <<Region 1>>, 1-2-3 assumes that the document is located in the default folder (the folder where 1-2-3 automatically places documents when you save them). If you want to use a document in another folder, you must specify the pathname (including the disk name) within the angle brackets. For example, if the default folder is Lotus 1-2-3 and you want to use a document named West in the Sales folder on a disk named Hd, you would first enter **<<Hd:Sales:West>>** in the formula. Next, you enter the cell address, range address, or range name in the other document that contains the data you want to use, as in **<<Report>>A10** and **<<Hd:Sales:West>>Sales**. When you finalize the formula, 1-2-3 converts a cell address to a range address and adds sheet references, so <<Report>>A10 becomes <<Report>>A:A10..A:A10.

A Link Example

If you want to create a consolidation sheet for the total company expenses, you can consolidate the lower level totals with link formulas. You can try this by creating a worksheet and saving it with different document names after entering new numbers, as shown here:

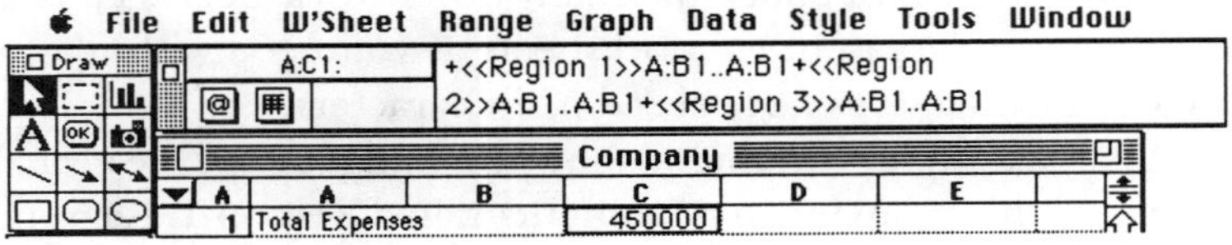

To try this, follow these steps:

1. Type **Expenses** in A1, and click B1 or press tab.
2. Type **100000** in B1, and click the confirm button or press enter.
3. Choose Save in the File menu or press ⌘-S, type **Region 1** as the document name, and click OK or press return.
4. Type **150000** in B1 to replace 100000, and click the confirm button or press enter.
5. Choose Save As in the File menu, type **Region 2** as the document name, and click OK or press return.

If you want to save an existing worksheet with a different document name, you must use the File Save As command instead of File Save.

6. Type **200000** in B1, and press enter or click the confirm button.
7. Choose Save As in the File menu, type **Region 3** as the document name, and click OK or press return.

Now you have documents for the three regions. All you need now is the worksheet that totals these values.

8. Click the close box or press ⌘-W to close the worksheet.

9. Choose New in the File menu or press ⌘-N to open a new worksheet.
10. Type **Total Expenses** in A1 and click C1 or press (tab) twice.
11. Type **+<<Region 1>>B1+<<Region 2>>B1+<<Region 3>>B1** and click another cell or press (return).

The result of 450000 is the total of the entries in B1 of the three worksheets.

12. Choose Save in the File menu or press ⌘-S, type **Company** as the document name, and click OK or press (return).
13. Click the close box or press ⌘-W, and then choose New in the File menu or press ⌘-N to close this worksheet and open a new one.

If you revise the expenses in any of the region worksheets, the next time you retrieve the Company worksheet, the result shown in C1 will include the new values in the regional worksheets. Rather than typing all of this formula, it is easier to point to the entries in the other worksheet and have 1-2-3 add the document name and range for you. You will learn how to do this as you learn how to work with multiple worksheet documents in Chapter 8, "Managing Documents and Sheets."

@Functions

Your 1-2-3 worksheets have already shown you the importance of formulas. Formulas are actually the power behind a spreadsheet package like 1-2-3; they record your calculations and use them over and over again. However, there is a problem with formulas: it takes a long time to record them, and when you are recording a long series of calculations, it is easy to make a mistake. Also, formulas are oriented toward working with one or more individual cell addresses. Many times you want to reference a group of cells with one entry and use each value in the calculation. Fortunately, 1-2-3 has *built-in functions* to reduce these drawbacks. These functions are prerecorded formulas that have already been verified for accuracy. All you need to do is specify which data they should operate on each time you use them. The built-in functions also provide features that go beyond the capabilities of formulas, such as accessing the system date and calculating square roots and tangents.

To use these functions, you need to learn the syntax and the rules that provide a powerhouse of 104 prerecorded calculations that you can access easily. In the following discussion, you learn about the various function categories into which all 1-2-3 functions are grouped. You examine a variety of functions from the different categories and learn how to use them in worksheets.

Built-in @Function Basics

A few general rules apply to all functions, regardless of their type, yet individual functions can differ from one another in how they expect you to convey the data with which you want them to work. You need to know the general rules and the individual exceptions, as well as which category of function is likely to handle the task you wish to address. This section provides such information. Read it before addressing the individual function categories; it is an important first step.

General Rules

Since built-in functions are formulas, they are value entries in worksheet cells. There are several rules for functions that do not apply to formulas, all of them pertaining to the syntax of recording the different components. A diagram of these components is shown in Figure 4-1. The first rule for function entry is that all functions must start with an @ symbol. This is why they are called *@functions.* After entering the @ symbol, you must include

Figure 4-1. *Function format*

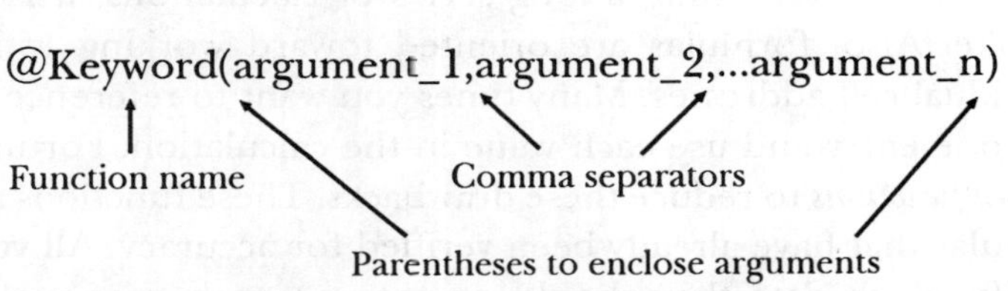

the special keyword that 1-2-3 uses to represent the function. This *keyword* is the function's name. You can enter it in either upper- or lowercase letters, but it must follow 1-2-3's spelling exactly. You can even have 1-2-3 supply it for you using the @Function pop-up menu. You can select a function category in the @Function pop-up menu and then one of the specific functions of that category and 1-2-3 will add the function keyword and any parentheses necessary to your entry. 1-2-3 can even add brief descriptions of the function arguments you must use. The @Function menu appears when you select the @Function pop-up button, which looks like [@].

Rules for Function Arguments

The next component within a function is its arguments. *Arguments* specify the data with which the function will work. Arguments are required by most functions since most functions use values or entries to determine the function's result. Arguments must be enclosed within parentheses, but if the function you are using does not require arguments you do not need to use them.

When using a function that requires multiple arguments, use a comma (,) or a semicolon (;) to separate the arguments. Spaces cannot be used within a function, so they are not valid as separator characters.

Function arguments can be provided as cell addresses, range addresses, range names, values, text, or even formulas or other built-in functions. The examples you enter in this chapter may include some values in the functions to expedite data entry. However, it is preferable to store the data needed by the function in worksheet cells and to reference these cells within the function, since a change in an argument's value will not require you to edit the function. Much variety is possible; look at these examples of the @SUM function, which totals the values you provide as arguments:

```
@SUM(9,4,8,7)
@SUM(A1;D3;Y6;Z10)
@SUM(Salaries,Rent_Exp,Equipment)
@SUM(A1..H4)
@SUM(A1,@SUM(B2..B3),<<Budget>>A:Z2..A:Z2)
```

All five are valid function entries. The last two examples reference a range of cells and use each value within the range. Ranges of cells must always form a rectangular area of contiguous worksheet cells.

Most built-in functions expect value entries for arguments. Other built-in functions require text or character data for arguments. You cannot substitute a type of data for an argument that is different from what 1-2-3 is expecting. For example, if you use 1-2-3's @UPPER function, which converts letters in a string to uppercase, you need to provide text as an argument. If you substitute a value for the argument, @UPPER cannot convert it and returns ERR, indicating an error.

Different Types of Function Arguments

Different functions require different arguments and use them in different ways. The three basic types of functions are those that require no arguments, those that expect a list of arguments in any sequence, and those that require a specific number of arguments in a specific order.

Examples of functions that require no arguments are @NOW and @PI. @NOW supplies the current date and time number. @PI represents the special mathematical constant 3.14159265, which is used in geometric problem solving.

There are also a number of functions that expect a list of values for arguments. The entries in the list can be single cells or ranges of cells and can be provided in any order you like. All of the statistical functions fall within this category of argument types. For example, these two functions are equivalent:

```
@SUM(A1,B4,C5,D2..D10,F1,H2..M4)
@SUM(F1,H2..M4,A1,C5,D2..D10,B4)
```

In both cases, all individual values, as well as each of the values in the ranges, are totaled to produce a single sum. Functions that allow this interchangeability of argument order specify a *list* as their argument. For example, since @SUM accepts this type of argument, you can expect to see @SUM(*list*) when the syntax of this function is discussed.

The last type of function argument is position dependent. Functions that require arguments in a specific order cannot have their arguments reordered without erroneous results. For example, the @PMT function is designed to calculate the amount of a loan payment. The function requires three arguments: the principal, the interest, and the term of the loan. Later in this chapter, you will see the functions specified like this:

@PMT(*principal,interest,term*)

When using the function, you must provide the three arguments in this exact order. For example, if you enter the formula @PMT(100000,30*12,.1/12) instead of @PMT(100000,.1/12,30*12) for a $100,000 loan for 30 years at a ten percent annual rate, 1-2-3 will return the incorrect result of $751,733,483.33 instead of the correct monthly payment of $877.57.

A Close Look at Each Function Category

There are eight categories of functions in 1-2-3, excluding the special database functions covered in Chapter 12, "Data-Management Basics." Built-in functions are grouped into categories in which each of the functions within a category has some similarity of purpose. The various function categories form the organizational structure of the rest of this chapter. You can use the remainder of the chapter in two ways. The preferred approach is to work through the exercises in each function category to become familiar with each function's category use. There may be function categories that apply to your worksheets, but unless you take an in-depth look at what they can do, you might not realize their potential. A second alternative, if your time is limited, is to focus on those function categories for which you have immediate use and come back and take a look at the other categories as you need them.

Statistical Functions

"Statistics" is a word that causes many people to be apprehensive—perhaps they recall statistics as complicated mathematical procedures from a required college math course. 1-2-3's statistical functions need not invoke this sense of alarm. They are simple to use, and they compute the most basic statistical measures, computations that you perform every day without even thinking about them as "statistical." They include computations for such operations as finding the average, summing, counting, and finding the minimum and maximum value. Table 4-1 provides a list of the *statistical functions.*

1-2-3's statistical functions perform their magic on lists of values. These lists are often a contiguous range of cells on the worksheet. They can also be a series of individual values or a combination of a range and individual values. Blank cells can be included within the list, but all values in the blank range will count as zeros. When a range contains multiple blank cells, 1-2-3 ignores the cells that contain blanks.

Table 4-1. *Statistical Functions*

Function Entry	**Description**
@AVG(*list*)	Computes an average for the values in *list*
@COUNT(*list*)	Counts the nonblank entries in *list*
@MAX(*list*)	Returns the maximum value in *list*
@MIN(*list*)	Returns the minimum value in *list*
@STD(*list*)	Calculates the standard deviation of the values in *list*
@STDS(*list*)	Calculates the sample standard deviation of the values in *list*
@SUM(*list*)	Totals the values in *list*
@SUMPRODUCT(*list*)	Multiplies the parts of *list* and adds their results
@VAR(*list*)	Computes the variance for the values in *list*
@VARS(*list*)	Computes the sample variance for the values in *list*

Follow these steps to create a worksheet to try out the @SUM function:

1. Place the following entries in the cells listed:

C1:	**High Profits Inc. Sales**	A12:	**Total:**
C2:	**Region 4**	C5:	**"Sales**
A5:	**Salesperson**	C6:	**95800**
A6:	**Jason Rye**	C7:	**56780**
A7:	**Paul Jones**	C8:	**89675**
A8:	**Mary Hart**	C9:	**91555**
A9:	**Tom Bush**	C10:	**92300**
A10:	**Jane Hunt**		

Rather than entering a formula to total sales, you can use the @SUM function.

2. Move to C12, type **@SUM(C6.C10)**, and click the confirm button or press (return) (or (enter)).

The formula you have just entered is equivalent to the formula +C6+C7+C8+C9+C10. The advantage of this formula is that it is easier to enter. Also, in Chapter 7, "Changing Row and Column Options," you will learn how to insert rows. When you insert rows in the middle of a range, 1-2-3 automatically expands the range to include the inserted rows. This means that if you add another salesperson between Jason Rye and Jane Hunt, 1-2-3 will automatically include their sales in the @SUM formula.

The @COUNT function is an exception to the others in the statistical category since it often used with value and text entries. You can add this function to the worksheet.

3. Move to A13, type **Number of Salespeople:**, and move to C13.
4. Select the @Function pop-up menu, Statistical, and COUNT().

1-2-3 adds @COUNT(list) to the entry and highlights "list" so your entry will replace 1-2-3's description of the function arguments this command uses. These function argument descriptions provide a reminder of the information you must supply. With other functions that use multiple arguments, you must check that you remove the text of 1-2-3's description of the function arguments. The function arguments are provided as you add functions to an entry through the @Function pop-up menu when the Add Arguments option in the @Function pop-up menu is turned on (a check mark appears next to it).

5. Type **C6..C10** as the range to use in place of "list," and click the confirm button or press (enter) to finish the worksheet, as shown in Figure 4-2.
6. Choose Save in the File menu or press (⌘)-(S), type **High Profits** and click Save or press (return).
7. Click the close box or press (⌘)-(W) to close the worksheet and then choose New in the File menu or press (⌘)-(N) to open a new one.

Applications: *You can use the statistical functions to create a management summary report. Rather than showing all the detail, you can use these functions to compute sums, averages, and counts.*

Figure 4-2. *Totaling values with the @SUM function and counting entries with the @COUNT function*

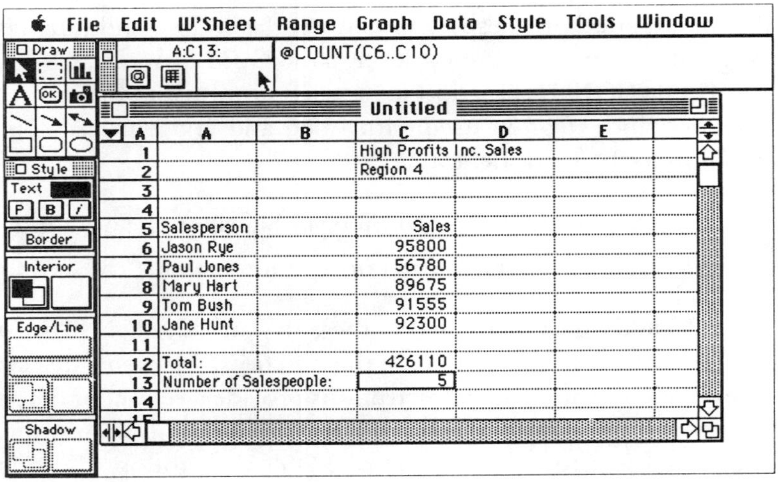

Calendar Functions

Date information and time information are important parts of many business decisions. You need date information to know if a loan is overdue or if there is still time remaining in the discount period for an invoice. You can use time information to calculate the service time for various tasks or to log the delivery time for various carriers. In Chapter 2, "Entering Text and Numbers," you learned how to enter dates and times. The calendar functions are an alternative approach for making these entries and allow you to work with one component of a date or time, such as the year or minute for the entry. Many of the date and time functions expect a time or date number as their argument. The *calendar functions* are shown in Table 4-2.

Table 4-2. *Calendar Functions*

Function Entry	**Description**
@D360(*start_date,end_date*)	Calculates the number of days between two dates using a 360-day year
@DATE(*year,month,day*)	Creates a date number
@DATEVALUE(*string*)	Converts *string* in a valid date format to a date number
@DAY(*date_number*)	Extracts a day number from *date_number*
@HOUR(*time_number*)	Extracts an hour from *time_number*
@MINUTE(*time_number*)	Extracts the minute number from *time_number*
@MONTH(*date_number*)	Extracts a month from *date_number*
@NOW	Returns the current date and time number
@SECOND(*time_number*)	Extracts a second from a *time_number*
@TIME(*hour,minutes,seconds*)	Creates a time number
@TODAY	Enters the current date number
@TIMEVALUE(*string*)	Converts *string* in a valid time format to a time number
@YEAR(*date_number*)	Extracts a year from *date_number*

You can enter **@NOW** in a worksheet cell to generate a date and time stamp. 1-2-3 accesses the system clock in your machine and places a date/time number in the cell to represent the current date and time. If the date is December 31, 1991 and the time is noon, the date/time number will be 33603.5. The whole-number portion of the entry represents the date, and the decimal fraction represents the time. The result of the @NOW function is updated when you open the document containing the @function and when the worksheet is recalculated, since the time is constantly changing. In Chapter 6, "Changing the Appearance of Worksheet Entries," you will learn how you can display the date and time numbers as the dates and times they represent.

To try one of these functions, type **@YEAR(@NOW)** and click the confirm button or press (return). The result, in this case 91, indicates the year for the date number created by @NOW.

Applications: *The calendar functions allow you to build applications that age accounts receivable, determine if an invoice is past due, compute charges for services performed on an hourly or daily basis, and determine how many days remain before an important presentation.*

Text Functions

Text functions provide a variety of character-manipulation formulas that give you flexibility in rearranging text entries. With text functions, you can work with the entire text entry for a cell or with just a part of it. The functions in this category can be real lifesavers when you have to correct data-entry errors. The same function you create for one entry could be copied down a column to correct a large portion of a worksheet. Table 4-3 provides a list of all the text functions.

You can use the @UPPER function to correct data-entry errors involving the inconsistent use of capital letters. The syntax of the function is @UPPER(*string*) to convert an entry to uppercase. An example of the @UPPER function might look like this:

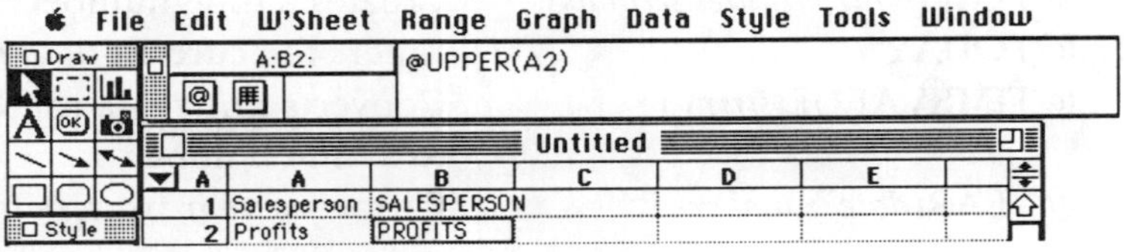

Table 4-3. *Text Functions*

Function Entry	Description
@CHAR(*x*)	Returns a LMBCS character corresponding to the number *x* to create foreign characters and special symbols
@CLEAN(*string*)	Removes non-printable characters from *string*
@CODE(*string*)	Returns the LMBCS code of the first character in *string*
@EXACT(*string1*,*string2*)	Returns 1 if *string1* and *string2* are identical and 0 if they are not identical
@FIND(*search_string*,*string*, *start_number*)	Returns the position of *search_string* in *string*
@LEFT(*string*,*n*)	Extracts *n* number of characters from the left side of *string*
@LENGTH(*string*)	Returns the number of characters in *string*
@LOWER(*string*)	Converts *string* to lowercase
@MID(*string*,*start_number*,*n*)	Returns *n* characters from the middle of *string* beginning with the position *start_number*
@N(*range*)	Returns the entry in the first cell of *range* as a value
@PROPER(*string*)	Converts *string* to propercase (first letter of each word is capitalized and the rest is lowercase)
@REPEAT(*string*,*n*)	Repeats *string* *n* times
@REPLACE(*original_string*, *start_number*,*n*,*new*)	Replaces *n* characters in *original_string* with *new* string beginning at position *start_number*
@RIGHT(*string*,*n*)	Extracts *n* characters from the right side of *string*

4

Table 4-3. Text Functions (continued)

Function Entry	**Description**
@S(*range*)	Returns the entry from the first cell in *range* as a text entry
@STRING(*x*,*n*)	Converts the value *x* to a text entry with *n* decimal places
@TRIM(*string*)	Removes beginning, trailing, and extra spaces from *string*
@UPPER(*string*)	Converts *string* to uppercase
@VALUE(*string*)	Converts *string* that looks like a value to a value

You convert the entries in A1 and A2 to uppercase by placing @UPPER(A1) and @UPPER(A2) in B1 and B2. Once you convert the entries, you can replace the original entries with the function results using the Convert to Value command in the Range menu that you will learn about in Chapter 9, "Making 1-2-3 Do Your Work."

Applications: *You can use text @functions to split lengthy entries into smaller parts such as splitting a name into its first and last components. You would use text @functions for this purpose when you want to put data entries into a consistent format.*

Mathematical Functions

1-2-3's *mathematical functions* perform both simple calculations and more complex operations such as logarithms. Table 4-4 is a complete list of mathematical functions.

You can overcome rounding problems where the total of numbers displayed differs from the total because the displayed numbers do not include digits after the decimal point while the total calculation uses these values after the decimal point in the calculation. The @INT function returns the whole-number portion of an entry. @INT requires only a single argument, the number that you want to work with. The function accepts a number, a formula, or another @function that returns a value for this entry. If you enter

Table 4-4. *Mathematical Functions*

Function Entry	Description
@ABS(*x*)	Returns the absolute value of *x*
@EXP(*x*)	Calculates the value of 2.718282 raised to the *x* power
@INT(*x*)	Returns the integer portion of *x*
@LN(*x*)	Calculates the natural log of *x*
@LOG(*x*)	Calculates the base 10 log of *x*
@MOD(*x*,*y*)	Returns the remainder when *x* is divided by *y*
@RAND	Returns a random number between 0 and 1
@ROUND(*x*,*n*)	Rounds the value *x* to the *n*th place
@SQRT(*x*)	Returns the square root of *x*

@INT(@NOW), 1-2-3 returns the date number portion of the date/time stamp. If you enter **@INT(B3/B6)**, 1-2-3 divides the value in B3 by the value in B6 and then discards any decimal fraction in the result before returning it. For example, **@INT(10/3)** would return a 3 rather than 3.3333333.

Trigonometric Functions

1-2-3's *trigonometric functions* return values for commonly used trigonometric functions. Most of these functions are specifically designed for engineering and scientific applications. Table 4-5 is a complete list of trigonometric functions.

For example, you can calculate the perimeter of a circle five feet across using the value of PI. To make this calculation, you would enter **@PI*5** to produce the results of 15.707963.

Special Functions

1-2-3's special functions are grouped together because they do not fit neatly into any of the other function categories. Some of them trap error conditions; others count the number of rows in a range or allow you to choose a value from a list of options. Still others let you examine the contents of worksheet cells closely, thus providing information about a cell's value or other attributes. For the most part, this group can be thought of as a

Table 4-5. Trigonometric Functions

Function Entry	Description
@ACOS(*x*)	Returns the arccosine of the value *x*
@ASIN(*x*)	Returns the arcsine of the value *x*
@ATAN(*x*)	Returns the arctangent of the value *x*
@ATAN2(*x,y*)	Returns the arctangent of *y/x*
@COS(*x*)	Returns the cosine of the angle *x* (radians)
@PI	Returns the value 3.1415926536
@SIN(*x*)	Returns the sine of the angle *x* (radians)
@TAN(*x*)	Returns the tangent of the angle *x* (radians)

smorgasbord of sophisticated features. Table 4-6 provides a complete list of the special functions.

Table 4-6. Special Functions

Function Entry	Description
@@(*location*)	Returns the address of the contents of the cell or range specified by *location*
@CELL(*attribute,location*)	Returns specific information about the first cell in the cell or range *location* as indicated by the string *attribute*
@CELLPOINTER(*attribute*)	Returns information about the active cell as specified by the string *attribute*
@CHOOSE(*offset,list*)	Returns the *offset* entry from *list*
@COLS(*range*)	Returns the number of columns in *range*
@COORD(*worksheet,column, row,absolute*)	Creates a cell address from the *worksheet, column,* and *row* numbers you provide
@ERR	Returns the value ERR
@HLOOKUP(*x,range, row_offset*)	Returns a value from *range* from the *row* indicated by *row_offset*

Table 4-6. *Special Functions* (continued)

Function Entry	Description
@INDEX(*range,column, row_offset,sheet*)	Returns an entry from the table range as indicated by the three offsets provided
@INFO(*attribute*)	Returns information about the current 1-2-3 session
@NA	Returns the value NA
@ROWS(*range*)	Returns the number of rows in *range*
@SHEETS(*range*)	Returns the number of sheets in *range*
@VLOOKUP(*x,range, column_offset*)	Returns a value from *range* from the column indicated by *column_offset*

One of the more interesting special @functions is the @VLOOKUP function. This function uses a table of values like the one in rows 11 through 14 of the worksheet in Figure 4-3. When you use this function, it looks in the first column of the table for either the text that exactly matches a text entry or the highest value that is equal to or less than the value you are looking for. When it finds this text or value, it returns an entry from the same column or another column of the table, using the row from the table containing the entry it found. The format of this function is @VLOOKUP(*x,range,column_offset*). *X* is the text or value you are trying to find in the table. *Range* is the worksheet range that contains the table. *Column_offset* selects from which column of the table the function returns the value. The first column has an offset of 0, the second column has an offset of 1, and so on. To try this function and see how it works, follow these steps:

1. Place the following entries in the worksheet cells listed:

C1:	**High Profits Inc.**	C6:	**19**
C2:	**Invoice Listing**	C7:	**16**
A5:	**"Invoice #**	C8:	**11**
B5:	**"Amount**	A10:	**"Number**
C4:	**"Salesperson**	A11:	**11**
C5:	**"Number**	A12:	**15**
D4:	**Salesperson**	A13:	**16**

D5:	**Name**	A14:	**19**
A6:	**1001**	B10:	**Salesperson**
A7:	**1002**	B11:	**J. Rye**
A8:	**1003**	B12:	**P. Jones**
B6:	**15167**	B13:	**M. Hart**
B7:	**78312**	B14:	**T. Bush**
B8:	**45377**		

2. Enter the following formulas in the worksheet cells listed:

D6:	**@VLOOKUP(C6,A11..B14,1)**
D7:	**@VLOOKUP(C7,A11..B14,1)**
D8:	**@VLOOKUP(C8,A11..B14,1)**

Your worksheet now looks like Figure 4-3. For each formula in column D, 1-2-3 searched the table in A11..B14 for the entry that matched the entry in column C. When 1-2-3 found a match, 1-2-3 returned the entry stored in the second column of the table (column B), which has a column offset of 1.

3. Choose Save in the File menu or press (⌘)-(S), type **High Profits Inventory**, and click Save or press (return).

Figure 4-3. *Using the @VLOOKUP special function*

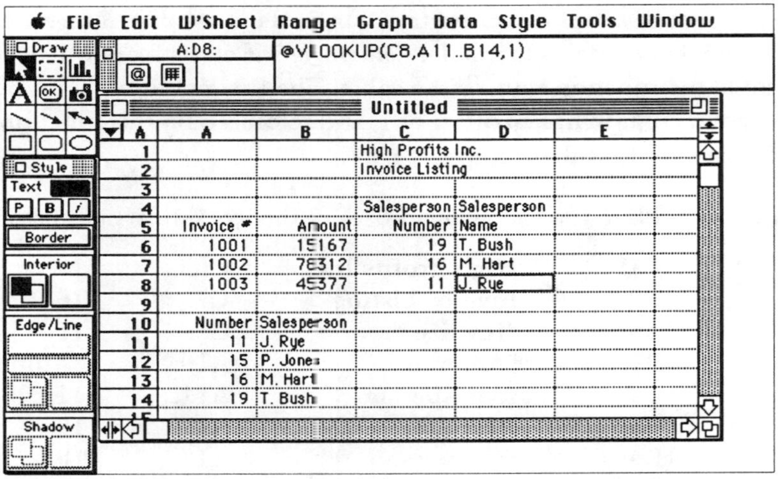

4. Click the close box or press ⌘-W to close the worksheet.
5. Choose New from the File menu or press ⌘-N to open a new worksheet.

Applications: *The @VLOOKUP function can be used to compute federal or state tax withholding, shipping rates, commissions, part prices, or hourly rates for various skilled employees.*

Financial Functions

1-2-3 provides an entire category of functions to use in investment calculations and other calculations concerned with the time value of money. You can use these *financial functions* to calculate loan payments, annuities, cash flows, and depreciation. You can quickly compare various financial alternatives since you can rely on the function to supply the correct formulas. As with the other functions, all you need to supply are arguments to tailor the calculations to your exact needs. Table 4-7 lists all of the financial functions and the arguments they use.

When you use financial functions, it is very important that all of the arguments and the result use the same unit of time. For example, the @PMT function, which computes a loan payment, requires you to decide whether you want to calculate the payment amount on a yearly, quarterly, or monthly basis. Once you decide on some unit of time, you must apply it consistently across all arguments. If you choose to compute a monthly payment amount, the interest rate is a monthly rate. Likewise, the term is the number of months of the loan.

The following illustration shows the computation of a loan payment:

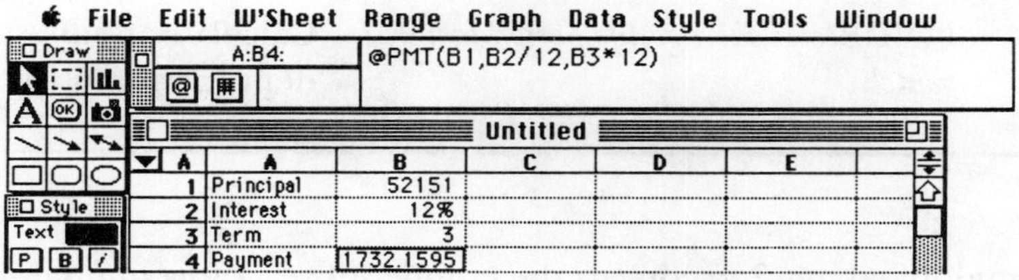

The principal in B1 is used as the first argument. The interest rate in B2 is divided by 12 to convert the yearly rate to a monthly rate. The term in B3 is

Table 4-7. Financial Functions

Function Entry	Description
@CTERM(*int,future_value, present_ value*)	Calculates the number of compounding periods *present_value* requires to attain *future_value*
@DDB(*cost,salvage,life,period*)	Calculates depreciation with the double-declining balance method
@FV(*payments,interest,term*)	Calculates a future value for an annuity investment
@IRR(*guess,range*)	Calculates an internal rate of return
@NPV(*interest,range*)	Calculates the net present value of a series of cash flows
@PMT(*principal,interest,term*)	Calculates a loan payment
@PV(*payments,interest,term*)	Calculates the present value
@RATE(*future_value,present_value, term*)	Calculates the interest rate *present_value* needs to reach *future_value*
@SLN(*cost,salvage,life*)	Calculates the straight-line depreciation
@SYD(*cost,salvage,life,period*)	Calculates the sum-of-the-years'-digits depreciation
@TERM(*payments,interest, future_value*)	Calculates the number of periods needed for an annuity to reach *future_value*
@VDB(*cost,salvage,life,period,factor, switch*)	Calculates double- declining depreciation using a variable rate

multiplied by 12 to convert the number of years to a number of months. The complete function entry is

@PMT(B1,B2/12,B3*12)

Applications: The financial functions are used in many financial applications, including computing loan payments and calculating the value and yield in investments.

Logical Functions

1-2-3's *logical functions* build conditional features into your worksheets. The functions in this category return logical values (true or false) as the result of the condition tests they perform. They are a powerful addition to 1-2-3 because they allow you to alter calculations based on conditions in other locations of the worksheet. This flexibility lets you construct worksheets patterned after real-world business conditions, where exceptions are prevalent. Table 4-8 is a complete list of the logical functions.

Logical functions let you have more than one calculation for commission payments, purchase discounts, FICA tax, or any other computation requiring multiple calculations that depend on other values in the worksheet. The @IF function is the most popular logical function, since it allows you to test a condition to determine what you want to use as the result of the @function. Use the @IF logical @function when you need to decide which of two entries should be in a cell based on some condition. The function syntax is

@IF(*condition_test,value_if_true,value_if_false*)

Valid entries would include

@IF(B4>100,.15,.08)
@IF(D4>500,D4*.15,D4*.08)

To create a worksheet using the second example of the @IF function, follow these steps:

1. Place the following entries in the worksheet cells listed:

B1:	**ABC Inc.**	F4:	**+D4–E4**
B2:	**Product Order Form**	A5:	**Printer**
A3:	**Item**	B5:	**800**
B3:	**"Cost**	C5:	**5**

Table 4-8. *Logical Functions*

Function Entry	Description
@FALSE	Returns the logical value 0
@IF(*condition,x,y*)	Tests *condition* and returns *x* if it is true and *y* if it is false
@ISERR(*x*)	Tests *x* for the value ERR and returns 0 for false and 1 for true
@ISNA(*x*)	Tests *x* for the value NA and returns 0 for false and 1 for true
@ISNUMBER(*x*)	Tests *x* to see if it is a value and returns 0 for false and 1 for true
@ISRANGE(*range*)	Tests *range* to see if it is a valid range address or range name and returns 0 for false and 1 for true
@ISSTRING(*x*)	Tests *x* to see if it is a string and returns 0 for false and 1 for true
@TRUE	Returns the logical value 1

C3:	**"Quantity**
D3:	**"Subtotal**
E3:	**"Discount**
F3:	**"Total**
A4:	**Computer**
B4:	**6780**
C4:	**3**
D4:	**+B4*C4**
D5:	**+B5*C5**
F5:	**+D5–E5**
A6:	**Cables**
B6:	**5.99**
C6:	**25**
D6:	**+B6*C6**
F6:	**+D6–E6**

2. Enter the following formulas in the worksheet cells listed:

E4:	**@IF(D4>15000,D4*.15,D4*.08)**
E5:	**@IF(D5>15000,D5*.15,D5*.08)**
E6:	**@IF(D6>15000,D6*.15,D6*.08)**

Now the worksheet looks like this:

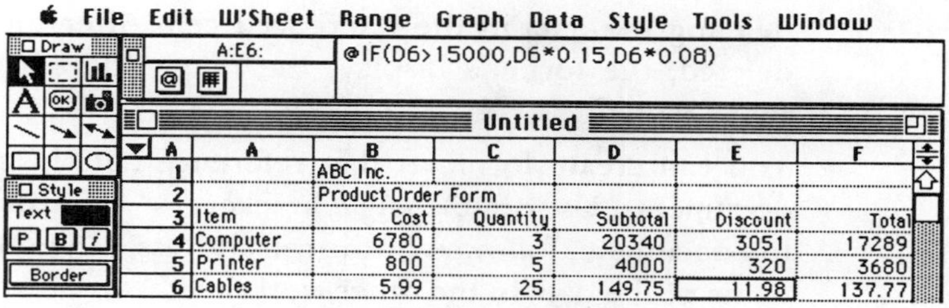

The formulas in column E compute the purchase discount. The discount is 15 percent for orders over $15000 and 8 percent for orders of $15000 or less. The formula compares the order total in column D to the $15000 amount and provides true and false alternatives for the comparison. For the first item, the 15 percent discount applies, while for the other two, the 8 percent discount is used. The @IF function lets 1-2-3 make the decision, based on the values stored in other cells.

3. Choose Save in the File menu or press ⌘-S, type **ABC Product Order** and click Save or press return.
4. Click the close box or press ⌘-W to close this worksheet and then choose New in the File menu or press ⌘-N to open a new one.

Applications: *Use @IF to give different discounts, depending on purchase levels; to calculate vacation days, depending on years of service; to calculate overtime pay; and to see if you are eligible to pay the discounted amount on an invoice.*

Review

In this chapter, you learned more advanced 1-2-3 features that you can use with formulas. These advanced features include range names, link formulas, and functions. Specifically, you learned the following:

- A range name can be assigned to any cell or range on the worksheet. To access an existing range name, use the Range pop-up menu when building a formula or to move to the named range.

- A range name that is no longer needed can be deleted without deleting the data in the referenced cell. After the range name is deleted, the formula displays the range address rather than the range name.
- You can create formulas that reference data in other worksheet documents. Use double angle brackets (<< >>) around the name of the document, followed by the cell address, range address, or range name of the data in the other worksheet.
- @Functions are prerecorded formulas. You access them by typing @ followed by a keyword. Most @functions also have arguments that define your specific needs to 1-2-3. These arguments are enclosed in parentheses and separated by commas.
- You can select the @Function pop-up menu to add an @function to an entry. You can also have 1-2-3 add the arguments the @function uses to the @function.
- There are nine categories of @functions. Statistical functions perform basic statistical calculations. Calendar functions work with date and time numbers. Text functions manipulate character strings. Mathematical functions access mathematical operations. Trigonometric functions access functions that work with angles. Financial computations involve the time value of money or depreciation. Special functions are miscellaneous functions that do not fit into other categories. Logical functions test conditions. Data management functions, which are covered with databases in Chapter 12, "Data-Management Basics," perform selective computations with 1-2-3 database records.

Keys and Commands

The keys you learned to use in this chapter help you build link formulas. You also learned commands that assign names to worksheet ranges and save a worksheet with a different document name. These keys and commands are

Entry	Action
<< >>	Encloses a document name as part of reference to data in another document
[@] (@Function pop-up menu)	Displays a list of @function names that you can add to a formula
[▦] (Range pop-up menu)	Displays a list of range names that you can select or add to a formula
File Save As	File Save As saves a document with a name you provide
Range Name Create (⌘-R)	Assigns a name to a cell or range
Range Name Delete	Removes the assignment of a name to a range without affecting the data in the range

5

Menus, Dialog Boxes, and Palettes

Although you can make entries on the worksheet without using menus, you cannot access any of 1-2-3's other features without them. Menus are your initial interface for telling 1-2-3 exactly what you want it to do for you. You can use either your mouse or keyboard to make menu selections, although most Macintosh users prefer the mouse.

If you have used 1-2-3 for DOS in the IBM environment you will find that the menu that you see at the top of your screen does not match the menu you used under DOS. While you are mastering its new structure, you will still be able to access the familiar menu from the past, which is called the 1-2-3 Classic menu in the Macintosh version.

With 1-2-3 for the Macintosh's menu structure you can make an initial menu selection and then define your specific requirements through pull-down menus, submenus, or dialog boxes. *Pull-down menus* pull down from the menu bar and allow you to see the commands in the menu at a glance. The pull-down menu display also indicates whether a selection will finalize a command or display a submenu menu or dialog box. *Submenus* display next to the pull-down menu and allow you to look at the entire chain of command entries within an entry. *Dialog boxes* present many items in a concise format. Dialog boxes are especially useful with a mouse, since you can make changes to a number of items with a quick click of the mouse and an entry or two to fill in needed information. You will find that dialog boxes organize all your selections on one screen and provide a quick way to handle all the details.

Palettes are actually another form of commands available in 1-2-3 for the Macintosh. Palettes offer more flexibility than other menus since you can locate them anywhere you wish. Palettes are used for drawing, selecting graph types, and choosing styles.

1-2-3's Menus

1-2-3's menu bar is designed to make 1-2-3's commands easy to access and remember. A quick mouse action or a key combination is all you need to access the menu commands. Lotus has chosen menu titles that represent their functions, making it easier to decide which menu and command to choose.

While 1-2-3 may have a wide variety of commands, do not be overwhelmed. You can accomplish 90 percent of your work by using only a small percentage of the total menu. The other commands are there to provide sophisticated options for 1-2-3's power users. The menu bar, although inactive, is always visible, as shown here:

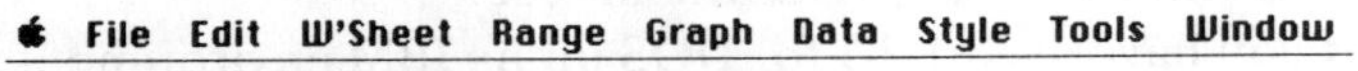

Your menu bar may not exactly match the one shown since there are several variations that could add a few extra menu titles. Depending on your monitor's resolution, Worksheet may be abbreviated as W'Sheet. If you are using System 7 on your Macintosh, you will have a Help menu title at the far right side of the menu bar. If you are using MultiFinder features (always in System 7 and available in System 6), you will have an icon for the Finder that shows 1-2-3 since it is the current application. The menu bar with System 7 looks like this:

Activating a Menu

You activate any 1-2-3 menu in the menu bar by moving the mouse to the desired menu title and pulling down its menu. Once the pull-down menu appears you can continue dragging down until you reach the desired selection. Selections followed by ... (an ellipsis) have a dialog box that must be completed before you see the effect of your selection. Selections with a ▶ will display a submenu; for these you can drag across and down until the desired selection is made and release the mouse button. Pull-down menu items without ... or ▶ will complete the requested command as soon as you release the mouse button. Some of the selections in a pull-down menu have ⌘ and a letter to the right of this. This is a *keyboard shortcut.* You have learned about a few of these such as ⌘-S, ⌘-W, and ⌘-N in prior chapters. Other commands have these shortcuts so you can quickly perform a command by holding down the ⌘ key while you type a letter.

Although using the mouse seems to be the preferred approach to menu selections, you can use the keyboard if you wish by pressing option-/ to activate the menu bar. Next, type the first letter of the desired pull-down menu or use the arrow keys to choose a pull-down menu associated with the menu bar's menu titles.

1-2-3 lets you know which menu commands you cannot choose by *dimming* them. If the letters are printed in gray instead of black, the command is unavailable. For example, most of the selections in the Graph pull-down menu cannot be chosen until you select an existing graph or create a new one so most of the commands in the Graph pull-down menu are initially dimmed.

Most of the 1-2-3 commands should be started from Ready mode. If the mode indicator is not Ready, you may need to take an action to return the indicator to Ready before choosing a command. This may include completing an entry, waiting for 1-2-3 to finish its current task, or finishing a dialog box. The mode indicator will read Menu, Edit, or Point while you are using the menu.

Menus Accessible from the Menu Bar

The menu titles in the menu bar each provide a number of selections. Like selections are grouped under the menu titles to make it easy to find the information that you are looking for. Each of these menu selections will be discussed in more detail as you proceed through this book. Before you examine any one particular menu choice in further detail, take a quick look at each of the menu choices and the category of tasks it performs:

Menu	**Selection**
	Works with Apple desk accessories. This menu allows you to access help if you are not using System 7 and other applications set up as aliases if you are using System 7.
File	Gets and puts data on disks, combines data, and prints your data.
Edit	Moves and copies data between areas on a worksheet, between worksheets, and between applications; undoes entries or commands.
Worksheet (W'Sheet)	Makes changes that affect the entire worksheet, including adding and removing columns, rows, and sheets; adjusts colors, column widths, and row heights.
Range	Makes changes to an area within a worksheet, including formatting numbers and assigning names; also allows you to change the active cell.
Graph	Creates and names graphs created with worksheet data.
Data	Sorts data, searches data for matching information, and performs other data management.
Style	Adds word processing formatting such as fonts, lines, colors, and shading to worksheet cells.
Tools	Provides drawing and layout features, changes global settings and provides macro and Backsolve features.
Window	Changes the display of worksheet windows.
	Available with System 7 only. Opens and displays a help window on different 1-2-3 topics. Allows you to turn System 7's balloon help on and off.
	Available only with Multitasking. Switches between applications and determines which ones appear on the screen.

Choosing Commands from a Menu

As mentioned previously, using the mouse is the technique of choice for most Macintosh users. All menu titles in the menu bar can be chosen by dragging down a pull-down menu to the desired command. If the command requires a selection from a submenu, you must complete the dragging process into the submenu choice before releasing the mouse button.

You learned that you could activate the menu bar from the keyboard by pressing option-/. Next, you can choose a pull down menu by typing the first letter in the pull-down menu. If the keyboard is used to pull down a menu, the menu will remain on the screen until you make a selection. To choose a command from a pull-down menu, use the ↑ and ↓ to highlight it or type the first letter of the command and then press return when the desired command is selected. Typing a letter moves to the next command that starts with that letter.

A list of choices in a pull-down menu might look like this:

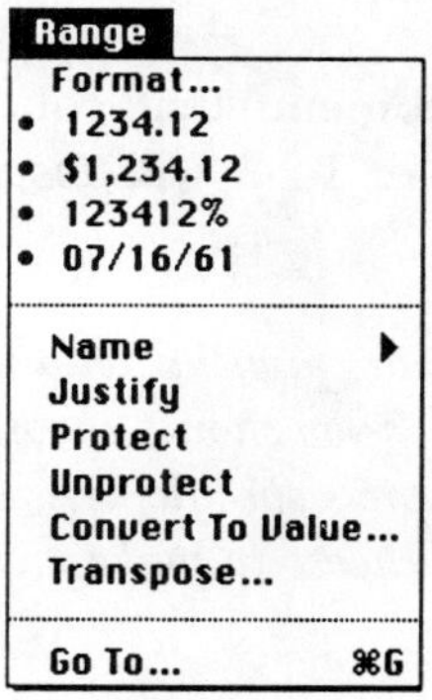

Pull-down menus let you further refine your request. When you choose a command in a pull-down menu, 1-2-3 may perform the command, display another menu (called a submenu), or display a dialog box to prompt for more information. You can tell what will happen by looking at any characters to the right of the command. For example, next to Name in the Range pull-down menu, 1-2-3 displays a triangle. This indicates that if you choose Name, 1-2-3 will display a submenu. Next to Format, 1-2-3 displays three dots (an ellipsis). This indicates that if you choose Format, 1-2-3 will display a dialog box.

Commands like Protect do not have any characters after them, indicating that 1-2-3 will perform the Protect command in the Range menu as soon as you choose Protect.

You can try making menu selections by following these directions:

1. Drag down the Range pull-down menu or press option-/ and press R.

If you are using a mouse you will need to continue to press the mouse button. 1-2-3 displays the Range pull-down menu, which includes Format, several common range format selections, Name, Justify, Protect, Unprotect, Convert to Value, Transpose, and Go To. Name has a triangle next to it indicating that if you choose Name, 1-2-3 will display a submenu. Format, Convert to Value, Transpose, and Go To have ellipses to indicate that if you choose one of them, 1-2-3 will display a dialog box.

2. Continue dragging down to Name, or press N to choose Name if you are using the keyboard.

1-2-3 displays a submenu that contains Create, Label Create, Delete, Notes, and Paste Table. 1-2-3 will display a dialog box for any of these selections.

Note: *As you become more familiar with menu selections, this book will give only the names of the commands you should choose for each exercise; you will no longer be told to use the mouse or press specific keys. It does not matter how you activate the menu or which way you choose to make menu selections–use whatever method you prefer.*

Canceling a Selection

Since you are just examining the menu structure, do not make any additional selections at this time. You can cancel your selections up to this point by releasing the mouse or pressing ⌘-. or esc. If a dialog box is on the screen, click the Cancel button or press ⌘-. or esc. If a selection within one dialog box causes another dialog box to display, you will need to click the Cancel button in both dialog boxes to close them. You can start over in making a new selection.

1-2-3's Classic Menu

If you have used 1-2-3 for DOS, you may not be comfortable with the Macintosh 1-2-3 menu. To make 1-2-3 easier for you to use, 1-2-3 has included both menus. When you press (/), 1-2-3 displays the 1-2-3 Classic menu:

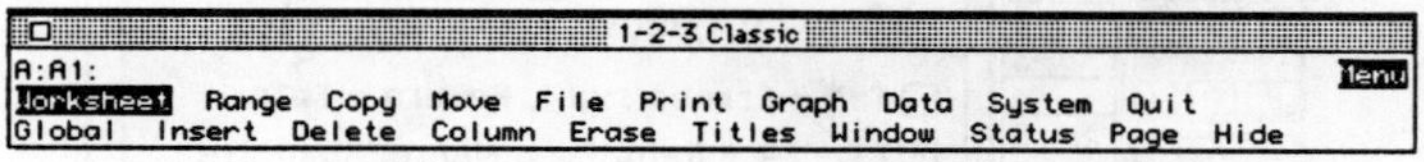

This is the same menu that 1-2-3 Release 3 for DOS uses. If you are accustomed to earlier releases, you will find all of your old commands there, as well as the new features that were added in later releases. This menu behaves just like the menu in 1-2-3 for DOS. This menu helps you make the transition between 1-2-3 for DOS and 1-2-3 for the Macintosh at a pace you find comfortable.

If nothing happens when you press (/), your copy of 1-2-3 is not set to display the 1-2-3 Classic menu. To change this, choose User Setup in the Tools menu and then choose Preferences. Next, with / selected in the first box, select 123 Classic in the second box by pressing (⌘)-(C), highlighting 123 Classic, and pressing (return) or dragging down on the arrow to change Nothing or Menu to 123 Classic. Finally, click OK or press (return).

Dialog Boxes

Some of 1-2-3's menu selections display dialog boxes. Dialog boxes let you provide additional information that 1-2-3 needs to perform a command for you. For example, when you want to open a document, 1-2-3 needs to know the name of the one you want and where it is located. Figure 5-1 shows a dialog box.

Dialog boxes contain title bars that you can use to move the dialog box on the screen just as you can move worksheet windows. The dialog box is filled with the various components that allow you to make different types of entries.

Figure 5-1. *User Setup Preferences dialog box showing dialog box components*

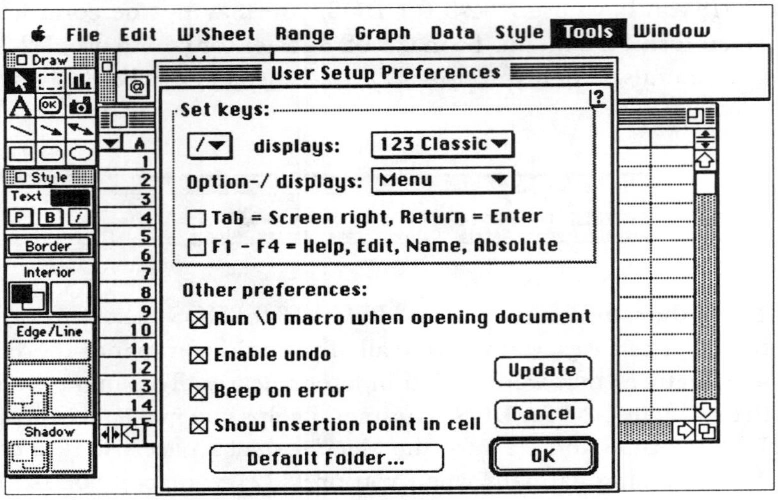

You can use the mouse to select different dialog box components or, in some cases, a key combination consisting of a letter and the ⌘ key. You can hold down the ⌘ key until you see the key combination that will activate different areas of the box. Dialog boxes contain the following types of components:

- *Check boxes* add or remove features. They appear as boxes that are blank, are selected with an X, or are shaded. You can see check boxes under Other preferences in Figure 5-1. Check boxes can be clicked with the mouse to change the setting. You can also press the ⌘ key combination to toggle the setting between an X and blank.
- *Buttons* perform an action, such as finalizing a command, closing a dialog box, or switching to another dialog box. Most dialog boxes contain the OK button to finalize selections and the Cancel button to return to Ready mode or a previous dialog box without performing the command. You can click a button like Cancel to select it, or you can use a combination such as ⌘-. to make the selection. If

you press return, you will select the default button, which is the one with an extra outline around it (usually OK).

- *Pop-Up menus* display a list that you can select from by dragging the arrow or by using the ⌘ key combination to activate the menu, highlighting the desired selection, and pressing return. In Figure 5-1, the two boxes after "displays:" are pop-up menus. You can select whether pressing / and option-/ will display nothing or the 1-2-3 Classic menu, or you can activate the menu bar by pressing the box and highlighting a new selection. If you use the ⌘ key combination (⌘-C and ⌘-M in these cases), the menu will pop up and remain until you highlight your selection with the ↑ and ↓ keys and press return.
- *Information boxes* list information without letting you make any changes. In Figure 5-2, the box in the Style Font dialog box that shows "Sample 123" with the selected font is an information box.
- *List boxes* provide a list of options that you can select from. The list of typeface styles under Font: in Figure 5-2 is a list box. When a list box has more options than fit in the box, the list box will include a scroll bar for changing the section of the list that appears in the list box. You can click on the desired selection in a list box or use the mouse to drag the scroll box to see another area of the list. To use the keyboard, use the ↑ and ↓ keys and return to select.
- *Radio buttons* select features from a group of exclusive choices (that is, only one can be selected at a time). The radio buttons that make up an exclusive set are grouped together. You can click any radio button or its text or press its ⌘ key combination to select it. Radio buttons are the ones shown here next to Formulas, Text, and Both:

Figure 5-2. *Style Font dialog box*

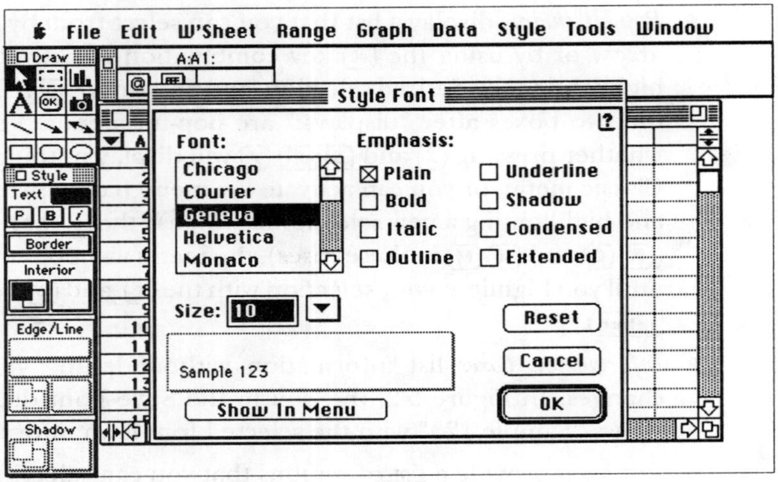

- *Text boxes* accept lengthy entries. The type of entry you should make is described next to the text box. You must make text box entries with the keyboard. The Search for and Replace with text boxes shown earlier are two examples of text boxes. You can also use (tab) to switch between text and list boxes or between text boxes.

To try using the different components of a dialog box, follow these steps:

1. Choose User Setup in the Tools menu, then choose Preferences to display the dialog box in Figure 5-1.

The extra border around OK indicates that it is the default button that is selected if you press (enter) or (return). This dialog box has two check boxes under Set keys and four under Other preferences, three pop-up menus under Set keys, a button that will activate a dialog box for Default Folders, and buttons for Update, Cancel, and OK. With the exception of OK, every component has a (⌘) key sequence that you can use from the keyboard.

2. Click the check box for Beep on Error or press ⌘-B to deselect this check box.

When a check box has an X in it, it is selected. When the check box is empty, it is deselected.

3. Repeat step 2 to select this check box again.
4. Click the button for Default Folder or press ⌘-D.

The ellipsis in this button indicates that another dialog box will display.

5. Click Cancel in this new dialog box or press ⌘-..
6. Point to the first pop-up menu box containing the / then press the mouse button to look at the other choices. Although you could drag to the other selection to make a change, you will want to leave the current setting in effect and should release the mouse button with the check next to the /.

7. Press ⌘ until you can view the assignment for each dialog box component.
8. Press ⌘-I to select the first pop-up menu under Set Keys.
9. Press ⌘-. to remove the pop-up menu.
10. Click the Cancel button, press ⌘-., or press esc to return to Ready mode.

Palettes

1-2-3 for the Macintosh provides three palettes. Two are on the screen when you start 1-2-3. These two palettes offer features for drawing and changing style characteristics. The Draw palette adds arrows, rectangles, or lines to worksheet data to highlight important areas or to create a custom form. The Style palette can change the style of cells and entries including adding boldface and color. You can use the palette to change the border around cells or the frame around a graph. You will learn more about using the various palettes in later chapters as their features are discussed.

A Graph palette that shows the graph types will set the graph type of an existing graph or one you create. Initially this palette is not visible, although you can choose New Graph or Change Type in the Graph menu and drag the palette to any location on the screen. Figure 5-3 shows the screen with the two initial palettes and the Graph palette. You can drag any of these palettes to new locations or close any or all of them. If you close the Draw palette you can use the Draw command in the Tools menu or press ⌘-D to bring it back again. If the Style palette is not displayed, you can use the Show Palette command in the Style menu or press ⌘-Y to open it again.

Applications: *On a large worksheet application, such as a monthly budget, you might want to click the close buttons on the palettes, drag your worksheet to the left, and enlarge it to fill the extra space.*

Figure 5-3. *Three palettes displayed*

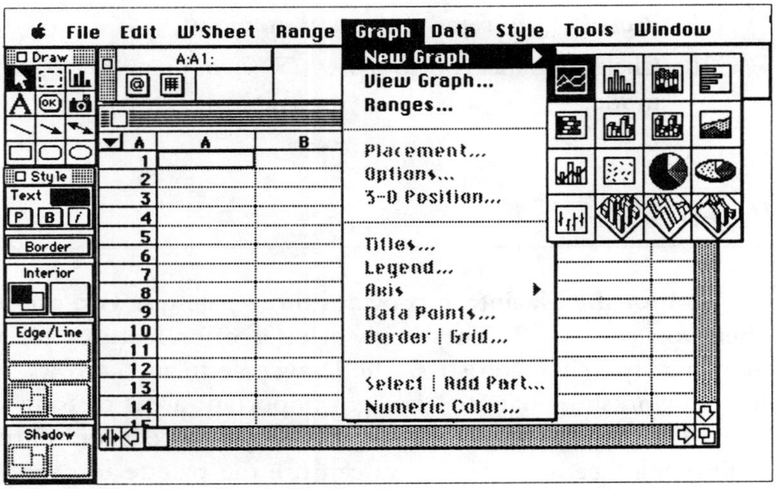

Undoing Menu Commands

You have looked at 1-2-3's Undo feature for eliminating a cell entry, but Undo has even more power. 1-2-3 keeps track of all the activities that occur. Most of the activities you do in 1-2-3 can be undone. Only a few activities cannot be undone. If you open a worksheet, format a range, or alter the width of a range of columns, 1-2-3 can undo these actions as long as you use Undo before performing a new activity. Once you invoke another command or make a new entry, that action is the latest action and is the work that will be undone when you use Undo.

The Undo command in the Edit menu will have additional descriptive entries indicating what action will be undone. When you choose Undo in the Edit menu again, the last action is undone. When you display the Edit pull-down menu, the Undo command is replaced with Redo since 1-2-3 can toggle the last action's effect. If you choose Redo from the Edit menu, 1-2-3 reinstates the effect that you removed by choosing Undo. To see how Undo can help you, first check that Undo is enabled, as described in Chapter 2, "Entering Text and Numbers," and then follow these steps:

1. Choose Open in the File menu, Salary from the list of documents in the list box, and the Open button.
2. Move to column A.
3. Choose Delete in the Worksheet menu, select the Column radio button, and the OK button.
4. Choose Undo Delete Columns in the Edit menu.

1-2-3 restores the deleted column.

5. Choose Redo Delete Columns in the Edit menu.

The deleted column disappears from the worksheet again.

6. Choose Close in the File menu and select No when 1-2-3 asks if you want to save the changes.
7. Choose Undo File Close in the Edit menu.

1-2-3 opens the closed worksheet document.

Review

Now you have learned how to use 1-2-3's menus. As you learn the features the different commands offer, using the new commands will be as easy as using the commands you already know. The specific skills you have learned for using menus include the following:

- Other than basic entries, you can access all of 1-2-3's features with selections from a series of menus. You invoke the menu by clicking a menu title displayed in the menu bar or by pressing (option)-(/) and typing the letter of the desired menu choice. From the pull-down menu, you can select one of the commands by dragging the mouse to the command. With a keyboard, type the first letter of the command until it is highlighted and press (return).
- You can choose a submenu option by dragging the highlight to your selection and releasing the mouse button or by typing the first letter of the desired selection and pressing (return). You can use (⌘)-(.) or (esc) to back out of a menu level.
- When 1-2-3 displays a dialog box, you can enter the additional information that 1-2-3 needs to perform the command. The type of selections you can make in a dialog box varies with the command, since different commands require different types of information. When you select the OK button, 1-2-3 performs the command.
- You can display the 1-2-3 Classic menu, which behaves exactly as 1-2-3 Release 3's menu does, by pressing (/) (slash) if the User Setup Preferences dialog box is set to display the 1-2-3 Classic menu when you press (/).
- You can undo the effect of the last menu command by Edit Undo.

Keys and Commands

The keys you used in this chapter let you use menus and make selections as you used the menus. You also learned how you can remove the effect of the last command with the Edit Undo command. These keys and commands are

Entry	Action
/	Displays the 1-2-3 Classic menu. (If it does not work, use Tools User Setup Preferences to change / to display 1-2-3 Classic.)
⌘	When held down in a dialog box, displays the ⌘ key combinations you can use to make selections.
option-/	Activates the menu bar.
esc (⌘-.)	Backs you out of the menu.
Edit Undo (⌘-Z)	Removes the effect of the last command or entry.

6

Changing the Appearance of Worksheet Entries

Up to this point, you have accepted 1-2-3's choices for how to present your entries. You have used 1-2-3's *default* for the format in which the data is displayed. It is great to have this default available; it lets you build a worksheet that produces completely accurate results without worrying about how your entries appear. But it is also great to know that 1-2-3 provides a set of powerful formatting commands that let you change the appearance of your entries. These are commands that let you select how the characters appear and whether 1-2-3 adds numeric formatting such as currency symbols to values. Other 1-2-3 commands change the alignment of text, either before or after you enter them. You will find that each of these 1-2-3 commands is easy to use and provides significant improvements in the appearance of your worksheets. You will be able to use the new menu selection and dialog box skills that you learned in Chapter 5, "Menus, Dialog Boxes, and Palettes," to make your selections.

Using a Range of Cells

Everything you have accomplished with 1-2-3 so far has focused on individual cells. However, 1-2-3 also allows you to work with any contiguous rectangle of cells, called a range, to accomplish tasks. Chapter 4, "@Functions and Other Formula Options," introduced ranges when you used them in formulas that use more than one cell. Figure 6-1 shows groups of cells that are valid ranges, as well as some groups that are not. The groups on the left are invalid ranges because they do not contain contiguous cells that form rectangles. The cell groups on the right are valid ranges because each one forms a contiguous group. As long as this rule is met, the range can be as large as you wish or as small as one cell. Most commands that you use require that you select a range before you choose the command.

You can use several methods to specify cell ranges. In some cases, you can type them in like a cell address but most of the time you will select them

Figure 6-1. *Invalid and valid ranges*

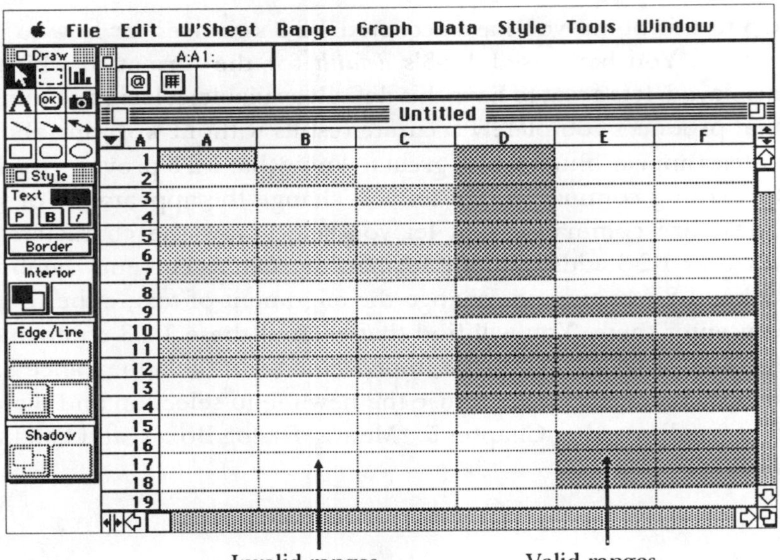

with the mouse or keyboard. Ranges are specified by any two diagonally opposite corners separated by one or more periods. For example, the cells in rows 11 through 15 of columns E, F, G, and H can be specified as E11..H15, E15.H11, H15..E11, or H11.E15. The most common way to specify a range is to use the upper-left cell first and the lower-right cell last, as in E11..H15.

For most commands that use ranges, you must first select the range, and then choose the command that uses the range. If you do not select the range first, the effect of the command is only applied to the active cell. To select a range, move to one corner of the range you will select. Next, drag the mouse to cover the range or hold down the (shift) key as you press the arrow keys to select the range. You can also select one cell with a mouse and then hold down (shift) while you click a cell to select a range defined by the two selected cells.

To try these three methods of selecting a range from Ready mode, follow these steps:

1. Move to B3.
2. Press (shift)-(→) three times and (shift)-(↓) twice to select B3..E5.
3. Click B3 and drag the mouse to E5 to select the same range.
4. Click B3 and hold down (shift) while you click E5 to select the same range.

This range remains highlighted so you can select a command that will use this range.

When you select a range from Ready mode, the range remains selected until you select another range or cell. When you choose a command, 1-2-3 automatically uses the range you have selected. The range remains selected after you use the command.

Collections

Another grouping of cells 1-2-3 sometimes uses is called a *collection.* A collection is a group of one or more cells and ranges that may not necessarily be part of the same range. For example, the invalid ranges on the left side of Figure 6-1 could be part of a valid collection. In the example of the invalid ranges in Figure 6-1, the collection of the shaded cells would be defined as A1;B2;C3;A5..B7;C6..C7;B10;A11..C12. You can see from this example that

6

you describe collections by separating the cell and range addresses with semicolons. When you are selecting a collection with a mouse, select the first cell or range part of the collection and then hold down the (⌘) key while you select the other cells and ranges that will be part of the collection. All ranges can be collections, although many collections are not ranges, since they are composed of multiple cells and ranges. Try this by following these steps:

1. Move to A5.
2. Select the range A5..A10.
3. Point to C5.
4. Hold down the (⌘) key while you select the range C5..C10.

1-2-3 still highlights the first range as you select the second range when you hold down the (⌘) key. If you want to use a collection for a command that prompts for a range, you can type the range address, for example, **A5.A10;C5.C10**.

While many commands use ranges rather than collections, you can use collections for several commands. These commands include the commands in the Style menu (this chapter); the range to print for Page Setup in the File menu (Chapter 10, "Printing Your Worksheet"); Clear or Clear Contents, Paste, Paste Special, Clear Styles in the Edit menu (Chapter 9, "Making 1-2-3 Do Your Work"), Column Width and Row Height in the Worksheet menu (Chapter 7, "Changing Row and Column Options"), Format in the Range menu (this chapter), and the input range of Query in the Data menu (Chapter 12, "Data-Management Basics"). Other 1-2-3 commands that can use collections that are not covered in this book include Protect and Unprotect in the Range menu and the Modify input range of the Query command in the Data menu.

Changing the Appearances of Entries

In Chapter 2, "Entering Text and Numbers," you learned how to make entries. 1-2-3 has several commands that change how text appears on the worksheet. You can change the alignment of existing cells without editing the cells individually. You can also change the appearance of the characters. This adds word processing character formatting to your 1-2-3 worksheet. You can also add borders and colors.

Applications: *You can use the commands and features you learn about in this section to create a professional looking report. For example, you can change the worksheet you have to calculate next year's budget into a formal budget report that still has all the calculations yet looks as if it is professionally typeset.*

Changing Entry Alignment

You already learned one method for changing the text alignment in Chapter 2 when you entered text by starting it with an alignment prefix. This method works, but if you have a large number of text entries, it is time consuming. It also requires you to edit the entries if you want to change the alignment of existing entries. Fortunately, 1-2-3 has two alternatives that can be real time savers. One option changes the alignment of entries that are already on the worksheet; this option can even change the alignment of values. The other option changes the default alignment prefix for the current worksheet so that any new text you enter will use the new alignment setting.

Changing Alignment of Existing Entries

1-2-3 has two methods for altering the existing text entries. You can use Edit mode to alter the alignment prefix character, or you can use the Align command in the Style menu. In Chapter 2 you learned how you can change the alignment prefix by using Edit mode. The Align command in the Style menu requires less work; you can change the alignment of many cells with a single command. Not only that, but you can also align values. When you choose Align in the Style menu, you can then choose from Left, Right, Center, and General. The General option left aligns text and right aligns values. Look at the effect of altering entry alignments by using the Align command in the Style menu with this example:

1. Make the following entries in these cells:

B1:	**Jan**	B2:	**60000**
C1:	**Feb**	C2:	**70000**
D1:	**Mar**	D2:	**65000**
E1:	**Apr**	E2:	**80000**

The text is currently left aligned and the values right aligned with the default setting.

2. Select the range B1..E2.
3. Choose Align from the Style menu, and then Center, so your entries look like this:

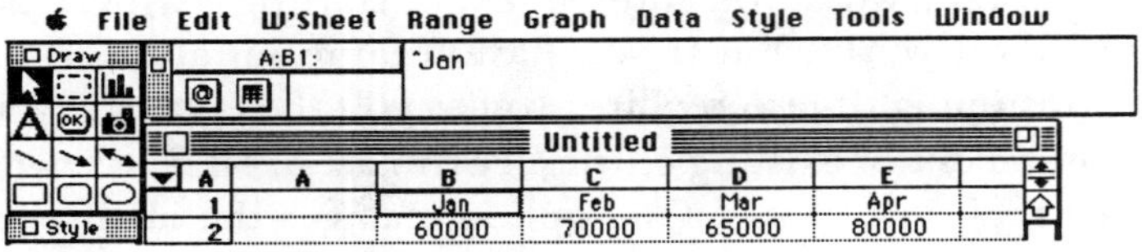

Each of the entries is now centered in its cell. Subsequent entries in these cells will not be affected since Align in the Style menu affects only existing cell entries. The Align command in the Style menu changes only the alignment of the entries that are in the range at the time you use the command. If you later make new entries in the range that you have used with an Align command in the Style menu, the new entries will use the default alignment prefix, rather than the alignment prefix you chose with the Align command in the Style menu. The Align command in the Style menu is also the only way you can change the alignment of values, since changing the default alignment prefix only changes text entries but has no effect on values.

Applications: *Since the default alignment prefixes for text and numbers are different, you will need to use an alignment prefix for text column headings or change the alignment after entry to achieve a professional looking report.*

Changing Alignment Globally Before Making Entries

If you change the default alignment prefix, any new text you enter will use this setting. Existing text is not affected. This option is especially useful when you wish to enter a series of text entries with a different alignment. You can alter the default alignment without converting the data already on the worksheet, make your entries, and then change the alignment back to its original setting. To try this feature, follow these steps:

1. Choose Global Settings from the Worksheet menu, select Right from the Align Text pop-up menu, and select the OK button.
2. Move to A4 and type **Div. A**. Then move to A5.
3. Type **Div. B** and move to A6.
4. Type **Div. C** and click the confirm button or press enter so your entries are right aligned, as shown here:

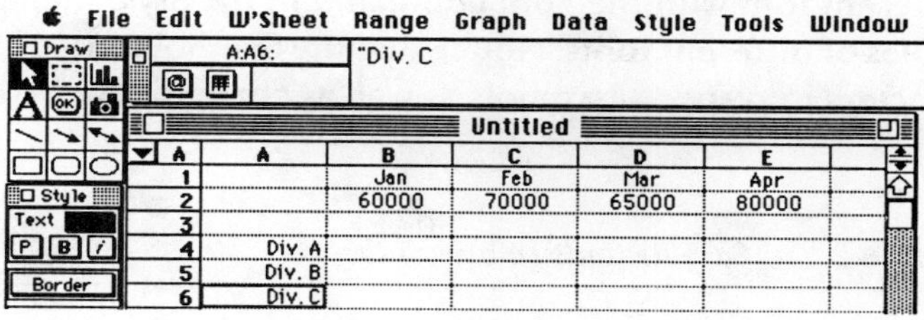

Each entry is now preceded by ", automatically generated by 1-2-3 since you have changed the default alignment prefix for the worksheet to right alignment.

5. Click the close box or press ⌘-W to close the window and select the No button when 1-2-3 asks if you want to save the changes.
6. Choose New from the File menu or press ⌘-N to open a new worksheet.

Changing Worksheet Fonts

A *font* is the typeface and size of the characters 1-2-3 uses to display and print your data. So far your worksheet entries have used only one font, but you can use multiple fonts to enhance your data's appearance. You can use any fonts that are installed in your Macintosh, including some of the fonts that are added when you install 1-2-3.

Typeface refers to the style of print characters. Some of the options you may have include Chicago, Courier, Geneva, and Helvetica. The *size* of the characters is another important component of a font. Size is measured in points. A point is 1/72 of an inch. Normally, you use 10- or 12-point fonts for regular entries, 18- or 24-point fonts for headings, and 6- or 8-point fonts for fine print. 1-2-3 also lets you add emphasis like boldface, underlining, and shadow.

Using Different Fonts

You can use many fonts in a worksheet. The default font for all entries is 10-point Geneva with no emphasis (Plain). All entries use it unless you select a different font with the Font command in the Style menu. Figure 6-2 shows samples of different fonts. Notice that the Symbol font in D7..D9 changes the characters into special symbols as well as changing the style.

Figure 6-2. *Sample fonts in a worksheet*

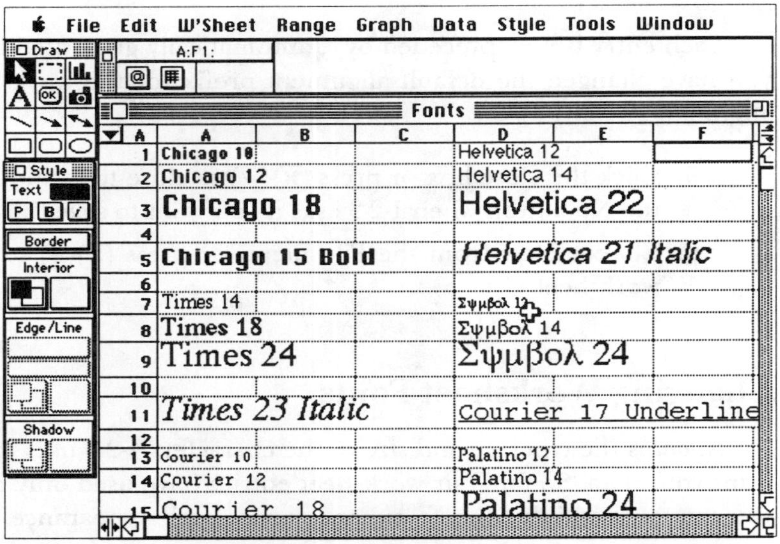

To look at using different fonts in a worksheet, complete the entries shown in Figure 6-3. Follow these directions:

1. Move to C2, type **ABC Company**, and move to C3.
2. Type **Sales Projections** and move to A6.
3. Complete the following entries.

A6:	**Unit Price**	D5:	**1993**
A7:	**Unit Sales**	D6:	**4.75**
A8:	**Sales**	D7:	**+C7*(1+C10)**
A10:	**Percent Growth**	D8:	**+D6*D7**
C5:	**1992**	E5:	**1994**
C6:	**5**	E6:	**4.8**
C7:	**60000**	E7:	**+D7*(1+C10)**
C8:	**+C6*C7**	E8:	**+E6*E7**
C10:	**.12**		

Figure 6-3. *Worksheet for demonstrating font features*

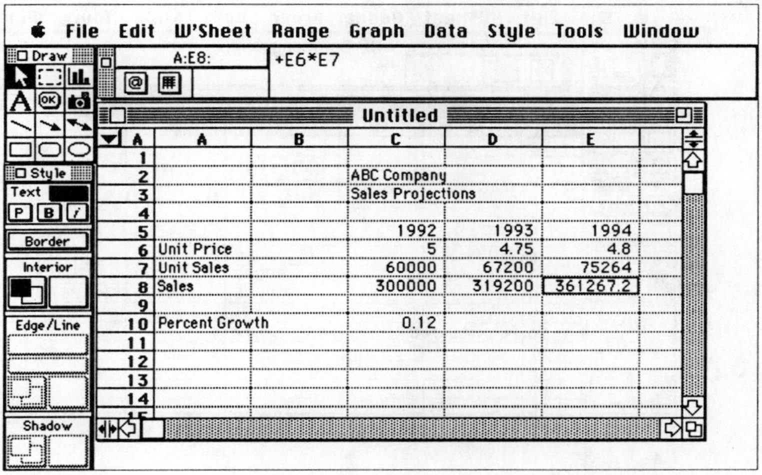

4. Select the range C2..C3.
5. Choose Font in the Style menu or press (⌘)-(T) to change the font of the range.

The dialog box lets you select the font typeface, size, and emphasis for the selected range.

6. Select Chicago from the list box under Font, 14 from the Size pop-up menu, the Bold check box, and the OK button so the entries now look like the ones in Figure 6-4.

You can change the font size two ways. You can use the pop-up menu as you have done here or you can type the size in the text box. The pop-up menu contains the most common font sizes, but you can type any number in the text box.

The attribute applies to the entire entry even though part of it displays in other cells. When cell entries use a different font, your entries may become wider or narrower. In Chapter 7 you will learn how you can change the column's width so it will fit the wider or narrower entries. 1-2-3 automatically

Figure 6-4. *Worksheet showing a font change*

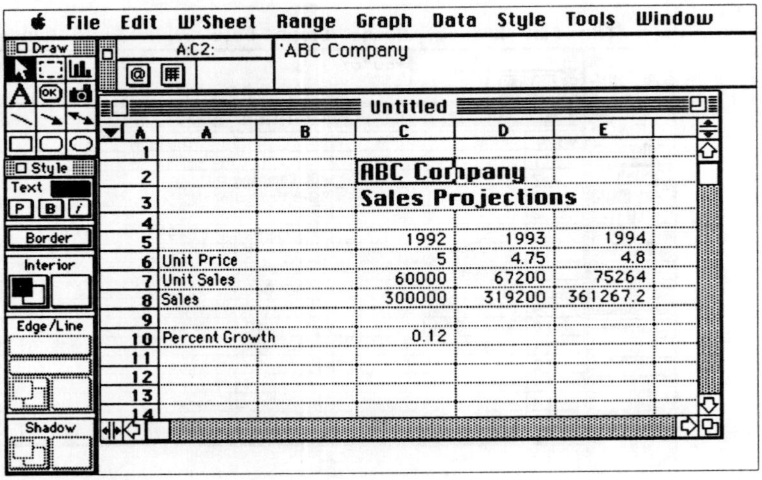

adjusts a row's height to match the tallest character in the row, although in the next chapter you will learn how you can change the row's height yourself.

7. Select the range C5..E5.
8. Choose Font in the Style menu or press ⌘-T, then select Chicago from the list box under Font, 12 from the Size pop-up menu, the Bold check box, the Show In Menu button and the OK button, so the entries now use a new font, size, and emphasis.

The next time you use the Style menu, 1-2-3 will include Chicago 12 boldface in the Style menu. You can add a font typeface, size, and emphasis selection to the Style menu.

9. Select the collection A6..A10;C10.

As a reminder, you will select the range A6..A10 and then hold down the ⌘ key as you select C10.

10. Choose **Chicago 12** in the Style menu.

In addition to changing fonts and emphasis with the Font command in the Style menu, you can alter the appearance of cell entries using the Style palette. You can boldface, italicize, and reset text.

11. Select the range C8..E8.

The Style palette has P, **B**, and *i* buttons to represent plain text, boldface, and italics. To use these buttons, select the range that will use the attribute and then click the button for the attribute you want.

12. Select the **B** button.

Now your entries look like the ones in Figure 6-5.
Depending on your monitor's resolution, your entry in E8 may still display as 361267.2.

When you want to remove text emphasis, you can choose Font from the Style menu and deselect the check box to turn the emphasis off. Another

Figure 6-5. *Worksheet after changing fonts and adding attributes*

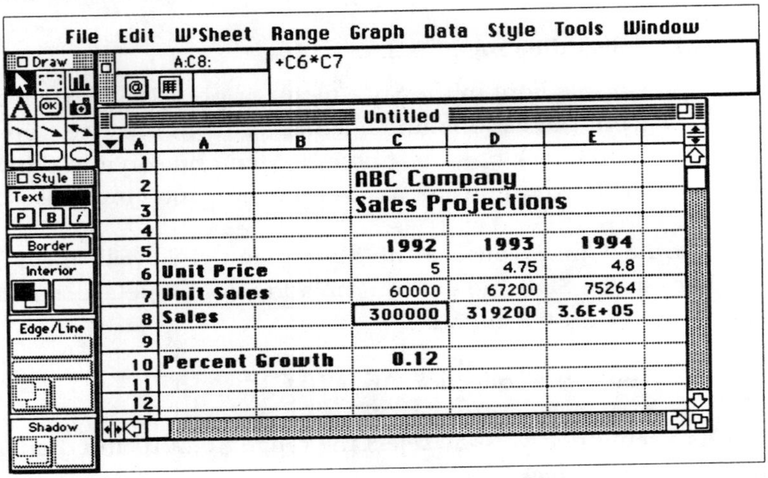

alternative is to select the range and the P button in the style palette to return it to plain text.

Applications: *Although some variation in typeface, style, and point size is important, too many changes can distract from your message. A good rule of thumb is to limit yourself to two compatible typefaces and three point sizes.*

Adding Borders

You can add a border on any side of a cell or range of cells. You can outline a range to put lines on all four sides of a range or select the side of a range where 1-2-3 will add lines. For example, you can add a border around the entries in A8..E8 by following these directions:

1. Select the range A8..E8.
2. Press the mouse on the Border button in the Style palette.

The options for the border select where the border is added.

3. Select Outside to add a border around the selected range like that shown in Figure 6-6.

You can also add this border by choosing the Border command in the Style menu and then selecting the Outside check box and the OK button. The options for border placement are the same regardless of whether you use the Border button in the Style palette or choose Border from the Style menu.

You can remove the borders by using the Border command in the Style menu again and turning off the check boxes for the borders you want to remove. You can also remove all borders by selecting the range and selecting None after pressing the Border button in the Style palette.

Adding Colors and Shading

1-2-3 will let you change the color or shading of cells and their entries. With Text in the Style palette, you can select the color of the text. Under

6

Figure 6-6. *Border added to worksheet range A8..E8*

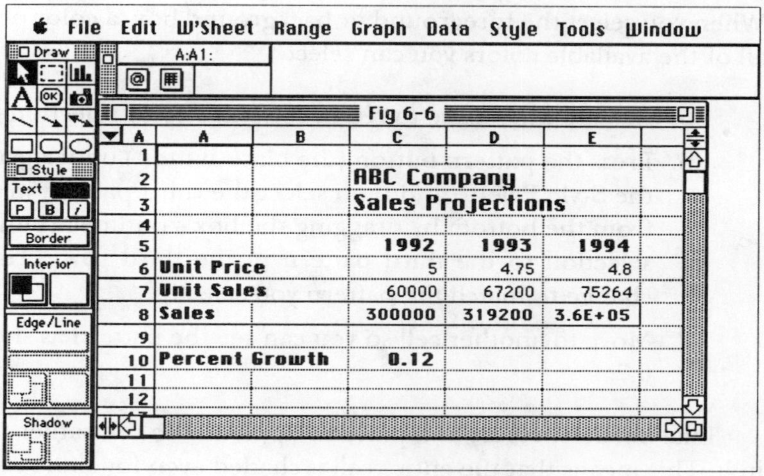

Interior in the Style palette you can select the foreground color, the background color, and pattern. If you do not have a color monitor, you will be selecting the shade rather than the color. To use light shading on numbers in the 1994 column, follow these steps:

1. Select the range E5..E8.
2. Press the text color pop-up menu, which is the black box to the right of Text in the Style palette.

The text color pop-up displays all of the available colors you can select for the text. The color you select from the palette selects the color of the text in this range.

3. Release the mouse so you do not change the text's color selection.
4. Press the bottom of the two interconnected boxes underneath Interior.

This button lets you select the color for two parts. The box in the front selects the foreground color, which is the color used for the front of objects. Some of the objects include objects you see in a graph. You will learn about graphs in Chapter 11, "Creating Graphs." The button in the back selects the background color, which includes the background color of a cell. For example you can set the background color to display the contents of E5..E8 in red. When you select the foreground or background box, a color pop-up displays all of the available colors you can select.

5. Release the mouse to retain the text's color selection.
6. Press the pattern button (the black button) underneath Interior in the Style Palette and then select the third pattern in the third row from the bottom by dragging the box's outline around the current selection to the third pattern in the third row. (The button will change to match the pattern you select.)
7. Move to another cell so you can see the pattern as shown in Figure 6-7.

Like borders, colors and patterns apply to the cell rather than the entry in it. This means that the entire cell is shaded even for short entries and that

Figure 6-7. *Range E5...E8 with pattern added as a background*

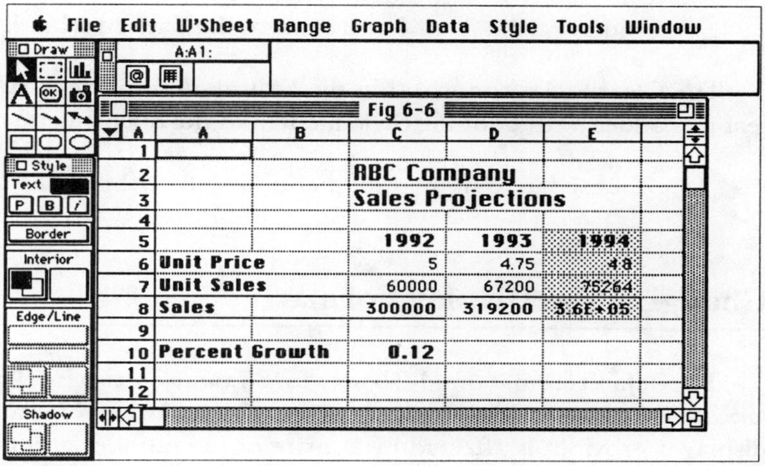

the cells used for displaying text wider than the cell are shaded only if they are included in the range when you change the range's pattern. Be careful—a cell that is shaded with a very dark shading can be hard to read.

Applications: *Consider using borders, colors, and patterns to create your own preprinted forms to record manual entries. Although your 1-2-3 document contains only a few text entries to indicate the information that should be recorded manually, you can draw attention to the areas requiring completion with these special effects.*

Removing Styles

You can remove many of the style enhancements you add to worksheet entries using the same command or similar Style palette selections. If you want to remove all of the style enhancements, you can use the Clear Styles command in the Edit menu. This command removes all styles you have added to a worksheet entry. Try removing some styles by following these steps:

1. Select the range A8..E8.
2. Choose Clear Styles in the Edit menu to remove the outline and boldface from A8..E8 and remove the pattern from E8.

The Clear Styles command in the Edit menu removes many formatting features added with both the Style menu and the Style palette at once.

3. Choose Undo in the Edit menu to restore the formatting.

Changing the Display Format

The default format that 1-2-3 uses for all value entries is called the *General format.* This format does not provide consistent formats for all entries. The display it provides is affected by the size of the number and the number of digits after the decimal point. Some numbers display as they are entered, while others have leading zeros added or are rounded to the number of decimal digits that will fit in the cell width. The general format also suppresses trailing zeros after the decimal point, so a column of numbers may have varying numbers of digits after the decimal point. Very large and very small numbers are displayed in scientific notation, as described in Chapter 2.

The General format handles a wide variety of formats, but it often results in a display whose results have varying numbers of decimal places. These inconsistencies make this format less than desirable for many business worksheets. However, this inconsistency does not mean that the General format is useless; it is ideal in many situations. The General format is useful when you want to minimize the space used to display very large or very small numbers. It is *not* the display to use when you need to control the number of decimal places shown or when you want to add *formatting characters,* such as %, $, and commas. To add these formatting characters, you must assign one of 1-2-3's formats to the cells. Since 1-2-3 uses the number as it is stored in the cell rather than as the number appears, changing the format does not affect the results of calculations.

Formatting Options

1-2-3 has many alternatives to the General display format, providing a wide range of formatting options that allow you to display your data with everything from dollar signs and commas to percent symbols. You can even specify the number of decimal places for some of the formats. The specific formats supported by 1-2-3 and their effects on worksheet entries are shown in Table 6-1. The examples under Display show two decimal places selected,

Table 6-1. *1-2-3's Format Options*

Format	Cell Entry	Display
Comma	5678	5,678.00
	-123.45	(123.45)
Currency	5678	$5,678.00
	-123.45	($123.45)
Fixed	5678	5678.00
	-123.45	-123.45
General	5678	5678
	-123.45	-123.45
Hidden	35000	
Label	+A2*A3	'+A2*A3
Percent	5	500.00%
	.1	10.00%
Scientific	5678	5.68E+03
	-123.45	-1.23E+02
Text	+A2*A3	+A2*A3
+/-	4	++++ 3
	-3	---
	0	
Date Short Intn'l	33678	03/15
Date Long Intn'l	33678	03/15/92
DD-MMM	33678	15-Mar
DD-MMM-YY	33678	15-Mar-92
MMM-YY	33678	Mar-92
HH:MM AM/PM	.75	06:00 PM
HH:MM:SS AM/PM	.75	06:00:00 PM
Time Short Intn'l	.75	18:00 PM
Time Long Intn'l	.75	18:00:00 PM

where appropriate. The Mixed option, which you will see in 1-2-3's list of format options, is really not a formatting option, but rather it is combined with the options that have check boxes in the Format command in the Range menu.

Scope of the Formatting Change

You can choose how extensive an impact you want a particular format command to have by formatting the entire worksheet or a range of cells in the worksheet. First you will examine the procedure for changing the format for a range of the worksheet.

Changing the Format for a Range of Cells

When you want to change how values in a range of worksheet cells appear, you can assign one of 1-2-3's formats to the range. Changing the format of a range affects only the appearance of the values that are part of the range.

You can try some of these formatting changes using the worksheet you created earlier in the chapter. To try some of the formats you can apply to a range, follow these steps:

1. Select the range C7..E7.
2. Choose Format in the Range menu.

The list box of formats lists the different formatting options you can select.

3. Select Comma from the list box.

Several of the format options, such as Comma, let you select the number of digits that are displayed after the decimal point. The default for these formats is 2, but you can enter a number between 0 and 15 in the Decimal Places text box.

4. Type **0** in the Decimal Places text box and select the OK button so each of the values in C7..E7 appears with a comma to separate the thousands, with no digits after the decimal point.

Table 6-2. *Examples of Format Abbreviations*

Abbreviation	Format in Effect
(F6)	Fixed with six decimal places
(P2)	Percent with two decimal places
(T)	Text
(G)	General
(C0)	Currency with zero decimal places
(,2)	Comma with two decimal places
(D1)	Date format 1
(D6)	Time format 1

Notice that next to the cell address in the console is (,0–). The information in parentheses indicates the format assigned to the cell with a Format command in the Range menu. Table 6-2 presents examples of some of the commonly used format abbreviations. For formats that allow you to specify the number of decimal places, like Comma in this example, a numeric digit follows. The – in the parenthesis indicates that negative numbers are displayed in a different color.

Another shortcut is to select one of the format selections displayed in the Range menu. 1-2-3 initially provides four: Fixed with two digits after the decimal point, Currency with two digits after the decimal point, Percent with no digits after the decimal point, and Date Long Intn'l. Like style font selections, you can add these to the menu by selecting the format and the Show in Menu button. You can try these shortcuts by following these steps:

5. Select the range C6..E6.
6. Choose 1234.12 from the Range menu.

You could also have chosen Format from the Range menu and then selected Fixed in the list box, typed **2** in the Decimal Places text box, and selected the OK button.

7. Move to C10.

6

Figure 6-8. *Worksheet with range format changes*

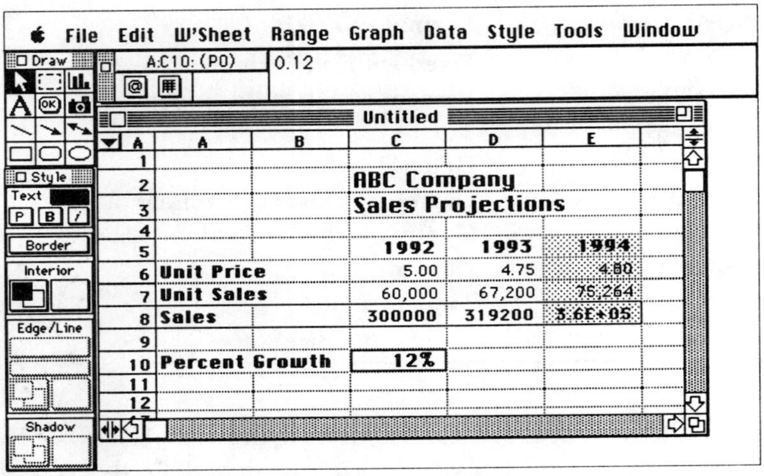

8. Choose 123412% in the Range menu so your entries look like those in Figure 6-8.

You could have also chosen Format in the Range menu, selected Percent in the list box, typed **0** in the Decimal Places text box, and selected the OK button.

The formats you select remain with the cells unless you reset the range by selecting the range, the Format command in the Range menu, and the Reset button. You can also reset the range with the Clear Styles command in the Edit menu, since it removes the format added with the Format command in the Range menu, as well as styles added with the Style menu or the Style palette.

Making a Global Format Change

When you wish to alter the format of the entire worksheet or even most of it, a *global format* change is the ideal solution. A global format change alters the default format for every cell on the current worksheet, including both cells with entries and cells that are currently empty. The only cells that do not use the global format are the cells that you have formatted with the Format command in the Range menu. For an empty cell, this global format is used as soon as you place a value entry in the cell. Global formatting is especially useful when most of the worksheet is formatted with the same option. You can choose a global format that meets the requirement for most of the cells and then go back and format the exceptions with the Format command in the Range menu.

To alter the global format for the worksheet, follow these steps:

1. Choose Global Settings in the Worksheet menu.
2. Select the Format pop-up menu and Currency from the menu.
3. Type **0** in the text box to the right of the Format pop-up menu to specify zero decimal places, and select the OK button.

The entries in C8..E8 now appear as asterisks, although the edit region still displays the formulas in these cells. The asterisks are how 1-2-3 tells you that the column is not wide enough to display the value using the format you have selected. When this happens, you have two choices–you can either select a different format that takes less space or widen the column, as you will learn how to do in Chapter 7. The years also appear as currency, even though this format is inappropriate for these numbers, since these values did not use the Format command in the Range menu.

4. Choose Undo in the Edit menu to restore the numeric format setting to General.
5. Choose Save from the File menu, type **ABC Sales** in the Save As text box, and select the OK button to save this worksheet.
6. Click the close box or press or ⌘-W to close this worksheet.
7. Choose New in the File menu or ⌘-N to open a new worksheet.

Automatically Formatting a Worksheet

1-2-3 has an *Automatic format,* which converts a number that you enter with numeric formatting characters into one of 1-2-3's numeric formats. For example, if you enter $5,432.09 in a cell with an Automatic format, 1-2-3 changes the cell's format to currency with two digits after the decimal point and stores 5432.09 in the cell. When the Automatic format is selected, it remains with the cell until you enter something that 1-2-3 formats. After you make an entry that uses the automatic formatting, and 1-2-3 uses one of the other acceptable formats for the cell, the cell's assigned format changes to the one it used when you made the entry. To try this formatting option, follow these steps:

1. Select the range C1..C8 and choose Format in the Range menu. Select Automatic in the list box and the OK button.
2. Make the following entries so the resulting worksheet looks like the one in Figure 6-9.

A1:	**Date**	C1:	**12/31/92**
A2:	**Time**	C2:	**12:41 PM**
A3:	**Old Sales**	C3:	**$671,500**
A4:	**Growth %**	C4:	**8.0%**
A5:	**New Sales**	C5:	**+C3*(1+C4)**
A6:	**Units Sold**	C6:	**170,000**
A7:	**Price**	C7:	**3.95**

3. Move to each of the entries in C1..C7 and to see how each cell is formatted.

1-2-3 converted the entries in C1 and C2 into their date and time numbers. When you move to cells in column C, you can see that the format description has changed from (A) for Automatic format to the format description that is appropriate for the entry you have made. For each of the cells, 1-2-3 used your entry to determine the format you want to use. 1-2-3 performed a Format command in the Range menu on each cell in which you made an entry. Once 1-2-3 selects a format for a cell, the format does not change unless you execute another Format command in the Range menu. The only cells that retained the Automatic format are C5, since the formula does not provide the formatting information 1-2-3 needs to assign a format to the cell, and C8, since it is empty.

4. Type **$60.3** in C7, and press (enter) or click the confirm button.

Figure 6-9. *Automatic format for values*

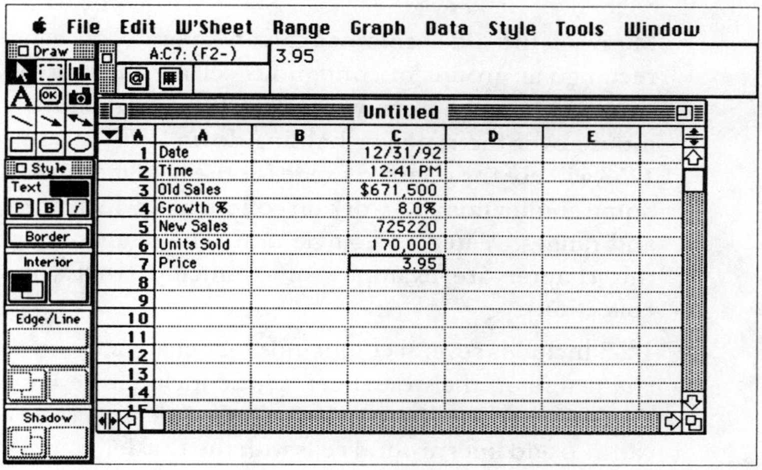

Notice that the format did not change to currency with one digit after the decimal point because the cell is already formatted to Fixed with two digits after the decimal point.

5. Click the close box or press (⌘)-(W) and select No when 1-2-3 asks if you want to save the worksheet before you close it.

Applications: *The Automatic format allows you to design a new worksheet quickly since you can use this format and allow the entries in individual cells to control the format, rather than needing to customize the format for many small ranges.*

Review

In this chapter you learned how you can add spreadsheet publishing features to your worksheets by specifying fonts and adding boldface, colors, and lines. You also learned how you can set 1-2-3 to add formatting characters to numbers to give a consistent appearance.

- Many of the 1-2-3 commands can operate on ranges, which are rectangular groups of contiguous cells. You can select the range a command uses before you select the command by dragging the mouse over the range or holding down (shift) as you select a range. 1-2-3 will use the selected range for the next command you perform. Some commands also work on collections, which are a group of cells and ranges treated as a single unit. The commands you learned in this chapter are examples of commands that you can use with collections.
- 1-2-3 includes several commands that change the appearance of the characters on the worksheet. These include the Font command in the Style menu to change the font typeface, style, and emphasis. You can also add lines around cells with the Border command in the Style menu.
- Use Align Text in the Worksheet Global Settings dialog box to change the alignment for entries you are about to make. Use the Align command in the Style menu to alter the alignment of existing entries.
- You can format numeric entries to match your needs. The Format command in the Range menu formats a range or collection. The Format setting in the Worksheet Global Settings dialog box sets the default format and formats any numeric entry not formatted with a Format command in the Range menu. Formats added with the Format command in the Range menu are shown in the console.
- The Style palette provides shortcuts to adding spreadsheet publishing to your worksheet. With the buttons under Text, you can boldface or italicize text or return it to plain text. You can also use the Style palette to add a border to a range and set the text, foreground and background color as well as setting the pattern.

Keys and Commands

The commands you learned in this chapter add formatting to a worksheet. You also learned how you can select the range to use before you format it. The commands and keys are

Entry	**Action**
⌘	While selecting cells and ranges, adds the current selection to the existing selection to create a collection
Edit Clear Styles	Removes styles and formatting added with Range Format, Style commands and the Style palette
Range Format	Applies a consistent format to mostly numeric entries
Style Align	Changes the alignment of existing worksheet entries
Style Border	Adds lines around a range or around individual cells
Style Font (⌘-T)	Sets the font style, size, and font attributes for cells
Worksheet Global Settings	Sets the global settings of the worksheet, such as the default text alignment and numeric format

7

Changing Row and Column Options

In Chapter 6, "Changing the Appearance of Worksheet Entries," you examined some of the changes you can make to the appearance of individual entries in cells. There are also several commands that allow you to make changes to one or more columns or rows at a time. 1-2-3 provides options that let you determine the width you wish to use for one or more columns and the row height for one or more rows. You can also hide or display columns on your document, and you can insert or delete columns and rows.

Altering Column Widths

When you begin a new 1-2-3 document, the default width of columns is nine characters. This is adequate for values displayed with the General format; often, however, it is not wide enough when you want to display formatted numbers or long text entries. At other times, the opposite might be true. Even though you might have a column that never contains more than one character, the full width of nine characters is always reserved for the column. If you make some columns narrower, you can view more columns in the window. 1-2-3 lets you make a column wider or narrower. In fact, 1-2-3 even lets you choose whether to change the width of all the columns at once or to alter a range of columns.

Changing the Width of One or More Columns

The ability to alter the width of individual columns lets you tailor your display to meet your exact needs. This is the preferred approach when you have only a few columns to change. Any change you make for individual columns will take precedence over the global column width. Follow these steps for making changes to some of the document columns:

1. Choose Open from the File menu, select ABC Sales from the list box, and select the OK button.

This is the worksheet that you created in Chapter 6. If you did not complete the worksheet entries, you can use the data in Figure 7-1 to complete the entries (E8 contains 361267.2).

2. Select the range C8..E8.

To change the width of one or more columns, the range you select before choosing the command must contain at least one cell from each column to change. Any range that contains cells from columns C, D, and E would work just as well.

3. Choose Column Width from the Worksheet menu.

With the radio button for Set Width selected you can type a new width in characters.

Figure 7-1. *Worksheet for trying row and column options*

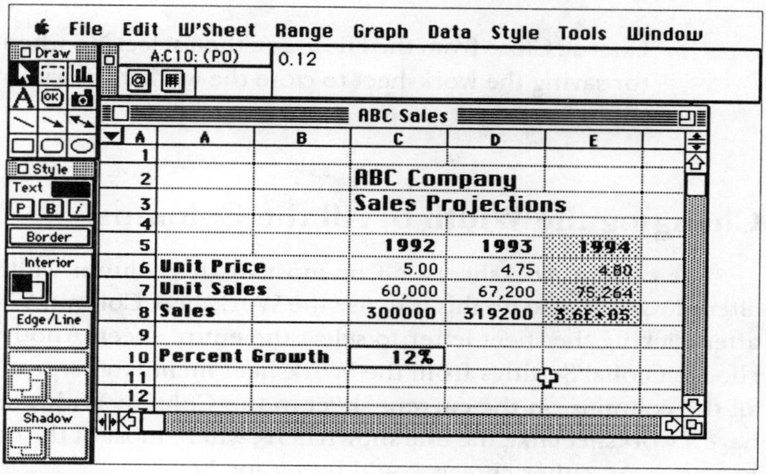

4. Type **12** in the Set Width To text box.
5. Select the OK button.

The change is made to all of the selected columns. Since the width for these columns is different from the default for the worksheet, 1-2-3 displays the column width in brackets, as in [W12], in the console.

With a mouse, you can also change column widths using the vertical line separating columns in the worksheet frame:

1. Move the pointer to the vertical line separating column A from column B in the worksheet frame so the mouse looks like the cross hair shown here: ✛
2. Drag the mouse to the right so the temporary line 1-2-3 draws to indicate the column's new border is on top of the B and release the mouse when the column is the desired width.

You do not see the number of characters the column is set to, but you can see where the column's boundaries will be.

3. Choose Close from the File menu then select No when 1-2-3 prompts for saving the worksheet to close the worksheet without saving your changes.

Changing the Width of All the Columns

For certain worksheets, all or most of the column widths need to be altered. One way to do this is to use the Worksheet Column Width command after clicking the sheet letter to select the entire sheet. Another option is to choose Global Settings from the Worksheet menu and type a new width for all the columns on the current sheet in the Column Width text box. If you have a worksheet like the one shown here, where most of the columns should be narrower, either choice would be acceptable:

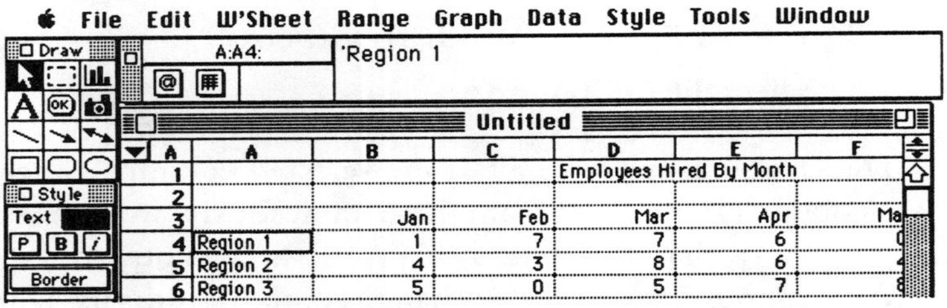

You can create this worksheet by entering the months in B3..M3, the regions in A4..A6, and random numbers in B4..M6.

When you change the global column width, column widths set with Column Width in the Worksheet menu or set by dragging the mouse on the worksheet frame are not affected. The following entries alter the above worksheet so more months can be viewed. Follow these steps to make the global column width change.

1. Choose Global Settings from the Worksheet menu, type **5** in the Column Width text box, and select the OK button.

Now all of the columns are five characters wide. The only problem with this display is that column A has also become smaller and does not display the region numbers. To fix this problem, do the following:

2. Move to column A.
3. Choose Column Width from the Worksheet menu, select the Set Width To radio button, type **7** in the Set Width To text box, and select the OK button.

This change to an individual column width fixes the problem and produces the result shown here:

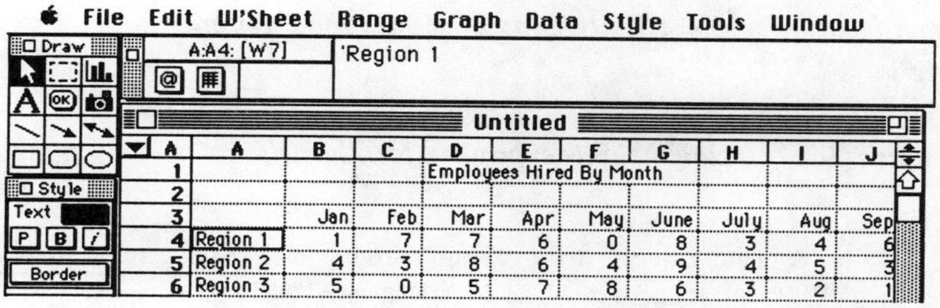

Unlike when you change the width of a range of columns, 1-2-3 does not display the global column width in the console.

4. Choose Close from the File menu then select No when 1-2-3 prompts for saving the worksheet to close the worksheet without saving your changes.

Applications: *When you need to record head counts or survey data, narrow columns are often appropriate, since they maximize the number of columns of information that you can view at once. Documents such as financial reports often have lengthy entries in column A, so you will want to make this one column wider than the rest of the columns.*

Changing Row Heights

1-2-3's initial row height for documents is .181 inches, which is the same as 13 points. If you use a different font size, 1-2-3 automatically adjusts the row height to accommodate new font sizes. You may want to change row heights to accommodate your specific needs. You can select a range and apply the change to all the rows within the range.

Applications: *If you need to duplicate a custom form with 1-2-3, you will want to use the row height features to create a matching document. This feature is especially important for custom forms since you may not want to increase the font size for the text in the form–only the space where users will write on the form. Figure 7-2 shows part of a document that might be printed and used to record changes to employee information. The expanded row height makes it easy to label what will be placed in each location while still allowing adequate room for entries.*

Figure 7-2. *Row heights expanded to .75 inch*

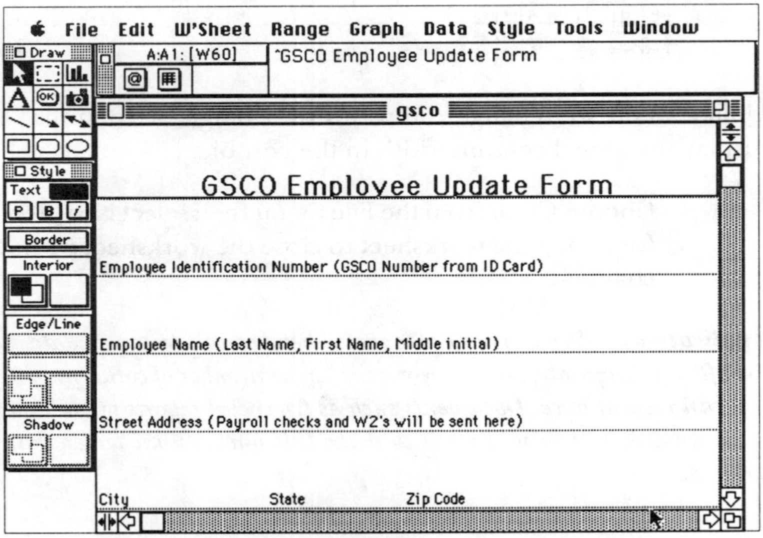

Changing the Height of One or More Rows

You can change the height of one or more rows. It is not necessary to select an entire row to change its height. Having even a single cell from a row as part of the range when you choose the command will change the height of the entire row. Follow these steps to make a change:

1. Select at least one cell from each row whose height you want to change.
2. Choose Row Height from the Worksheet menu.
3. Type a new height in the text box with the Set Height To radio button checked.

The row height is expressed in inches as the default setting.

4. Select the OK button.

Resetting the Row Height

The default font size established with Global Settings in the Worksheet menu determines the row height. If you want to return the row height for rows that you have changed to the default row height, follow these steps:

1. Select the range that you want to change.
2. Choose Row Height from the Worksheet.
3. Click the Reset radio button.
4. Select the OK button.

Applications: *You can design 1-2-3 documents to match preprinted forms with the ability to change fonts and row heights. Rather than allow 1-2-3 to establish row heights based on your font selections, you can define them to exactly match a form.*

Inserting and Deleting Rows and Columns

No matter how thoroughly you plan your worksheet applications, sometimes you need to make substantial changes to a worksheet. You might need to add an employee to a worksheet, delete accounts that are no longer used, or add some blank space to make the document more readable. 1-2-3 accommodates each of these needs by means of commands that let you insert or delete blank rows or columns in the document.

Inserting Rows and Columns

You can insert blank columns and rows at any location you choose in the document. When you add columns or rows to the document, they are placed at the location of the active cell. New rows are added above the active cell, and new columns are placed to the left of the active cell. 1-2-3 determines the number of rows or columns to insert based on the size of the range selected before choosing the command. The first column or row in this range is where the new columns or rows are inserted. The number of columns or rows in this range selects the number of columns or rows inserted. If you specify a range that includes three columns or rows, three columns or rows are inserted. If you specify a cell, only one column or row is inserted.

When 1-2-3 inserts rows into a document, the cell references of the data below this location are changed. It is as though 1-2-3 pushes the data down on the sheet to make room for the new blank rows. 1-2-3 automatically adjusts all the formulas that reference this shifted data. The same is true for data stored in cells to the right of the location at which columns are inserted.

Seeing the insertion in action will clarify the way it works. Let's add a column and a few blank rows to the ABC Company sales projections. Follow these steps to complete the changes:

1. Choose Open from the File menu, select ABC Sales from the list box, and select the OK button.
2. Move to D7.

Notice that the formula that projects the next year's sales is +C7*(1+C10). Be sure to look at this formula again after inserting a column and notice how 1-2-3 has adjusted it for you.

3. Move to any cell in column A.
4. Choose Insert from the Worksheet, or press its keyboard shortcut, ⌘-I.

You will notice that the Insert Selected Range check box is not selected. You will want to leave it *deselected,* or 1-2-3 will insert a portion of a column rather than an entire column. Since you do not have a range of cells selected, the default is not to check this box. If you selected a range before invoking this command, the 1-2-3's default setting would be to check the box–you would need to remember to deselect it or your results would not be what you expected.

5. Select the OK button to insert a single column. (The Column radio button is already selected.)
6. Move to E7. Your document should look like that shown in Figure 7-3.

Notice how 1-2-3 adjusted the document: the entries that were in C7 and C10 are now in D7 and D10, and formulas that referenced C now reference D.

7. Select the range D8..D9. (Any range that contains cells from rows 8 and 9 would work just as well.)
8. Choose Insert from the Worksheet menu, select the Row radio button, select Insert Selected Range to deselect the box, then select the OK button to insert two rows.

1-2-3 adds two rows, as shown in Figure 7-4.

9. Choose Save from the File menu to save your changes.

Figure 7-3. *New column added for column A*

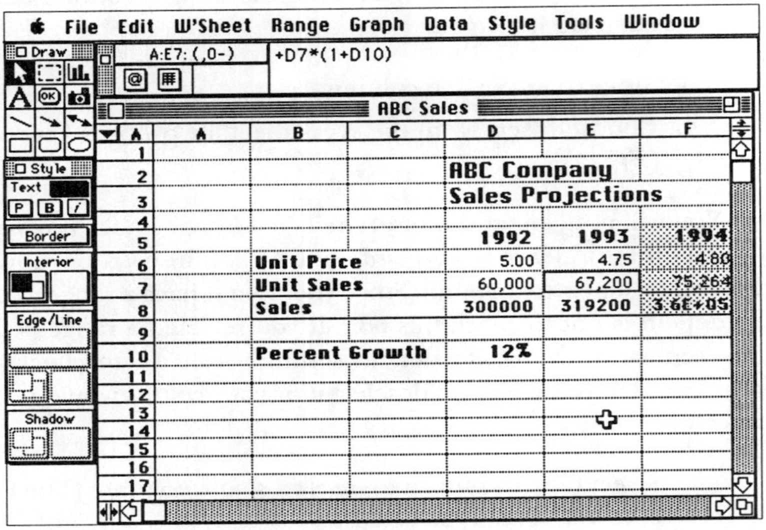

Figure 7-4. *Two new rows added*

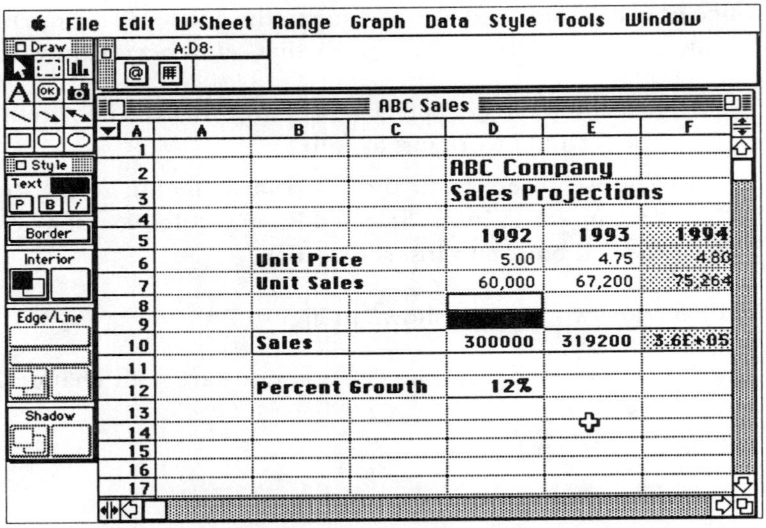

Applications: *Most of the time you will want to insert an entire row or column in a document. You can avoid the confusion of dialog box options for inserting a range rather than a complete row or column and use a shortcut approach by selecting column letters or row numbers from the frame to select entire rows or columns and then pressing* ⌘-I. *This approach will insert the desired number of rows or columns immediately without the need for dialog box selections.*

Deleting Rows and Columns

You can delete rows and columns at any location in a sheet. This allows you to eliminate blank rows and columns or rows and columns that contain entries you no longer need.

When 1-2-3 deletes rows or columns in a sheet, the cell references of the data below and to the right of the deleted rows or columns are changed. It is as though 1-2-3 pushes the data up or to the left on the sheet to replace the deleted rows or columns. 1-2-3 automatically adjusts all the formulas that reference this data. Cell references in formulas that refer to a cell in the deleted rows change to ERR. When this happens, you must edit the formula to refer to a correct range. If a formula references a range that spans the deleted rows or columns, the range the formula uses shrinks to a smaller size because of the deleted rows or columns.

Just as when you insert columns or rows, you must select the range containing the columns or rows to delete before you choose the command. You invoke the delete command by choosing Delete in the Worksheet menu and then selecting the Column or Row radio button. To ensure that 1-2-3 works with the entire row or column specified by the selected range, you need to check to ensure that the Delete Selected Range box is not checked. If you specify a range that includes three columns or rows, three columns or rows are deleted (as long as Delete Selected Range is not checked). If you specify a cell, only one column or row is deleted.

Follow these steps to make the changes:

1. Select the range D8..D9 (any range that contains cells from rows 8 and 9 would work just as well).
2. Choose Delete from the Worksheet menu or press its keyboard shortcut, ⌘-K.

3. Select the Row radio button, deselect the Delete Selected Range check box, and select the OK button to delete two rows.

1-2-3 deleted the two rows you just added.

Deleting columns is just as easy. To delete a column, use the Delete command in the Worksheet menu and select the Column radio button, and check to be certain that Delete Selected Range is not checked. This deletes the columns in the range you select before choosing the command. You can also save time by selecting the row numbers or column letters on the frame of the worksheet and deleting.

Hiding and Displaying Columns

1-2-3 can temporarily conceal columns from view on the display screen. The data in these columns is not altered in any way and can be displayed again at any time with the entry of another command. This feature is particularly useful if you are working with sensitive information, like salary data, and do not wish it to be in plain view of anyone who walks by your computer.

Applications: *Since hidden columns do not print, you can hide a column to narrow a report to a size that will fit on one sheet of paper. The data in the hidden columns is not lost and can be used in another report, once it is redisplayed.*

You can hide the entries in column E by following these steps:

1. Move to any cell in column E.
2. Choose Hide|Show from the Worksheet menu, select the Column button, and the Hide button, since the Range text box shows the active cell for the range 1-2-3 will hide.

1-2-3 hides the entries in column E, as shown in Figure 7-5.

3. Move to F7.

Notice that the formula still uses a value in column E. When a column is hidden, it is removed only from the display and not from the worksheet.

To display the hidden column, follow these steps:

1. Select the range D7..F7 to select a range that contains at least one cell from columns D, E, and F.
2. Choose Hide|Show from the Worksheet menu, the Column radio button, and the Show button to display the hidden column, E.

As this example shows, you can include columns in the range you select that are not hidden without affecting them.

With a mouse, you can use the worksheet frame to hide and display columns. To hide columns, select the columns to hide and then drag the right border of the last column to hide all the way to the left border of the first column to hide. To hide column E in the above example, drag the right side of the column on top of the left side. If you are hiding columns C and D, drag the right side of column D to the left side of column C.

Figure 7-5. *Column E hidden*

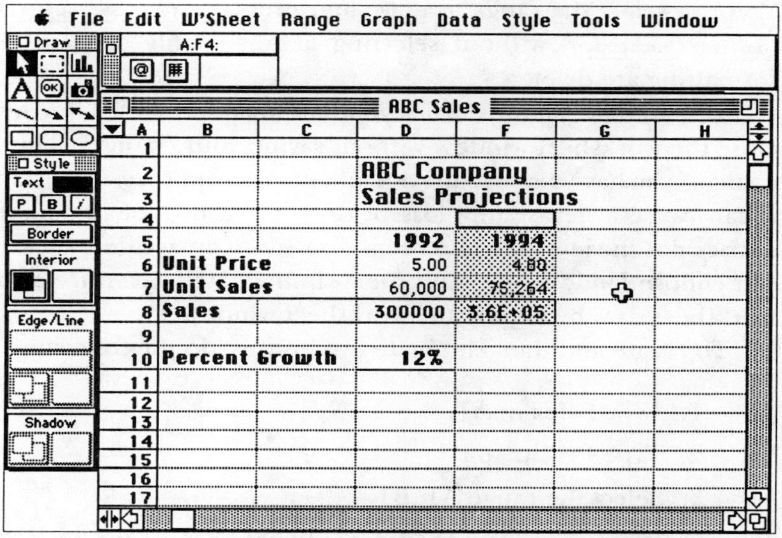

Erasing Worksheet Data

You have learned how to change worksheet entries and completely replace them with other data. However, you may want to eliminate entries completely; they may be mistakes or old data that is no longer required. Pressing (⌘)-(.) does not eliminate entries once they are finalized.

You have already learned how to eliminate attributes from cells with the use of Clear Styles in the Edit menu. This command removes numeric format and text styles but leaves the data intact. Two additional commands let you clear both the data and attributes or just the data. When you use these commands 1-2-3 does not even care what types of entries the cells contain; 1-2-3 erases text, numbers, and formulas with equal ease. Normally you will clear only a small range of cells on the sheet. A second, more extensive approach would clear the entire document.

To erase a range of cell entries yet retain their attributes, select the range you want to erase and choose Clear Contents in the Edit menu or press (⌘)-(L). This eliminates only the cell entries and retains any attributes assigned with the Format command in the Range menu or the commands in the Style menu. To erase the attributes, as well as the contents, select the range and then choose Clear in the Edit menu or press (⌘)-(B). You also have another choice. You can select the range to erase and press (delete)/(backspace). If you press (delete)/(backspace) without selecting a range, only the active cell and its formatting are deleted.

To eliminate all the entries you have made in a 1-2-3 document, you can close the worksheet window without saving your changes. This removes any changes you have made to the document. This option is more dangerous since it can cause a devastating loss of data if you do not remember important entries not in view on you screen. To restore an accidental clear option you can choose Undo in the Edit menu immediately, even if you removed the worksheet data by closing the worksheet window.

To create and then eliminate two entries, do the following:

1. Type **Sales** in A1.
2. Type **Profits** in B1.
3. Select the range A1..B1.
4. Press (delete)/(backspace) or choose Clear from the Edit menu.

You can use either of these methods, and the results are the same.

5. Choose Close from the File menu and select No when 1-2-3 prompts if you want to save the worksheet.

Closing a worksheet to erase data has a much more destructive capability, since it eliminates everything from the document, assuming you have not saved the worksheet. You close a worksheet window when you have saved a worksheet and are ready to start a new task (in which case you lose no data) or if you have made a complete mess and want to start over. To close a window, choose Close from the File menu, click the close box, or press ⌘-W. 1-2-3 displays a message about saving the worksheet if you have made changes that have not been saved. You can select Yes to save the worksheet under its current name and then close it, No to close the worksheet without saving, Save As to specify a new name to use when saving and close it, or Cancel to leave the worksheet open. When you close a document without saving it, if the worksheet was saved previously, the version of the worksheet that was put into the folder is still there. If you want to remove the worksheet document from the folder, you must move the document from the folder to the Trash from the Finder or Desktop.

Review

In this chapter, you learned how you can rearrange your sheet by adding and deleting columns and rows. You can also set the widths of the columns and indicate which ones to display. The procedures you learned include the following:

- You can change the column width of one or more columns. Use the Column Width command in the Worksheet menu to change the width of columns in a selected range. Use the Column Width setting in the Worksheet Global Settings dialog box to set the width of all columns that you have not individually changed. Column widths changed from the default column width display their width in the console.

- You can change the height of rows so they are smaller or larger than what 1-2-3 has selected, based on the font the worksheet uses. Use the Row Height command in the Worksheet menu to change the height of rows in a selected range or to reset them to use 1-2-3's setting.
- You can insert and delete rows and columns with the Insert and Delete commands in the Worksheet menu. When you delete a row or column, you delete the contents of all the cells in the row or column. Be certain that the Insert or Delete Selected Range boxes are not checked or 1-2-3 may insert or delete a portion of a row or column rather than the entire one.
- You can hide columns of data and redisplay them with the Hide|Show command in the Worksheet menu. Use this feature to hide confidential information on the screen.
- You can erase a group of cells with the Clear command in the Edit menu or by using (delete)/(backspace). To erase the contents but retain cell attributes from a range, choose the Clear Contents command from the Edit menu. To erase the changes you have made to a worksheet, choose Close from the File menu then No. (The document as it was last saved will remain in the folder.)

Keys and Commands

This chapter focused on the commands you will use as you build more advanced worksheets. You have also learned about keys that are shortcuts to commands. These keys and commands are

Entry	Action
(delete)/(backspace)	Shortcut for the Edit Clear command
Edit Clear ((⌘)-(B))	Erases the selected range's contents and its formats
Edit Clear Contents ((⌘)-(L))	Removes the cell's entry while retaining the attributes (numeric format and text styles)
File Close ((⌘)-(W))	Closes the worksheet window

Worksheet Column Width	Changes the width of columns in a selected range
Worksheet Delete	Deletes a contiguous group of selected rows or columns
Worksheet Global Settings	Changes the global settings of the sheet, such as the default column width (in the Column Width text box)
Worksheet Hide|Show	Hides columns from display without removing their contents and allows you to redisplay them
Worksheet Insert	Inserts blank columns and rows at the active cell

8

Managing Documents and Sheets

New computer users frequently find the concept of files or documents on a disk a little difficult to understand. This is partly because you cannot *see* a document on a disk the way you can see documents in a drawer. However, computer documents are really quite simple to work with. They are very similar to the documents you use every day in your office. The main difference is that computer documents are stored on a disk instead of in a drawer.

When you perform tasks without the computer, documents and papers are the normal media for organizing your information. Often you need several different folders available at once to accomplish a job. 1-2-3 lets you have several worksheets open at once so you can access information in the different locations easily. 1-2-3 even makes it easy for you to build formulas that use entries you have stored in other worksheets.

Just as you usually need more than one sheet of paper for each task or activity, 1-2-3 lets you have multiple sheets in one worksheet document. You can use multiple sheets in a worksheet to help organize your information. You might store salary information on one sheet and travel expenses on another. Or perhaps you are overseeing several branch operations and want to organize the data for each branch separately. Once you have added the extra sheets, you can access information in all of the sheets as if it were on one sheet by specifying the sheet level as part of the cell's address.

In this chapter, you learn about basic document concepts and explore the basic commands that 1-2-3 has to offer to store and obtain your data. Next, you learn about using multiple worksheet documents simultaneously. Finally, you learn about using more than one sheet in each worksheet document.

Document Concepts

Every day, you undoubtedly work with a number of different pieces of paper. Periodically, you probably place some of these papers into folders in a cabinet or desk drawer to make space for new information on your desktop. Then, when you want to review these papers, you search for them in the cabinet or you ask your secretary to bring you the folder you wish to see. Assuming that you have an organized filing system, the papers you want will arrive back on your desk.

Your computer uses very similar procedures to maintain its information. Taking a look at the similarities and differences will help you understand the important role that documents can play for you.

Storing Information on Disk

When you store information in your computer, you provide the machine with an organizational challenge similar to the one faced by you or your secretary. In the computer's case, the working area where it puts the information it is currently using is *random access memory*, or *RAM*, the temporary memory of the system; like your desktop, it has a limited amount of space. How much space is available in memory dictates how much information you can place in memory at any one time. You can use part of this space for applications such as 1-2-3; you can use another part to store the data the applications use.

Just as you use folders to store papers, your computer uses folders to store documents. The computer's folders are maintained on disk rather than in a cabinet.

When working with a computer, you need to save your worksheet; 1-2-3 does not automatically maintain a permanent record of your worksheet. As soon as you quit 1-2-3 (whether deliberately or accidentally), the worksheet is lost. In order to use this worksheet again, you must already have stored a copy of it in a document on your disk. The disk provides more permanent storage because its contents are not lost when the power is off in your computer. As long as you store the document on disk, you can open a copy of the document from disk into RAM, where the computer can work on it. The prompt when you attempt to exit from 1-2-3 or close a window reminds you to save the changes to your worksheets.

When you work with data in the form of papers stored in your office folders and you retrieve those papers so you can work with them again, the folder is empty and no longer contains the data. But storing data on computer disks works differently. Once you store a worksheet on disk, it remains there until you take some special action to remove it from the disk. When you open the worksheet, you are placing a *copy* in working or temporary memory, but the original is maintained on the disk. This feature offers a tremendous advantage over paper storage methods: if you accidentally destroy the copy in the computer's memory, you can always open another copy of the worksheet from the disk.

Organizing the Disk Data

When you create folders for your office, you probably have a system—at least a rudimentary one—for labeling these folders. One rule of your system is probably that no two folders should have exactly the same label. If they did, you would have a lot of difficulty finding the papers you needed once they were filed. Perhaps your system for labeling folders is quite organized. It may include color coding or some other scheme that makes it easy to categorize your folders.

Storing data on disk also requires a system. Part of this system involves rules you must follow. There is also room for some flexibility, however, so you can personalize the system to suit your needs. You need not be concerned with the specifics of how the data is stored on disk. Your only concern is the rules you need to follow when working with these documents, especially the rules that center around the names you use for your documents and the location of these documents when they are stored.

Applications: *Using a folder for each application lets you find individual 1-2-3 documents relating to this application quickly. If you use 1-2-3 for sales budgeting, payroll, and inventory, you might have folders for each of these areas with numerous worksheets in each folder.*

Document Names

To store a document on your disk, you must give it a name. Since the naming process follows particular, although flexible, rules, first review the rules you must follow for naming a document. Each document on a disk must have a unique name. This name consists of from one to thirty characters. You can create a name by using any character (including blank spaces) except a colon (:), backslash (\), or slash (/). It is best to develop some consistent rules for naming your data because consistency can help you determine a document's contents when you see the document name later on. If you are storing sales data for a number of years and keeping one year's worth of data in each document, you could create names such as Sales 1991 and Sales 1992. You could also use names such as 1992 Sales or Sales-92. It really does not matter what pattern you select for your names; what is important is that once you decide on a naming pattern, you apply it consistently for each document that you create. Naming documents 1989 Sales, Sales 1990, Sales 1991, and Sales-92 is not a good strategy; the pattern is too inconsistent. You can enter document names in uppercase or lowercase letters or in any combination of the two.

Storing Your Data

Documents can be stored on either hard or floppy disks. Hard disks, thanks to today's technology, are popular storage media for business computer systems. A floppy disk holds from 800,000 to over 1,400,000 characters, depending on the capacity of the disk and the disk drive. Today's typical hard disk installed in a computer system has a capacity of over 40,000,000 characters of information. The hard disk reads and writes considerably faster than the floppy. However, the floppy is very portable.

When new documents are added to a disk, they can be placed loose on the disk, or their names can be added to a *folder* on the disk. Although you could put all of your worksheets loose on a disk, the disk's window would have so many items that finding the one you want would be difficult. This would be like having a single index to catalog a whole library of reference volumes; it would take a long time to read. It would be better if each book in the collection had its own index and if books had chapter outlines that could be referenced for contents.

To lessen the burden of the main disk index, called the *disk window,* you can set up folders on your disk. A folder can contain other folders, so the folders you add into a given folder function as a second-level index to group documents further. You can create these folders on any basis you like, such as one for each individual that uses the system, one for each application, or any other basis. Certain documents and folders, such as the System folder, are always maintained in the disk window. 1-2-3 has created several folders for their files. When folders are added, their names are placed in the disk window or the folder that is active when you add the folder. Disks and folders are organized in a hierarchical structure, as shown in Figure 8-1. Here, the entries in the disk window include several folders. These folders are created using the Finder menu, the Macintosh's operating system interface. Although 1-2-3 cannot create folders, it can use any folder that is available.

1-2-3 always assumes that you want to work with documents in the *current,* or *default, folder*—the disk and folder you are using. This means that if you are content to use the default folder, you do not need to specify where you want your documents saved. However, if you want to use a different disk or folder, you can either change the default or provide the disk or folder location along with the document name. You look at both of these possibilities in the following section on 1-2-3 commands.

1-2-3 Commands for Document Management

The commands on 1-2-3's File menu help you handle your document management tasks. There are menu selections for saving your data to disk and for opening copies of these documents to place in memory. You have an opportunity to try these commands to save and open your worksheets in the

Figure 8-1. *A hierarchical folder structure*

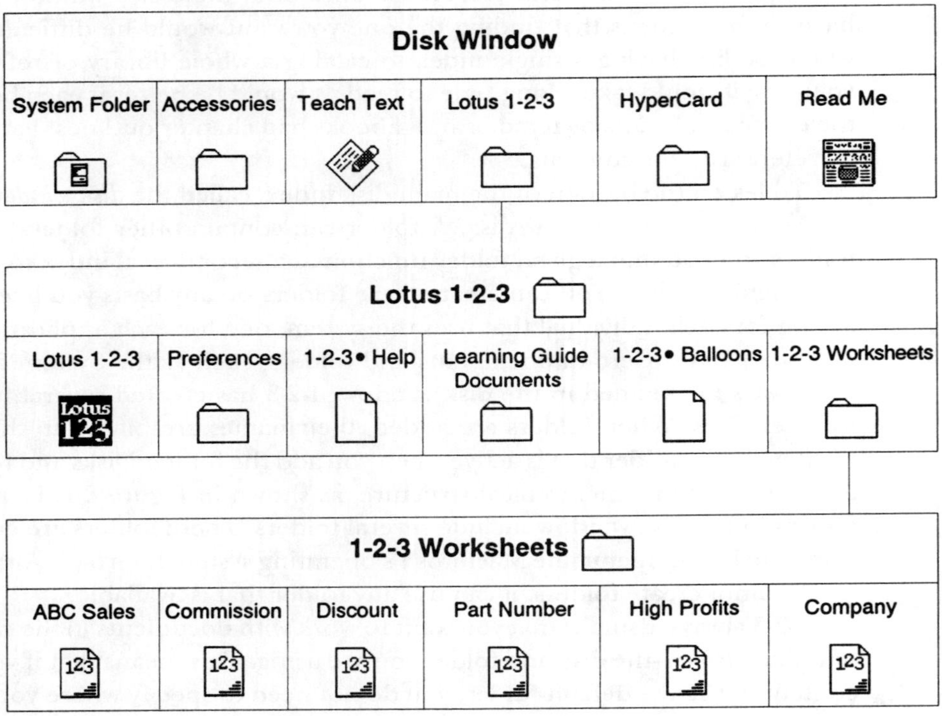

following sections. 1-2-3 also has other commands in the File menu for printing and other advanced document commands. You will learn about these commands in other chapters.

Changing the Folder

1-2-3's use of the default folder saves you a considerable amount of time. The default folder is the location that 1-2-3 assumes you are referencing unless you specify otherwise. If you keep the default folder set to the folder containing your data, you will not need to change the folder most of the time. Since you are working with a hard disk system, your data is probably stored in the same folder as 1-2-3 or in a folder within 1-2-3's folder. To work with 1-2-3 for a period of time, you need to be able to change the folder you are using. You will see how you can change the folder for a single command and also change the default folder.

Using Another Folder

1-2-3 may use a hard disk for storing its program, but you can select any available disk and folder for storing your data. If you change the default drive to a floppy disk, you must insert the disk into the drive before you can select it. To change from the current folder to a floppy disk, follow these steps in 1-2-3:

1. Put an initialized disk into the floppy disk drive.

If the disk you put in the drive is not initialized for the Macintosh, you will see a dialog box telling you so and providing you the option of initializing or ejecting the disk.

2. Choose User Setup from the Tools menu and then choose Preferences.
3. Select the Default Folder button.
4. Select the pop-up menu under Select Current Folder and select Drive (System 6) or Desktop (System 7) from the pop-up menu.
5. Select the name of the disk in the floppy disk drive and then select the Select Current Folder button.
6. Select the OK button.

This change lasts only until you quit 1-2-3. If you want to permanently change the location where 1-2-3 saves and opens documents, select the Update button in the User Setup Preferences dialog box before selecting the OK button.

1-2-3 combines the disk, the folder names and a document name into a *path*. You saw an example of a path in Chapter 4 when you built formulas containing references to other worksheet document data. Most of the time you do not need to think of the path since you are visually selecting the disk and folder you are working with. Follow these steps to return to the previous folder setting:

1. Choose User Setup from the Tools menu and then choose Preferences.
2. Select the Default Folder button.
3. Select the pop-up menu under Select Current Folder and select Desktop (System 7) or Drive (System 6) from the pop-up menu.
4. Double-click the name of your hard disk, as in MacintoshHD, as the disk you want to use and then double-click the names of the folders that lead to the folder where you want to put your 1-2-3 documents.
5. Select the Select Current Folder button, and then the OK button.

Saving Documents

1-2-3 does not save your documents automatically—it is your responsibility to save the data you enter. It is best to do this periodically; do not wait until you are ending your 1-2-3 session before you save data for the first time. A good guideline is to save every 20 to 30 minutes so you can never lose more than 20 to 30 minutes of your work, even if the power goes off unexpectedly. In previous chapters, you were briefly introduced to the Save and Save As commands in the File menu to save your data.

Saving for the First Time

When you save a document for the first time, 1-2-3 suggests a document name but you can provide a different one. The document name 1-2-3 suggests is Untitled-*x*, where *x* is replaced by the next unused sequential number (as in Untitled-5) after it has used Untitled. You can either accept this document name or provide one of your own. In the following example, you make a few entries on the worksheet and then save the data.

1. Make the following entries:

B1:	**"Qtr 1**	B2:	**80000**
C1:	**"Qtr 2**	C2:	**85000**
D1:	**"Qtr 3**	D2:	**90000**
E1:	**"Qtr 4**	E2:	**105000**
A2:	**Sales**		

Your entries look like this:

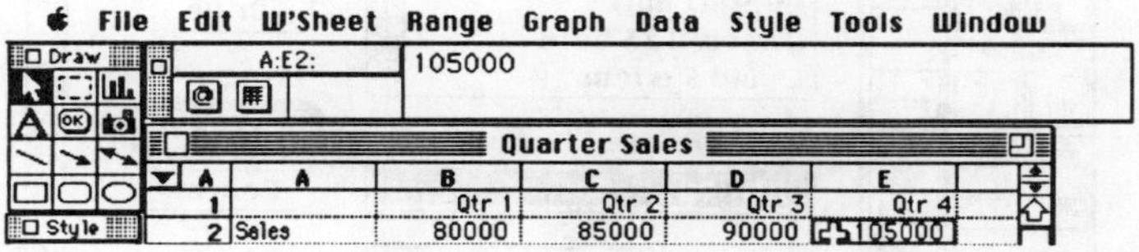

2. Choose Save in the File menu to display the dialog box shown in Figure 8-2 (System 7's dialog box looks slightly different). This figure shows that you will save the worksheet in the disk window of MacintoshHD.

While you can use 1-2-3's suggested document name, you will want to provide a more meaningful name for the document by typing a new name.

3. Type **Quarter Sales** in the Save As text box and select the Save button to save the worksheet document.

Once you select the Save button, 1-2-3 writes the worksheet document to the folder displayed in the pop-up menu at the top of the dialog box. 1-2-3 replaces the title bar entry with the document's name. At this point, you can continue to work on the worksheet or close it since you know that the worksheet is saved. For now, you will make some additions to it to see how the process differs for subsequent saves.

Applications: *Meaningful document names allow you to locate needed information quickly. Try to develop naming standards so that all similar documents have names that follow the same pattern. Budget 1991 and Budget 1992 are better choices that Budget 91 and 92 Budget.*

Figure 8-2. *The Save As dialog box for saving a worksheet*

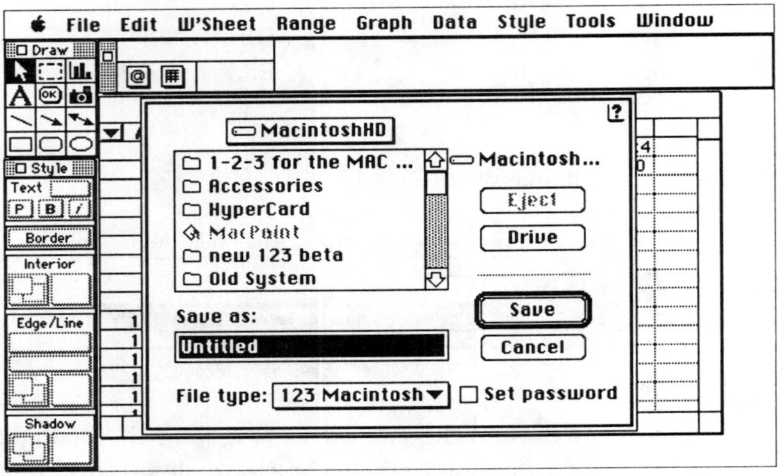

Subsequent Saves

Each time you save a worksheet you have saved before, you can replace the copy on the disk with the information that is currently stored in memory or you can save the data to another worksheet document. If you saved the worksheet previously, 1-2-3's default is to save the worksheet under the same name. You can also copy the old version of the worksheet to a backup document before saving the new version of the data. Make a few changes to the worksheet and save the worksheet again with these steps:

1. Move to A3 and type **Profit**. Type **10000** in B3, **15000** in C3, **10000** in D3, and **20000** in E3.
2. Choose Save in the File menu or press ⌘-S to save the document again using the same settings.

You do not need to complete a dialog box because 1-2-3 already knows the name of the document and where the document is stored. When you save the document using the Save As command in the File menu the steps are different.

3. Type **15000** in E3 and click the Confirm button or press (enter).
4. Choose Save As in the File menu and the Save button. 1-2-3 presents this dialog box:

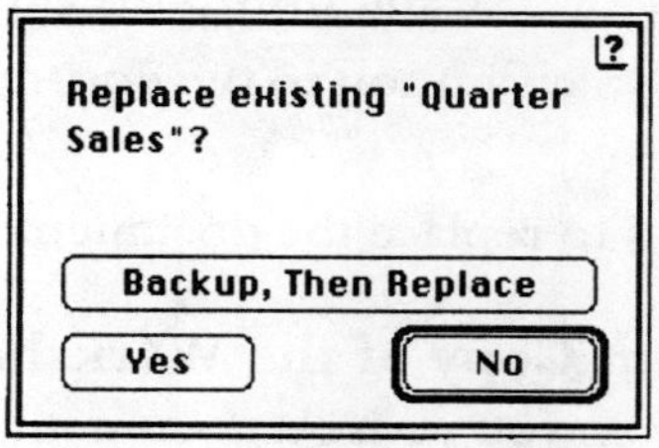

1-2-3 is asking if you wish to replace the Quarter Sales document with the one currently displayed (Yes), cancel the request (No), or back up the original document before replacing it.

5. Select Yes. 1-2-3 saves the updated worksheet under the name you used previously.

If you want to save a worksheet under a new name, use the Save As command in the File menu and enter or edit the document name in the Save As text box. When you select the Save button, the document is saved under the new name. This feature is especially useful when you need to create two similar copies of a worksheet; you can enter the data that is the same for both worksheets and then save the worksheet under two different names before adding the entries that are different.

Saving to Another Location

You can also use the Save As command from the File menu to save a document to a folder other than the default. To do this, use the pop-up menu at the top of the dialog box when you save the document. For example, to save the document to a floppy disk, do the following:

1. Choose Save As from the File menu.
2. Select the Drive button (System 6) or Desktop button and the name of the disk from the list box (System 7).

3. Select the Save button to save the worksheet in the new location.
4. Choose Save As from the File menu.
5. Select the Drive button (System 6) or select Desktop button (System 7) and the name of the hard disk. Next select the folders that lead to the one where you previously saved Quarter Sales.
6. Select the Save button so the document is saved again in its original location.
7. Select Yes to replace the document.

Making a Backup Copy of the Worksheet

Sometimes when you revise a document, you keep the previous version of the document in the file cabinet along with the current version. If you revise a budget projection, for example, you may keep the previous projection for comparison purposes. You can then refer to the previous copy in case you want to revert to any of the old projections, or you can use it as a backup in case you lose the later copy.

1-2-3 offers the same feature for your worksheets. When you select Backup, Then Replace in response to the Yes, No, or Backup, Then Replace prompt, the worksheet stored on disk is renamed to add .BAK to the end of the document name. Then 1-2-3 saves the current worksheet with the selected name. Using the Backup, Then Replace option allows you always to access the current document and its most recent previous version. As an example, make several changes to the worksheet and save the worksheet again with these steps:

1. Move to A1 and type **ABC Company** and click the confirm button or press (enter).
2. Choose Save As in the File menu and the Save button.

1-2-3 displays the Yes, No, and Backup, Then Replace buttons.

3. Select Backup, Then Replace.

1-2-3 saves the updated worksheet as Quarter Sales. The previous version of the document is saved as Quarter Sales.BAK.

4. Click the close box or press ⌘-W to close this worksheet.

For a closer look at what the Backup feature offers, imagine looking inside the Quarter Sales and Quarter Sales.BAK documents. Their contents are shown in Figure 8-3. On the top, the Quarter Sales document has "ABC Company" in A1—it is created by the most recent save operation. Quarter Sales.BAK on the bottom does not have "ABC Company" in A1; this document contains the worksheet as it existed after the previous save operation. If you ever need to use the backup version, you can open it just as you would open other worksheets.

Opening Worksheets

Opening a worksheet reads a worksheet document from the disk and places it in a new worksheet window. You can open documents from any

Figure 8-3. *A worksheet and its backup*

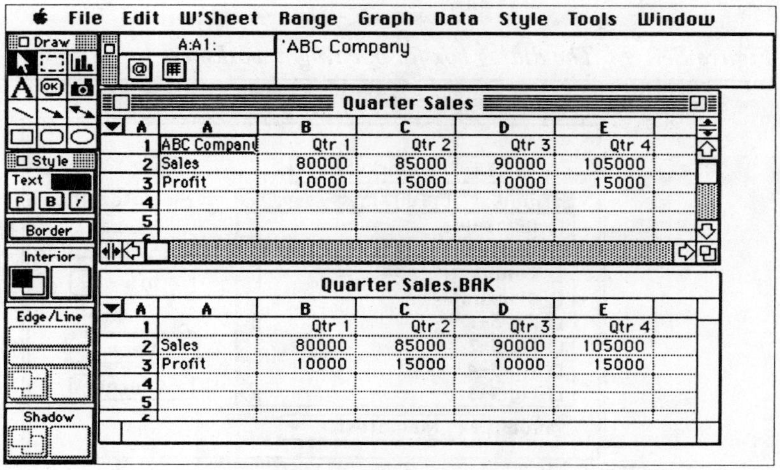

location. While 1-2-3 initially lists documents to open in the default folder, you can always open a worksheet from another location. Follow these steps to open the Quarter Sales worksheet:

1. Choose Open in the File menu or press ⌘-O to display the dialog box shown in Figure 8-4 (this figure shows System 6).

The list box lists the worksheets that are stored in the current folder. By changing the folder in the pop-up menu, you can change which folder of documents is listed. Many of components in this dialog box are identical to the ones in the dialog box when you save a worksheet.

2. Select the Drive button (System 6) or Desktop button (System 7) after putting a disk in the drive and then select the name of the disk from the list box.

Now the worksheets shown in the list box include the Quarter Sales worksheet document you saved earlier to the floppy disk.

3. Double-click Quarter Sales in the list box, or press ↓ to highlight it and return to open this worksheet.

Figure 8-4. *The dialog box for opening a worksheet*

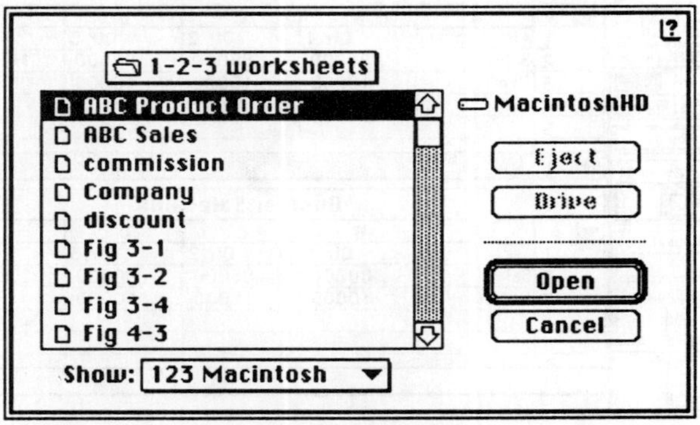

4. Click the close box or press ⌘-W to close this worksheet.
5. Choose Open in the File menu.
6. Select the Drive button (System 6) or Desktop button and the name of your hard disk in the list box (System 7). Next, return to the folder where your 1-2-3 worksheets are stored.

Now the list box contains all of the 1-2-3 worksheets you have created to this point. Since 1-2-3's default folder has more worksheets than can fit in the list box, you can scroll through the list to find the one you want. 1-2-3 displays the document list in alphabetical order to make it easy for you to find the one you want.

7. Click the scroll bar in the list box so Quarter Sales is visible, or type Q to move to the first item in the list that starts with the letter you type (in this case, Q).

You can also see the Quarter Sales.BAK backup document. If you need to open a backup, select the document with .BAK at the end of its name from the list box.

8. Select the Open button by clicking it or pressing RETURN.

Opening New Worksheets

In addition to opening existing worksheets, you can open a worksheet window that contains an empty worksheet so you can start creating new worksheets. The New command in the File menu creates a new worksheet in a new worksheet window. As soon as you choose the New command in the File menu, 1-2-3 opens a new window with a default document name (Untitled-*x*). Later, you can give it a better name with the Save or Save As command in the File menu. 1-2-3 creates a document on disk for the new document; if you look at the default folder, you will see the new document you are using. If you close the worksheet without saving it, 1-2-3 deletes the empty worksheet document placeholder.

Try the New command in the File menu now by choosing File and then New or pressing ⌘-N. Choose File and New again to add another worksheet window, as shown in Figure 8-5. 1-2-3 lets you continue adding new and existing worksheet documents to the desktop until your computer runs out of memory to hold the data or until the total number of sheets in all the open worksheets is 256.

Working with Multiple Worksheets

As you can see by the three title bars in Figure 8-5, when you open a worksheet window, you are not putting away the one that was active before you chose the Open or New commands in the File menu. 1-2-3 lets you open as many as worksheets as you like, as long as the total number of sheets is 256 or fewer. Realistically, the true limit is likely to be the amount of memory in your machine; you may run out of memory in which to store the data in every open sheet before you reach the absolute limit of 256 sheets.

Figure 8-5. *Opening a new worksheet*

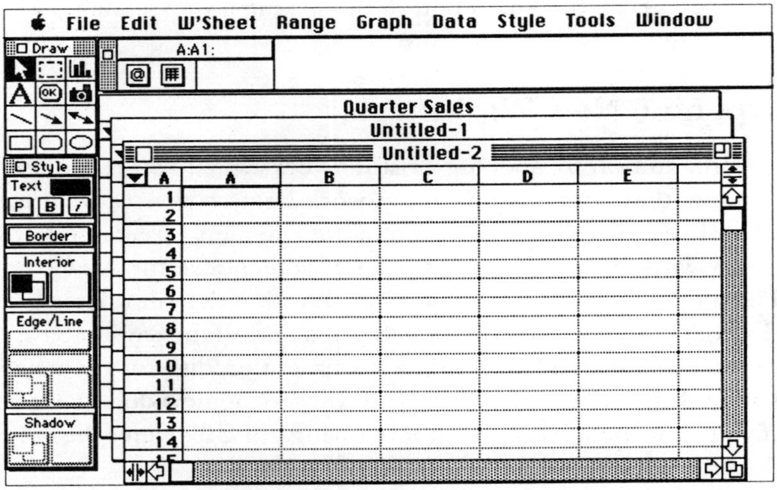

Since 1-2-3 keeps worksheet windows open as you open more, you must close the worksheet windows as you no longer need them. You do this with the close box in the window title bar, the Close command in the File menu, or ⌘-W, as you learned in Chapter 2, "Entering Text and Numbers."

Each worksheet window is separate, which means you can position and size the windows separately. The Macintosh features you use to size and move windows are described in Appendix B, "Using the Macintosh." 1-2-3 has some of its own commands that select how the windows appear on the desktop, as described in the next section. As you open more worksheets, you will need to learn how to switch between them and how you can use the data from the open worksheets.

Switching Between Worksheet Windows

1-2-3 lets you work with any worksheet window you want. You can switch to another window when 1-2-3 is in Point or Ready mode. With a mouse, the easiest way to switch to a worksheet window is to click any part of the one you want. You can also switch to another window by choosing the name of the worksheet you want from the Window menu. You can try some of these options as well as some of 1-2-3's options for displaying multiple worksheets by following these steps:

1. Click the title bar of the first Untitled-*x* worksheet (Untitled-1) you created.

You can tell this is now the active window because there are lines in its title bar, while the other title bars have only the document name.

2. Choose Arrange from the Window menu and choose Vertical Tile, so your worksheets look like Figure 8-6.

Tiling divides the desktop between the worksheets. 1-2-3 has two tiling options.

3. Choose Arrange from the Window menu and then choose Horizontal Tile to tile your worksheet horizontally.

8

Figure 8-6. *Vertical tiled worksheets*

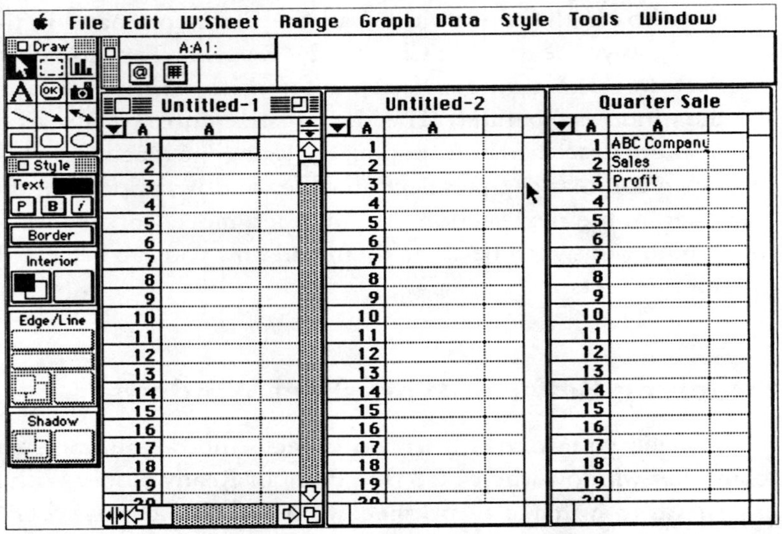

4. Choose Arrange from the Window menu and then choose Stack to return your worksheets to look like Figure 8-5.

Stacking arranges each window so you can see only the title bar for each application except the top one.

5. Click the title bar of the Untitled-1 worksheet you created.
6. Click the close box or press ⌘-W to close this worksheet without saving it.

If you press the option key while you click the close box or press ⌘-W, you will close all open windows instead of just the active one.

7. Choose Quarter Sales from the Window menu.
8. Choose Untitled-1 from the Window menu.

You can also use the following keys to move between worksheets:

control-end home	Moves to the first worksheet document
control-end end	Moves to the last worksheet document
control-end control-page up	Moves to the next worksheet document
control-end control-page down	Moves to the previous worksheet document

9. Press control-end end to move to the Quarter Sales worksheet.
10. Press control-end control-page down to move to the Untitled-1 worksheet.

Using Multiple Worksheet Documents in Formulas

You can create a formula in the new worksheet using some of the values in the Quarter Sales worksheet. You can also build this formula by using Point mode, just as you learned how to use Point mode to build formulas in the same worksheet in Chapter 3, "Defining Your Calculations." To create a formula that uses values from the Quarter Sales worksheet, follow these steps:

1. Type **Total Sales** in A2 of the new worksheet.
2. Move to B2 in the new worksheet and type **@SUM(**.
3. Click the Quarter Sales worksheet or press control-end control-page up and move to B2 in the Quarter Sales worksheet so the formula looks like this:

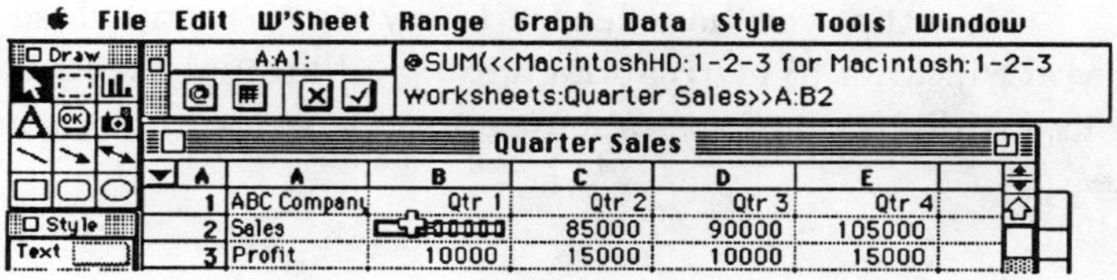

MacintoshHD will be replaced by the name of your hard drive. Notice that the same angle brackets you used when you built linking formulas in Chapter

4, "@Functions and Other Formula Options" and the information in them are automatically added for you.

4. Select the range B2..E2 by dragging the mouse or pressing (shift)(→).
5. Type) and click the confirm button or press (enter) to finalize the formula, which looks like this:

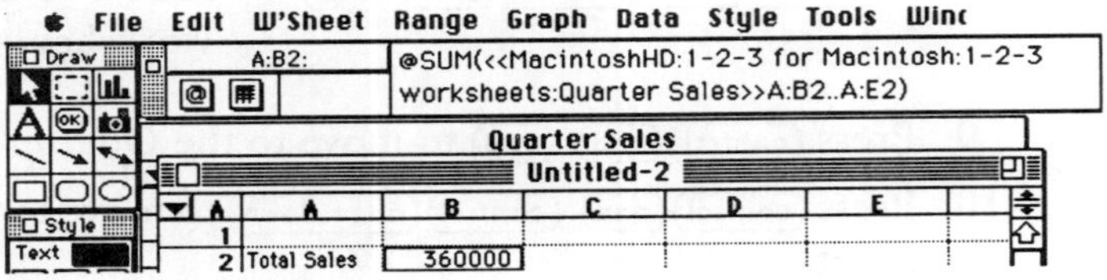

While you can type the information in the << >>, pointing to the cells provides visual confirmation of the cells you are using and requires less typing. For example, you could have typed

@SUM(<<Quarter Sales>>B2.E2)

which is the formula you entered by pointing to the range in the other worksheet. (1-2-3 will add the sheet references for you.)

6. Choose Save in the File menu, type **Total Sales** in the Save As text box, and select the Save button.

This saves the document with a better name than 1-2-3's default document name, but it does not save the other open worksheets. To save the other worksheets, you must make the worksheets active and then use the Save or Save As command in the File menu.

Now that you have learned how to open and close worksheet windows, you will want to learn about adding additional sheets to a worksheet. This is like adding pages to a tablet to provide you with areas to put data.

Adding Sheets to a Worksheet

Adding a sheet to a worksheet is like adding another sheet to a notebook: you go to where you want to add the new sheets and then add one or more sheets before or after the current sheet. To try adding more sheets to the Total Sales worksheet, use the following steps:

1. Choose Insert from the Worksheet menu or press its keyboard shortcut, ⌘-I, to display this dialog box:

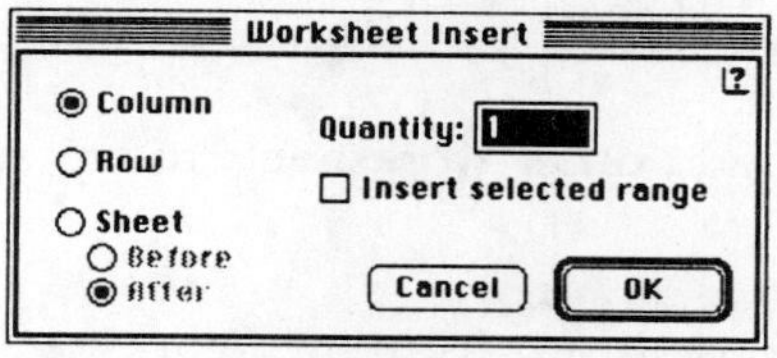

2. Select the Sheet radio button and the Before radio button below that.

The Quantity text box is where you type the number of sheets to add. The number 1 is the default, but you can enter a higher number to add more sheets.

3. Select the OK button to add one sheet.

The sheet indicator in the worksheet border is still an A but you do not see your entries. This is because 1-2-3 added this sheet in front of the one with entries. The new sheet is sheet A and the sheet with the entries is sheet B. As mentioned in Chapter 1, "Worksheet Basics," 1-2-3 labels sheets with letters just like it labels columns. The first sheet is sheet A, and labeling can continue up to IV if you have 256 sheets in one worksheet.

4. Press the Sheet pop-up icon, ▼, in the worksheet border and select B from the Sheet pop-up menu or press control-page up.

As the preceding step describes, you can press (control)-(page up) to move to the next sheet. (control)-(page down) moves you to the previous sheet. Now you can see the worksheet with your entries on sheet B. The top of your worksheet looks like this:

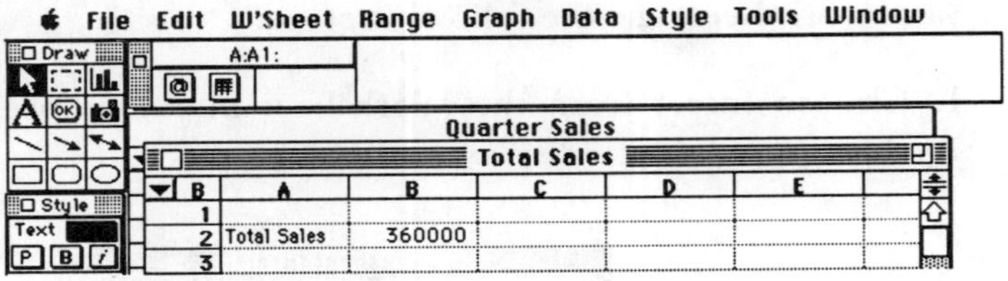

You can add other worksheets to try inserting sheets after the current one.

5. Choose Insert from the Worksheet menu or press (⌘)-(I); select the Sheet radio button and the After radio button; type **3** in the Quantity text box, and select the OK button.

1-2-3 inserts three blank sheets after sheet B.

6. Use the Sheet pop-up menu or press (control)-(page up) and (control)-(page down) to move through new sheets labeled C, D, and E.

At this point, you can see only one sheet at a time. You can look at two or more sheets at a time by splitting the window into panes.

Applications: *Add new sheets for new kinds of information. If you are recording detailed budget information, consider using a sheet for each expense category, then create a summary sheet.*

Using Panes to Help Monitor Data

1-2-3 allows you to split the window into two or four different sections, called *panes,* and to view a different portion of the worksheet in each section. You have the option of splitting the window vertically or horizontally or both. If you want to see columns in two different areas, you split the window vertically. If you want to view rows from two different locations, you choose a horizontal split. If you want to see rows and columns from four different locations, split the window four ways into panes.

The command that creates the panes is Split in the Window menu. Next, select the Horizontal radio button if you want two horizontal panes, the Vertical radio button if you want two vertical panes, or 4-Way if you want to split the window into four panes. 1-2-3 evenly splits the window into two or four panes.

Try creating two panes in your window by following this exercise:

1. Move to sheet B.
2. Choose the Split command from the Window menu, the four-way radio button, and the OK button to split the window into four panes, as shown in Figure 8-7.

You can have each pane display a different section of the sheet. The active pane has a dark border around it. Each pane has its own scroll bar and sheet pop-up.

Figure 8-7. *Window split into four panes*

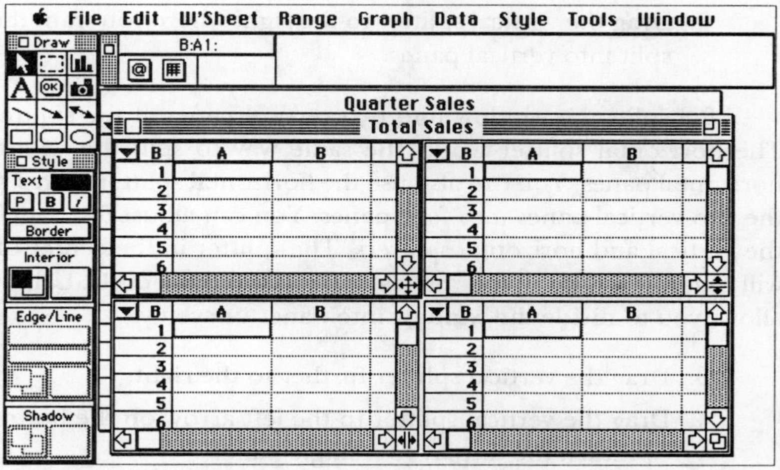

8

3. Click the upper-right pane or press ⌘-option-X or, on an extended keyboard, F6 (Window) to move to the upper-right pane.

⌘-option-X and F6 (Window) take you to the next pane. You can also select a pane by clicking any part of the pane you want.

4. Move to I29 in the upper right pane.

As you move to the right, the lower right pane also scrolls to the right since the panes' movements are synchronized. This is also why, as you move down, the upper left pane also scrolls down.

5. Choose the Split command from the Window menu, the Clear All Splits radio button, and the OK button to return to a single pane.

You can also split a window into panes by using the splitters in the window's scroll bars. Try creating two panes in the window with the splitters by following these steps:

1. Point to the vertical splitter on the scroll bar on the bottom of the worksheet window, which looks like 

The mouse changes to look like the vertical splitter.

2. Drag the vertical splitter to the right where you want the window to split into vertical panes.

1-2-3 splits the window into two vertical panes at the splitter's location. The horizontal splitter works the same way to split the window into two horizontal panes. You can also use the horizontal splitter at this point to split the two vertical panes into four panes. You can adjust the pane's split using the vertical and horizontal splitters. The splitter in the center of four panes will redefine where all four panes are split simultaneously. Using the splitters allows you to divide the window into panes unevenly.

3. Drag the vertical splitter further to the right.
4. Drag the vertical splitter to the left arrow on the bottom scroll bar to return the display to a single pane.

Using Panes with Multiple Sheets

Displaying your data by using panes is especially useful when you are working with multiple sheets. You can use each pane to display a separate sheet in the worksheet. To look at the worksheets you have added, follow these steps:

1. Select A from the Sheet pop-up menu or press (control)-(page up).
2. Choose the Split command from the Window menu, the Horizontal radio button, and the OK button to split the window into two horizontal panes.
3. Select B from the Sheet pop-up menu in the top pane or press (control)-(page up). Your worksheet now looks like the one in Figure 8-8.

1-2-3 moved to sheet B in the active pane while keeping the second pane on sheet A. You can use horizontal and vertical panes to look at two different sheets within the same worksheet just as you can use panes to look at two different areas of the same sheet.

Figure 8-8. *Using horizontal panes to view two sheets*

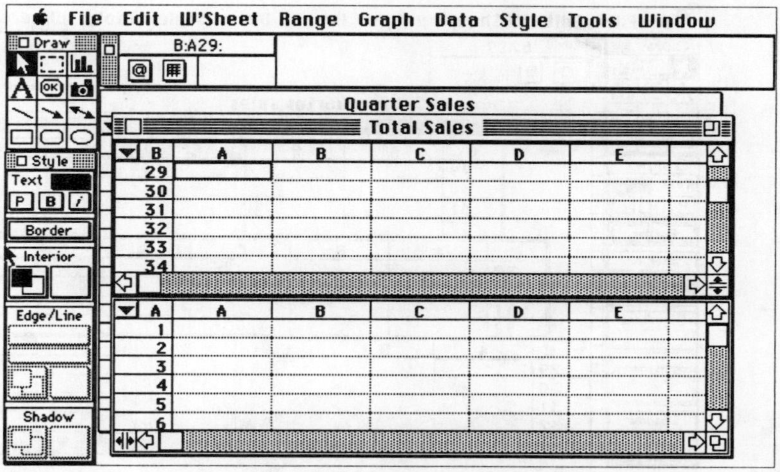

8

1-2-3 has another option in the Window Split dialog box that displays two to nine sheets in a worksheet at once. To see how 1-2-3 will display your worksheet when you use this option, follow these steps:

4. Choose the Split command from the Window menu, select the Perspective Sheets radio button, and select the OK button.

The default is to show three sheets but you can show from two and nine sheets by selecting a different number from the pop-up menu after the Perspective Sheets radio button. 1-2-3 changes the display to look like the worksheet in Figure 8-9. The current sheet appears first. You can use the Sheet pop-up in the first sheet to select the first sheet in the perspective display. You can also click a displayed sheet to make it the active sheet. You can also press ⌘-option-3 (3 on the numeric keypad), ⌘-option-9 (9 on the numeric keypad), ⌘-option-X, F6 (Window), on an enhanced keyboard, control-page down (on an enhanced keyboard), and control-page up (on an enhanced keyboard) to move through the sheets. If the perspective view displays more sheets than your worksheet has, some of them will appear empty.

Figure 8-9. *Using Window Split to view three sheets*

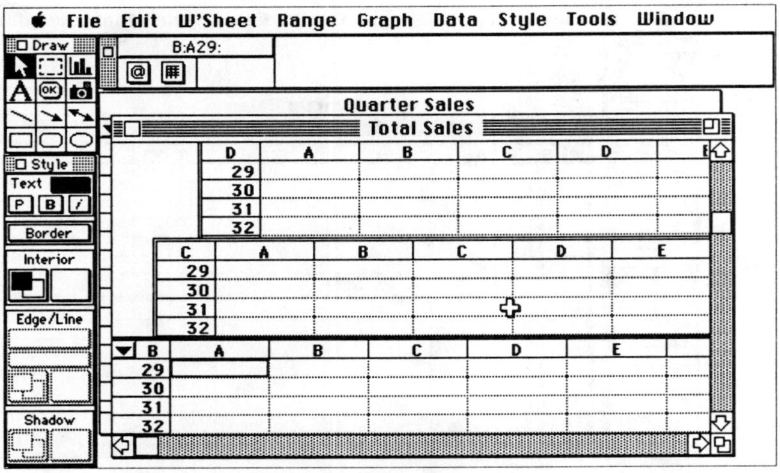

You can temporarily expand one of the sheets to use the full window and then contract it when you want to return to the pane display.

5. Click the zoom box, choose Zoom Pane Out from the Window menu, or press ⌘-option-Z or option-F6 (Zoom) to make sheet B, the active sheet, fill the window.

You can also use this command or the keystroke combinations with panes.

6. Click the zoom box again, choose Zoom Pane In from the Window menu, or press ⌘-option-Z or option-F6 (Zoom) again to return the display to the three sheets.

When you want to remove the perspective view, select the Clear All Splits from the Window Split dialog box.

Using Worksheet Functions with Multiple Sheets

Just as you can build formulas that reference data in other worksheets or on the same sheet, you can also build formulas that use data on different sheets in the same worksheet. For example, you can consolidate data by creating a formula that sums or averages data in a range that spans sheets. You can reference cells outside the current sheet by pointing to them or by typing the address, making sure that you include the sheet letter.

To create formulas in the Total Sales worksheet that uses multiple sheets, follow these steps:

1. Move to A:B1 and type **@SUM(** as the beginning of the formula.
2. Select B:A1 by clicking it or pressing control-page up and moving to B:A1.
3. Select B:A1..C:B2 by pressing shift when you select C:B2, or by typing a period and pressing the →, the ↓, and control-page up.

As mentioned in Chapter 6, "Changing the Appearance of Worksheet Entries," pressing shift and the arrow keys selects a range using the selected cell as one corner of the range and the current cell as the First diagonal corner.

8

4. Type), and click the confirm button or press (return) to complete the formula, @SUM(B:A1..C:B2).

1-2-3 automatically includes the sheet letter with the cell address when you point to cells on other sheets. Instead of pointing to cells on other sheets for cell addresses in a formula, you can type the address, but you must be sure to include the sheet letter and a colon as part of the address.

Deleting Sheets in a Worksheet

Just as you can insert and delete columns and rows in worksheets, you can also insert and delete sheets within a worksheet. The steps for deleting a sheet are just like those for deleting columns and rows. When you delete sheets, you do not enter the number of sheets to delete. Instead, like deleting columns and rows, you select a range containing at least one cell in each sheet that you want to delete. You have created more sheets than you need, so follow these steps to remove three of the sheets:

1. Choose C from the Sheet pop-up menu or press (control)-(page up) twice to switch to sheet C.
2. Select C:A1 and then hold down (shift) while you select E:A1 by selecting E from the sheet pop-up menu and then selecting E:A1 or press (shift)-(control)-(page up) twice, and (enter) once to select the range C:A1..E:A1.
3. Choose Delete from the Worksheet menu or press its keyboard shortcut, (⌘)-(K). Select the Sheet radio button and the OK button.

When 1-2-3 deletes a sheet, it reassigns letters to the remaining sheets. If you had a sheet F, it would become sheet C after you delete sheets C through E. Now the slots that previously displayed the later sheets are empty, and you can only see sheet B.

4. Choose the Split command from the Window menu, the Clear All Splits radio button and the OK button to return to a single pane in the window.
5. Choose Save in the File menu.

6. Press (option) while you click the close box or press (⌘)-(W) twice to close both worksheets.

Designing Multilevel Applications

1-2-3 lets you include up to 256 sheets in one worksheet, but you want to use multiple sheets only when they provide you with benefits. You want to plan how you lay out your data in the worksheet so you can easily access your information. While you have unlimited possibilities for arranging your worksheet, this chapter considers only two different arrangements of information.

Storing the Same Type of Information

When you need to store data containing the same information for different branches, regions, or departments within the same company, use separate sheets in a worksheet for each one. Multiple sheets with similar information are useful in expense reports for different departments, where each department uses the same format and design but the department numbers and expenses differ. Figure 8-10 shows an example of multiple sheets that contain the same type of data. Sheet A contains the summary information for all of the departments. Sheets B and C contain the detailed information for the accounting and advertising departments. The worksheet also contains the same type of information for all the remaining departments in the company. As numbers are entered in the sheets for the individual departments, the formulas in the summary sheet are immediately updated.

Storing Different Types of Information

Sometimes you have different types of information that you want to store on the same worksheet. When you create databases, as you will learn how to do in Chapter 12, "Data-Management Basics," you can store the database, the entries that select database information you want to find, and the reports created with the database on different sheets. This leaves room on each sheet for the database and allows the reports to grow without interfering with the other information. Also, you can add and delete columns and rows in one section without affecting the other data stored in the worksheet. Figure 8-11 shows such a database worksheet that has the three parts on separate sheets, minimizing the chance that a user will accidentally enter data in the wrong place.

Figure 8-10. *Multiple sheets containing the same type of data*

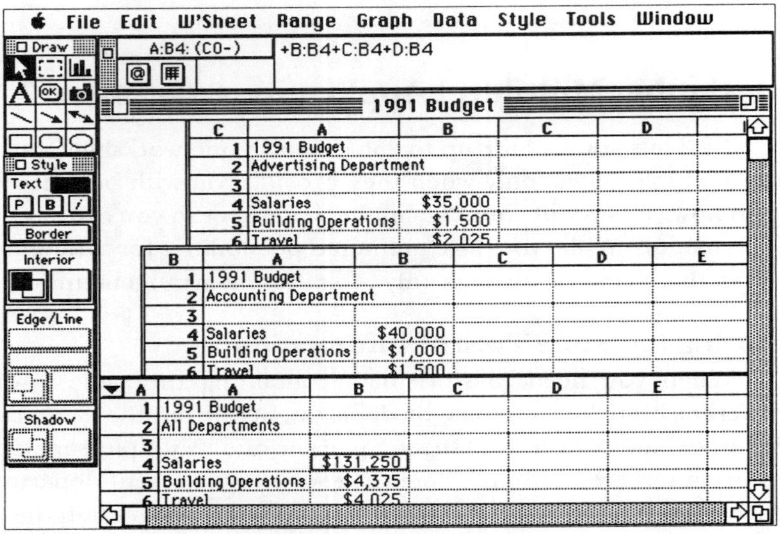

Figure 8-11. *An employee database using multiple sheets*

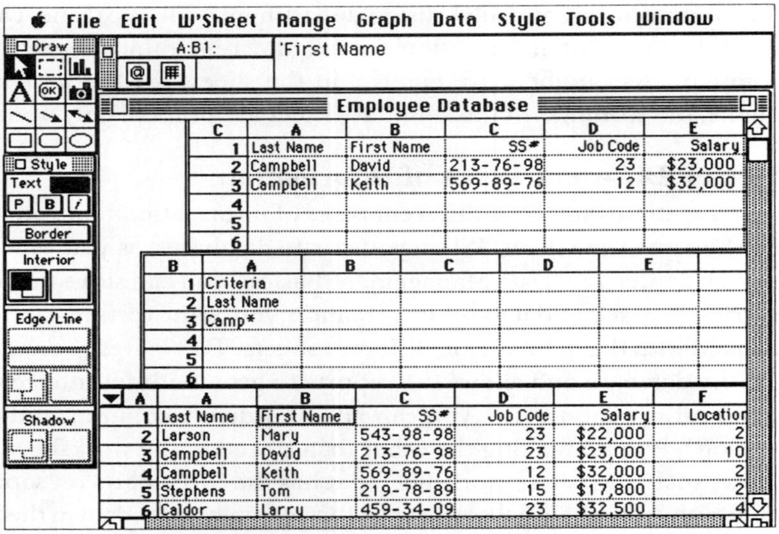

Review

Documents are the basic units for storing your information. You learned some of the commands you will use to work with the documents you create. The 1-2-3 features you have learned for working with documents include the following:

- Documents provide permanent storage for your worksheets. You can save and open worksheets to and from a floppy or hard disk.
- You can select where 1-2-3 looks for the documents that you work with by using the User Setup command in the Tools menu and choosing Preferences. When you use this command, you can provide a new default folder with the Default Folder button.
- You can save a worksheet with the Save As command in the File menu. When you save a worksheet for the first time, 1-2-3 displays a suggested name (Untitled followed by the next unused number). The name currently assigned to the document displays in the Save As text box. You can use this document name or type a new one. You can also select a new location for the document to be saved. When you save the document again, you must choose from Yes, No, and Replace, Then Backup.
- You can save a worksheet using the same document name and location with the Save command from the File menu.
- You can open a worksheet with the Open command from the File menu. When you execute this command, select a document from the list box, using the folder pop-up menu to change the location of the listed documents.
- A worksheet can contain up to 256 sheets. The total number of sheets may be limited by the other open worksheets and your computer's memory. Sheets are added with the Insert command in the Worksheet menu and removed with the Delete command in the Worksheet menu.
- You can open multiple worksheets at once. You can switch between these worksheets. 1-2-3 limits the sheets in memory to 256, regardless of how many worksheets make up the 256 sheets. The actual

limit may be less, depending upon the worksheets' contents and the computer's memory.

- You can use the Split command in the Worksheet menu to divide your worksheet window into panes to look at two or more sheets in a worksheet window at once. You can move in each pane to look at different sections of the same sheet.
- 1-2-3 lets you select ranges that span sheets in the same document to use in commands and formulas.

Keys and Commands

You learned about the commands that let you work with multiple sheets and worksheets at once. You also learned about commands that save and open your data. You were introduced to the keys you can use to switch between windows and worksheets. These keys and commands are

Entry	**Action**
F6 (Window) or ⌘-option-X	Moves to the next pane
option-F6 (Zoom) or ⌘-option-Z	Expands the active pane to fill the entire window
control-end end	Moves to the last worksheet
control-end home	Moves to the first worksheet
control-end control-page down	Moves to the previous worksheet
control-end control-page up	Moves to the next worksheet
control-home	Moves to A:A1 of the active worksheet
control-page down or ⌘-option-3	Moves to the previous sheet
control-page up or ⌘-option-9	Moves to the next sheet
File New (⌘-N)	Opens a new worksheet in a window
File Open (⌘-O)	Opens a file from disk and places it in a worksheet window
File Save (⌘-S)	Saves the active worksheet using the previously defined settings

File Save As	Saves the document with the name and location you select
Tools User Setup Preferences	Sets many 1-2-3 defaults including the default folder after you select the Default Folder button
Window *worksheet name*	Activates the window chosen by *worksheet name*
Window Arrange	Sizes each open window either so each window is the same size or so you can see only the title bar of each one except the active one at the top
Window Split	Splits the worksheet window into two or more panes
Worksheet Delete (⌘-K)	After you select Sheet, removes sheets from a worksheet
Worksheet Insert (⌘-I)	After you select Sheet, adds sheets to a worksheet

9

Making 1-2-3 Do Your Work

Until now, you entered every worksheet entry that you needed for your worksheets by yourself. While that is similar to using a columnar pad for your entries, it does not take advantage of the features offered by a package like 1-2-3. This chapter introduces you to some of these features. After making only a few entries, you often can complete your worksheet by putting 1-2-3 to work.

Copying worksheet entries has more potential to increase your productivity than any other command. In this chapter, you learn the ins and outs of copying both text and formula data. You also learn that 1-2-3 has other commands that can move worksheet data to a new location. This means that if the requirements of your application change, you can easily restructure the worksheet. You can also restructure the data stored in a column to row orientation and vice versa. Again, this is quite an improvement over the "eraser method" that manual spreadsheets require. Many of these commands use the *Clipboard*, a location that all Macintosh applications can use to store data temporarily.

Once you have mastered rearranging your worksheet entries, you will want to learn about some of the tools that can help you monitor your expanded worksheet. You can create repeating text and generate a series of numeric entries. 1-2-3 can search your worksheet for an entry rather than your having to search visually for the data you want. Once 1-2-3 locates the data you want, you can have 1-2-3 replace it with another entry. You can control the recalculation of worksheet formulas. You can also freeze some of the information on your worksheet window, which helps you keep track of your location in a large worksheet.

Copying Worksheet Data

Copying entries on a manual worksheet is a laborious task. To make an additional set of entries that duplicate existing ones, you must pick up your pencil and physically copy each entry that you wish to make. Naturally, duplicate entries take just as long to make as the original entries.

When you make duplicates with 1-2-3, this is not the case. For any entry that you wish to duplicate, 1-2-3 completes 95 percent of the work for you. Tell 1-2-3 the entries you want to copy and where you want them, and 1-2-3 does all the remaining work. 1-2-3 can take a column of text entries and copy it to ten new columns. It can even take a row of formulas that calculate all your sales projections for the month of January and copy it down the page to the next eleven rows, thus giving you all the calculations for February through December. 1-2-3 even adjusts the formulas as it copies them.

This chapter uses a building-block approach to cover all of the features of copying and moving worksheet data. First, you learn to duplicate a text entry. Then you look a little more closely at copying and moving entries as you examine 1-2-3's ability to adjust formulas.

Applications: *You can create a 12-month budget projection where 1-2-3 does over 90% of the work. Enter the basic numbers for month 1, a formula that projects the budget for month 2, and then copy the formula to the other 10 months.*

Copying Text

There are many situations in which copying text can save you time. Perhaps you want to create a worksheet that uses account titles or months of the year in two different locations. Rather than typing the text again, you can copy it. Not only does this save you time, it also guarantees that both sets of entries are identical. Copying text is also useful when you have a number of similar entries to make; you can often copy your original entries and make minor editing changes in less time than it would take to type each of the entries.

Telling 1-2-3 Which Data to Copy

The copy operation is split into two commands. The first step selects the entries to copy and puts them on the Clipboard with the Copy command in the Edit menu. The second step copies the entries from the Clipboard to the worksheet location with the Paste command in the Edit menu. For both of these commands, you must select the range to copy to the Clipboard and where you want to copy the entries *before* you select the command.

An example will help clarify how easy it is to copy text. Follow these steps:

1. Move to A1 in a new worksheet and type **Sales - Product A**. Then click the confirm button or press enter.
2. Choose Copy in the Edit menu, or its keyboard shortcut, ⌘-C.

Notice that nothing appears to have happened at this point. This is because you do not see that 1-2-3 has copied this text to the Clipboard.

3. Choose Show Clipboard in the Edit menu to see a Clipboard window with the current contents as shown here:

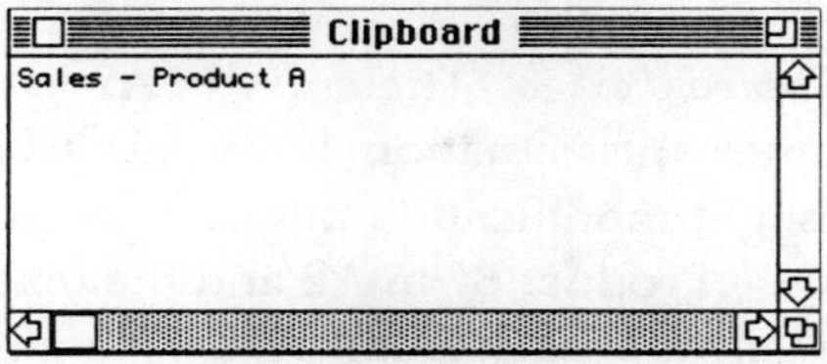

4. Click the Clipboard window's close box or choose Hide Clipboard from the Edit menu to remove the Clipboard window.

5. Move to A2, which is where you want the copy.
6. Choose Paste in the Edit menu, or its keyboard shortcut, (⌘)-(V), to generate these results:

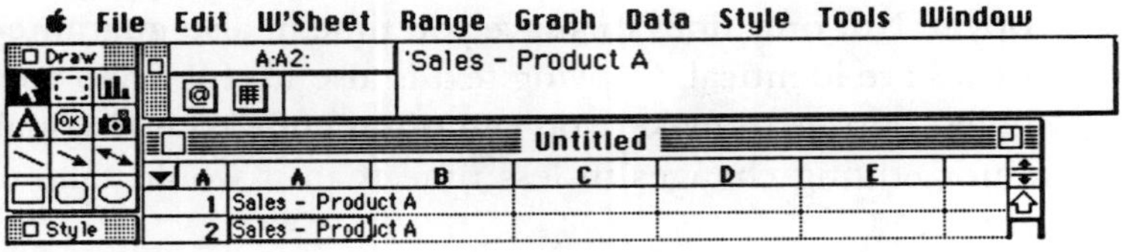

The new text is identical to the original entry, but you used far fewer keystrokes to create it. If A2 had contained an entry before you copied the entry, the previous entry would have been erased.

The advantage of using the Clipboard to copy worksheet entries is that the contents remain on the Clipboard (until they are displaced by a subsequent copy). You can paste another copy of the Clipboard's contents simply by moving to another location and pasting it onto the worksheet.

7. Move to A3, which is where you want the next copy.
8. Choose Paste in the Edit menu to make another copy of the entry.

Later in this chapter, you learn how to extend this productivity even further by copying to many locations at once. You can also press some keystroke combinations that make copying entries easier. When you copy cells, you are not only copying the actual entries, you are also copying the numeric formats and appearance settings that you learned about in Chapter 6, "Changing the Appearance of Worksheet Entries."

Modifying Copied Text The entry in A2 is currently identical to the original. Sometimes this situation is exactly what you need; at other times, however, a slight modification might be required. For example, if you want the text "Sales - Product B" in A2 and the text "Sales - Product C" in A3, the copying the text approach is still best. Changing the text requires these steps:

1. Move to A2 and press (⌘)-(E).
2. Press (delete)/(backspace), type **B**, and click A3 or press (return).

3. Press (⌘)-(E).
4. Press (delete)/(backspace), type **C**, and click the Confirm button or press (enter). Your altered entries look like this:

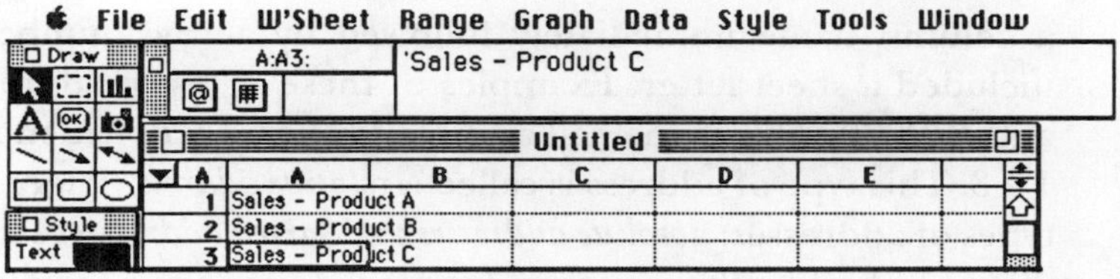

Keep this possibility in mind when you look for opportunities to copy; copying entries followed by a quick edit can still be much quicker than making new entries. Since you can use this feature with numbers as well, one potential application is to generate a list of numbers with only one digit different.

5. Click the close box or press (⌘)-(W) to erase the current worksheet. Select the No button so the current worksheet entries are not saved.
6. Choose New in the File menu or press (⌘)-(N) to open a new worksheet.

Copying Formulas

In one sense, copying formulas is no different from copying text or numbers. It is accomplished with the same commands. With formulas, however, you need to control how 1-2-3 copies the references in formulas. If you have one constant interest rate and want all formulas to refer to it, you must be able to direct 1-2-3 to leave the reference to the interest rate unchanged as it copies the formula. You need a different approach if you enter a formula for January profit that subtracts the cost of goods sold in January from the sales for January, and you want to copy this formula for the other 11 months. You cannot calculate February's profit by subtracting the January cost-of-goods-sold figure from January sales—you need to subtract February's cost of goods sold from February sales. Fortunately, 1-2-3 can handle both situations. You handle these different types of calculations by using *address types* in the original formula; they are not an option during the copying process. Let's examine the different reference types to help clarify this.

Address Types

All the cell addresses you have entered in formulas so far have contained a column name immediately followed by a row number; sometimes you included a sheet letter. Examples of these types of addresses are A1, B:E4, and IV2000. This is the cell address type that you use most frequently with 1-2-3. This type of address is called a *relative address.* There are two additional types of addresses: *absolute addresses* and *mixed addresses*. These three types are distinguished by the way they are recorded in your formulas and the way in which 1-2-3 performs a copy operation for each of them. It is important to master the differences between these address types as you learn how to copy formulas; the address type you use is critical in determining how 1-2-3 copies your formulas to new worksheet locations.

Relative Addresses Relative addresses are the only type of cell address you have used prior to this chapter. You can enter them easily in formulas by using the typing or pointing method of formula creation. When 1-2-3 records your entry, it appears to store the formula exactly as you entered it. If you move to any cell that holds one of the formulas you have entered, you will see the exact formula you entered in the console.

However, 1-2-3 remembers your instructions in a slightly different way from what it displays. If you store the formula +A1+A2 in cell A3, 1-2-3 interprets your instructions in this way: "Take the value that is located two cells above this cell and add the value that is located one cell above this cell." When your formula contains relative references, 1-2-3 remembers everything in terms of relative direction and distance from the cell that will contain the result.

When you copy this type of formula to another location, 1-2-3 adjusts the formula in the new location to reflect the same relative distance and direction. This means that 1-2-3 remembers the formula, using the same relative terms the original version of the formula uses. For example, if you copy the formula stored in A3 to B3, the formula you would see in the console for B3 is +B1+B2. The cell addresses are different from the original, but the formula still records the same relative directions: "Take the value that is located two cells above this cell and add the value that is located one cell above this cell." 1-2-3 automatically makes this adjustment as it copies formulas containing relative addresses.

Let's build a worksheet that allows you to practice copying a formula that uses relative references. This worksheet records profits for the current year and projects them for the next five years. The final result of your entries will look like the worksheet in Figure 9-1. Follow these steps to create the worksheet:

1. Move to B1, type **Sales Projections 1992 - 1995,** and then click the confirm button or press (return).
2. Move to A4 and make these entries:

A4:	**Sales**	E3:	**1994**
A5:	**COGS**	F3:	**1995**
A6:	**Profit**	B4:	**100000**
B3:	**1991**	B5:	**45000**
C3:	**1992**	B6:	**55000**
D3:	**1993**		

Figure 9-1. *The completed sales projection worksheet*

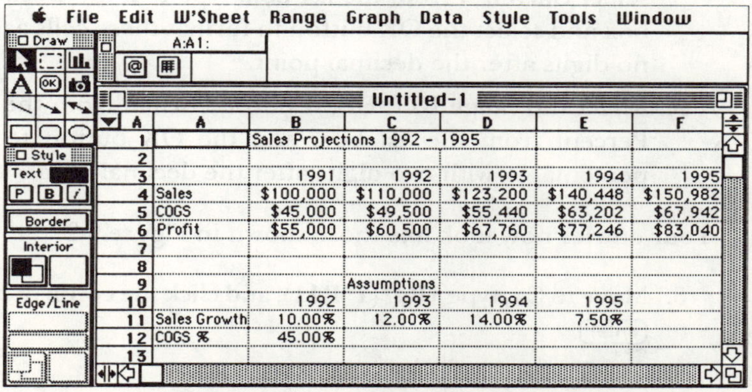

These numbers in B4..B6 are not computed, as they are assumed to be the actual numbers at the end of 1991.

It is time to think about how you want to project sales for the remaining years. You can use a constant growth rate that would apply to all years, or you can assume that sales will grow at varying percentages each year. You must also decide how to compute the cost of the goods sold (COGS) each year. One method is to use a percentage of sales. Even if you select this method without evaluating other options, you must again decide whether to use one percentage rate for all years or vary the percentage by year. The profit calculation does not require you to make a decision, since it is the sales minus cost of goods sold. This example assumes that sales will grow at varying rates but that cost of goods sold will be the same percentage of sales each year. You must enter these assumptions before projections can be made.

3. Complete these entries:

C9:	**Assumptions**	B11:	**.1**
B10:	**1992**	C11:	**.12**
C10:	**1993**	D11:	**.14**
D10:	**1994**	E11:	**.075**
E10:	**1995**	A12:	**COGS %**
A11:	**Sales Growth**	B12:	**.45**

4. Select the range B4..C6. Choose Format from the Range menu, select Currency from the list box, type **0** in the Decimal Places text box and select the OK button to format these cells as currency with no digits after the decimal point.
5. Select the range B11..E12. Choose Format from the Range menu, Percent from the list box, and the OK button to format these percentages with two digits after the decimal point.

Your entries now look like those shown in Figure 9-2.

6. Move to C4, type **+B4*(1+B11)**, and click the confirm button or press (enter).

Figure 9-2. *The worksheet after initial entries*

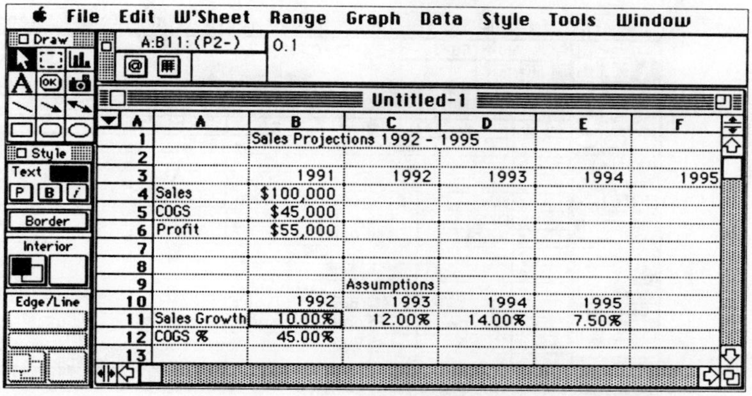

This computes the sales projection for 1992 by multiplying the 1991 sales by the sum of 1 plus the percentage increase in B11. Rather than typing this formula for each year, a better option is to copy it.

7. Choose Copy from the Edit menu, or press F3 (Copy) or ⌘-C.

If your keyboard has function keys, you can use them, as well as the commands or the keyboard shortcuts. F3 (Copy) is the function key for the Copy command in the Edit menu. F4 (Paste) is the function key for the Paste command in the Edit menu. When you copy data to the Clipboard, it replaces the data that was previously on the Clipboard; the Clipboard now contains the formula that is in C4 rather than the text you copied earlier. If you look at the Clipboard's contents at this point, you will see $110,000, the result of the formula, but the Clipboard contains both the formula's result and the formula.

8. Move to D4 and choose Paste from the Edit menu, or press ⌘-V or F4 (Paste).

Now you can see the copied formula, which is shown in Figure 9-3.

Figure 9-3. *The copied formula*

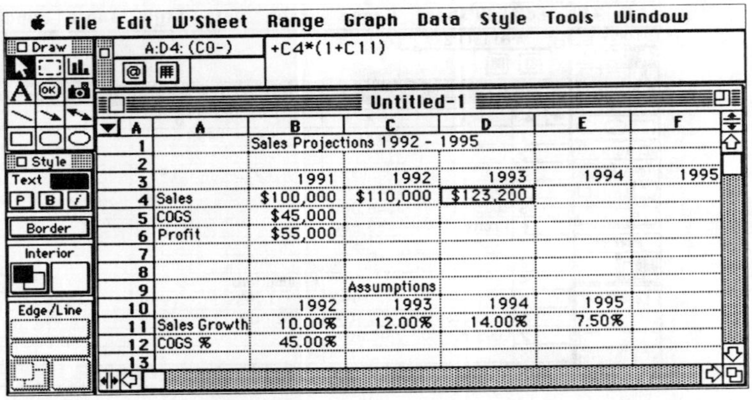

Notice that 1-2-3 adjusted each of the cell references to take the new location of the result into account. Each reference in the formula is the same distance and direction from the result in D4 as the original references were from C4, where the original result was computed. Before completing the copy process for the other years, you will want to look at an absolute reference—a reference that is not updated by a copy operation.

Absolute Addresses *Absolute addresses* are references that remain the same no matter where the formula is pasted. The reference in the formula is effectively frozen in place and is not allowed to change. To create this type of reference, you must place the $ character in front of the row, column, and sheet portions of the address. $A:$A$10 or $A:$D$8 are examples of absolute cell references. You can create an absolute reference in one of two ways: by typing or pointing. Both parallel the creation method for relative references. If you choose to build the formula by typing, you can type the dollar signs. You can also choose Absolute from the @Function pop-up menu or press ⌘-4 in Edit, Value, or Point mode; 1-2-3 then adds the dollar signs in front of the row, column, and sheet portions of the address.

Use this approach to build the cost-of-goods-sold formula. Follow these steps to enhance the sales-projection worksheet you have been working on:

1. Move to C5.
2. Type + and move to C4 to select this cell for the formula.
3. Type * and move to B12.
4. Choose Absolute from the @Function pop-up menu or press (⌘)-(4) to add the $ signs to the cell you are pointing to.

Your formula is now +C4*$A:$B$12, which multiplies the projected 1992 sales in C4 by the cost of goods sold percentage of sales in B12. You can also use Absolute in the @Function pop-up menu or (⌘)-(4) to add the $ signs to the current cell address in the Edit and Value modes. If you make a range address absolute, 1-2-3 changes both corners of the address.

5. Click the confirm button or press (enter) to complete the formula.
6. Choose Copy from the Edit menu to copy this formula to the Clipboard.
7. Move to D5 and choose Paste from the Edit menu to copy the formula from the Clipboard to the worksheet.

You can see that the new formula also references B12 for its cost-of-goods-sold percentage, as shown in Figure 9-4.

Figure 9-4. *The copy operation completed for the COGS formula*

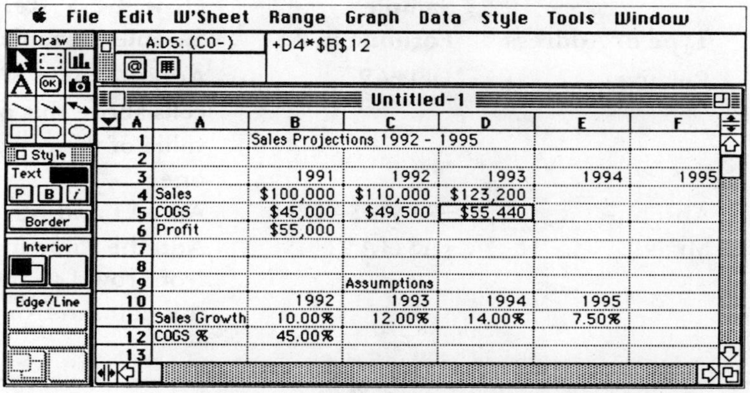

Applications: *If you have one interest rate, commission percentage, shipping charge, tax rate, or discount percentage, you will want to reference this number as an absolute reference in any formulas. If you need to copy the formula at a later time, the correct cell reference will automatically be maintained for you.*

Mixed Addresses *Mixed addresses* borrow something from each of the other two types of addresses. A mixed address is "mixed" in that one part is absolute and the other parts are relative. This means that the row, column, or sheet portion of the address can be fixed, but not all three. When you copy a formula that uses mixed address types, the fixed portion behaves like an absolute address, and the other portion functions like a relative address and is adjusted based on the location it is copied to.

Examples of mixed addresses are A$5, $D7 and $B:A20. In A$5, the column portion of the address is adjusted as the formula is copied to different columns, but the row portion always remains fixed. In $D7, the exact opposite takes place: the column portion of the address remains fixed, regardless of where the formula containing it is copied, and the row portion is updated when the formula is copied to a different row. In $B:A20, the address always refers to sheet B, regardless of the sheet the formula containing this cell reference is copied to.

Table 9-1. *Address Reference Types*

Type of Address	Sample Formula in A3	How 1-2-3 Remembers the Sample Formula
Relative	+A1+A2	Add the value of the cell two cells above this one to the value of the cell above this one
Absolute	+$A$1+$A$2	Add A1 and A2
Mixed	+A$1+A$2	Add the value in this column from row 1 to the value in this column from row 2

Mixed addresses are used only if you are building complex worksheets. Still, it is important to know that they work in case you ever see a mixed address in a formula. You will want to focus your time on the relative and absolute address types as you copy formulas. Table 9-1 shows an illustration of the three types of addresses in formulas.

The Scope of Copying Entries

You have learned how to copy an entry to a new location on the worksheet by completing the preceding steps. This is just one of the ways you can copy entries. Other options are copying the contents of one cell to many additional locations and copying many entries to many additional locations.

Copying One Entry to One New Location You have already copied the sales and cost-of-goods-sold projections for 1992 to create the same projections for 1993. Now you will copy a formula that calculates the profit for 1992 and 1993. Follow these steps to add a formula for profit and then to copy the formula to one additional location:

1. Move to C6, type **+C4–C5** and click the confirm button or press (enter).

Since you wish both cell addresses in this formula to be updated for the appropriate year when the formula is copied, both references are relative.

2. Choose Copy from the Edit menu or press (⌘)-(C) or (F3) to copy this formula to the Clipboard.
3. Move to D6 and choose Paste from the Edit menu, press (⌘)-(V) or (F4) to copy this formula to the Clipboard.

You have been making slow but steady progress in completing the worksheet. Now it is time to step up the pace and copy to more than one location at a time.

9

Copying One Entry to Many Locations Copying entries is not restricted to the single-copy approach you have been using. By expanding the size of the target range, you can copy the entry in one cell to a range that is as large as a row or column of the worksheet. You can put this expanded version of copying entries to use in completing the sales projections for the remaining years of the worksheet:

1. Move to D4 and choose Copy from the Edit menu, press ⌘-C, or F3 to copy this formula to the Clipboard.
2. Select the range E4..F4.
3. Choose Paste from the Edit menu or press ⌘-V or F4 to copy the formula on the Clipboard to each cell in the selected range.

The worksheet now looks like the one in Figure 9-5.

Copying Many Entries to Many New Locations You can step up the pace a little more and copy a column or a row of formulas to many columns or many rows all in one step. To accomplish this, you must select a range of cells to copy and paste. You can use this approach to complete the formulas for your worksheet. You can copy the two formulas in D5 and D6 to columns E and F. Follow these directions to complete the worksheet:

1. Select the range D5..D6 as the entries to copy.

Figure 9-5. *Copying the sales formula to many cells*

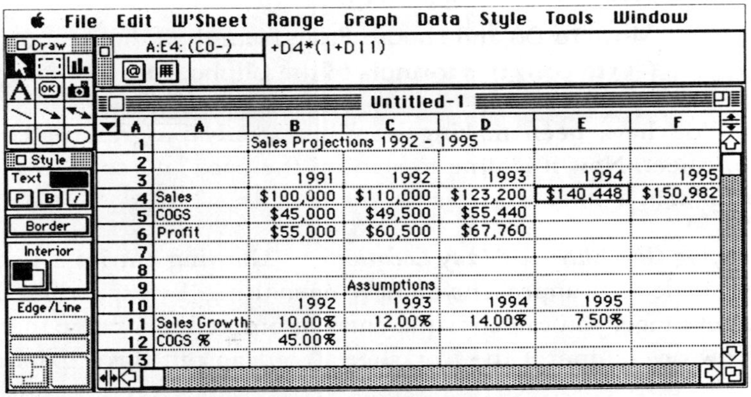

2. Choose Copy from the Edit menu, press (⌘)-(C) or (F3) to copy these formulas to the Clipboard.
3. Select the range E5..F5.

You are probably thinking that E5..F6 would have been the range to select before pasting the formulas. Since 1-2-3 already knows from the entries on the Clipboard that you are copying a column of formulas, 1-2-3 only needs to know the first cell of every copy you want to make.

4. Choose Paste from the Edit menu, press (⌘)-(V), or (F4) to copy the formulas from the Clipboard and to see the results shown in Figure 9-6.

Copying a row of cell entries follows the same basic pattern as this example. First, you must select the row of cells to copy and copy it to the Clipboard. Next, you must select a range to tell 1-2-3 where to copy this row to and how far down the worksheet to copy it. Keep in mind that all these copy methods can be used for values and text just as easily as for formula entries. Also, after you make these multiple copies, the data is still on the Clipboard so you can make another copy by pasting it to a worksheet range.

Figure 9-6. *The result of the copy operation for COGS and Profit*

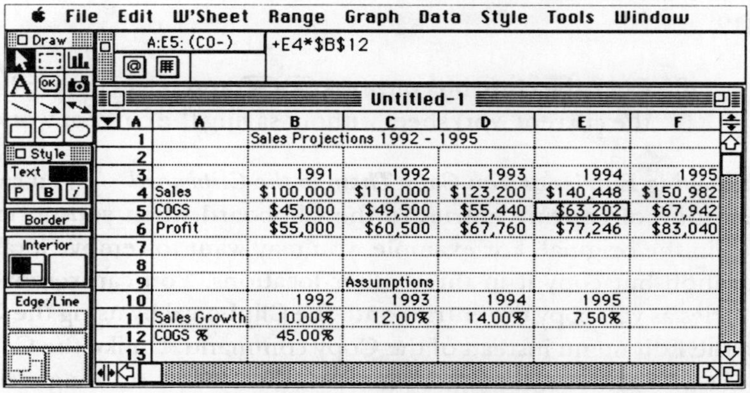

9

Copying to Other Worksheets So far, the examples of copying data have used the same sheet in the same worksheet. You can copy your cell entries to any sheet in any worksheet. You do this by using the Copy command from the Edit menu to copy the data to the Clipboard, switching to the sheet or worksheet where you want the entries copied to, and using the Paste command from the Edit menu. You can try out this operation by following these steps:

1. Select the range A1..F12.
2. Choose Copy from the Edit menu to copy these entries to the Clipboard.

You can use the d key combination, the function keys, or the commands in the Edit menu to transfer data between the worksheet and the Clipboard. The results are the same.

3. Choose New in the File menu to open a new worksheet window.
4. Move to A5, where you want to put the copy.
5. Choose Paste from the Edit menu to copy these entries from the Clipboard to the worksheet.

The new worksheet now looks like the one in Figure 9-7. As this example shows, once you copy data to the Clipboard, you can then transfer it from the Clipboard to any open worksheet. You will also notice that the numbers in C9..F9 are 0 because the absolute references in these formulas still refer to B12.

6. Click the close box or press ⌘-W and select the No button to erase the current worksheet without saving the current worksheet entries.

Removing Entries as You Copy Them to the Clipboard You can use another variation of copying entries to the Clipboard when you no longer want to retain the original. For example, you may want to remove a range from one location but copy it in three other locations. You can remove the original entries as you copy the entries onto the Clipboard by using the Cut command in the Edit menu instead of the Copy command. Unlike the Copy command, once you choose the Cut command, the entries no longer appear on the

Figure 9-7. *Copying entries to another worksheet*

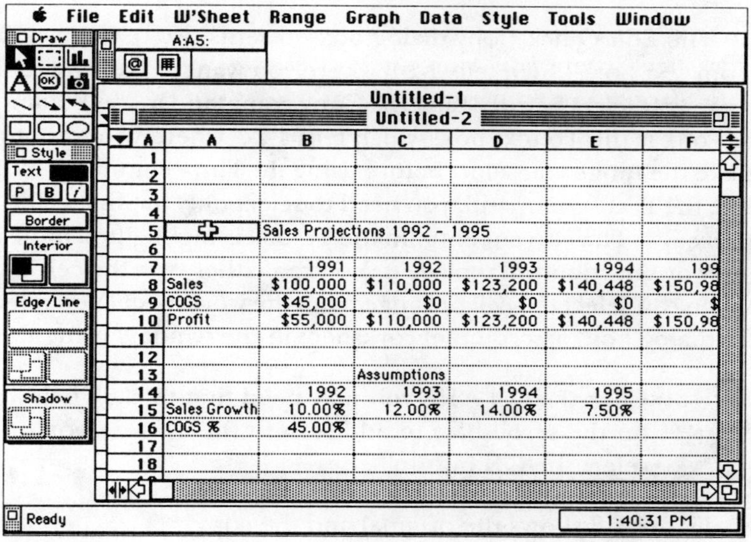

worksheet. After you copy the data to the Clipboard, you can move to the location where you want the entries copied and choose the Paste command in the Edit menu. The Cut command has the keyboard shortcut ⌘-X and is also assigned to the function key F2 (Cut).

Copying Without the Clipboard

So far you have learned how to copy entries by using the Clipboard. You may sometimes want to copy without using the Clipboard. For example, you may want to copy entries without removing the current Clipboard's contents. To copy entries without the Clipboard, choose Quick Copy in the Edit menu. This command has two text boxes to enter ranges, the From text box and the To text box. The range of entries you select to copy is the From range. The range to copy the entries in is the To range. You can try out this command by following these steps:

9

1. Select the range A9..E12.
2. Choose Quick Copy from the Edit menu.

The Edit Quick Copy dialog box presents two text boxes. The first is the From text box, which tells 1-2-3 where you want to copy from. This is like the range you select before using the Copy command in the Edit menu. The other text box is the To text box, which tells 1-2-3 where you want to copy to. This is like the range you select before using the Paste command in the Edit menu. Like the Paste command, you need to select only the first cell where you want each copy. The current entry in the To box is highlighted indicating that your entry or selection will replace it. You can either type the cell or range address or you can select the cell or range from the worksheet (You may need to move the dialog box or scroll the worksheet in the window using the scroll bars).

3. Click the cell A15 (you may need first to click below the scroll box on the scroll bar) to add A15 to the To text box or type **A15** and select the OK button.

Figure 9-8 shows the original and the copy.

4. Select the range A15..E18 and press (delete)/(backspace) to remove these entries.

Copying entries with the Quick Copy command from the Edit menu adjusts formulas in the same way as when you copy with the Clipboard. The disadvantage of the Quick Copy command from the Edit menu is that if you want to make copies in several noncontiguous locations, you must use multiple Quick Copy commands. Also, it is inconvenient to use the Quick Copy command when you want to copy data between worksheets.

Rearranging the Worksheet

Planning is the best assurance that your completed worksheet both looks good and meets your business needs. But even when you plan, there will be occasions when you want to rearrange the data contained in your worksheet.

Figure 9-8. *Formulas copied without the Clipboard*

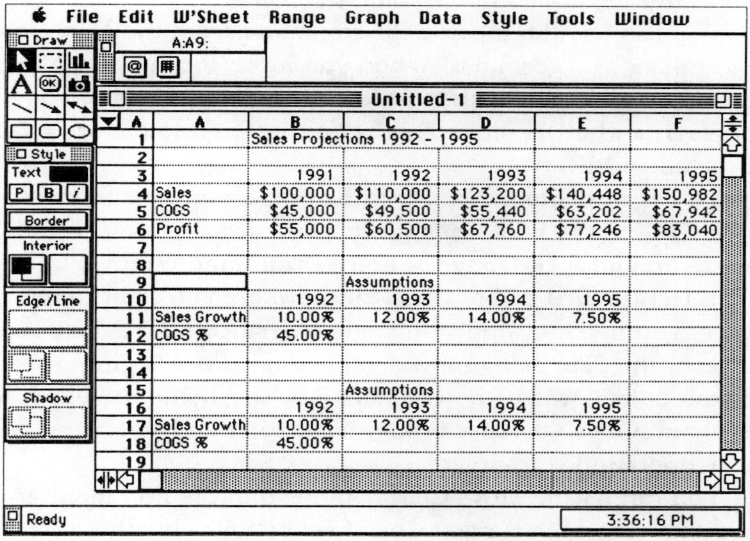

1-2-3 has commands that reorganize the worksheet for you so you do not have to reenter and erase entries the way you would with a manual version of your worksheet. These commands include two that can move any range of data to another range that is the same size and shape. Another command allows you to take a row of data and place it in a column or to take a column of data and place it in a row. You can also use another command to convert formulas to the numbers they represent.

9

Moving Worksheet Data

The Move Cells command in the Edit menu moves data in one range of the worksheet to another range. This range can be a single cell, a row of cells, a column of cells, or a rectangle with multiple rows and columns. The size and shape of the relocated data are determined by the original location of the data. This means that a row of data can be moved only to another row and cannot be placed into a column of cells.

You can use the Move Cells command from the Edit menu to relocate text, values, and formulas. When you move formulas, 1-2-3 adjusts the cell references in the formulas to reflect the cell's new location on the worksheet. This is true whether the cell addresses in the formulas are relative, absolute, or mixed address types.

To use this command, select the range you want to move. Next, choose Move Cells in the Edit menu, or its keyboard shortcut, ⌘-M. 1-2-3 uses the selected range as the range of entries you want to move. In the To text box, you select the first cell of the location where you want to move the selected range. You need to supply only one cell; since 1-2-3 determines the size and shape of the data being moved, all you need is a beginning location for the relocated data, which you can define by specifying the upper-left cell of the new area. Once you specify the destination and select the OK button, the move operation is complete.

You can try the Move Cells command in the Edit menu to relocate your assumptions on the current worksheet by following these steps:

1. Select the range A9..E12
2. Choose Move Cells in the Edit menu or press ⌘-M.
3. Click the cell B22 (you may need to first click below the scroll box on the horizontal scroll bar) or type **B22** to add B22 to the To text box and select the OK button.
4. Move to F25 to see where the range was moved.

The entire range of cells containing assumption data is relocated to B22..F25, as shown in Figure 9-9.

5. Choose Save in the File menu, type Sales Projections in the Save As text box, and select the Save button to save this worksheet.
6. Click the close box or press ⌘-W to close the current worksheet.
7. Choose New in the File menu to start a new worksheet.

Figure 9-9. *Moved data*

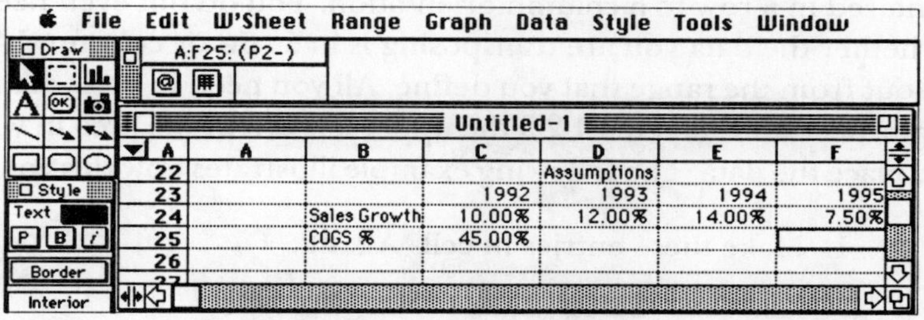

Applications: *A new look can often make an old report more useful. After getting feedback from users, try using Move and Transpose operations to create the new report from the old. Perhaps they will want to see summary information first rather than last.*

Transposing Data

1-2-3's Transpose feature offers another way to rearrange your worksheet data. Not only does the Transpose command in the Range menu copy data, it also alters its orientation. This command places data arranged in a row into a column. Likewise, it places data with a column orientation into a row. This command also has two options for transposing data between sheets. The power of this command will become apparent the first time you need to do major restructuring of a worksheet. In this section, you have an opportunity to try the first two types of transposition. Transposing between sheets is a more advanced topic than you will want to learn right now.

Transposition can be done with text, numbers, and formulas. When you transpose rows or columns containing formulas, 1-2-3 copies the results of the formulas to the new locations. The resulting copy contains numbers but not formulas. This allows you to transpose formulas without concern for whether or not the new orientation will damage the resulting entries. When you transpose worksheet data, the original entries remain intact.

9

Transposing Rows to Columns

The Range Transpose command makes it easy to change data that was entered in a row to a column orientation. You do not even need to tell 1-2-3 whether the data you are transposing is in a row or column; 1-2-3 can figure it out from the range that you define. All you need to do is define the data to transpose and then tell 1-2-3 the upper-left cell of the area in which you wish to place the data. The following example illustrates how this command works.

1. Make these entries in cells A2..E2:

A2:	**Sales - Balls**
B2:	**Sales - Kites**
C2:	**Sales - Rafts**
D2:	**Sales - Jacks**
E2:	**Sales - Blocks**

The entries appear as follows:

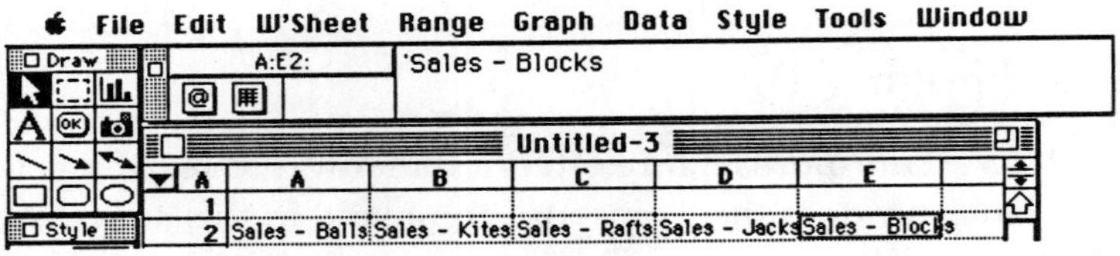

You can now try a different orientation by using the Transpose command in the Range menu.

2. Select the range A2..E2.
3. Choose Transpose in the Range menu.

1-2-3 has already put A2..E2 in the From text box. All you need to do is tell 1-2-3 where to start transposing the data. Since the entry in the To text box is highlighted, your selection will replace this entry.

4. Click the cell A3 or type **A3** to add A3 to the To text box and select the OK button.

This places the entries in column A, but the original entries are still in row 2. Your worksheet should match the display shown in Figure 9-10.

5. Click the close box or press ⌘-W and select the No button to erase the current worksheet without saving it.
6. Choose New in the File menu to start a new worksheet.

Transposing Columns to Rows

Transposing column data to a row is just as easy as the other way around. Try this example with the months of the year:

1. Using Figure 9-11 as your guide, enter the first six months in A3..A8.
2. Select the range A3..A8.
3. Choose Transpose in the Range menu.
4. Click B2 or type **B2** in the To text box and select the Ok button.

You can see five of the month names in Figure 9-12. The original entries remain unless you remove them.

5. Click the close box or press ⌘-W and select the No button to erase the current worksheet without saving it.
6. Choose New in the File menu to start a new worksheet.

Figure 9-10. *Data in a row transposed to a column*

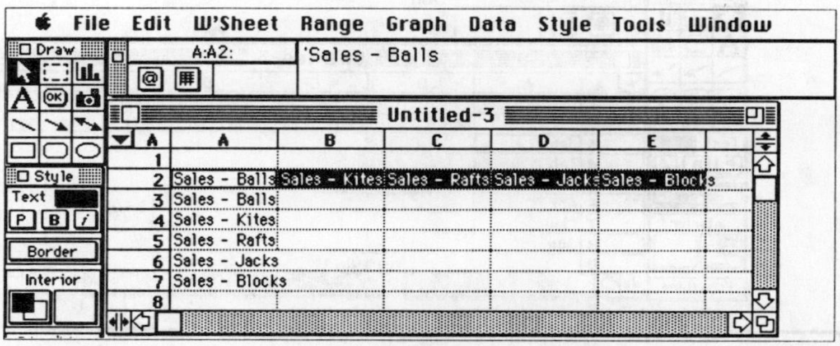

Figure 9-11. *Data entered in a column*

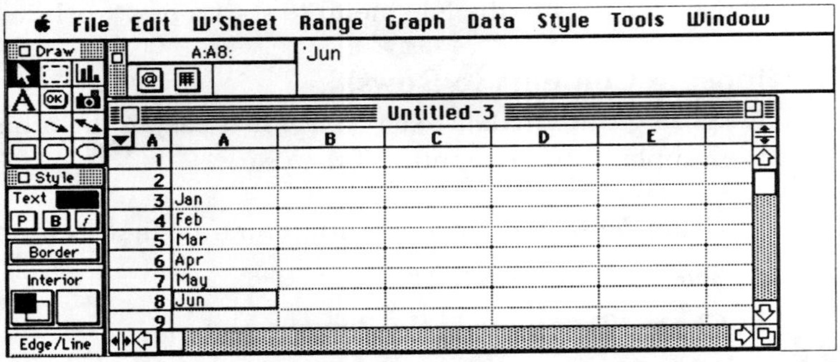

Freezing Formula Values

When you create formulas, you usually want to keep the formulas so they are always updated. However, sometimes, you may want to *freeze* the results of the formulas and replace the cells containing the formulas with their results. For example, if you have used string @functions to correct data entry

Figure 9-12. *Data in a column transposed to a row*

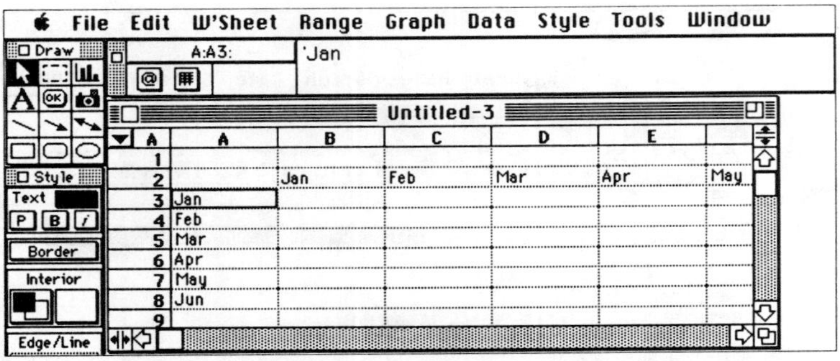

errors, you may want to replace the entries with the corrected versions. You can use the Convert To Values command in the Range menu to put a copy of the formula's results in another location or on top of the original formulas. Follow these steps to see how this command works.

1. Make these entries in cells A1..A5:

A1:	**JANE**
A2:	**Smith**
A3:	**@proper(A1)&" "&A2**
A4:	**1000*5.63**
A5:	**+A4*.075**

2. Select the range A1..A5.
3. Choose Convert To Value in the Range menu.

1-2-3 has already put A1..A5 in the From text box.

4. Click the cell C1 or type **C1** for where you want the copy of the formula's results and select the OK button to produce these results:

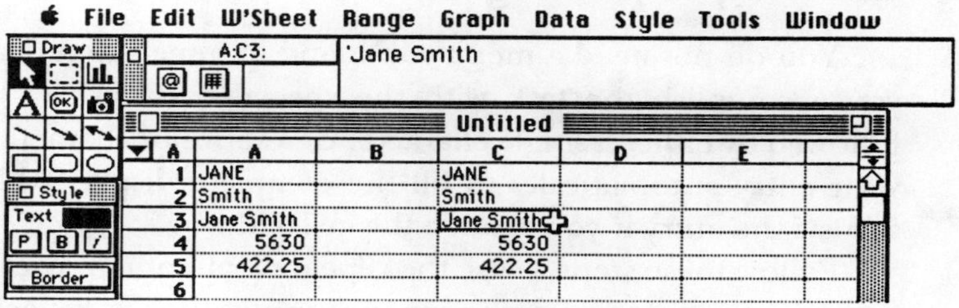

5. Move to C3 to see how this cell contains the text entry "Jane Smith" rather than the formula.

You can also replace the original formulas with their results.

6. Select the range A1..A5 and then choose Convert To Value in the Range menu and the OK button.

Since A1..A5 is the From range and A:A1 is the To range, the results of the formulas replace the formulas.

7. Click the close box or press ⌘-W and select the No button to erase the current worksheet without saving it.

Applications: *Freezing formulas is sometimes the key to data entry error correction. If you can develop a formula to correct a column or row of data entry errors, you can freeze the cells containing the formulas then move these entries over the original data.*

Generating Cell Entries

1-2-3's entry-generating features are so easy to use that it is like having someone perform data entry for you free of charge. The repeating text feature provided by 1-2-3 can generate dividing lines and other quick entries in worksheet cells. The other feature, a series generator, can generate a series of numbers that have the same increment between all the values in the series—for example, the series 1, 2, 3, 4 or 25, 50, 75, 100.

Creating Repeating Text

You do not need a menu command to generate repeating text. Instead, you accomplish the task with the special backslash (\) alignment prefix followed by either a single character or a series of characters. 1-2-3 duplicates your entry automatically to fill the complete display width of the cell and adjusts the entry if you change the cell width.

Follow these steps to use the repeating alignment prefix to draw a box of asterisks around the assumptions section of the worksheet:

1. Choose Open from the File menu, select Sales Projections in the list box and select the Open button, or double-click Sales Projections in the list box.
2. Move to A21, type *, and click the confirm button or press Enter.

Notice that the asterisks completely fill A21.

3. Choose Copy from the Edit menu to copy this entry to the Clipboard.
4. Select the range B21..G21, and then choose Paste from the Edit menu to copy the entry from the Clipboard to each of these cells.
5. Select the range A27..G27, and then choose Paste from the Edit menu to copy the asterisks to form the bottom of the box.
6. Move to A22, type *, and click the confirm button or press (enter).
7. Choose Copy from the Edit menu to copy this entry to the Clipboard.
8. Select the range A23..A26, and then choose Paste from the Edit menu to copy the entry from A22 to these cells.
9. Select the range H21..H27, and then choose Paste from the Edit menu to copy the entry from A22 to H21..H27.

The final result of your entries is a line of asterisks on all four sides of the assumptions, as shown in Figure 9-13 (the Draw and Style palette have been hidden).

Figure 9-13. *A box generated with the repeating alignment prefix*

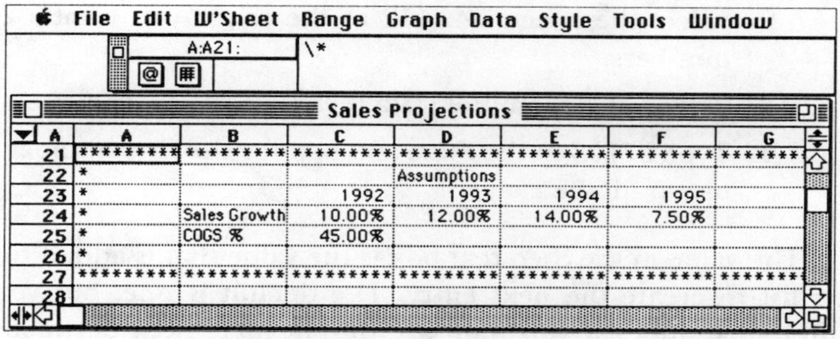

10. Choose the Save command in the File menu.
11. Click the close box or press ⌘-W to close the current worksheet.
12. Choose New from the File menu to open a new worksheet.

***Applications:** You can create a border around worksheet information with a few entries and four copy and paste operations. First enter a label such as \-, copy this entry then paste across the top row, copy the top row to the bottom row. Create an entry for the sides as '-. Copy these two entries then paste them to form the sides of the border you are placing around information.*

Generating a Series of Numbers

It can be tedious to enter a long list of numbers. In one special situation, you can assign this task to 1-2-3—when the list of numbers is a series with equal intervals. The interval can be either positive or negative, but it must be the same between all numbers in the series. This means that lists such as 10, 20, 30, 40; 7, 9, 11, 13, 15; 52609, 52610, 52611; and 30, 29, 28, 27 can be generated by 1-2-3. A list such as 1, 3, 7, 15 could not be generated because the intervals between the numbers in the list are not the same.

Follow these instructions to try this feature by generating a list of invoice numbers:

1. Type **"Inv. No.** in A3.
2. Select the range A4..A12 as the range you want 1-2-3 to fill with numbers.
3. Choose Fill from the Data menu.
4. Type **57103** in the Start text box for the first number that 1-2-3 will use to fill the range.

The value in the Step text box is the value that is added to each value in the list to create the next entry. The default is one, but you can enter a different number if you want a different increment between the numbers 1-2-3 generates.

5. Type **59000** in the Stop text box so the dialog box looks like this:

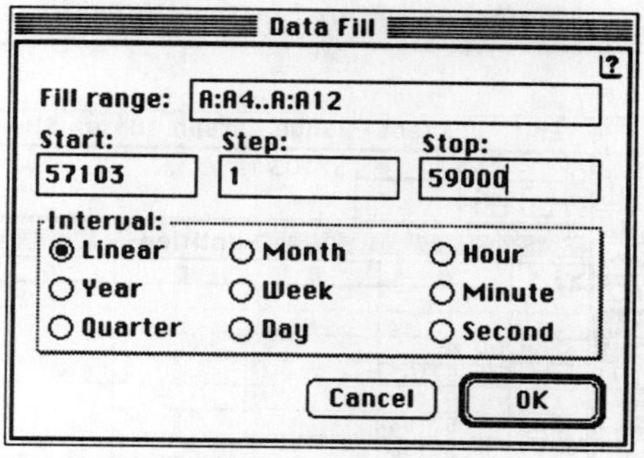

The stop value must always be as large as the last value in the list. This means that there are two factors that can end a list. 1-2-3 stops generating the fill numbers when it fills the range. The numbers can also stop sooner when the stop value is not large enough to generate numbers for all the boxes in the range.

6. Select the OK button.

The list of numbers generated is shown in Figure 9-14. Naturally, you can make your range larger to generate a larger list of numbers. You can also choose a horizontal range of cells and create an entry for each cell in the row.

7. Click the close box or press ⌘-W and select the No button to erase the current worksheet without saving it.

Applications: *Vendor ID numbers, purchase order numbers, invoice numbers, purchase orders, and weekly dates are all candidates for number generation.*

Searching for and Replacing Worksheet Data

As you create large worksheets that represent your business operations, it is more difficult to find a particular entry; it is no longer practical to scan the worksheet for a particular entry. You can have 1-2-3 scrutinize entries for you. 1-2-3 can find a string of characters in either text or formulas. Instead of just locating the matching characters, you can also have 1-2-3 change the

Figure 9-14. *Numbers generated by the Data Fill command*

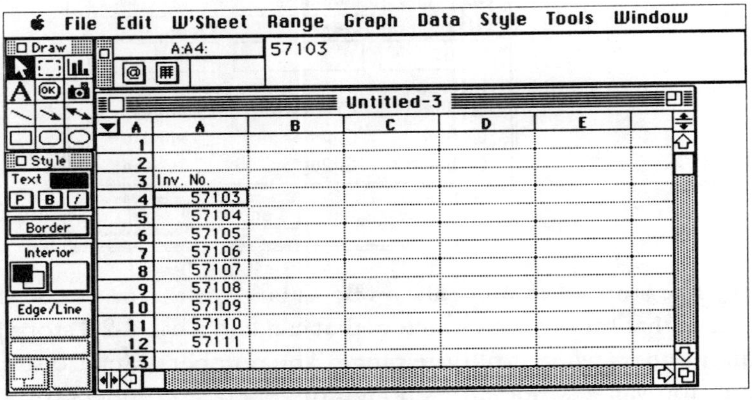

matching characters to another set of characters. These search and replace features can save you time in reviewing entries, as well as the editing time required for those you want to change.

The Find command in the Edit menu finds and replaces worksheet data. You can find text in cell formulas and text. Since 1-2-3 can replace text as well as find it, you can use this command to correct a misspelling and change a cell address that formulas use, as well as find a name in a worksheet. The options for replacing text or cell addresses allow you to make changes to all the affected cells at once. If you would prefer to move a little more slowly, you can select whether or not to make the replacement for each match 1-2-3 finds.

Searching for Worksheet Data

1-2-3 can find characters stored in formulas and text. 1-2-3 does not search cells that contain only numbers. Using the Search feature with the sales projection worksheet will show you how it works. Use these steps to find the text "Sales" in the Sales Projections worksheet:

1. Choose Open from the File menu, select Sales Projections in the list box and select the Open button, or double-click Sales Projections in the list box.
2. Select the range A1..F6 as the range that you will search.
3. Choose Find in the Edit menu or press its keyboard shortcut, ⌘-F, and type **Sales** in the Search For text box.

This step enters the characters you want to find. You can type **sales** or **SALES** with the same results.

4. Select the Text radio button and the Find button.

1-2-3 searches for the selected string of characters. 1-2-3 finds the word "Sales" in A4 (searching a column at a time) and displays the address and entry in the console.

5. Select the Next button.

1-2-3 continues the search, column by column, finds "Sales" in B1, and shows the address and entry in the console.

6. Select the Next button.

1-2-3 does not find another Sales entry in the range so 1-2-3 displays this alert:

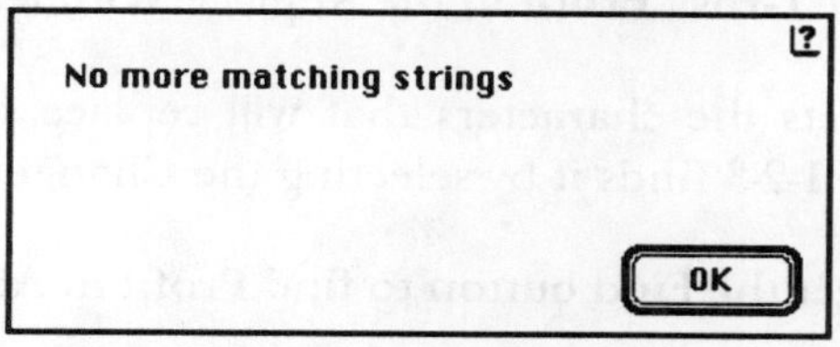

7. Select the OK button to return to Ready mode.

You can also use the Find command in the Edit menu to find text in formulas. To find which is the first cell that uses the 1994 sales growth figure stored in E24, you can search for a cell reference to E24 in formulas within the worksheet by using these steps:

1. Select the range A1..F6, choose Find in the Edit menu, and type **E24** in the Search For text box.

Typing **E24** replaces the word "Sales" from the previous search operation.

2. Select the Formulas radio button and the Find button.

Now 1-2-3 searches only formulas in the selected range for the cell reference E24. It finds E24 in E4 and displays the cell address and entry in the console and makes it the active cell.

3. Select the Done button to return to Ready mode.

Replacing Worksheet Data

If you make a few mistakes when reentering text and formulas, the Find command in the Edit menu can handle the corrections for you by replacing the characters it finds with another ones. You can use the Sales Projections worksheet and follow these steps to replace "Profit" with "Gross Profit":

1. Select A1..F6, choose Find in the Edit menu, type **Profit** in the Search For text box, and select the Text radio button.
2. Type **Gross Profit** in the Replace With text box.

This selects the characters that will replace occurrences of the string "Profit" after 1-2-3 finds it by selecting the Change or Change All button.

3. Select the Find button to find Profit in A6.
4. Select the Change button.

1-2-3 replaces "Profit" in A6 with "Gross Profit" and searches for the next occurrence of "Profit". Since 1-2-3 cannot find another occurrence of

"Profit", it displays an alert dialog box indicating that it cannot find the search string.

5. Select the OK button to return to Ready mode.

When you use the Find command in the Edit menu to replace characters in formulas or text, you must be careful about what you supply in the Search For text box. If the text that you search for is not clearly defined, you may wind up replacing text that you did not want to replace. As an example of an unintentional replacement, suppose you want to use the sales-growth rate for 1994 in 1995. One method of doing this is to replace the F24 cell reference with E24. If you use a search string of "F" and a replacement string of "E", 1-2-3 returns unexpected results since it finds many unexpected matches. To show how this happens, follow these steps:

1. Select A1..F6, choose Find in the Edit menu and type **F** in the Search For text box, and select the Both radio button.
2. Type **E** in the Replace With text box, and select the Find button.

1-2-3 finds F in Profit in A6.

3. Select the Change All button.

1-2-3 finds all occurrences of the letter "F" in A1..G6 and replaces them with the letter "E". When 1-2-3 cannot find another "F", it returns to Ready mode. The worksheet looks like the one in Figure 9-15. You can see how results have changed.

4. Move to F6.

Since the search string is not specific enough, every F changed to an E, including the formula in F6 that should subtract F5 from F4. The entry in F6 highlights the error. The solution is to type **F24** in the Search For text box and **E24** in the Replace With text box. Although you must type more characters, you exclude cells that you do not want to alter.

Figure 9-15. *The worksheet after supplying an inadequate search string*

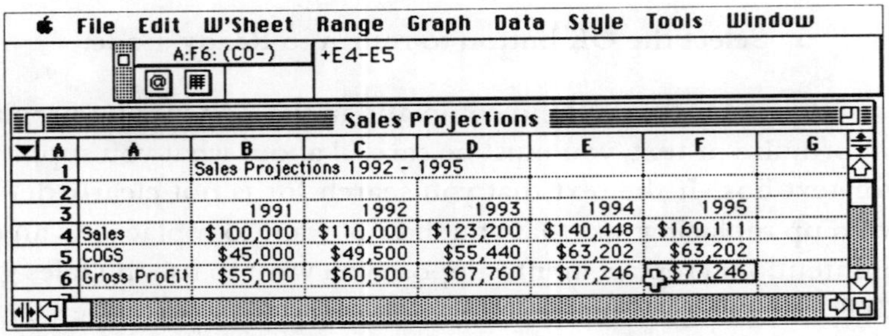

5. Choose Undo from the Edit menu to return to formulas to their original state.

Other Worksheet Commands for Expanded Data

Now you have learned how to create worksheets quickly. You will also want to learn some of the tricks that make working with these worksheets easier, such as controlling recalculation. This is a helpful trick because, as your worksheets grow larger, 1-2-3 takes longer to recalculate after each of your entries. 1-2-3's speed seems quite good, compared to manual alternatives, when you do what-if analyses; but if you are entering a long list of account names or invoice numbers, the constant recalculation can lower 1-2-3's performance. You also need to use additional tools for large worksheets since the entire worksheet cannot be shown in the worksheet window. You need to learn how you can freeze certain information on the worksheet and how you can have 1-2-3 find entries on the worksheet for you.

Recalculation

You access 1-2-3's recalculation options with the Tools User Setup Recalculation dialog box. This dialog box has three parts. You can select when the worksheet is recalculated, the order in which 1-2-3 recalculates formulas, and how many times 1-2-3 recalculates the worksheet. The latter two options are seldom altered. If you are curious about these, check your 1-2-3 manual. The first option can be a real time-saver with any large worksheet. 1-2-3 uses *minimal recalculation,* allowing 1-2-3 to recalculate only those formulas affected by worksheet changes. 1-2-3 also uses *background recalculation,* which means that 1-2-3 performs the recalculation in between the times you are entering and editing data. Minimal and background recalculation enable you to update your worksheet formulas as quickly as possible.

You can alter the timing of recalculation for the sales projection worksheet by following these steps:

1. Choose User Setup from the Tools menu and Recalculation to display the User Setup Recalculation dialog box.

The Automatically and Manually radio buttons let you choose whether 1-2-3 automatically updates the worksheet after a change or whether you control recalculation.

2. Select the Manually radio button once and the OK button.

This selection means that 1-2-3 does not recalculate formulas after a worksheet change.

3. Move to C4, type **120000**, and click the confirm button or press (enter).

Notice that this change does not affect the formulas, although Calc does appear in the status window. The Calc status indicator is a warning that the worksheet has not been recalculated since changes have been made.

4. Choose Calculate from the @Function pop-up menu or press (⌘)-(=).

Choosing Calculate from the @Function pop-up menu or pressing (⌘)-(=) updates the formulas in the worksheet. Now you will see the results of the change.

5. Change the value in C4 back to 110000 by typing **110000** and pressing (enter) or clicking the confirm button.

9

Again, the results are not affected.

6. Choose Calculate from the @Function pop-up menu or press ⌘-=.

Your display should again show the results you started with.

7. Choose User Setup from the Tools menu, Recalculation, the Automatically radio button, and the OK button.

From this point on, every worksheet entry will cause recalculation. Keep this easy-to-make change in mind; it is a great option when you have a significant amount of data to enter.

Using Titles with Large Worksheets

One of the problems with large worksheets is that you cannot see all the data in the worksheet window at one time. This problem is magnified when you move your cell pointer to the right or down and find that the column and row headings at the top and left scroll out of the worksheet window. You can find yourself in a sea of numbers with no visible indication of what each of these numbers represents. The solution in 1-2-3 is to freeze some of the information on the worksheet. Freezing information is another feature, like splitting a window into panes (as you learned in the Chapter 8, "Managing Documents and Sheets"), that you may want to use with larger worksheets.

The Titles command in the Worksheet menu freezes titles on the worksheet. The active cell at the time you invoke this command determines the columns and rows in the title. The command has four options: to fix titles both vertically and horizontally, to fix them vertically, to fix them horizontally, and to clear all fixed titles from the worksheet. This last option does not eliminate the data in titles themselves, but it ensures that neither vertical nor horizontal titles are frozen any longer.

If you freeze vertical titles with either the Vertical or Both radio button of the Titles command in the Worksheet menu, any columns to the left of the active cell become fixed on the worksheet. The situation is similar for horizontal titles, whether you choose Horizontal or Both. All rows above the active cell will remain frozen on the window. When you scroll down the worksheet, the rows that are not frozen disappear from the window, but the rows in the titles do not. When you scroll to the right, any frozen columns remain on the worksheet although the other columns may disappear. If A1 is the active cell, you cannot create either vertical or horizontal titles—there is no information above or to the left of the cell pointer.

Looking at an example of this command with the Sales Projections worksheet will show you how it works. Use these steps for freezing columns A and B and rows 1 and 2:

1. Move to C3.
2. Choose Titles in the Worksheet menu, the Both radio button, and the OK button.
3. Move to H28 to produce the display shown in Figure 9-16.

Notice that columns A and B are frozen in the worksheet window, yet columns C, D, and E have scrolled out of the window. Rows 1 and 2 are still visible although some of the ones below them are not. You cannot move into these columns and rows in the titles. You cannot select a cell into these columns and rows in the titles. The pointer has changed to become a pencil with a line through it when it is in the titles area to indicate that you cannot make any entries here.

4. Choose Titles in the Worksheet menu, the None radio button, and the OK button.

This unfreezes the titles, and frozen columns and rows scroll out of the worksheet window.

5. Click the close box or press ⌘-W and select the No button to close the Sales Projections worksheet without saving it.

Applications: *These title-freezing features are useful when you want to see totals at the bottom of a long column or on the right side of a long row. By freezing titles, you can check the total and still keep the corresponding text in the window for readability.*

Figure 9-16. *Titles displaying columns A and B and rows 1 and 2 frozen*

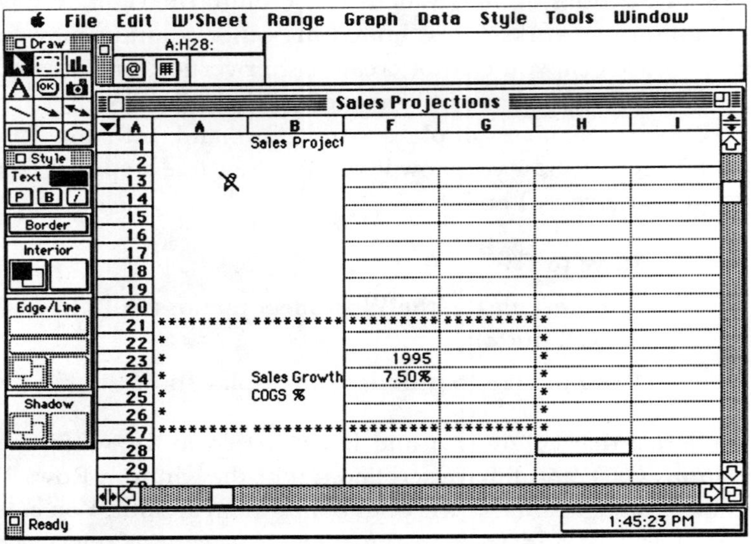

Review

In this chapter you learned the 1-2-3 commands and features that increase your productivity. These 1-2-3 features include the following:

- You can use the Macintosh's Clipboard to copy data. You can use the Clipboard to copy worksheet entries from one location to another. To copy data into the Clipboard, select the range and then choose the Copy command in the Edit menu, press ⌘-C or F3 (Copy). To copy data from the Clipboard, select the cells where you want the Clipboard's contents to start being copied and then choose the Paste command in the Edit menu, press ⌘-V or F4 (Paste). After copying data from the Clipboard, the Clipboard's contents are still intact, so you can make additional copies.

- You can make copies without using the Clipboard by using the Quick Copy command in the Edit menu. For this command, you must enter the range to copy from and the range to copy to in the two text boxes in the dialog box.
- When you copy entries, you can copy one cell to one cell or one cell to many cells. You can also make one copy of an entire range of cells or make many copies of the same range. When you copy cells, 1-2-3 adjusts the formulas in the range according to whether the formulas use absolute, mixed, or relative cell addresses.
- The Move Cells command in the Edit menu moves cells within a worksheet. When you move cells, 1-2-3 adjusts the formulas so that all formula references refer to the same cell contents as they did before cells were moved.
- The Transpose command in the Range menu copies a range of cells and changes the cells' orientation from row to column or column to row. If you transpose formulas, this command copies and transposes the results of the formulas rather than the formulas themselves.
- The Convert To Value command in the Range menu copies the results of formulas to the same or a new location.
- You can create repeating text by using the backslash (\) alignment prefix. The characters that you enter after the backslash are repeated for the width of the cell.
- The Fill command in the Data menu generates a series of numbers that are evenly increased or decreased. To use this command, you must provide the worksheet range that you want to fill with numbers, the number that you want to start the series, the increment between values (positive for ascending and negative for descending), and the last value that may appear in the series.
- The User Setup Recalculation dialog box determines whether 1-2-3 recalculates the worksheet whenever a worksheet entry is made, or when you choose Calculate from the @Function pop-up menu or press ⌘-=. This command is used when you have many values to enter and do not want 1-2-3 to recalculate all the formulas after every entry.

9

- The Titles command in the Worksheet menu freezes rows and columns in the worksheet window so you can always see the column or row titles. You can create horizontal titles (rows that always appear in the window), vertical titles (columns that always appear in the window), or both titles (columns and rows that always appear in the window), and you can clear titles (unfreeze them in the window).
- The Find command in the Edit menu can search for characters in text or formula entries. The Replace option allows you to replace the characters the command finds with different ones.

Keys and Commands

This chapter introduced you to the 1-2-3 commands that duplicate and move entries as well as other commands that make working with large worksheets easier. You learned to use keys that affect text and formulas. These commands and keys are

Entry	Action
\	As an alignment prefix, repeats the string that follows until the column width is filled
⌘-4 or Absolute in @Function pop-up menu	In Edit, Point, or Value mode, converts an address to an absolute, mixed, or relative address
⌘-= or Calculate in @Function pop-up menu	Updates the calculations in the worksheet
Data Fill	Generates a series of numbers a specific interval apart
Edit Copy (⌘-C)	Copies the selected range to the Clipboard
Edit Cut (⌘-X)	Copies the selected range to the Clipboard and removes the original from the worksheet
Edit Find (⌘-F)	Finds, or finds and replaces, characters in formulas and text entries
Edit Move Cells (⌘-M)	Moves a range to another location

Edit Paste (⌘-P)	Copies the Clipboard's contents to the worksheet
Edit Quick Copy	Copies cell entries to another location without the Clipboard
Edit Show Clipboard	Opens a Clipboard window to display the contents of the Clipboard
Range Transpose	Copies one or more cells to a new location and changes the column and row orientation
Range Value	Copies the results of formulas to the same or different location
Tools User Setup Recalculation	Sets when and how 1-2-3 recalculates the worksheet
Worksheet Titles	Sets the rows and columns that are frozen on the worksheet window

10

Printing Your Worksheet

In this chapter you have an opportunity to explore 1-2-3's printing features. You can use them to create a quick copy of your worksheet with only a few instructions. When you are ready for a final copy, you can change the page setup to create a professional-looking report.

You will first learn to use the basic printing features. Then you will learn more complex printing options, each skill building on those before it, until you have a set of printing features that you can use for all of your printing needs. You will learn about previewing your worksheet so you can see how it will appear when you print it. You also have the opportunity to explore options to use worksheet commands to further customize your print output.

Printing Basics

1-2-3's basic printing features are designed to give you quick access to a printed copy. This quick access is made possible by default values that 1-2-3 has set for options such as page size and margins. Later in this chapter, you learn to override these default settings, but for now you might as well appreciate their presence; they make it easy for you to print your worksheets.

When you print, 1-2-3 assumes you want to print to the printer that is currently installed through the Macintosh System. You can change which printer you will use to another one. As long as this printer is turned on and has paper when you tell 1-2-3 to begin printing, your print output is sent to this printer. Normally, the printer has a series of small lights to indicate that the printer is ready to accept data. If the printer is nearby, verify that the printer is turned on and has paper before you start to print. It is also a good idea to understand the defaults that will apply to your output before you learn about the instructions that actually start the printing.

The Print command in the File menu is the command you use to print your data. The Print dialog box this command displays looks something like this:

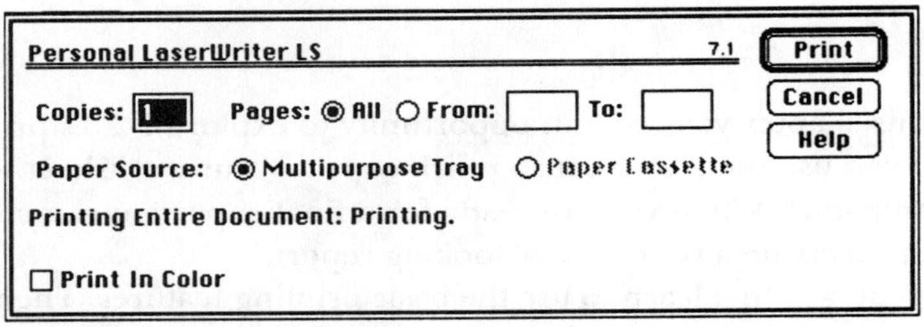

The options you will see depend on the printer you are using. This is the same Print dialog box you will see if you select a worksheet from a disk or folder window and choose Print from the Finder's File menu. 1-2-3 remembers the print settings from the last time you printed the worksheet. To have 1-2-3 remember what you want to print or any changes that you make to the print options, first complete the definition of your print specifications, and then save the worksheet. This saves the print settings with the worksheet for the next time you want to print the data.

The Default Settings

One of the things that simplifies printing a worksheet the first time is the default print settings. These defaults affect how 1-2-3 prints the worksheet and the amount of white space, or the *margin*, on all four sides of a printed page. 1-2-3 fits a number of lines on the page based on the row heights in the worksheet range you select and a number of columns across based on the column widths in the selected range. The Font command in the Style menu you learned about in Chapter 6, "Changing the Appearance of Worksheet Entries," sets the size of the characters used in the worksheet, and the Column Width and Row Height command in the Worksheet menu sets the width of the columns and heights of the rows.

The default print settings defined by 1-2-3 has several areas affecting the amount of data that prints on a page. A sample printed worksheet is shown in Figure 10-1 with several print settings labeled. Not all of the page contains printed data. Some of the area on all four sides is reserved for margins. 1-2-3 initially sets the margins to one-half inch on each side. In addition to the top and bottom margins, 1-2-3 reserves room at the top and bottom for a header and footer if you use them. You can use other print settings, but initially, try the Print operation without modifying any of these defaults.

The Basic Printing Process

The first part of printing is telling 1-2-3 how much of the worksheet you wish to print. You can print all of the worksheet's entries with the Print command in the File menu or you can select a range and use the Print Selection command in the File menu to print a subset of the worksheet's data.

The size of the range affects how 1-2-3 prints your data. If the range contains more data than will fit on one page, 1-2-3 breaks the data into pages. If the width of the range exceeds the number of characters that will print across one page, 1-2-3 prints as many columns across the first page as possible. The remaining columns are printed on subsequent pages. If the number of rows in the range exceeds the number of rows that can print on one page, 1-2-3 generates a page break when the data prints. Once you select a range to print, 1-2-3 displays dashed lines indicating the boundary of each page.

You can try several printing options with the following steps. You will copy entries more than once to build a large worksheet quickly so you can try out the extensive printing features covered in this chapter. Follow these steps to create a worksheet and print it.

Figure 10-1. *The layout of a printed page (default print settings)*

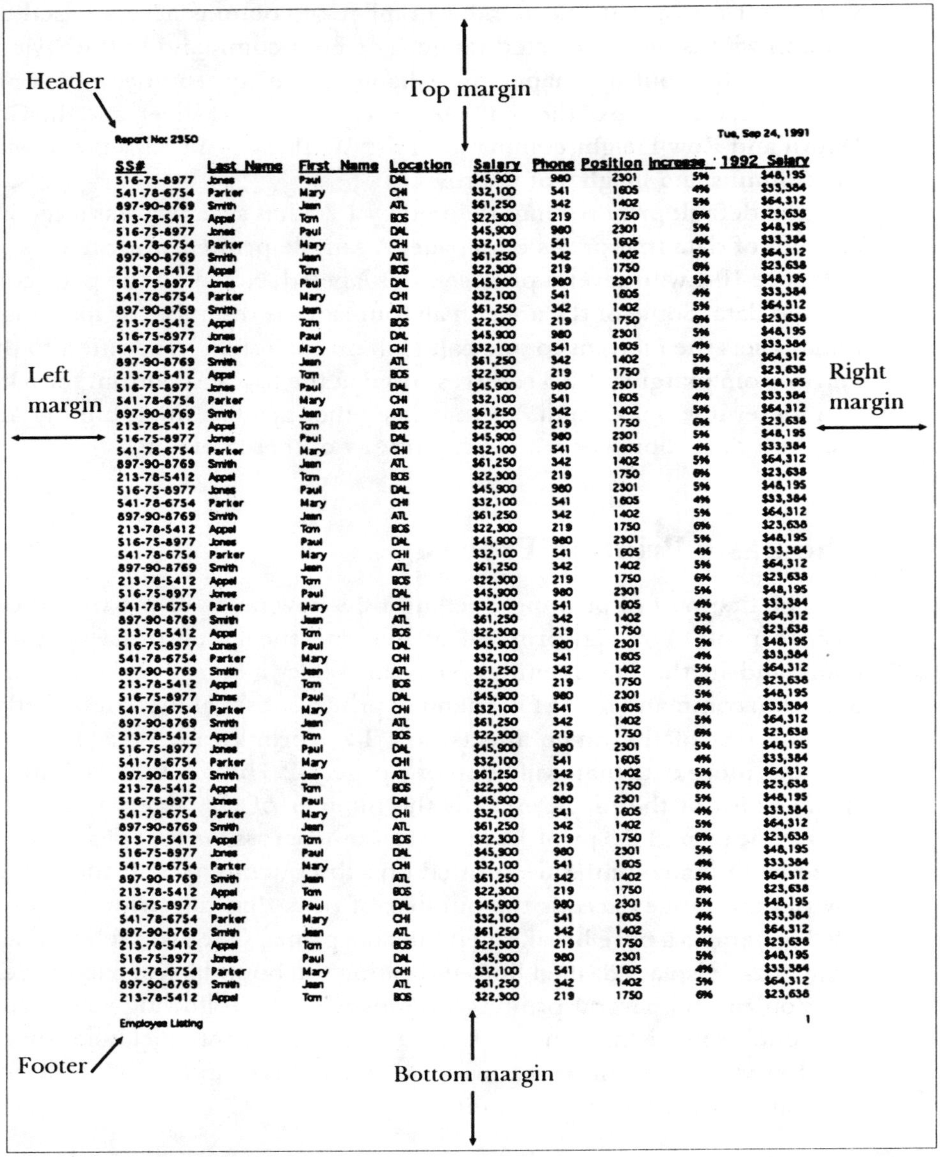

Report No: 2350

Tue, Sep 24, 1991

SS#	Last Name	First Name	Location	Salary	Phone	Position	Increase	1992 Salary
516-75-8977	Jones	Paul	DAL	$45,900	980	2301	5%	$48,195
541-78-6754	Parker	Mary	CHI	$32,100	541	1605	4%	$33,384
897-90-8769	Smith	Jean	ATL	$61,250	342	1402	5%	$64,312
213-78-5412	Appel	Tom	BOS	$22,300	219	1750	6%	$23,638
516-75-8977	Jones	Paul	DAL	$45,900	980	2301	5%	$48,195
541-78-6754	Parker	Mary	CHI	$32,100	541	1605	4%	$33,384
897-90-8769	Smith	Jean	ATL	$61,250	342	1402	5%	$64,312
213-78-5412	Appel	Tom	BOS	$22,300	219	1750	6%	$23,638
516-75-8977	Jones	Paul	DAL	$45,900	980	2301	5%	$48,195
541-78-6754	Parker	Mary	CHI	$32,100	541	1605	4%	$33,384
897-90-8769	Smith	Jean	ATL	$61,250	342	1402	5%	$64,312
213-78-5412	Appel	Tom	BOS	$22,300	219	1750	6%	$23,638
516-75-8977	Jones	Paul	DAL	$45,900	980	2301	5%	$48,195
541-78-6754	Parker	Mary	CHI	$32,100	541	1605	4%	$33,384
897-90-8769	Smith	Jean	ATL	$61,250	342	1402	5%	$64,312
213-78-5412	Appel	Tom	BOS	$22,300	219	1750	6%	$23,638
516-75-8977	Jones	Paul	DAL	$45,900	980	2301	5%	$48,195
541-78-6754	Parker	Mary	CHI	$32,100	541	1605	4%	$33,384
897-90-8769	Smith	Jean	ATL	$61,250	342	1402	5%	$64,312
213-78-5412	Appel	Tom	BOS	$22,300	219	1750	6%	$23,638
516-75-8977	Jones	Paul	DAL	$45,900	980	2301	5%	$48,195
541-78-6754	Parker	Mary	CHI	$32,100	541	1605	4%	$33,384
897-90-8769	Smith	Jean	ATL	$61,250	342	1402	5%	$64,312
213-78-5412	Appel	Tom	BOS	$22,300	219	1750	6%	$23,638
516-75-8977	Jones	Paul	DAL	$45,900	980	2301	5%	$48,195
541-78-6754	Parker	Mary	CHI	$32,100	541	1605	4%	$33,384
897-90-8769	Smith	Jean	ATL	$61,250	342	1402	5%	$64,312
213-78-5412	Appel	Tom	BOS	$22,300	219	1750	6%	$23,638
516-75-8977	Jones	Paul	DAL	$45,900	980	2301	5%	$48,195
541-78-6754	Parker	Mary	CHI	$32,100	541	1605	4%	$33,384
897-90-8769	Smith	Jean	ATL	$61,250	342	1402	5%	$64,312
213-78-5412	Appel	Tom	BOS	$22,300	219	1750	6%	$23,638
516-75-8977	Jones	Paul	DAL	$45,900	980	2301	5%	$48,195
541-78-6754	Parker	Mary	CHI	$32,100	541	1605	4%	$33,384
897-90-8769	Smith	Jean	ATL	$61,250	342	1402	5%	$64,312
213-78-5412	Appel	Tom	BOS	$22,300	219	1750	6%	$23,638
516-75-8977	Jones	Paul	DAL	$45,900	980	2301	5%	$48,195
541-78-6754	Parker	Mary	CHI	$32,100	541	1605	4%	$33,384
897-90-8769	Smith	Jean	ATL	$61,250	342	1402	5%	$64,312
213-78-5412	Appel	Tom	BOS	$22,300	219	1750	6%	$23,638
516-75-8977	Jones	Paul	DAL	$45,900	980	2301	5%	$48,195
541-78-6754	Parker	Mary	CHI	$32,100	541	1605	4%	$33,384
897-90-8769	Smith	Jean	ATL	$61,250	342	1402	5%	$64,312
213-78-5412	Appel	Tom	BOS	$22,300	219	1750	6%	$23,638
516-75-8977	Jones	Paul	DAL	$45,900	980	2301	5%	$48,195
541-78-6754	Parker	Mary	CHI	$32,100	541	1605	4%	$33,384
897-90-8769	Smith	Jean	ATL	$61,250	342	1402	5%	$64,312
213-78-5412	Appel	Tom	BOS	$22,300	219	1750	6%	$23,638
516-75-8977	Jones	Paul	DAL	$45,900	980	2301	5%	$48,195
541-78-6754	Parker	Mary	CHI	$32,100	541	1605	4%	$33,384
897-90-8769	Smith	Jean	ATL	$61,250	342	1402	5%	$64,312
213-78-5412	Appel	Tom	BOS	$22,300	219	1750	6%	$23,638
516-75-8977	Jones	Paul	DAL	$45,900	980	2301	5%	$48,195
541-78-6754	Parker	Mary	CHI	$32,100	541	1605	4%	$33,384
897-90-8769	Smith	Jean	ATL	$61,250	342	1402	5%	$64,312
213-78-5412	Appel	Tom	BOS	$22,300	219	1750	6%	$23,638
516-75-8977	Jones	Paul	DAL	$45,900	980	2301	5%	$48,195
541-78-6754	Parker	Mary	CHI	$32,100	541	1605	4%	$33,384
897-90-8769	Smith	Jean	ATL	$61,250	342	1402	5%	$64,312
213-78-5412	Appel	Tom	BOS	$22,300	219	1750	6%	$23,638
516-75-8977	Jones	Paul	DAL	$45,900	980	2301	5%	$48,195
541-78-6754	Parker	Mary	CHI	$32,100	541	1605	4%	$33,384
897-90-8769	Smith	Jean	ATL	$61,250	342	1402	5%	$64,312
213-78-5412	Appel	Tom	BOS	$22,300	219	1750	6%	$23,638

Employee Listing

1

1. Enter the following text across row 1:

A1:	**SS#**	F1:	**"Phone**
B1:	**Last Name**	G1:	**"Position**
C1:	**First Name**	H1:	**"Increase %**
D1:	**Location**	I1:	**"1992 Salary**
E1:	**"Salary**		

2. Select the range A1..I1, then click the bold button in the Style palette or choose the Font command in the Style menu, the Bold check box, and the OK button.

When you print, 1-2-3 prints the worksheet with all of the cell formats you have added to the worksheet, including fonts and styles such as boldfacing and underlining. This means that before you print your data, you should make any enhancements you want in the worksheet's appearance.

3. Make these entries in the cells shown:

A2:	**'516-75-8977**	A4:	**'897-90-8769**
B2:	**Jones**	B4:	**Smith**
C2:	**Paul**	C4:	**Jean**
D2:	**DAL**	D4:	**ATL**
E2:	**45900**	E4:	**61250**
F2:	**980**	F4:	**342**
G2:	**2301**	G4:	**1402**
H2:	**.05**	H4:	**.05**
I2:	**+E2*(1+H2)**	A5:	**'213-78-5412**
A3:	**'541-78-6754**	B5:	**Appel**
B3:	**Parker**	C5:	**Tom**
C3:	**Mary**	D5:	**BOS**
D3:	**CHI**	E5:	**22300**
E3:	**32100**	F5:	**219**
F3:	**541**	G5:	**1750**
G3:	**1605**	H5:	**.06**
H3:	**.04**		

4. Move to I2 and choose Copy from the Edit menu. Select the range I3..I5 and choose Paste from the Edit menu.

This completes the first four records. You need more rows of data to get the full effect of 1-2-3's printing features, but typing the entries would take too long. Instead, copy these entries until you have a sufficient number to print more than one page. You will, of course, have many duplicates.

5. Select the range A2..I5 and choose Copy from the Edit menu. Move to A6 and choose Paste from the Edit menu.
6. Move to A10 and choose Paste from the Edit menu.
7. Repeat step 6 after moving to cells A14, A18, A22, A26, A30, A34, A38, A42, A46, A50, A54, A58, and A62.

Another option is to increase the size of the range each time you repeat step 6 since this reduces the number of copy operations that you need to perform.

8. Drag the right edge of column A so the worksheet has a space between the social security numbers and the last names, or move to column A and choose Column Width from the Worksheet menu and type **12** in the Set Width To text box, and select the OK button.
9. Select the range E2..E65. Choose the Format command in the Range menu, select Currency in the list box, type **0** in the Decimal Places text box, and select the OK button.
10. Select the range H2..H65. Choose 123412% in the Range menu.
11. Select the range I2..I65. Choose the Format command in the Range menu, select Currency in the list box, type **0** in the Decimal Places text box, and select the OK button.
12. Drag the right edge of column I so 1992 Salary fits entirely in column I; or move to column I, choose Column Width from the Worksheet menu, type **11** in the Set Width To text box, and select the OK button.

The upper portion of your entries should match Figures 10-2 and 10-3.

Figure 10-2. *The left side of the entries*

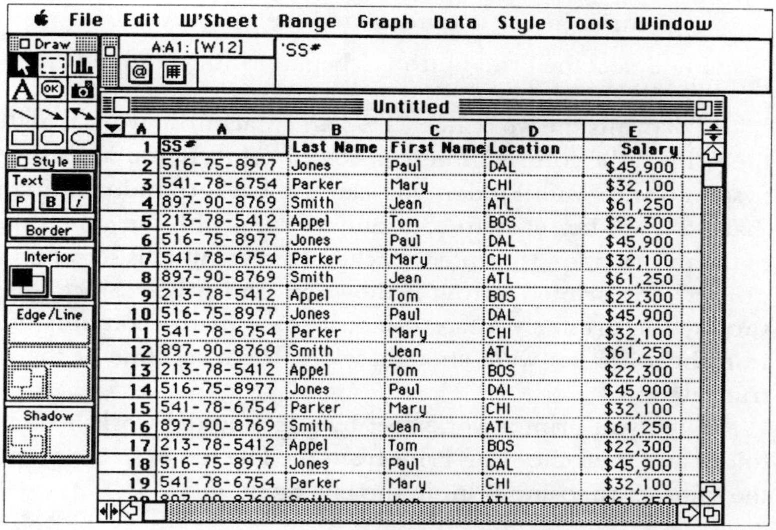

A	A	B	C	D	E
1	SS#	Last Name	First Name	Location	Salary
2	516-75-8977	Jones	Paul	DAL	$45,900
3	541-78-6754	Parker	Mary	CHI	$32,100
4	897-90-8769	Smith	Jean	ATL	$61,250
5	213-78-5412	Appel	Tom	BOS	$22,300
6	516-75-8977	Jones	Paul	DAL	$45,900
7	541-78-6754	Parker	Mary	CHI	$32,100
8	897-90-8769	Smith	Jean	ATL	$61,250
9	213-78-5412	Appel	Tom	BOS	$22,300
10	516-75-8977	Jones	Paul	DAL	$45,900
11	541-78-6754	Parker	Mary	CHI	$32,100
12	897-90-8769	Smith	Jean	ATL	$61,250
13	213-78-5412	Appel	Tom	BOS	$22,300
14	516-75-8977	Jones	Paul	DAL	$45,900
15	541-78-6754	Parker	Mary	CHI	$32,100
16	897-90-8769	Smith	Jean	ATL	$61,250
17	213-78-5412	Appel	Tom	BOS	$22,300
18	516-75-8977	Jones	Paul	DAL	$45,900
19	541-78-6754	Parker	Mary	CHI	$32,100

Figure 10-3. *The right side of the entries*

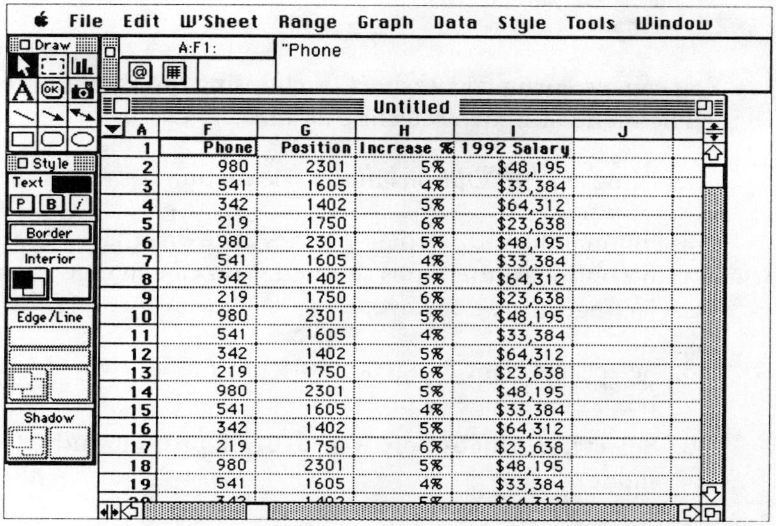

A	F	G	H	I	J
1	Phone	Position	Increase %	1992 Salary	
2	980	2301	5%	$48,195	
3	541	1605	4%	$33,384	
4	342	1402	5%	$64,312	
5	219	1750	6%	$23,638	
6	980	2301	5%	$48,195	
7	541	1605	4%	$33,384	
8	342	1402	5%	$64,312	
9	219	1750	6%	$23,638	
10	980	2301	5%	$48,195	
11	541	1605	4%	$33,384	
12	342	1402	5%	$64,312	
13	219	1750	6%	$23,638	
14	980	2301	5%	$48,195	
15	541	1605	4%	$33,384	
16	342	1402	5%	$64,312	
17	219	1750	6%	$23,638	
18	980	2301	5%	$48,195	
19	541	1605	4%	$33,384	

13. Choose Print from the File menu or press its keyboard shortcut, ⌘-P, and you see that 1-2-3 plans to print all of the worksheet entries just as if you selected the range A1..I65.
14. Select the Print button to begin printing and return to Ready mode.

1-2-3 prints the worksheet. 1-2-3 and Macintosh work together to provide the printer the information it needs to print. If you are using System 7 or System 6 with MultiFinder, you can use background printing which means that 1-2-3 will be ready to continue working with the spreadsheet before all of the information is printed. Background printing is set when you select the printer. The printed output is shown in Figure 10-4. Since the printout may vary by the printer you are using, if some of the columns of your printed worksheet are not wide enough, widen them so none of the information is truncated.

When you print a worksheet by selecting the worksheet document in a folder and then choosing Print from the File menu in the System menu, it is the same as choosing Print in the File menu in 1-2-3.

15. Select the range A1..G10.
16. Choose Print Selection from the File menu and you see that 1-2-3 plans to print only A1..G10. Select the Print button to print this smaller range.

You can also print a worksheet by choosing the Print Options command in the File menu and then selecting a range.

17. Choose Print Options in the File menu.

This command has three dialog boxes. The one that appears depends on which radio button at the top is selected. You can change to another dialog box by selecting Include or Layout.

18. Select the Print Range(s) radio button and type **A1.I25** in the text box as the range to print.
19. Select the Print button twice to begin printing and return to READY mode.

Figure 10-4. *The output from the print operation*

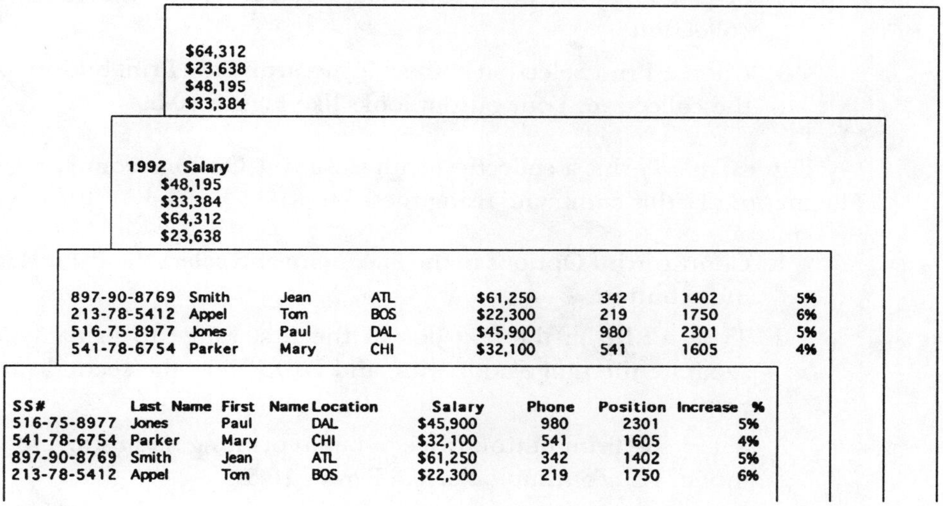

$64,312
$23,638
$48,195
$33,384

1992	Salary
	$48,195
	$33,384
	$64,312
	$23,638

897-90-8769	Smith	Jean	ATL	$61,250	342	1402	5%
213-78-5412	Appel	Tom	BOS	$22,300	219	1750	6%
516-75-8977	Jones	Paul	DAL	$45,900	980	2301	5%
541-78-6754	Parker	Mary	CHI	$32,100	541	1605	4%

SS#	Last Name	First Name	Location	Salary	Phone	Position	Increase %
516-75-8977	Jones	Paul	DAL	$45,900	980	2301	5%
541-78-6754	Parker	Mary	CHI	$32,100	541	1605	4%
897-90-8769	Smith	Jean	ATL	$61,250	342	1402	5%
213-78-5412	Appel	Tom	BOS	$22,300	219	1750	6%

When you select the worksheet data to print in the Print Options dialog box, the selected range is retained with the worksheet, so the next time you use the Print command in the File menu, you will see the range address in place of Entire Document.

Printing Collections

In Chapter 6, "Changing the Appearance of Worksheet Entries," you learned about collections, which are multiple cell and range addresses that are treated as a unit. You can print collections rather than printing several ranges separately. You can either select the collection with the mouse or type the collection address using semicolons (;) or commas (,) to separate the range and cell addresses in the collection. When 1-2-3 prints the ranges, it prints them in the order in which they were provided. To see how this feature works, follow these steps to print two sections of the worksheet:

1. Select the range A2.D6.
2. Press the ⌘ key while you select B10.F15 to add this range to the collection.
3. Choose Print Selection in the File menu and the Print button to print the collection. Your output looks like Figure 10-5.

You can also print a collection with the Print Options command in the File menu. Try this command using these steps:

1. Choose Print Options in the File menu and select the Print Range(s) radio button.
2. Type **A2.D6** in the text box as the first range to print, type ; to separate the range addresses, and **B10.F15** as the second range to print.
3. Select the Print button twice to begin printing and return to Ready mode. Your output looks like Figure 10-5.

Applications: *Collections let you selectively print tables on a worksheet without printing all of the detail. You can also print a collection to skip confidential data in the middle that you do not want to print.*

Figure 10-5. *Printing a collection*

516-75-8977	Jones	Paul	DAL	
541-78-6754	Parker	Mary	CHI	
897-90-8769	Smith	Jean	ATL	
213-78-5412	Appel	Tom	BOS	
516-75-8977	Jones	Paul	DAL	
Jones	Paul	DAL	$45,900	980
Parker	Mary	CHI	$32,100	541
Smith	Jean	ATL	$61,250	342
Appel	Tom	BOS	$22,300	219
Jones	Paul	DAL	$45,900	980
Parker	Mary	CHI	$32,100	541

Selecting Pages to Print

Initially, when you want to print your worksheet, you will want to print all of the pages in the range you select. If you then discover that one page out of several has an error, such as a misspelled name, you will not want to waste time and paper reprinting all of the pages in order to print the corrected page. You can easily print a single page or a group of pages by using the text boxes in the Print dialog box. To try this, follow these steps:

1. Choose Print Options in the File menu, the Entire Document radio button and the Print button.
2. Type **3** in the From text box and **3** in the To text box after Pages.
3. Select the Print button to print page 3.

1-2-3 and the Macintosh return these settings to the default of printing every page.

Printing to a Different Printer

Usually you want to print to the printer that is currently selected. You can also print to any printer that is available to your system. If you want to print to a different printer, choose Chooser from the menu. Next, select the printer from the list of printer types on the left side. If network zones are listed, select the one you want to use and make sure the AppleTalk Active radio button is selected. Next, either select the name of the printer you want to use, or, if your printer is directly connected to the computer, select how the printer is connected to the computer by selecting the icon representing the port the computer uses to send information to the printer. (It will match the symbol above the cord at the back of the computer that is connected to the printer.) If you are using System 7 or System 6 with MultiFinder, you can also select whether the printer uses background printing, which allows you to continue working with the computer as the computer continues to send information to the printer. Now click the Close box, and 1-2-3 will print to this selected printer.

Previewing Your Printed Worksheet

As you start changing your worksheet, you probably will be curious as to how the changes will appear when you print the data. You can see how the output will appear by *previewing* it, or displaying the worksheet data as it will appear when you print it. Previewing a worksheet before you print it lets you save time and resources since you can see if the printout is what you want before you actually print it. This is especially important if you are using a network printer and must wait for a print job in a long print queue.

To preview a worksheet you are printing, you can use the Preview command in the File menu or select the Preview button from the Print Options or Page Setup dialog box. While you preview a worksheet, you can change the page that is previewed, look closely at a section of the previewed page, and select whether to preview the entire worksheet or just a selected range. Try previewing your worksheet by following these steps:

1. Choose Preview in the File menu to display the Print Preview window, as shown in Figure 10-6.

You can advance through the pages by clicking either scroll arrow. If you select the Use Selection check box, 1-2-3 switches between displaying the

Figure 10-6. *Previewing a worksheet before printing it*

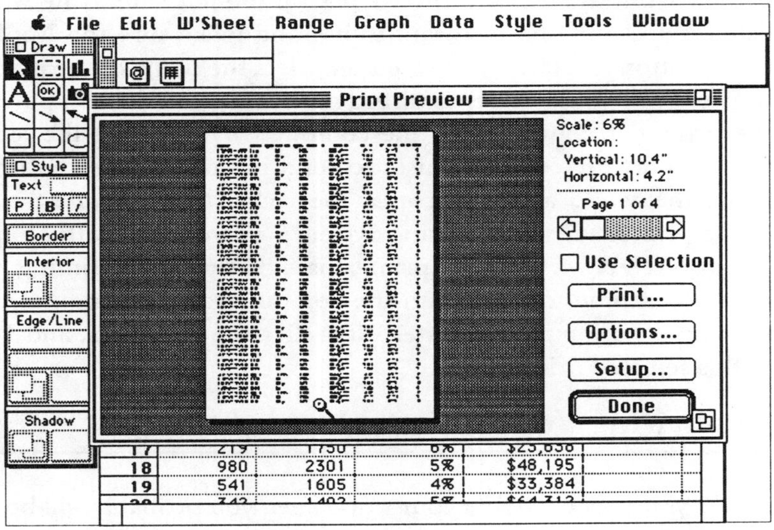

preview for the entire document or the range selected. You can also use the mouse to select the part of the previewed document that you want to look at more closely. In a Print Preview window, when the pointer is on top of the previewed document, it looks like a magnifying glass.

2. Click the right arrow in the scroll bar to see the second page.
3. Click the left arrow in the scroll bar to see the first page.
4. Click any part of the previewed page.

Clicking part of the previewed page displays that part of the worksheet in its actual size when it is printed.

5. Click the zoomed area of the page again to return the page to its original size.

You can also select the Use Selection check box to switch between previewing the document or range selected in the Print Options dialog box and previewing the range selected before you choose the Preview command in the File menu. This Print Preview window has several buttons to display dialog boxes you may use to print the worksheet data. The Print button will transfer you to the Print dialog box so you can print what you see in the Print Preview window. The Options and Setup buttons switch to dialog boxes so you can change the print settings the worksheet uses to print.

6. Select the Done button to return to Ready mode.

Adding Printing Options

You have already mastered the basics of printing; you do not need any other commands to get a printed copy of your data. But you may not be content with the appearance of your printout. If you want to improve it, the Print and Page Setup options can assist you. The Print options are defined in the three Print Options dialog boxes that appear with the Print Options command in the File menu, or when you select the Options button from the Print Preview window or the Print Options button from the Page Setup dialog box. From these dialog boxes, you can change many printing options, including margins, headers and footers, titles, and grid lines. The page setup is defined in the dialog box that appears when you choose Page Setup in the File menu or when you select the Setup button from the Print Preview window. From this Page Setup dialog box, you can select the page size, orientation, scale and printer effect. The specific options vary with the printer you are using. This is the same Page Setup dialog box you will see when you select a document from a folder window and choose Page Setup from the Finder's File menu. The changes you make to the print options and page setup are retained with the worksheet.

Margin Settings

The margin settings are displayed in the Top, Left, Bottom, and Right text boxes under Margins in the Print Options dialog box after you select Layout. The number in each text box represents the distance, for the appropriate side, from the edge of the paper to the edge of the area where 1-2-3 can print your data. To change a margin setting, type a new number in the text box. The top and bottom margins can range from 0 to the length of the paper. The right and left margins can range from 0 to the width of the paper. By default, 1-2-3 expects your entry to be in inches.

Try the following steps with the employee data to see how margins can affect the output:

1. Choose Print Options in the File menu and select the Layout radio button to display the dialog box in Figure 10-7.
2. Type **1** in the Left text box under Margins.
3. Type **.75** in the Right text box and select the Print button to switch to the Print dialog box.
4. Select the Print button to print the worksheet.

You should find that one fewer column prints across the first page because you have reserved more space for the right and left margins.

Applications: *If you are printing worksheet data to insert in a word processing report, you will want to change the margins to match the ones you are using in your word processor.*

Figure 10-7. *One of the Print Options dialog boxes*

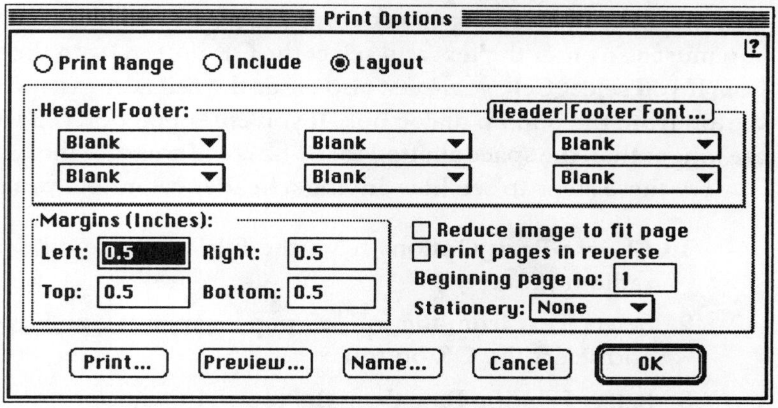

Headers and Footers

Headers and *footers* are lines of text that can appear at the top and bottom of every page of printed output. Information placed in the header (at the top of a page) can include the date or time, an identifying report number, a report title, the preparer's name, or a page number. The most frequent entry in a footer (at the bottom of the page) is the page number. A header or footer has three different sections to it, and you can put different information in each section.

Headers and footers can contain the date, time, page number, document name, text, or the contents of a cell. 1-2-3 allows you to define entries for the left, middle, and right sections of a header or footer. In other words, each header or footer is divided into three sections, so you have six pop-up menus under Header|Footer when the Layout radio button is selected in the Print Options dialog box. The top three pop-up menus are for the header, and the bottom three are for the footer. The two on the left are left aligned in the print area, the two in the middle are centered and the two on the right are right aligned. You create a header or footer by selecting what you want to appear in each third of the header or footer by making a selection from a pop-up menu. For each of these pop-up menus, you can select from Blank,

Text, Cell, Page Number, Printing Date, Printing Time, and File Name. The default is Blank, so as you add entries in the header and footer, you can later remove them by selecting Blank from the pop-up menu. If you select Text, you must also enter the text and select the OK button from the pop-up dialog box. If you select Cell, you must also enter the cell address and select the OK button from the pop-up dialog box. If you enter text or a cell whose contents are longer than the space allotted for it, 1-2-3 will truncate the extra characters.

Try these steps to see how adding a header can affect your output:

1. Choose Print Options from the File menu, and select the Layout radio button.
2. Select Text from the top left pop-up menu, type **Report No: 2350**, and select the OK button.
3. Select Printing Date from the top-right pop-up.
4. Select the Print button twice to return to the first dialog box and print the worksheet.

The header at the top of the first page looks like this:

Report No: 2350 Thu, Sep 24, 1992

SS#	Last Name	First Name	Location	Salary	Phone	Position
516-75-8977	Jones	Paul	DAL	$45,900	980	2301
541-78-6754	Parker	Mary	CHI	$32,100	541	1605
897-90-8769	Smith	Jean	ATL	$61,250	342	1402
213-78-5412	Appel	Tom	BOS	$22,300	219	1750
516-75-8977	Jones	Paul	DAL	$45,900	980	2301

Print Titles

The text you enter at the top and left side of a worksheet provide descriptive information on the first page of a printed report. When the rows in the worksheet exceed the length of one page, the rows at the top do not repeat automatically, and the second page may contain data that is meaningless without column headings. Similarly, when the columns in the worksheet exceed the width of one page, the columns at the left appear only on the first page. Data further to the right appears on subsequent pages but may be meaningless without row headings. When you look at worksheets that are wide and long in a worksheet window, you can freeze titles to continue displaying the identifying entries to the left and at the top. When you print worksheets that are wide and long, you can have *print titles,* which print the same columns and rows on each page that you would freeze with titles.

Print titles allow you to select rows or columns that will appear at the top or left side of every printed page. The columns or rows you select as titles should not be included in the print range. Otherwise, this data will print twice on the report: once as part of the print title, and once as part of the print range.

To select the columns and rows used for the print titles, select the Column Range or Row Range check box in the Print Options dialog box when the Print Range radio button is selected. Next, select or type a cell or range address in the text boxes after Column Range and Row Range that includes at least one cell from each column or row that you want to use for the column or row title. When you want to place row information on every page, select the Row Range check box and enter a range in the text box. To use column information on each page, select the Column Range check box and enter a range in the text box.

You can use column and rows titles with the employee worksheet; the worksheet has more rows than will fit on one page, and the second page has no identifying rows or column headings. Follow these steps to add column and row titles:

1. Choose Print Options in the File menu.
2. Select the Column Range check box, and type **A1..C1** or select the range A1..C1 in the text box.

This range only needs to contain cells from columns A, B, and C.

3. Select the Row Range check box, and select or type A1 in the text box.

This range only needs to contain cells from row 1.

4. Select the range D2..I65 or type **D2.I65** in the Print Range(s) text box which also turns off the Entire Document radio button and turns on the Print Range(s) one.

You want the range to print to exclude the columns and rows you will use for print titles.

5. Select the Print button twice to print the data.

The output contains entries at the top and left of each page, as shown in Figure 10-8. To remove these titles, deselect the Column Range and Row Range check boxes.

You can add a different type of title by adding *grid lines* and the frame to your printed worksheet. You can add grid lines and the row numbers and column letters using the same 1-2-3 features that let you hide or print different parts of worksheet data. You can also print the grid lines just as you see them

Figure 10-8. *Print titles places labels on all pages*

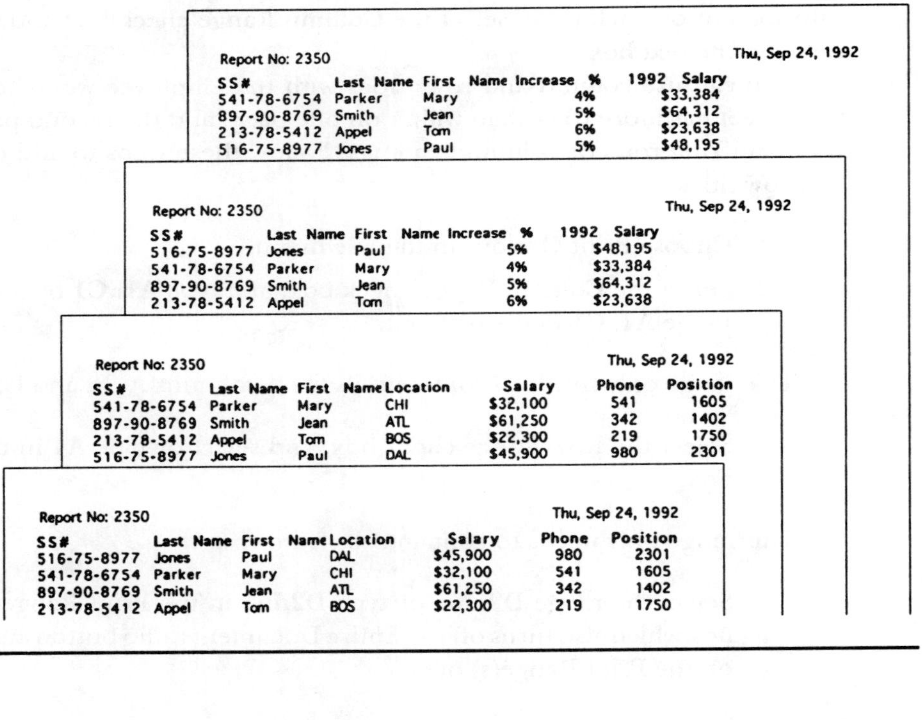

Report No: 2350 Thu, Sep 24, 1992

SS#	Last Name	First Name	Increase %	1992 Salary
541-78-6754	Parker	Mary	4%	$33,384
897-90-8769	Smith	Jean	5%	$64,312
213-78-5412	Appel	Tom	6%	$23,638
516-75-8977	Jones	Paul	5%	$48,195

Report No: 2350 Thu, Sep 24, 1992

SS#	Last Name	First Name	Increase %	1992 Salary
516-75-8977	Jones	Paul	5%	$48,195
541-78-6754	Parker	Mary	4%	$33,384
897-90-8769	Smith	Jean	5%	$64,312
213-78-5412	Appel	Tom	6%	$23,638

Report No: 2350 Thu, Sep 24, 1992

SS#	Last Name	First Name	Location	Salary	Phone	Position
541-78-6754	Parker	Mary	CHI	$32,100	541	1605
897-90-8769	Smith	Jean	ATL	$61,250	342	1402
213-78-5412	Appel	Tom	BOS	$22,300	219	1750
516-75-8977	Jones	Paul	DAL	$45,900	980	2301

Report No: 2350 Thu, Sep 24, 1992

SS#	Last Name	First Name	Location	Salary	Phone	Position
516-75-8977	Jones	Paul	DAL	$45,900	980	2301
541-78-6754	Parker	Mary	CHI	$32,100	541	1605
897-90-8769	Smith	Jean	ATL	$61,250	342	1402
213-78-5412	Appel	Tom	BOS	$22,300	219	1750

on the worksheet. To include the grid lines and frame in the print range, follow these steps:

1. Choose Print Options from the File menu and select the Include radio button.

Now the dialog box has various options for the features you can display or hide. The check boxes that are turned on are printed–such as the header, footer, and worksheet data. The ones that are turned off are ignored.

2. Select the Grid Lines, Row Numbers, and Column Letters check boxes and then select the OK button.
3. Select the range A1..F6 and then choose Print Selection in the File menu and the Print button to print the data with the grid lines as shown here:

A	A	B	C	D	E	F
1	SS#	Last Name	First Name	Location	Salary	Phone
2	516-75-8977	Jones	Paul	DAL	$45,900	980
3	541-78-6754	Parker	Mary	CHI	$32,100	541
4	897-90-8769	Smith	Jean	ATL	$61,250	342
5	213-78-5412	Appel	Tom	BOS	$22,300	219
6	516-75-8977	Jones	Paul	DAL	$45,900	980

4. Choose Print Options from the File menu and select the Include radio button. Select the Grid Lines, Row Numbers, and Column Letters check boxes to turn these off, and then select the OK button to return to Ready mode.

Setting the Orientation

When you print a document, 1-2-3 initially prints from the top of the page to the bottom. An alternative is printing sideways. You may want to print sideways on the page so you can print a wider but shorter document. To try it, follow these steps:

1. Choose Page Setup from the File menu, the Landscape icon (the one on the right under Orientation), and the OK button.

2. Choose Print from the File menu, and select the Print button to print the worksheet sideways.

This command sequence prints the worksheet in Landscape mode. 1-2-3 automatically adjusts the range that is printed on each page to fit in the sideways area of print space on each page, so the worksheet page divisions will be different.

3. Choose Page Setup from the File menu, the Portrait icon (the one on the left under Orientation) and the OK button to return the page orientation to its original setting.

Other 1-2-3 Commands that Affect Printing

1-2-3 has three commands that affect printing that are not found in the File menu. These commands are for adding page breaks and hiding columns. You learned about hiding columns in Chapter 7, "Changing Row and Column Options," but you can also use hidden columns to select which columns are printed.

Adding Page Breaks

You can add a page break at any location within a worksheet to ensure that the information following the page break starts a new page. This feature can prevent awkward breaks that can occur, for example, between the last number in a column of numbers and the total beneath it. 1-2-3 adjusts the automatic page breaks based on the size of the range and where you add manual page breaks. If you do not want automatic page breaks where 1-2-3 puts them, you must insert additional manual breaks to interrupt the automatic page-processing feature. You can add page breaks either between rows or between columns.

To insert a horizontal page break between rows, move to a cell in the row that you want to be at the top of a new page. Then choose Page Break Row in the Worksheet menu. To insert a vertical page break between columns, move to a cell in the column that you want on the next page and choose Page

Break Column in the Worksheet menu. 1-2-3 adds dotted lines to indicate where the worksheet will be divided.

Follow these steps to insert a page break in the employee listing:

1. Move to F31.
2. Choose Page Break Row from the Worksheet menu.
3. Choose Page Break Column from the Worksheet menu.

Now the pages are divided between rows 30 and 31 and between columns E and F. When you display the Worksheet menu, you see checks next to Page Break Row and Page Break Column.

4. Choose Print from the File menu and select the Print button to print this range with the new page breaks.
5. Choose Page Break Row from the Worksheet menu and Page Break Column from the Worksheet menu to remove these manual page breaks and return to 1-2-3's automatic ones.

Applications: *Add a page break at the end of each new report section. It makes it easier for the user to see where the detail and the summary data end.*

Hiding Columns

1-2-3's Hide|Show command in the Worksheet menu can enhance the features of printing by letting you define a wide print range and by hiding columns that you do not want printed. 1-2-3 cannot print two separate ranges side by side. However, you can effectively print separated columns of information in the same row by hiding the columns that lie between the areas you want to print.

This feature is especially advantageous when a worksheet contains confidential information. You can hide a column that contains salary information or a projected increase percentage, yet you can still create a list of employee names, locations, and phone numbers, even when the salary information is in the midst of the data columns you need. As mentioned in Chapter 7, "Changing Row and Column Options," hiding the column does not destroy the salary data—it merely removes the unwanted data from view temporarily.

When you want to restore hidden data, use the Worksheet Hide|Show command. You can try this by following these steps to print a copy of the employee data without the salary or social security number columns:

1. Move to column A.
2. Choose Hide|Show from the Worksheet menu and the Hide button to hide column A.
3. Move to column E, where the salary information is stored.
4. Choose Hide|Show from the Worksheet menu and the Hide button to hide column E.
5. Choose Print from the File menu and the Print button to print the worksheet with the hidden columns.

The beginning of the printed report looks like that shown in Figure 10-9.

6. Move to F1, type + and press (home), if your keyboard has it, or the (←) five times.

When you select a range in Point mode, 1-2-3 displays the hidden columns with an asterisk next to the column letters as shown here.

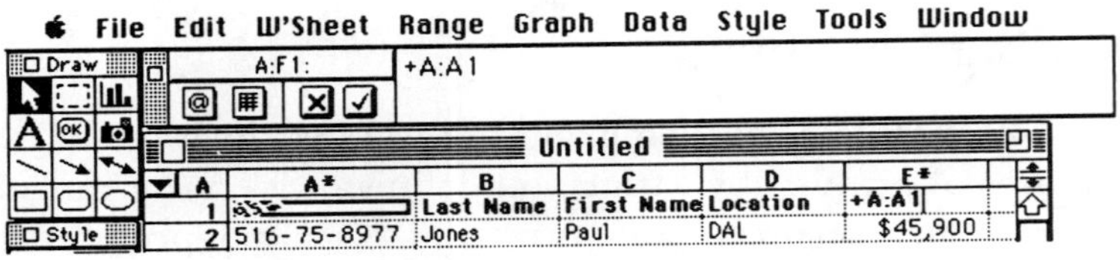

7. Click the Cancel button or press (⌘)-(.) to cancel the entry.
8. Choose Hide|Show from the Worksheet menu, type **A1..E1** or select the range A1..E1 in the Range text box and select the Show button to redisplay your hidden columns.
9. Choose Save in the File menu, type **Printing** in the Save As text box, and select the Save button to save this worksheet.

Figure 10-9. *A printed worksheet with hidden columns*

Report No: 2350 Thu, Sep 24, 1992

Last Name	First Name	Location	Phone	Position	Increase %	1992 Salary
Jones	Paul	DAL	980	2301	5%	$48,195
Parker	Mary	CHI	541	1605	4%	$33,384
Smith	Jean	ATL	342	1402	5%	$64,312
Appel	Tom	BOS	219	1750	6%	$23,638
Jones	Paul	DAL	980	2301	5%	$48,195
Parker	Mary	CHI	541	1605	4%	$33,384
Smith	Jean	ATL	342	1402	5%	$64,312
Appel	Tom	BOS	219	1750	6%	$23,638
Jones	Paul	DAL	980	2301	5%	$48,195
Parker	Mary	CHI	541	1605	4%	$33,384
Smith	Jean	ATL	342	1402	5%	$64,312
Appel	Tom	BOS	219	1750	6%	$23,638
Jones	Paul	DAL	980	2301	5%	$48,195

Review

Printing your reports transfers your worksheet data from your monitor to paper. 1-2-3's printing features use the worksheet features you have learned in other chapters so you can design your worksheet in the worksheet window and print it as it appears there when you want a printed copy. These 1-2-3 features include the following:

- The dialog boxes available with the Print, Print Selection, Preview, Page Setup, and Print Options commands in the File menu provide the options that you use to print your worksheets. Only the Print button in the Print and Print Selection dialog boxes start sending information to your printer. The changes that you make with any of these commands are reflected in the settings for the other commands. Print settings are saved with the worksheet data.
- You can select whether to print some or all of your entries. You can print all of your entries with the Print command when the Print Options command is set to Entire Document. When the Print

Options command is set to Print Range(s), you will print the selected range or collection entered in its text box. You can also select a range and use the Print Selection command to print this selected range.

- You can preview a printed worksheet with the File Preview command or the Preview button in the Print Options dialog box to see how 1-2-3 will print your data.
- You can change the printer used to print the worksheet using the Chooser desk accessory available from the menu.
- 1-2-3 makes several assumptions about how it should print a worksheet. These are the default print settings. The default print settings include the margins and how the information is printed. You can change these with the Page Setup and Print Options commands in the File menu. Changes you can make include altering the margins, adding a header or footer, selecting print title columns and rows, setting the orientation, printing the worksheet frame, and printing grid lines indicating cell boundaries.
- A report can contain headers and footers that appear on every page. Headers and footers are divided into three sections, and in each section you can choose between leaving it blank or printing the date, time, document name, the page number, text, or the contents of a cell.
- Print titles let you select the rows and columns that print at the top and left of every page. Titles allow lengthy reports to retain their row and column headings from page to page.
- You can prevent columns from printing by hiding them with the Worksheet Hide|Show command.
- The Page Break Column and Page Break Row commands in the Worksheet menu insert a page break at a column or row in the worksheet. These manual page breaks override the automatic ones 1-2-3 adds.

Keys and Commands

In this chapter, you learned the 1-2-3 commands you will use to print. These commands and keys are

Entry	Action
File Page Setup	Sets the page setup that 1-2-3 uses when you print the worksheet. This includes the page size, orientation, and reduction scale.
File Preview	Displays the worksheet data in the Print Preview window as it will appear when it is printed.
File Print (⌘-P)	Prints the entire worksheet or range(s) selected with the Print Options command in the File menu.
File Print Options	Sets the print options that 1-2-3 uses when you print the worksheet. This includes headers and footers, titles, and includes different parts of the worksheet.
File Print Selection	Prints the selected range or collection.
Worksheet Hide|Show	After selecting Column, hides or displays columns which do not print when hidden.
Worksheet Page Break Column	Inserts a page break at the current column.
Worksheet Page Break Row	Inserts a page break at the current row.

11

Creating Graphs

The worksheet provides an excellent way to *perform* all your financial projections, but it is not always the best way to *present* the results from these calculations. Important numbers that you want to highlight often get lost in a sea of other figures. How can you make sure that you and others who read your report, which contains hundreds of numbers, will focus on those conditions and trends that you think are important?

One solution is to use 1-2-3's graphics features, which let you present your data in an easy-to-interpret format. Graphs do not present all of the specific numbers; instead, they summarize your data in a way that lets you focus on general patterns and trends. When you find something in a graph that warrants more detailed analysis, you can still return to the supporting worksheet for a closer look.

You do not have to reenter your 1-2-3 data to use the graphics features; you can use the data already entered for your spreadsheet application without making any changes. Nor do you need to learn a new system to create your graphs; you access 1-2- 3's graphics features through menus that are just like 1-2-3's other menus. Once you enter your worksheet data, you need to learn only a few new commands to present the data in a graph format. Any changes you make to your data will be reflected in your graph.

Creating a basic graph is easy to do. Initially, you need only select the data you want to appear in the graph. Once you have created a graph with this data, you can proceed to change the graph type and text. After you complete the basic graph, you can add further enhancements.

This chapter introduces you to the basics of defining a graph. You learn about some of the special options that produce a professional-looking product. You find out how to create and save multiple graphs in a single worksheet. You also learn how to add a graph in a worksheet range and how to obtain a printed copy of your graph.

Basic Terms

Before you can begin to create your first graph, there are a few basic terms to understand. A sample graph, with the key terms and components marked, is shown in Figure 11-1. A discussion of each of the basic terms is presented here; more specialized terms are covered along with the implementation of specific features later in the chapter.

Data Sets

1-2-3's graphs are designed to show from one to 23 sets of data values, depending on the type of graph that you select. A series of data values is referred to as a *data set* and must consist of a worksheet range in a column or row. A data set can represent sales of a product for a period of 6 months, the number of employees within the company each year for the last 10 years, or the number of rejects on a production line for each of the last 16 weeks. Most graphs can use up to 23 data sets. To distinguish the data sets, they are labeled A through W.

Figure 11-1. *A bar graph with titles, labels, and legend*

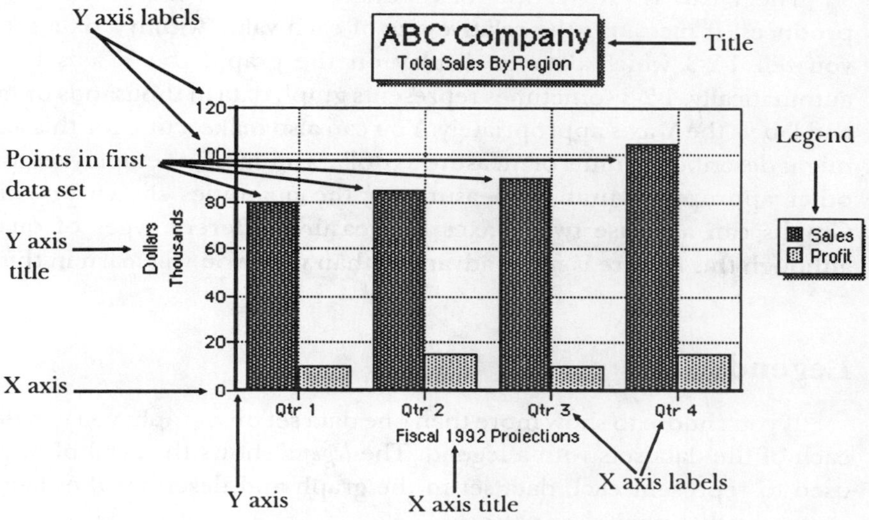

X Axis

The individual values in the data set are represented as data points along the *X axis,* which is the horizontal axis at the bottom of the graph. Each point along this axis might represent a year, a month, or a quarter. It could also represent a division, a product, or a project. You can label points along the X axis to make it clear what they represent. In addition, you can place a title along the X axis to describe the general category of data it shows. For example, if each of the points on the X axis represents a month between January and December, an appropriate title for the X axis might be Fiscal 1992 Projections, which describes the category to which each of these months belongs.

Y Axis

The *Y axis* is the vertical axis found on most of the graphs that 1-2-3 produces. It measures the relative size of each value within a data set. Once you tell 1-2-3 which data to display on the graph, the Y axis is labeled automatically. 1-2-3 sometimes represents graph data in thousands or millions and labels the Y axis appropriately. You can also make a title for this axis; you might describe the units of measure as dollars, number of employees, or some other appropriate unit of measure for the quantities shown on this axis. Graphs can also use two Y axes to measure different types of quantities although this feature is more advanced than what you will learn in this book.

Legends

If you choose to show more than one data set on a graph, you can describe each of the data sets with a legend. The *legend* shows the symbol or pattern used to represent each data set in the graph and describes the data represented by that symbol or pattern.

Creating a Graph

If you have worked through the examples in this book from Chapter 1 on, you already have a number of worksheets that 1-2-3's graphics features could represent nicely. Even though you have some data for a graph, here you enter a short new worksheet designed to let you work with a small amount of data and still apply all the graphics features. Follow these steps to enter the required data for the examples in this chapter.

1. Make the following entries in the worksheet cells shown:

D1:	**ABC Company**	B8:	**39550**
D2:	**Sales By Region**	C4:	**Feb**
A5:	**North**	C5:	**+B5*1.035**
A6:	**South**	C6:	**+B6*1.05**

A7:	**East**	C7:	**+B7*1.02**
A8:	**West**	C8:	**+B8*.98**
B4:	**Jan**	D4:	**Mar**
B5:	**50000**	E4:	**Apr**
B6:	**45000**	F4:	**May**
B7:	**62800**	G4:	**Jun**

2. Choose Global Settings from the Worksheet menu, Currency from the Format pop-up menu, and type **0** in the text box to the right of the pop-up menu, type **7** in the Column Width text box, and select the OK button.
3. Move to D1 and select Font from the Style menu, Chicago from the Font list box, 14 from the Size pop-up menu, the Shadow check box, and the OK button.
4. Select the range B4..G4 and then choose Align from the Style menu, and then Right to align the months with the numbers below them.
5. Select the range C5..C8, choose Copy from the Edit menu, select the range D5..G5, and choose Paste from the Edit menu to copy the formulas from column C to columns D through G.
6. Move to the following cells and type these numbers:

D5:	**41000**
E6:	**50000**
F7:	**75000**

When you add these numbers, they replace the formulas in those cells and provide more variety in the graph than would a growth at a constant rate. Your entries should look like those in Figure 11-2.

7. Choose Save in the File menu, type **My Graph** in the Save As text box, and select the Save button to save the worksheet.
8. Select the range A4..G8 as the worksheet data you want in the graph, choose New Graph from the Graph menu, and select the second graph type on the first row (drag the mouse from New Graph to the second one on the first row and release the mouse button).

Figure 11-2. *Worksheet for using graph features*

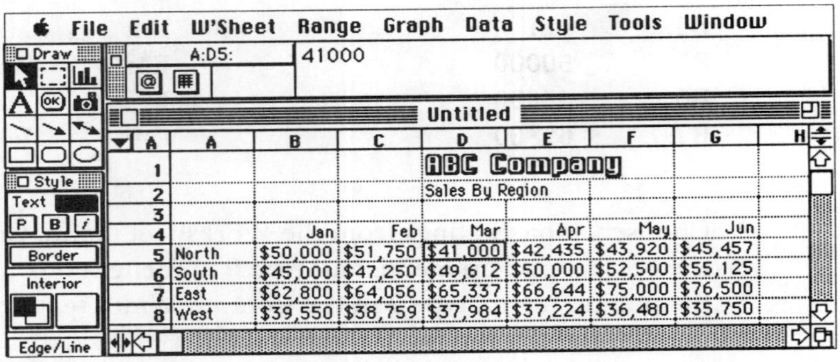

1-2-3 creates a bar graph with the data in the range and puts it in the middle of the worksheet area, as you can see in Figure 11-3. 1-2-3 divides the range you select by rows, since the range you selected has more columns than rows. 1-2-3 decides whether it should divide the range according to rows or columns, with the assumption that you want more data points than data sets. When the range has more columns than rows, 1-2-3 divides the range by rows and vice versa. The X axis labels, which appear along the X axis, uses the data in row 4. The remaining four data sets, A through D, use the data in rows 5 through 8. Later in this chapter, you learn how you can instruct 1-2-3 to override its initial decision of how to divide the range you graph.

This graph is on top of your worksheet data but the entries below it are still available. The overall graph is the currently selected part which you can tell by the small squares, called *handles*, at the corners of the graph. As you select parts of the graph, 1-2-3 will mark the part with handles.

You can move this graph to a new location by dragging it. To make sure that you do not accidentally select another graph part, drag the graph by a part of the empty area that does not contain other parts of the graph.

9. Drag the graph from its current location to below the worksheet data.

Figure 11-3. ***Graph created with worksheet data***

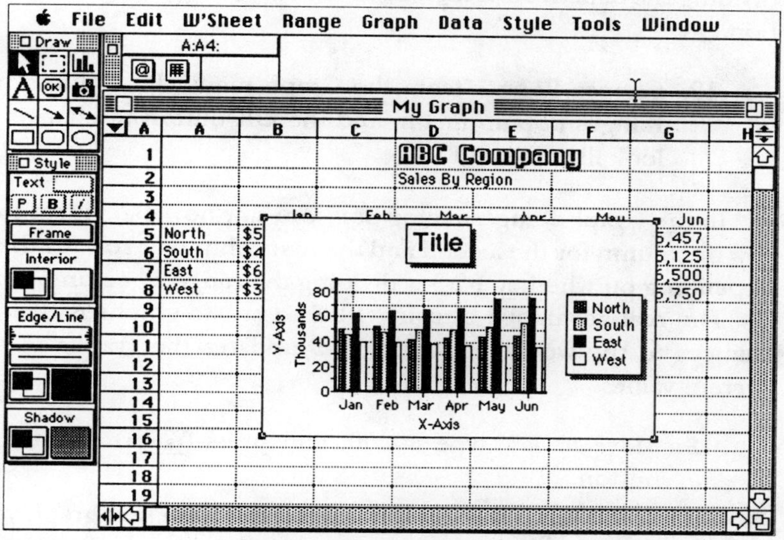

Another way of creating a graph is by selecting range of data to graph and then the graph tool in the Draw palette. 1-2-3 creates a graph using the selected data and the preferred graph type (a line graph). The graph tool in the Draw palette looks like 

10. Select the range A4..G8 again and then select the graph tool in the Draw palette.

Now 1-2-3 needs to know where you want to display this graph and how large you want it to be.

11. Select the cell D35.

1-2-3 uses this cell as the center of the graph using the default graph size. Another option is to drag the mouse from one corner of the area you want the graph to fill to the other corner. This method selects both the size and position of the graph. At this point, this graph uses the same data from the first graph in the same way, but you can change how it displays the data by dividing the data by rows instead of columns, overriding 1-2-3's initial suggestion.

12. Choose Ranges from the Graph menu, By Column in the Assign Ranges pop-up menu, and the OK button to change the graph to look like Figure 11-4.

In the Graph Ranges dialog box, you saw how 1-2-3 is set to use the first row or column for the legend and the first column or row for the X axis labels depending on whether 1-2-3 is dividing the range by columns or rows.

The real advantage of using 1-2-3 to create graphs is that as you make changes to the worksheet data, 1-2-3 updates the graphs to use the most current values.

13. Move to B8, type **80000**, and press (return) or click the confirm button.
14. Scroll down the worksheet to display the first graph you created to see the graph with the updated values for the West region.
15. Scroll down further on the worksheet to display the second graph you created to see the graph with the updated values which are the higher data points for the West region.

Changing the Range of a Graph in the Worksheet

When you create a graph and have it display on the worksheet, 1-2-3 either uses the range you have selected or a predetermined size. You can change the size of a graph on the worksheet as well as move it. Try these steps to change the range of the two graphs you have created:

1. Scroll up the worksheet to see the first graph you created, and select it by selecting any empty area of the graph.
2. Move the pointer to the lower-right handle so the pointer looks like four arrows.
3. Drag this handle down and to the right, so the graph's lower-right corner is in G27.

Figure 11-4. *Graph created by dividing the worksheet range by columns*

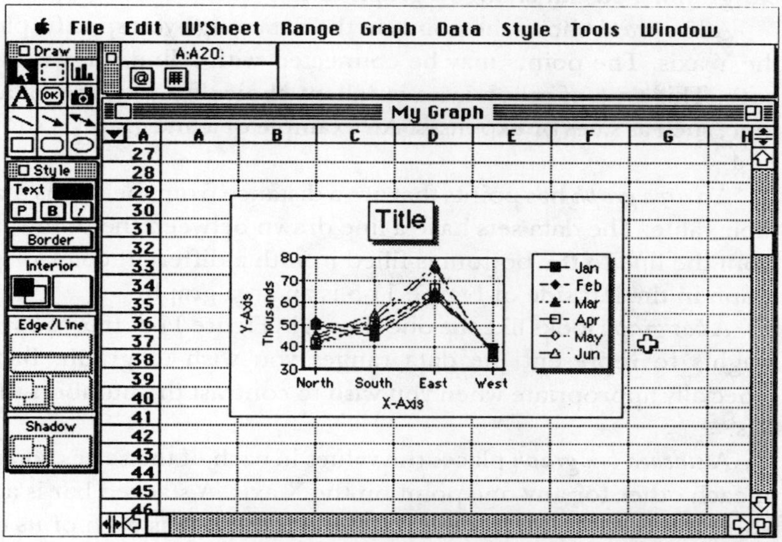

4. Move the pointer to the upper-left handle and drag this handle to the left, so the graph's upper left corner starts at the left edge of column A.
5. Scroll down on the worksheet and select the second graph you created.
6. Move the pointer to the lower-right handle and drag this handle down to G46.
7. Move the pointer to the upper-left handle and drag it to A28.

Deciding on a Graph Type

1-2-3 offers you ten different graph types: line, area, bar, stacked bar, horizontal bar, horizontal stacked bar, pie, scatter (XY), HLCO, and mixed graphs with some variation on these different types. For example, bar graphs can use the variations of a plain bar graph, a bar graph with depth, or a 3-D bar graph. You can change a graph to one of the other graph types.

A *line graph* shows the points in the data range you specify, plotted against the Y axis. The points may be connected with a line, shown as symbols, or both. This type of graph is an excellent choice for plotting data trends over time, such as sales or expenses. An example of a line graph is shown in Figure 11-4.

An *area graph* has points that are a distance from the X axis that represents their value. The data sets have a line drawn between the points, and the area from the line to the bottom is filled in with a different color or pattern. The graph in the left side of Figure 11-5 is an area graph.

A *bar graph* looks like the one shown in Figure 11-3. It uses bars of different heights to represent the data ranges you wish to graph. Bar graphs are especially appropriate when you wish to contrast the numbers in several data sets.

A *stacked bar graph* places the values in each of the series you select on top of each other for any one point on the X axis. A stacked bar is a good choice when you wish to see the level of the total as well as each of its components. You might use this type of graph to show the contribution to profit from each of the company's subsidiaries. The graph in the right side of Figure 11-5 is a stacked bar graph.

A *horizontal bar graph* looks like the one on the left in Figure 11-6. It is just like a bar graph where the graphed data is rotated. Unlike other graph types, the X axis is the vertical axis and the Y axis is horizontal. Horizontal bar graphs are appropriate for contrasting the numbers in several data sets.

A *horizontal stacked bar graph* is just like a stacked bar graph that is rotated ninety degrees. Like the horizontal bar graph, the X axis is the vertical axis and the Y axis is horizontal. A stacked bar is a good choice when you wish to see the total as well as the individual values. The graph on the right in Figure 11-6 shows a horizontal stacked bar graph.

A *pie graph* shows only one range of values. It represents each value as a percentage of the total, using a pie wedge to show the comparative size of the value. A pie graph is an effective way to show the relative size of different components of a budget or the contribution to profit from different product lines. An example of a pie graph is shown in the left side of Figure 11-7.

A *scatter (XY) graph* plots the values in one data set against the values from other data sets. You might use this graph type to plot age against salary, time

Figure 11-5. *An area graph and a stacked bar graph*

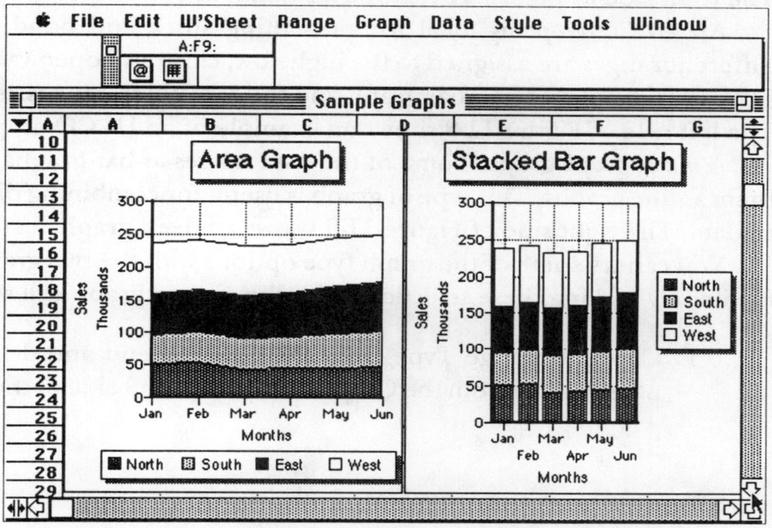

Figure 11-6. *A horizontal bar graph and a horizontal stacked bar graph*

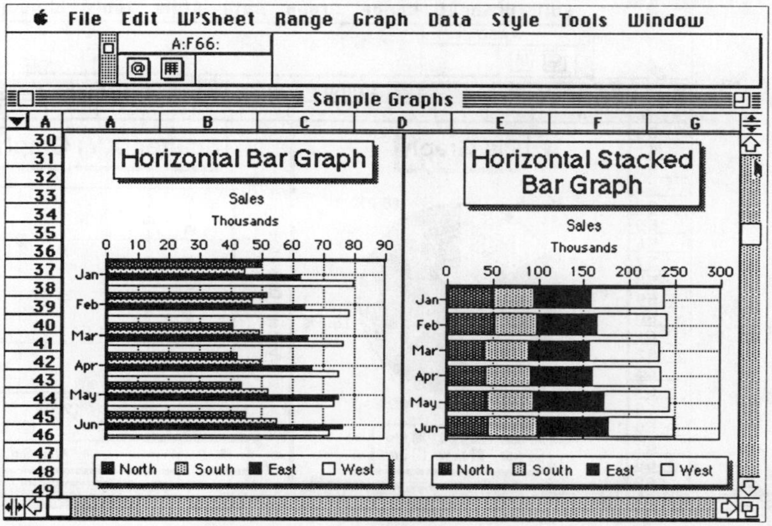

against temperature, or machine repairs against the age of the machinery. The right side of Figure 11-7 shows an example of a scatter graph.

An *HLCO graph* is ideal for presenting stock and bond prices. Four different ranges are assigned to the high, low, close and open values, with the fifth range displayed as a bar graph and the remaining ranges as line graphs. The left side of Figure 11-8 shows an example of an HLCO graph.

A *mixed graph* graphs some of the data ranges as bar graphs and some of them as line graphs. This type of graph is useful for combining different types of data. The right side of Figure 11-8 shows a mixed graph.

You can try some of the graph type options with the two graphs you have created by making these selections with the second graph still selected:

1. Choose Change Type from the Graph menu and drag the Graph palette away from the Graph menu to the left side of the screen. You

Figure 11-7. *A pie graph and a scatter graph*

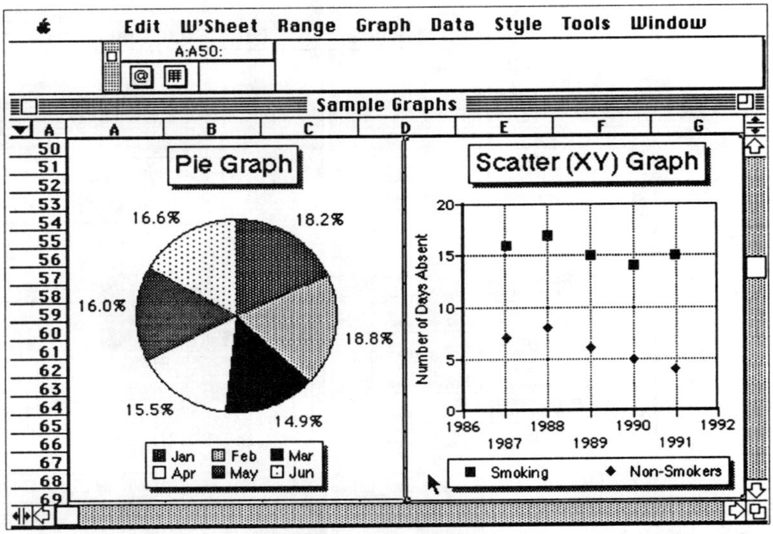

Figure 11-8. *An HLCO and a mixed graph*

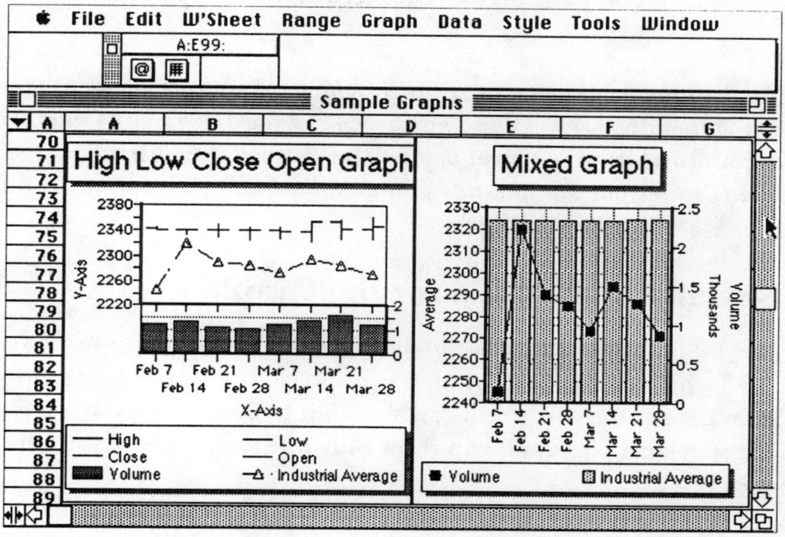

will have to drag the palette down and away from the Graph menu to pull it away from the Graph menu before you position it.

New Graph in the Graph menu has changed to Change Type because you currently have a graph selected rather than data.

2. In the Graph Types palette, select the 3-D bar graph icon, which is the second one on the last row, to change this graph's type.

Each time you make another selection from the Graph palette, you change the graph type of the currently selected graph.

3. In the Graph palette, select the horizontal bar graph icon, which is the last one on the top row, to change the graph type again as in Figure 11-9.
4. Scroll the worksheet up to see first graph you created and click any part of the white area of the graph to select it.

5. In the Graph palette, select the 3-D bar graph icon, which is the second one on the second row, to change the graph type as in Figure 11-10.

Applications: *When you create graphs for your own data, try different types of graphs to see which looks best. For example, if you are graphing sales of different areas of your company or different products, go through the different types of graphs so you can select the one that presents your data the best.*

Specifying the Data for the Graph

1-2-3 has no defaults for the data to show in a graph. If you do not tell 1-2-3 which data to display on the graph, your graph will be empty. Each graph type except the pie graph can show up to 23 data sets or ranges. Pie graphs are special; a pie graph can show only one data set, range A. So far, you have

Figure 11-9. *A horizontal bar graph and the Graph palette*

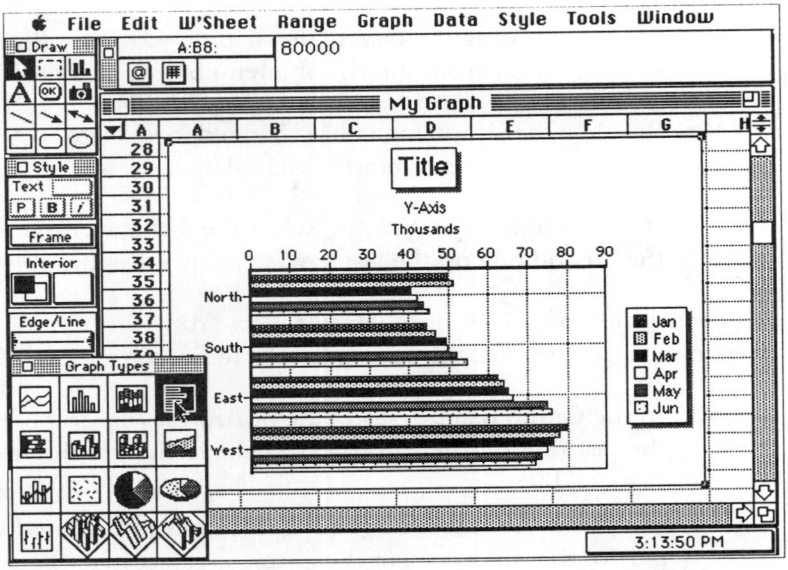

Figure 11-10. *A 3-D bar graph*

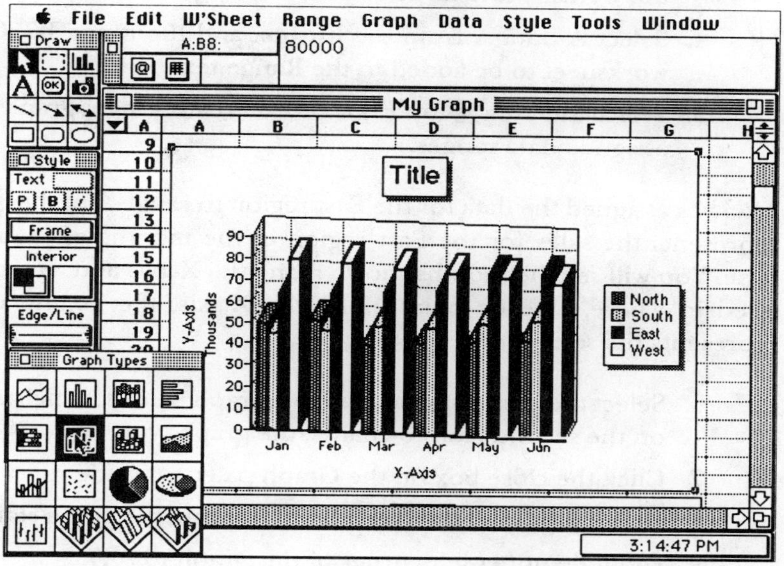

selected data to use in a graph by selecting a range that contains the X series and the data sets. You can also assign noncontiguous ranges one at a time to the data sets the graph uses.

Follow these steps to assign individual ranges to a new graph's X and A range:

1. Move to the top of the worksheet so you can see the worksheet data, and select a cell that is not part of a graph.
2. Choose Ranges from the Graph menu and drag the dialog box to the right so you have more room to select worksheet ranges. (You can move the dialog box to be partially below the screen and move it up when you want to use the lower half.)

Now the Assign Ranges pop-up menu is set to Individually because you did not select a range for 1-2-3 to divide into rows or columns.

3. Select X-Axis Labels from the list box and the range B4..G4 from the worksheet to be added to the Range text box.
4. Select A-Data A from the list box and the range B7..G7 from the worksheet to be added to the Range text box.
5. Select the New Graph button to create a new graph using these assigned data ranges.

1-2-3 has assigned the data for the East region to range A of the graph; it now represents the sales for the East region in the months of January through June. You will see the months shown along the X-axis and a color or pattern filled in where, at each point along the X-axis, the height at that point represents the sales for the East region.

6. Select the area graph icon in the Graph palette, which is the last one on the second row, to change the graph type.
7. Click the close box on the Graph palette to hide it.
8. Drag the graph down the worksheet until the graph starts in row 47.
9. Drag the upper-left corner of this graph to A47.
10. Drag the lower-right corner of the graph to G63.
11. Choose Save from the File menu to save the current worksheet and its graphs.

When you save a worksheet that has graphs, the graph settings are saved along with the worksheet data.

You assigned only two ranges, X and A, but you can assign up to 24 ranges for the graph to use (X and A through W). You do not have to use all the possible ranges a graph can use. Since you did not assign ranges to series B through W, they remain unassigned. You can remove an assigned range by selecting the range in the graph and choosing Clear from the Edit menu. For example, if you want to remove the data for the East region of the first graph you created, you would select one of the bars and then choose Clear from the Edit menu.

Named Graphs

1-2-3 keeps each graph separate by assigning each graph a name. 1-2-3 has given the graphs you have created the name Graph *n*, where *n* is the next unused number. You can continue using 1-2-3's suggested graph names or rename them. Each graph name is a collection of graph settings. 1-2-3 has special options for graphs and graph names. You can hide graphs, display hidden ones, and display them as icons. You can even rename the graphs to provide better names than the graph names like Graph 1, Graph 2, and Graph 3 for the graphs you have created. You can try these features by following these steps:

1. Choose View Graph from the Graph menu to display the Graph View dialog box.
2. Select Graph 1 in the list box. Replace Graph 1 in the text box below the list box with **Sales by Month** and select the Rename button to rename Graph 1.
3. Select Graph 2 in the list box. Replace Graph 2 in the text box below the list box with **Sales by Region** and select the Rename button to rename Graph 2.
4. Select Graph 3 in the list box. Replace Graph 3 in the text box below the list box with **East Region** and select the Rename button to rename Graph 3, which shows the sales for the East region.
5. Select Sales by Month in the list box, the Hide button, and the Done button.
6. Move to the top of the worksheet to see how the graph no longer appears underneath the worksheet data.
7. Choose View Graph from the Graph menu, Sales by Month in the list box, the Show button, and the Done button to display this graph again.
8. Scroll down further on the worksheet and select the second graph you created, Sales by Region.

9. Choose Layout from the Tools menu and then choose Make Icon from the submenu or press its keyboard shortcut, ⌘-J, to change this graph into an icon as shown here: 

This icon can be moved just like the graph by dragging it to a new location, and it can be expanded to return to its normal size.

10. Double-click the graph icon to return it to its normal size.

Enhancing the Display

The current graphs are not very useful—they lack text to tell the reader what the graph contains. Besides graph text, you will want to make other enhancements such as legends, grid lines and frames. You will also want to try some of the special features only available with pie graphs.

Adding Titles

You can use titles in your graph to improve its appearance. You can place titles along either of the axes and use one or two lines at the top of the graph. You can add two lines to the bottom of the graph as well. You can directly enter the text to use in the graph, or you can use an entry you have stored in a worksheet cell. Follow these steps to enhance the Sales By Region and East Region graph with titles:

1. Choose Titles from the Graph menu with the Sales by Region graph selected to produce the Graph Titles dialog box, which contains text boxes for entering the title, the second line of the title, a note, and the second line of the note.
2. Type **D1** in the Title text box and select the Cell check box.

This makes the current entry in D1 the title at the top of the graph.

3. Type **Total Sales by Region** in the Line 2 text box under Title and select the OK button.

This time, you add the text by typing it, since the worksheet does not have an entry that exactly matches the desired title.

4. Choose Axis from the Graph menu, and then X, to produce the Graph X-Axis dialog box, which includes selections for the axis title and setting the X axis or having 1-2-3 set it for you.
5. Type **Fiscal 1992 Projections** in the Axis Title text box, and select the OK button.
6. Choose Axis from the Graph menu and Y, type **Dollars** in the Axis Title text box, and select the OK button.

Now your graph has new text, as shown in Figure 11-11.

Figure 11-11. *Graph with new text*

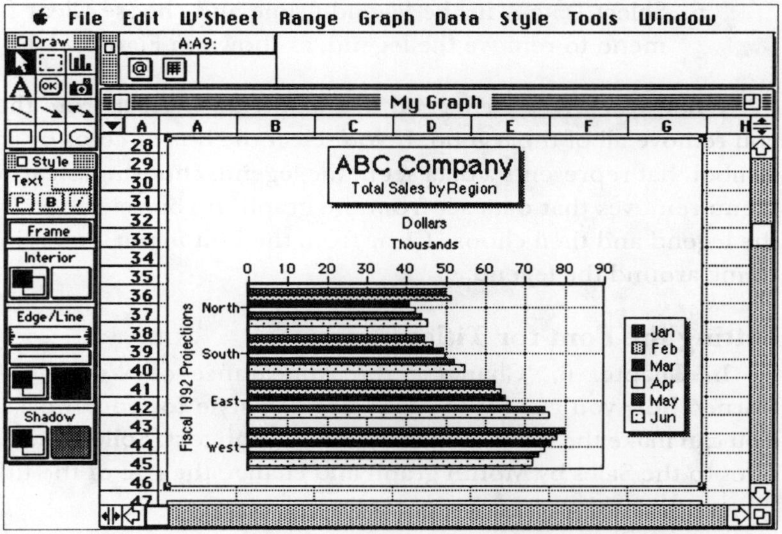

Try these steps to modify the East Region's titles:

1. Scroll down further on the worksheet and select the third graph you created, East Region.
2. Double-click Title in the graph to display the Graph Titles dialog box, type **East Region Sales** in the Title text box, deselect the Cell check box, type **First six months of 1992** in the Note text box, and select the OK button.

Double-clicking the graph part you want to change is a shortcut to using commands in the Graph menu, which displays the same dialog boxes that let you change the features of the part in the graph you have selected.

3. Double-click the title Y-Axis, type **Dollars** in the Axis Title text box, and select the OK button.
4. Select the title X-Axis in the graph and choose Clear from the Edit menu.

You can use the Clear command from the Edit menu to remove items in a graph you do not want.

5. Select Data-A in the legend frame and choose Clear from the Edit menu to remove the legend, as shown in Figure 11-12.

When you select the legend text and choose Clear from the Edit menu, you remove all of the legend. If you select the box of color or pattern or the symbol that represents a data set in the legend, choosing Clear from the Edit menu removes that data set from the graph. If you select the frame around the legend and then choose Clear from the Edit menu, you remove only the frame around the legend.

Setting the Font for Titles

In Chapter 6, "Changing the Appearance of Worksheet Cells," you learned how you can set the font size and style for your worksheet entries. You can make the same changes to your graph text. Follow these steps to add titles to the Sales by Month graph and change the size of the titles:

Figure 11-12. *East Region graph after changing text and removing the legend*

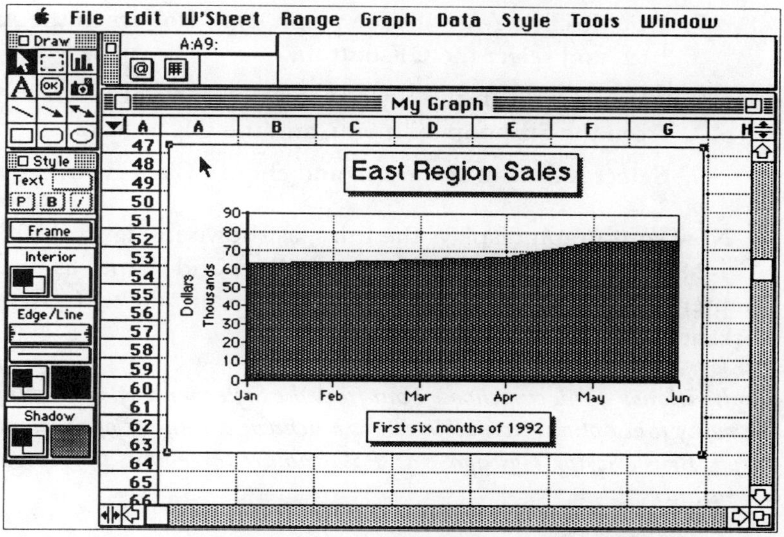

1. Scroll up on the worksheet and select the first graph you created, Sales by Month.
2. Double-click Title in the box, type **D1** in the Title text box, select the Cell check box, type **Sales by Month** in the Line 2 text box under Title, and select the OK button.
3. Select ABC Company in the graph and choose Font in the Style menu.

This is the same Style Font dialog box that you used for changing the font, size, and emphasis of worksheet entries. You can make the same types of changes to graph text.

4. Select Palatino in the list box, the Bold check box, and the OK button.
5. Select Sales by Month in the graph.

6. Choose Font in the Style menu, select Palatino in the list box, select 14 from the Size pop-up menu. Finally, select the OK button.
7. Double-click Y-Axis in the graph, type **Dollars** in the Axis Title text box, and select the OK button.
8. Choose Font in the Style menu, select Palatino in the list box, 12 from the Size pop-up menu, and the OK button.
9. Select X-Axis in the graph and choose Clear from the Edit menu.

Now your graph displays the titles, as shown in Figure 11-13.

1-2-3 will also let you add extra text, lines and shapes as you will learn in Chapter 13, "Advanced Techniques." You can add text anywhere on the worksheet, including on top of a graph.

Applications: *You can choose Font from the Style menu after selecting a title. With the many font options available you can achieve a number of different looks for one graph. Brush Script, Chicago, and Palatino are three fonts that have very different appearances.*

Figure 11-13. *Graph after adding titles and changing the font*

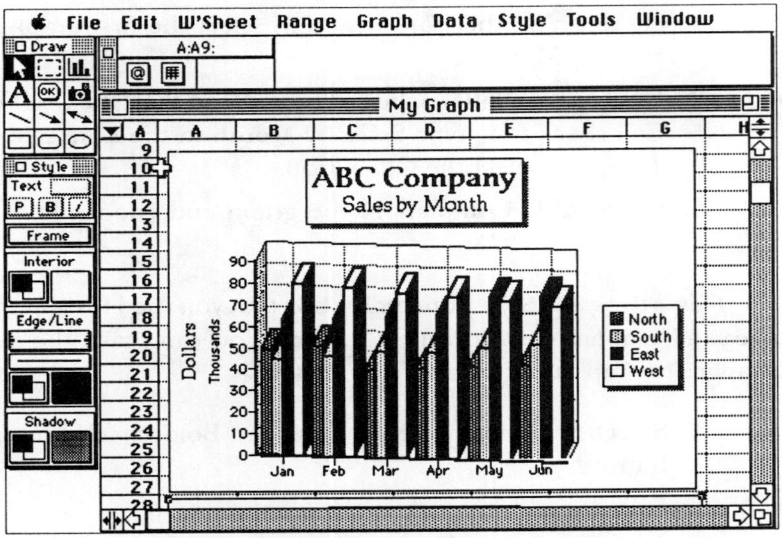

Adding Legends

Legends add clarity to any graph that presents more than one data set by identifying how each data set is represented on the graph. If you use symbols to distinguish the different data sets, the legend will consist of the series indicator and the text describing the data shown by that series. If color or patterns are used, a small square of the color or pattern is placed next to the description of the series. You can type the legend text for each series or use entries stored in one cell or a range for the legend for one or all series. With the graphs you have created, 1-2-3 automatically used some of the worksheet data as the legend text.

When you enter the text for a series, you can choose from the same 23 letters you used to assign worksheet ranges to the different data sets for the graph. Like entering titles, you can either type the text to use or a cell address. You can even use a worksheet range for the legend text for all the series.

Follow these steps to modify the legend for the Sales by Month graph:

1. Double-click North in the legend box or choose Legend from the Graph menu to display the Graph Legend dialog box.
2. Type **North Region** in the Legend Entry text box and deselect the Cell text box.

Previously, this graph used the entry in A:A5 for the legend text of the A data set. Now, this graph will identify this data set with the text North Region.

3. Select B-South in the list box, type **South Region** in the Legend Entry text box and deselect the Cell text box.
4. Select C-East in the list box, type **East Region** in the Legend Entry text box and deselect the Cell text box.
5. Select D-West in the list box, type **West Region** in the Legend Entry text box and deselect the Cell text box.
6. Select the OK button to display the graph with the modified legend.
7. Choose Placement from the Graph menu.

You can also display the Graph Placement dialog box by double-clicking an empty area of the graph. This dialog box selects where several graph parts

Figure 11-14. *Changing the legend of the bar graph*

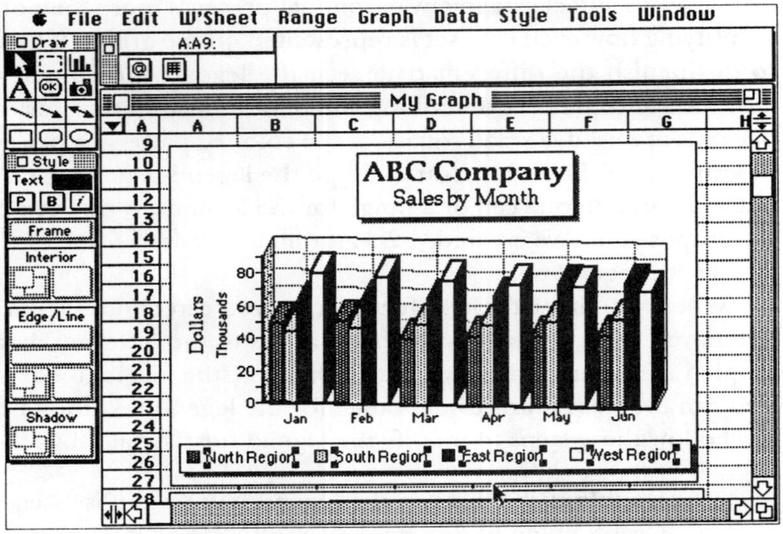

are positioned. For example, the title has five predefined positions, as well as Manual radio buttons that allow you to put the title in any location.

8. Select the bottom-center legend position which is the middle radio button of the three, just above the Inside Plot check box, and select the OK button.

The moved and modified legend is shown in Figure 11-14.

You will notice how 1-2-3 constantly adjusts the graph as you make changes. Another way of assigning ranges is to assign all of the ranges at once, when the text that you want to use for the series is stored in a worksheet range, just as 1-2-3 has stored it when you initially created the Sales by Month and Sales by Region. Follow these steps to reassign legend text for the Sales by Region graph:

1. Scroll down on the worksheet and select the second graph you created, Sales by Region.

2. Double-click one of the months in the legend box or choose Legend from the Graph menu.
3. Select All Ranges from the list box, the range B4..G4, and the OK button.

While the graph looks the same, these are the steps you will use when the text containing the legend text is not automatically assigned when you create the graph. This graph uses the first worksheet cell for the A series legend, the second worksheet cell for the B series legend, and so forth. This is the same legend assignment 1-2-3 made when you created the graph and used the first row as legend text when the range to graph was divided by rows.

Adding Grid Lines

Grid lines are lines that are parallel to either the X axis or the Y axis and that originate from the markers on the axis. They help you interpret the exact value of data points by extending either up or to the right from these markers. Using grid lines in both directions at once creates a grid pattern on your graph. Your graphs initially include grid lines but you can remove the ones you do not want.

Grid lines are added and modified with the Border|Grid command in the Graph menu. You can also display the same Graph Border|Grid dialog box this command displays by double-clicking any existing grid line on a graph. You can add grid lines to any graph except a pie graph. Try changing grid lines to the Sales by Region graph:

1. Double-click the grid lines in the Sales by Region graph or choose Border|Grid from the Graph menu.
2. Deselect the Show Plot Border check box, and select None from the X-axis pop-up menu, and the OK button.
3. Select the overall graph so you can see the changed grid lines as shown in Figure 11-15.

The plot border you have removed is the extra line that is a perimeter around the data in the graph. When it is not included, the only border lines around the graph data are where an axis has its labels.

Figure 11-15. *Adding vertical grid lines to the bar graph*

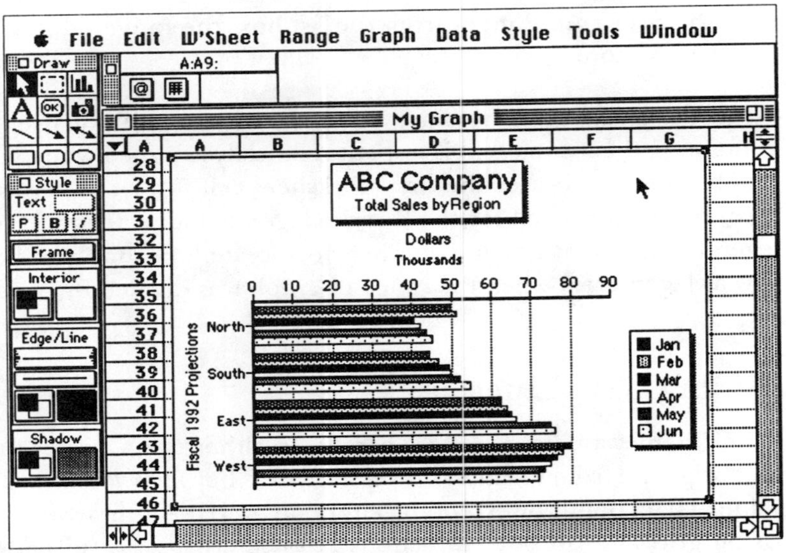

Applications: *If you need to quote a number from a graph, you will want to add grid lines, since they make it much easier to interpret the data points shown on the graph. A graph that shows the number of machines breakdowns per shift is one where horizontal grid lines might be helpful.*

Changing the Frame in Graphs

The graphs you have created have frames in several locations. You have a frame around the graph title, the legend, any note, and around the entire graph. 1-2-3 offers several options for frames so you can choose the one that looks best for your presentation. Frames are altered by selecting a frame on the graph and then either double-clicking it or choosing Frame from the Style menu. Try these steps to change the frames used on some of your graphs:

1. Scroll up the worksheet and select the frame around the Sales by Month graph.

3. Select None from the Edge pop-up menu, and the OK button to remove the graph's frame.
4. Scroll down to the Sales by Region graph and select its frame.
5. Double-click the frame or choose Frame from the Style menu, select Outer Thick from the Edge pop-up menu, Thin from the Shadow pop-up menu, and the OK button to change the graph's frame.
6. Scroll down to the East Region graph and select its frame.
7. Double-click the frame or choose Frame from the Style menu, select Outer Thick from the Edge pop-up menu, Thin from the Shadow pop-up menu, and the OK button to change the graph's frame.

Pie Graphs

Pie graphs are special graphs that only show one data set. Since this graph type is different than the others, you may want to try using it to see its unique features. One special pie graph feature is *exploding pie wedges,* which pulls the wedge away from the center. Explode pie wedges when you want to focus on specific values in the data set. To use a pie graph's features with the East Region graph, follow these steps:

1. Choose Change Type from the Graph menu and, from the Graph palette, select the 3-D pie graph icon, which is the last one on the third row.
2. Choose Options 3-D Pie from the Graph menu.

The Options command changes to match the current graph type. Depending on the current graph type, the options 1-2-3 presents will vary.

3. Select the Equally radio button and select 20 from the pop-up menu after it to equally explode all wedges of the pie.
4. Select the Values and Contents of X Data Range check boxes and deselect the Percentages check boxes, so 1-2-3 will label the pie wedges with the text in the X data range and the values of the pie wedges, rather than the percentages each value has to the total.
5. Select the OK button to display the graph as in Figure 11-16.

Figure 11-16. *East Region sales data as a pie graph with exploded pie wedges*

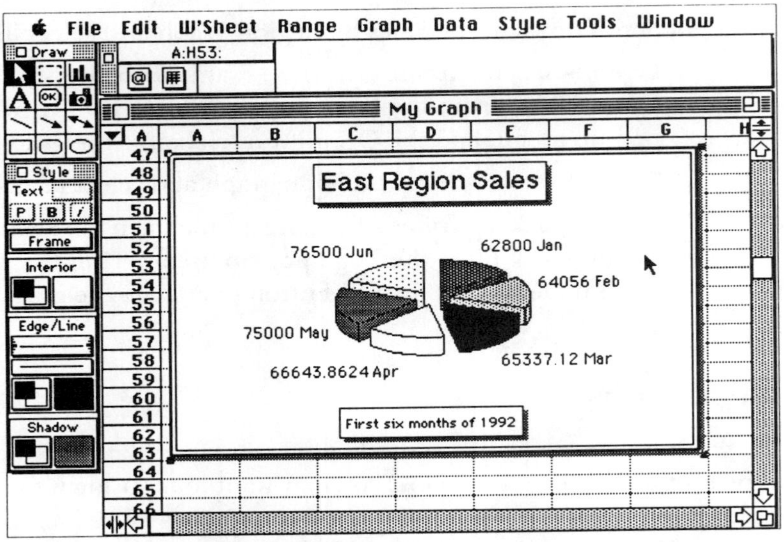

6. Move to the following cells and type these numbers:

H48:	**0**	H51:	**0**
H49:	**0**	H52:	**0**
H50:	**0**	H53:	**50**

1-2-3 can also selectively explode wedges. 1-2-3 will use these values as the percentage that each wedge should be exploded so the first five wedges are not exploded but the last one is exploded by 50 percent. The other option for exploding pie slices is using the B data range. When you use the B data range, you should select the same-sized range. 1-2-3 uses these values for wedges that are under 100 to tell 1-2-3 not to explode the pie wedge and the ones that are above 100 to tell 1-2-3 to explode the pie wedges.

7. Select the graph and then choose Options 3-D Pie from the Graph menu.

8. Select the By Range radio button, the range H48.H53 in the text box after it, and the OK button to see the graph with only the June wedge exploded.

Applications: *You can have the values that explode pie wedges updated as the values in the data set change. For example, if you are graphing product sales for a month, you may want to explode the product sales that are above their quotas. You can use the @IF function you learned about in Chapter 4, "@Functions and Other Formula Options," to create a formula like @IF(B5>50000,50,0) (assuming B5 contains the product sales for the first product) and then copy the formula for the other values in the data set. The @IF formulas will update the percentage each wedge is exploded as the product sales change.*

Printing Graphs

Printing a graph on a worksheet is no different from printing your other worksheet entries. To print a graph, you must include it in the range to print. 1-2-3 prints the range you select whether the range contains worksheet entries, graphs, or a combination of both. You use the same menu selections to specify the range of the worksheet that contains a graph. You can also make changes using the other commands for printing. When you are ready to print the worksheet range containing graphs and worksheet entries, select the OK button from the Print dialog box.

To print the worksheet data and the three inserted graphs in the My Graph worksheet, follow these steps:

1. Move to row 47 and choose Page Break Row from the Worksheet menu, so there is a page break between the second and third graphs and 1-2-3 does not print part of the third graph on page 1 and the remainder on page 2.
2. Select the range A1..G65.
3. Choose Preview from the File menu and the Use Selection check box in the Print Preview dialog box.

Since printing a graph takes longer than printing a worksheet, you should preview the graph before printing it, to ensure that the graph contains the information you want to print.

4. Select the Print button twice to switch to the Print dialog box and to print the worksheet data and graphs.

The first page is shown in Figure 11-17.

5. Select the Done button to leave the Print Preview window.
6. Choose Save from the File menu to save your worksheet.

Review

In this chapter you learned how to create graphs out of the worksheet data you already have stored in your worksheets. 1-2-3 has many graphics features so you do not need to learn a new package to create another way to visually present your data. These 1-2-3 features include the following:

- 1-2-3 can create ten different graph types from your worksheet data. It can create area, bar, horizontal bar, horizontal stacked bar, HLCO, line, mixed, pie, scatter, and stacked bar graphs.
- 1-2-3 can plot up to 23 sets of data in a graph with another data set along the X axis.
- You can create a graph by selecting a range of data and choosing New Graph in the Graph menu.
- Graphs have names to distinguish them. Initially, graphs have the name Graph *n*, where *n* is the next unused number. You can rename graphs using the View Graph command from the Graph menu. You can also use this command to hide, display and move to named graphs.
- When you select a part in a graph, that graph part is marked with handles. By double-clicking a graph part, you can display a dialog

Figure 11-17. *Printed graph and worksheet data*

ABC Company

Sales By Region

	Jan	Feb	Mar	Apr	May	Jun
North	$50,000	$51,750	$41,000	$42,435	$43,920	$45,457
South	$45,000	$47,250	$49,612	$50,000	$52,500	$55,125
East	$62,800	$64,056	$65,337	$66,644	$75,000	$76,500
West	$80,000	$78,400	$76,832	$75,295	$73,789	$72,314

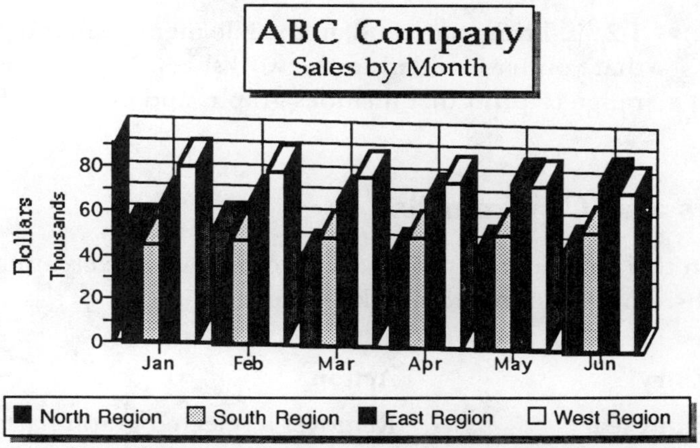

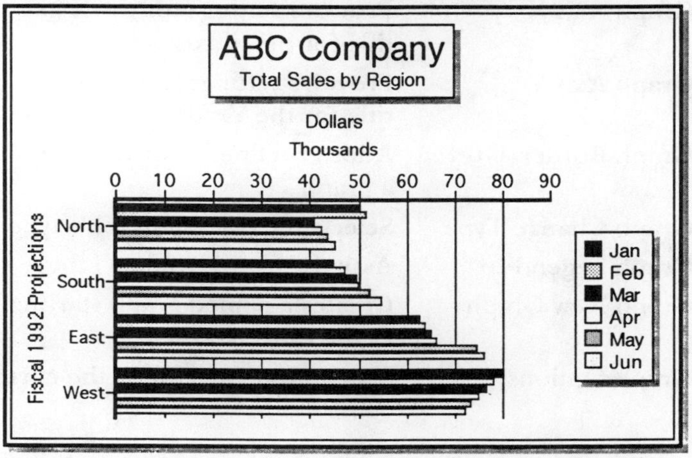

box for one of the commands in the Graph menu that lets you change the appearance of the selected graph part.

- You can position and size graphs. To move a graph, drag the interior of a graph to a new location. To size a graph, drag a handle or edge of the graph to a new location.
- A graph can contain legends to identify the data ranges, grid lines for identifying data values, and titles to enhance the graph's appearance.
- You can save the graphs by saving the worksheet.
- 1-2-3's Print command, in the File menu, lets you print 1-2-3 graphs that you have added to the worksheet. You can select a worksheet range to print that includes graphs and other worksheet entries.

Keys and Commands

In this chapter, you learned the commands for creating and using 1-2-3 graphs. These commands and keys are

Entry	**Action**
Edit Clear	Removes a selected graph part
Graph Axis X	Provides settings for the X axis, including the title for the X axis
Graph Axis Y	Provides settings for the Y axis, including the title for the Y axis
Graph Border|Grid	Adds grid lines to or removes grid lines from a graph
Graph Change Type	Selects the current graph's type
Graph Legend	Assigns legends to data ranges
Graph New Graph	Creates a named graph starting with the data in the range you select
Graph Options	Sets options specific to the current graph type

Graph Placement	Sets the location for various graph parts including the title, legend, and note
Graph Ranges	Assigns worksheet data to the graph series and selects whether 1-2-3 divides a range into data sets by rows or columns; uses the first row or column for legends and X axis labels
Graph Titles	Provides the text for titles and notes
Graph View	Displays, hides, renames, and shows graphs
Style Font (⌘-T)	Sets the font, size, and emphasis for text of the selected graph part
Style Frame	Sets the frame appearance of a selected graph part
Tools Layout Make Icon (⌘-J)	Reduces a graph to an icon

12

Data-Management Basics

All the work you have done with 1-2-3 until now has been concerned with calculating a numeric result, which is the usual application for 1-2-3. However, 1-2-3 also has features that are oriented more toward the management of information than toward calculations. These data-management features are a special group of commands that provide capabilities for the design, entry, and retrieval of information, with or without additional calculations. You can use these commands to keep track of information about your suppliers, clients, or employees.

Since this is a new area of 1-2-3 for you, the first step is to learn some new terms. A *database* is a collection of all the information you have about a set of things. These things can be customers, employees, orders, parts in your inventory, or anything else. If you created a database of employee information, you would place the information about each of your employees in it. All the information about one employee would be in one record of the database. A *record* is composed of all the pieces of information you want to record about each thing in the set, such as one employee. These individual pieces of information in the record are referred to as *fields.* Fields you might include in each record in an employee database are name, job classification, salary, date of hire, and social security number. Every time you design a new database, you need to decide what fields will be included in each record.

A 1-2-3 database is a range of cells on the worksheet. The database can be in any area of the worksheet, but you must put the field names in the top row of the range. The records in the database, which contain data for each field, must go in the rows beneath the field names. You can also make your data-entry tasks easier with the use of forms that lay out the fields on a sheet.

Creating a Database

To create a new database, first create a list of the fields you plan to use, and then you estimate the number of records the database will contain. A database in 1-2-3 for the Macintosh can contain up to 256 fields and 8191 records. Usually, computer memory is the limitation. If you run out of memory as your database expands, you will want to either split the database into separate worksheets with the Extract To command in the File menu introduced in Chapter 13,"Advanced Techniques," or use 1-2-3's advanced database features to transfer the database to another database application such as FoxBASE. (1-2-3 can use these databases directly; you can continue to use the database with 1-2-3's features.)

To create an employee database, you first decide the information you want to store for each employee. For the database you create to use the database features of this chapter, this information includes the last name, first name, social security number, job code, salary, and location of the employee.

Choosing a Location on the Worksheet

You can use any area of the worksheet for a database. Normally, when your worksheet serves a dual purpose (both for calculations and as a database), you should place the database below and to the right of the calculations so it can expand easily. If nothing else is stored on the worksheet, row 1 is as good a starting location as any other. Since you can have multiple sheets in a worksheet, you can put the database on one sheet and the other information the worksheet uses on separate sheets.

Applications: *Try to plan for future as well as current needs when you design your database. It is better to correct and record your data once than to have to do it repeatedly.*

Entering Field Names

Whatever area you select for your database, place your field names across the top row. Always choose meaningful names; you will use them again to invoke the data-management features. Meaningful names can be *self-documenting,* which means they can help clarify what you are doing. Each field name must be contained within a single cell. A field name stored in two cells is not acceptable. Neither are spaces at the end of a field name. Spaces or special characters in the cell immediately beneath the field name can also cause a problem with some of 1-2-3's data-management features.

To enter the field names in the chosen area, just type them in their respective cells.

1. Enter the field names for the employee database in these cells now:

A1:	**Last Name**	D1:	**"Job Code**
B1:	**First Name**	E1:	**"Salary**
C1:	**"SS#**	F1:	**"Location**

Pay special attention to the spelling of field names. When you use the field names in later tasks, they must match exactly if the job is to be completed properly.

2. Select the range A1..F1, and then select the Bold button in the Style palette so your entries look like this:

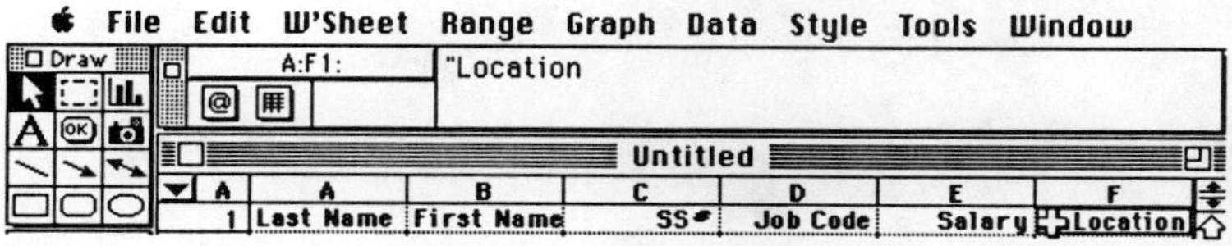

Applications: *Enter the database field names in the order they appear in the original form. For example, if you are recording invoices in a database, you would put the fields in the order they appear in the invoice so entering data for that database is easier.*

Entering Data

Now that you have entered the field names, you can begin entering the data beneath them. The first record should be entered immediately beneath the field names. Each record will occupy one row; do not skip rows as you begin to enter records. Another alternative is to use a form that prompts you for the different fields. With the form, you can design a custom entry form that provides a friendly interface to the database.

Make sure that the data you enter in each field is the same type. If a field contains value entries, the entries in all records for this field should be value entries. If you do not have all the data for a record, you can leave the field blank, as long as you do not leave the entire row blank. Except for these simple guidelines, everything is exactly the same as entering data in the worksheet environment.

You need to complete the data entry for the database used throughout the rest of this chapter by following these steps:

1. Enter the data for the first three records by making these entries:

A2:	**Larson**	A3:	**Campbell**	A4:	**Campbell**
B2:	**Mary**	B3:	**David**	B4:	**Keith**
C2:	**'543-98-9876**	C3:	**'213-76-9874**	C4:	**'569-89-7654**
D2:	**23**	D3:	**23**	D4:	**12**
E2:	**12000**	E3:	**23000**	E4:	**32000**
F2:	**2**	F3:	**10**	F4:	**2**

Creating a Form for Data Entry

While you can continue entering all of the entries by moving back and forth through the columns, you can also enter records by creating a form. Since the form will pick up the formatting information from the range you select, you will want to format the database records you have added before creating the form. As you add new records, the form will apply the formats to the new records. The form will use the default global width but you can change the width of the fields in a form by customizing it.

1. Select C2..C4, choose Format from the Range menu, Label in the Format list box, and the OK button.

This step makes the social security numbers that you will enter text entries so you do not have to enter the alignment prefixes.

2. Select E2..E4, choose the Format command in the Range menu, select Currency in the format list box, type **0** in the Decimal Places text box, and select the OK button.
3. Move to column C, choose Column Width from the Worksheet menu, type **12** in the text box, and select the OK button or drag the right edge of column C three characters to the right.
4. Move to column D, choose Column Width from the Worksheet menu, type **7** in the text box, and select the OK button or drag the right edge of column C two characters to the left.
5. Move to column F, choose Column Width from the Worksheet menu, type **7** in the text box, and select the OK button or drag the right edge of column C two characters to the left.
6. Select the range A1..F4 and then choose the New Form command from the Data menu to display the default form shown in Figure 12-1.
7. Click the zoom box to display all of the form.

Figure 12-1. *Initial form for the employee database*

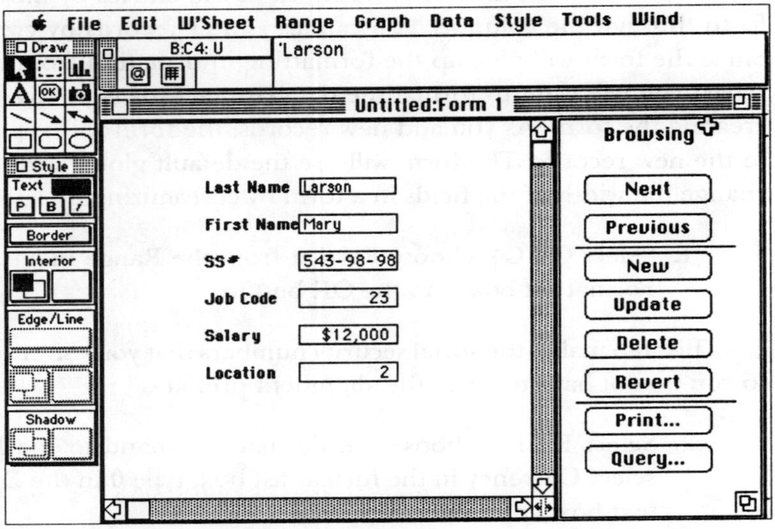

Applications: *Consider using a form any time you delegate your data entry tasks to someone else. It will make their job easier and much less error prone.*

Using the Form for Data Entry

This default form can be used to easily add records by selecting the New button, typing the record's information, and selecting the Update button. You can also make some formatting changes to this form so it will look nicer.

1. Choose the View Form command from the Data menu, type **Employee Data** in the text box, select the Rename button and the View button to rename the form from Form 1 to Employee Data.
2. Choose the Form Options command from the Data menu and select Customize Form so 1-2-3 makes available commands that let you change the form's appearance, such as range formats, styles, and column widths.

3. Choose Column Width from the Worksheet menu, type **12** in the text box, and select the OK button.
4. Choose the Form Options command from the Data menu and select Customize Form to switch from customizing the form to browsing through the database.
5. Select the New button to tell 1-2-3 that you want to add a new record to the bottom of the database and then enter the following database record so it looks like the one in Figure 12-2 (don't forget to finalize your last entry):

Last Name:	**Stephens**
First Name:	**Clara**
SS#:	**219-78-8954**
Job Code:	**15**
Salary:	**17800**
Location:	**2**

Figure 12-2. *Modified form completed for the next record to add*

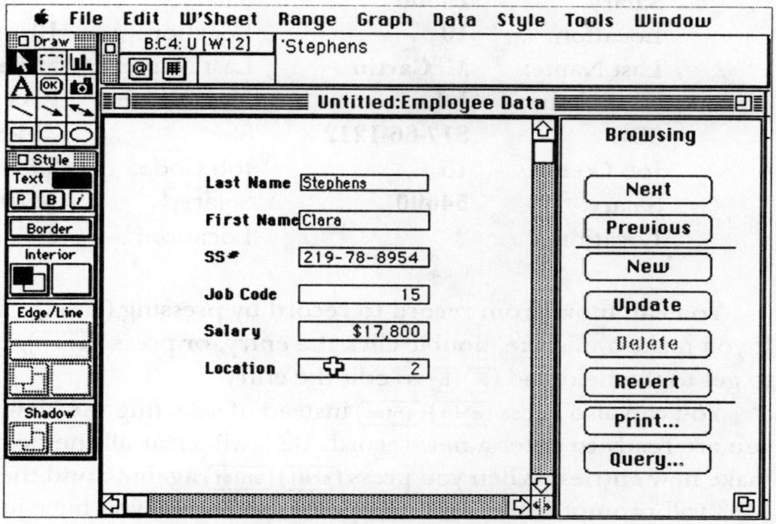

6. Select the Update button so 1-2-3 updates the new record you have added.

1-2-3 does not alter a database's record from the form until you select Update.

7. Add these remaining records to complete the database selecting the New button before you enter the information and Update after you enter it.

Last Name:	**Caldor**	Last Name:	**Justof**
First Name:	**Larry**	First Name:	**June**
SS#:	**459-34-0921**	SS#:	**431-78-9963**
Job Code:	**23**	Job Code:	**17**
Salary:	**32500**	Salary:	**41200**
Location:	**4**	Location:	**4**
Last Name:	**Lightnor**	Last Name:	**Patterson**
First Name:	**Peggy**	First Name:	**Lyle**
SS#:	**560-55-4311**	SS#:	**212-11-9090**
Job Code:	**14**	Job Code:	**12**
Salary:	**23500**	Salary:	**21500**
Location:	**10**	Location:	**10**
Last Name:	**McCartin**	Last Name:	**Miller**
First Name:	**John**	First Name:	**Lisa**
SS#:	**817-66-1212**	SS#:	**214-89-6756**
Job Code:	**15**	Job Code:	**23**
Salary:	**54600**	Salary:	**18700**
Location:	**2**	Location:	**2**

You can move from record to record by pressing (return), (tab), or (enter). If you make a mistake, double-click the entry, or press (return), (tab), or (enter) to get to the field and (⌘)-(E) to edit the entry.

You can also press (shift)-(enter) instead of selecting the New button when you are ready to enter a new record. 1-2-3 will clear all the fields so you can make new entries. When you press (shift)-(enter) again to add the next record, 1-2-3 will prompt if you want to update the record you have just entered so you can select the OK button to add this record instead of selecting Update.

8. Choose Untitled from the Window menu to switch from the form to display the database records added to the worksheet as shown in Figure 12-3.
9. Select Save in the File menu, type **Employee Database** in the Save As text box, and select the Save button to save the worksheet.

1-2-3 saves the form you have created as a *hidden sheet.* That is why when you choose the Form Options command from the Data menu and then choose Customize Form, you can use all of the same commands you use to change the appearance of a worksheet. The field names that appear in the form are separate from the ones in the database, so you change the field names without affecting the database field names. You might want to make changes such as making the names longer or adding colons after the field names. Since the form is separate from the database, you must select Update for 1-2-3 to update the database with the entries in the form. Also, since this form is a hidden sheet, you may see references to cells in the hidden sheet in the console while you use the form or see B* in the Sheet pop-up menu when you select it in Point mode.

Figure 12-3. *The employee database*

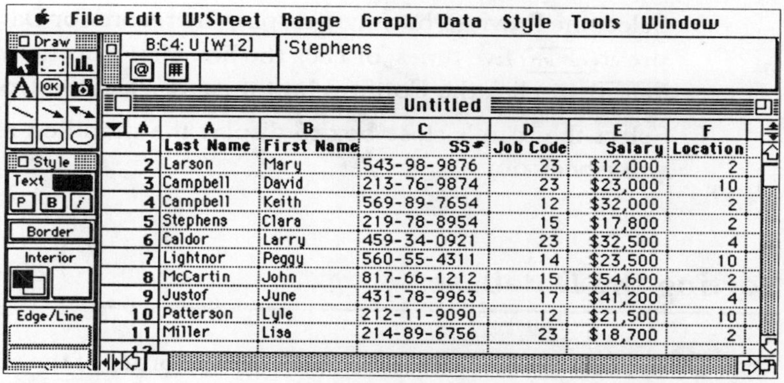

A	A	B	C	D	E	F
1	Last Name	First Name	SS#	Job Code	Salary	Location
2	Larson	Mary	543-98-9876	23	$12,000	2
3	Campbell	David	213-76-9874	23	$23,000	10
4	Campbell	Keith	569-89-7654	12	$32,000	2
5	Stephens	Clara	219-78-8954	15	$17,800	2
6	Caldor	Larry	459-34-0921	23	$32,500	4
7	Lightnor	Peggy	560-55-4311	14	$23,500	10
8	McCartin	John	817-66-1212	15	$54,600	2
9	Justof	June	431-78-9963	17	$41,200	4
10	Patterson	Lyle	212-11-9090	12	$21,500	10
11	Miller	Lisa	214-89-6756	23	$18,700	2

Making Changes

Making changes to entries in the database is no different from making changes in the worksheet data you use. You have two good choices: make the changes in the worksheet or use the form. Either way, you can retype any entry to replace it or use the Edit mode to make a quick correction. To feel at home with making changes, carry out the following steps to make changes to your database records:

1. Move to C2, press ⌘-E, and press delete/backspace twice, type **46**, and press return or click the confirm button to modify the social security number.
2. Move to E2, type **22000**, and finalize the entry by pressing return or clicking the Confirm button.
3. Choose Employee Database:Employee Data from the Window menu to display the form.
4. Select the Next button until you see the record for Keith Campbell; then press return or click the box after First Name, type **Kevin**, press return or click the Confirm button, and select the Update button.

This updates the database on the worksheet with the data you have in the form. If you forget to select the Update button, when you select the Next or Previous button, 1-2-3 will ask you if you want to update the record.

5. Select the Previous button to display the record for David Campbell, press return five times, or click the box after Location, type **4**, press return, or click the Confirm button, and select the Update button.
6. Select the form's close box to display the modified records in the worksheet.

Sorting the Database

1-2-3 provides a Sort feature that can alter the order of the records in your database to any sequence you need. If you decide that you would like an employee list in alphabetical order, 1-2-3 can do this for you. If you decide that you want the records in order by job code, salary, or location, 1-2-3 can make this change easily. You can use up to 255 fields to sort your database. You will find 1-2-3's Data Sort command easy to work with, and you will be amazed at how rapidly 1-2-3 can rearrange your data. To sort the data, you need to fill in the Data Sort dialog box shown in Figure 12-4, which you can activate by choosing Sort in the Data menu.

Applications: *Consider adding a field for record number before sorting your database the first time. You can fill this field with sequential numbers. After sorting in any sequence, you can always return the records to the original order by sorting by the record number.*

Defining the Database Location

The first step in resequencing your database is to tell 1-2-3 where the data is located. When you are sorting data, 1-2-3 is not interested in the field names, only in the data values that you expect it to sort. If you accidentally include the field names in this range, 1-2-3 sorts them, just as if they were intentionally included as data values.

In defining the area to be sorted, you have the choice of defining some of the records or all of them. Always include all of the fields, even if you want

Figure 12-4. *Data Sort dialog box*

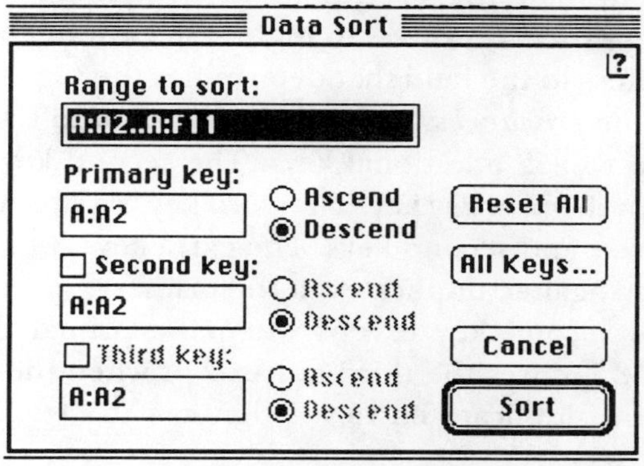

to exclude some of the records. Excluded fields remain stationary and do not remain with the rest of the record to which they belong, thus jeopardizing the integrity of your database. Therefore, it is a good idea to save the worksheet before sorting, in case you accidentally exclude some of the field names. Having Undo enabled is another safeguard, although it is effective only if you reverse the result of the sort operation before entering another command.

Follow these steps to tell 1-2-3 where the employee records are located:

1. Select the range A2..F11 as the range to sort.
2. Choose Sort in the Data menu.

As with other commands that use worksheet ranges, you can preselect a range and have 1-2-3 pick it up in the dialog box. Notice that the selected range does not include the entries in row 1. If you included the field names and sorted by the entries in column A, 1-2-3 would put the field names in the row between Larson and Lightnor.

Defining the Sort Sequence

You can sort your data in sequence based on any of the database fields. If you sort by the contents of column D, the database will be in sequence by job code. If you sort by column C, the social security numbers determine the *sort sequence*. Whichever field you choose to sort on, you also have to decide whether you want the entries to be sequenced from highest to lowest (descending order) or lowest to highest (ascending order).

1-2-3 refers to the field that determines the sequence of the records after the sort as the *primary key*. 1-2-3 also allows you to establish a *second key*, third key, and up to 252 additional keys. The second key is a precaution against duplicates in the primary key. The third key is a precaution against duplicates in the primary and second keys. The extra keys, which are also optional, are a precaution against duplicates in the primary, second, and third keys. 1-2-3 ignores the second key except when the primary key contains duplicate entries. 1-2-3 ignores the third key except when the primary and secondary keys contains duplicate entries. It ignores the extra keys except when the primary and second keys contain duplicate entries. The second key and extra keys are used to break the tie.

Choosing a Primary Key

The way you tell 1-2-3 how you want your data sorted is by selecting keys. The first key to select is the primary key, which selects the first column of values 1-2-3 will use to sort the data. The primary key depends on the entry you make in the Primary Key text box. You can point to a cell in the column you want to use, type a cell address, or enter a range name for a cell in the column you want to use to sort. While the following examples select the first entry to sort in a column, you can select any cell in the column, since 1-2-3 needs to know only which column the primary key is in. You can also select whether the entries are sorted in ascending or descending order according to their primary field values by selecting the Ascend or Descend radio button.

Follow these steps to select a primary key and sort the database:

1. Move to the Primary Key text box and either type **C2** or point to C2.

This selects the social security number as the primary sort key. The default primary key sort order is descending, so you do not need to change it.

2. Select the Sort button to sort the data and change the sequence of the records to match the database in Figure 12-5.

Choosing a Second Key

The second key is the primary tie breaker. It resolves duplicate entries and determines which one of the duplicates should be listed first, based on the value of the second field. In situations like the last example, where the social security number was the controlling sequence, a second key is not needed. The SS# field does not contain duplicates, so there is no need for a tie breaker. However, if you want to sort the employee data by last name, a second key is appropriate—last names sometimes are duplicated.

The process for specifying the second key is the same as for the primary key, except that you make your selections under Second Key. Try this feature by sorting the employee database by name:

1. Choose Sort in the Data menu, type **A2** or select A2 in the Primary Key text box, and select the Ascend radio button to use the last name as the primary sort key.

The range you selected to sort is still selected in the Range To Sort text box.

2. Type **B2** or select B2 in the Second Key text box and select the Ascend radio button.

When you select a cell for the second key, you also select the Second Key check box. This selects a cell in the First Name field as the second key. This key resolves the tie when more than one employee has the same last name. In this case, the first name field determines which record is placed first.

3. Select the Sort button to resequence the data as a name list in alphabetical order, as shown in Figure 12-6.

Since the database has two records with the last name of Campbell, 1-2-3 used the secondary key, the first name, to determine that David Campbell's record should be placed before Kevin Campbell's.

Figure 12-5. *Records in social security number sequence*

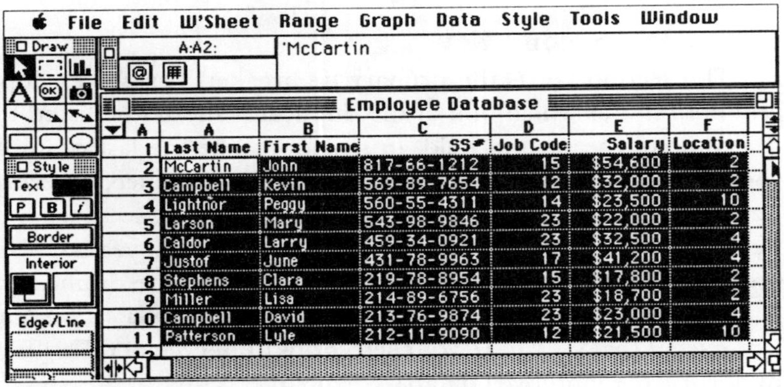

Choosing Additional Keys

1-2-3 can have up to 255 sort keys. This feature gives you up to 253 additional fields that you can use as tie breakers. It resolves duplicate entries with the primary key, second key, third key, and other extra keys and determines which one of the duplicates should be listed first, based on the value of the extra keys. In the last example, employees had the same last name but different first names, so extra keys were not needed; a second key was sufficient. However, if you want to sort the employee data by job code and location, an third key is appropriate—some employees have the same information for both fields, and you can use a third field to order these duplicate entries.

While you can add a third key using the Third Key text box in the Data Sort dialog box, you can also use the All Keys button to display a dialog box that lets you select the first through 255th key the same way. Try using three keys to sort the employee database by social security number within job code and location with these steps:

1. Select the range A2..F11, choose Sort in the Data menu, and then select the All Keys button and the Reset All button.

Figure 12-6. *Records in sequence by name*

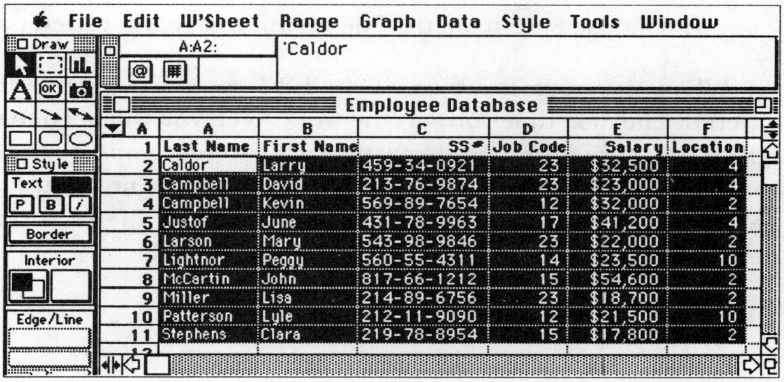

The Reset All button in the All Keys or Data Sort dialog boxes cancels the current settings for range and the sort keys. Since you selected a range before you selected Sort in the Data menu, 1-2-3 replaces the previous range to sort with the currently selected range (in this case, the same range).

2. Type **D2** or select D2 in the Key Range text box, select the Ascend radio button, and select the Accept Key button to use the job code as the first (primary) key.
3. Select 2 Next Key in the Key list box, type **F2** or select F2 in the Key Range text box, select the Ascend radio button, and select the Accept Key button to use the location as the second key.
4. Select 3 Next Key in the Key list box, type **C2** or select C2 in the Key Range text box, select the Ascend radio button, and select the Accept Key button to use the social security number as the third key.

When you select the keys to sort by with the All Keys dialog box, you can continue selecting keys to use in the sorting process for up to 255 sort keys. Any selections you have made for the first, second, and third keys in the Data Sort dialog box will carry over to this dialog box.

5. Select the Sort button to resequence the data, which now looks like Figure 12-7.
6. Choose Undo from the Edit menu to return the database to the last- and first-name sequence.
7. Choose Save from the File menu to save the sorted database.

When you save the worksheet, 1-2-3 saves the sort settings you just entered. The next time you sort the worksheet, you will need to set only those options that are different. Be particularly careful to update the data range to sort if you add more fields to the database; if you do not adjust the range, the new fields will remain stationary while the rest of the record is sorted to a new row.

Searching the Database

As your database increases in size, it becomes increasingly important to review selectively the information it contains. Once the employee database contains 500 records, it becomes extremely time consuming to locate all the records that have a job code of 23 by visually scanning the Job Code column.

1-2-3 gives you a way to work with information in your database selectively by means of *selective reporting*. This means you have a method of selectively presenting information that falls outside of a normal set of values you establish. This selective review feature provides an easy way to clean up the database or to create reports in response to unexpected requests. You can either *query* a database by using a form or by using the Query command in the Data menu.

Working with 1-2-3's selective reporting feature requires that you enter your specifications for record selection on the worksheet. These specifications

Figure 12-7. *Records in sequence by job code, location, and social security number*

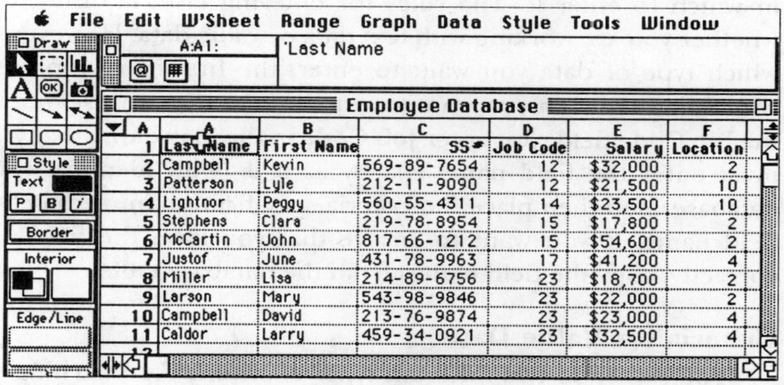

are known as *criteria*. If you query a database using a form, you enter your criteria on a form, and if you query a database using the Query command in the Data menu, you enter your criteria in the worksheet before you use the command and then make all of the entries required for working with 1-2-3's selective reporting feature in the Data Query dialog box. Since selective reporting has several steps, the best approach is to look at each step and then try a few examples that combine all of the features. You begin by exploring the rules for entering your criteria on the worksheet.

Entering Criteria

You enter criteria on the worksheet to tell 1-2-3 which records you want to work with. 1-2-3 ignores records that do not match these criteria when you use the Query command in the Data menu to perform a task with the database. You enter criteria in a different way when you are querying a database with a form, but the same types of entries must be made, so first we will look at querying a database with the Query command in the Data menu, and then apply the criteria you have created to forms.

The first step in creating criteria is choosing a blank area on the worksheet in which to enter it. The rules for entering criteria differ, depending on whether you are working with text data or value data. However, regardless of which type of data you want to enter, the first entry represents the field containing the data you want to search. If you want to search the entries in the Job Code field, you enter **Job Code** in the blank area that you chose. You must enter the field name exactly as it is (with identical spelling) in the database. You then place the criteria specification immediately beneath this field name. If you want to ensure that you have the field names spelled correctly, copy the field names from the database table.

Criteria for Value Data

You can enter two different types of criteria for matching records when you use a field that contains value entries. One option is to use *exact-entry-match criteria,* which places a value that could occur in the field beneath the field name. If you want to search for all records with the number 23 in the Job Code field, enter **23** beneath the Job Code in the criteria area.

Make the following entries to set up the exact-match criteria:

1. Choose Insert from the Worksheet menu, the Sheet radio button, and the OK button to add a sheet after the sheet containing the database.
2. Move to B:A1, type **Job Code**, and move to B:A2 to finalize the entry.

It does not matter to 1-2-3 if the field name has a different alignment or style (boldface or not) from the copy in the database, as long as the text after the alignment prefix is the same.

3. Type **23** and press (enter) to create the criteria entry shown here:

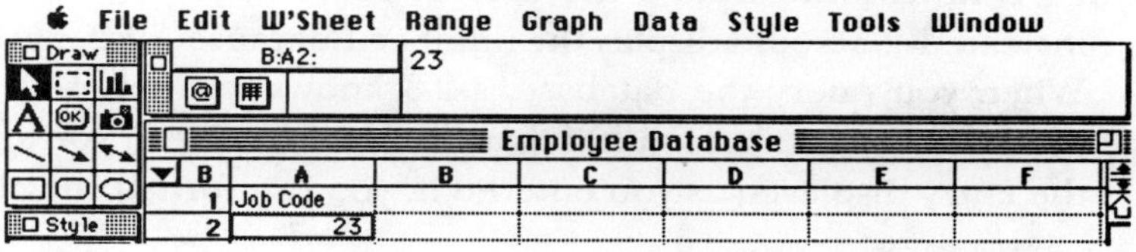

This criteria tells 1-2-3 that you want to use database records where the value in the Job Code field is 23. The entries you just made do not select any records; they only enable you to use the Query command in the Data menu to select the records you want. Before moving on to the remaining steps, look at the other types of criteria that are available. In fact, you can set up examples of several criteria on the worksheet at once.

The other type of value criteria is a *comparison formula.* This is more powerful than exact-entry criteria because it not only performs an exact match, but it also identifies records with values less than, greater than, and not equal to an established value. The logical operators that you can use to express these conditions are the same ones you were introduced to in Chapter 3, "Defining Your Calculations," to build logical formulas. You can still place the field name on the worksheet at the top of the criteria area, although 1-2-3 does not care what field name you use when you are entering formula criteria. However, it is worth entering the correct field to help document the basis of your selection.

The entry below the optional field name is the formula. The formula is designed to compare the values in a field against another value. For example, to select those records in which the salary is greater than $25,000, you could enter the formula **+Salary>25000**. In the formula, you can either use the field name, as in Salary, or the cell address of the first field value, as in E2. You can also use a shortcut approach and enter **'>25000** as long as you enter it as text beneath the field name it uses. You can use column C for this criterion by following these directions:

1. Move to B:C1, type **Salary**, and move to B:C2 to finalize the entry.
2. Type **+Salary>25000** and finalize the entry, which appears as ERR.

Your entry displays as ERR, but when you use it to query the database, 1-2-3 finds and displays the correct records. If you entered **+A:E2>25000** instead, 1-2-3 would display the number 1 because A:E2 is greater than 25,000. When you query the database, 1-2-3 knows to apply this formula to every record in the database rather than just the first one. If you are intent on seeing the entry displayed as you entered it, you can format the cell as text.

Criteria for Text Data

There are both similarities to and differences between value and text criteria. Exact-match entries work the same way as for value entries. You can place a field name in the criteria area and place the text entry you are looking for immediately beneath it. 1-2-3 is not concerned with differences in alignment, capitalization, or style between the two entries.

Wildcard characters are a special option with text entries. You can make a partial entry and use the asterisk (*) to tell 1-2-3 that you do not care which characters come at the end of the entry as long as the characters you have specified match. For example, to find all records in which the last name begins with"C," you would enter **Last Name** for the field name in the criteria area and immediately beneath it you would enter **C***. To find all the records in which the last name starts with"Camp," you would enter **Camp***. Enter a sample for this type of criterion:

1. Move to B:E1, type **Last Name**, and move to B:E2 to finalize the entry.

2. Type **Camp*** and finalize the entry to enter criteria in B:E1..B:E2.

The other type of wildcard character is the question mark, which represents any one character. For example, Mil??? matches Miller and Milton but does not match Million.

1-2-3 has one additional type of text criterion. This type uses string formulas. Since string formulas are an advanced topic, this chapter addresses the use of the criteria you have already entered.

Defining the Database Location

You must tell 1-2-3 where your database is stored before it can search the database for the information you need. In this case, you must include the field names in the range you provide since they are an integral part of identifying the information you want to select. You can select the employee database with these steps:

1. Switch to sheet A by selecting A from the Sheet pop-up menu or pressing control-page down.
2. Select the range A:A1..A:F11.
3. Choose Query from the Data menu.

The range A:A1..A:F11 tells 1-2-3 the location of the database to use as the input for the queries. This dialog box remains on the screen so you can continue to make additional selections, such as the criteria location and the type of query selection you want performed.

Telling 1-2-3 the Criteria Location

1-2-3 uses criteria to select the records from the database that will fill your request. You have already entered several sets of criteria on the worksheet. Now you need to choose one set that 1-2-3 can use to check each record in the database. 1-2-3 ignores records that do not meet these criteria.

To define the location of your criteria on the worksheet, enter the range in the Criteria Range text box. Remember that the criteria must already be stored on the worksheet before you can use this command effectively. Use the criteria that search all of the records to find those that contain a job code of 23:

1. Select the range B:A1..B:A2 or type **B:A1..B:A2** in the Criteria Range text box.

Now all you need to do is tell 1-2-3 what you want 1-2-3 to do with the records that match the criteria.

Finding Matching Records

The Find button selects records that match the criteria you have defined. If the database has multiple records that match, the records are selected one at a time. Now, when you select Find, 1-2-3 uses the database and criteria you have selected. Since the preliminaries have been completed, only one step is needed to select the first matching record: select the Find button to produce the display shown in Figure 12-8.

Notice that the first record containing a job code of 23 is classified as matching the criteria and that it is currently selected. 1-2-3 begins at the top of the database, selecting the first record that matches, and lets you use the ↑ and ↓ keys to move to other records that match the criteria. You can also use the → and ← keys to select other fields within a matching record. As you move around the database, you can edit the contents of the record just as you can from Ready mode by pressing ⌘-E or double-clicking the entry, after having selected the entry you want to edit. You cannot move to records that do not match the criteria; 1-2-3 automatically skips over them. You cannot use the mouse, so the pointer appears as a watch.

2. Press the ↓ key to move to the next record with a job code of 23.
3. Press the ↑ key to move back to the previous record.
4. Press return to return to Ready mode.

Figure 12-8. *Finding the first matching record*

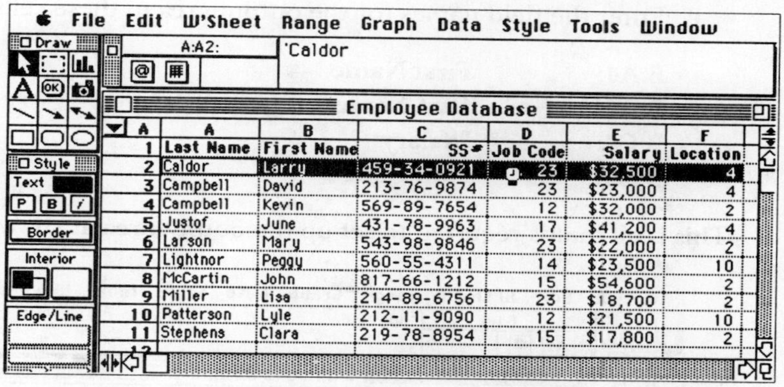

A	A	B	C	D	E	F
1	Last Name	First Name	SS#	Job Code	Salary	Location
2	Caldor	Larry	459-34-0921	23	$32,500	4
3	Campbell	David	213-76-9874	23	$23,000	4
4	Campbell	Kevin	569-89-7654	12	$32,000	2
5	Justof	June	431-78-9963	17	$41,200	4
6	Larson	Mary	543-98-9846	23	$22,000	2
7	Lightnor	Peggy	560-55-4311	14	$23,500	10
8	McCartin	John	817-66-1212	15	$54,600	2
9	Miller	Lisa	214-89-6756	23	$18,700	2
10	Patterson	Lyle	212-11-9090	12	$21,500	10
11	Stephens	Clara	219-78-8954	15	$17,800	2

Extracting Matching Records

The Find query operation is useful when you need to answer a question quickly or take a quick look at someone's record. You can specify the criteria to have these records selected for you. The problem with Find is that the data does not stay in the worksheet window. Often, when you move to the second record, the first record disappears from view (the database is probably larger than your small example). The Extract query operation can solve this problem; it selectively copies matching records from the database to a new area on the worksheet. As you *extract* this information, you can also use the fields in any sequence in the output area you are building.

To use Extract, you must complete a preliminary step from Ready mode: you must construct an output area in a blank area of the worksheet to store the copied records. You can put this output area in any location that will not interfere with the database, such as below the database, to the right of it, or on a separate sheet. After choosing an area, you create the output area by placing the field names in the top row of this area. Remember, you do not need to include every field, and the fields do not need to be in the same sequence as in the database.

Try extracting matching records by following these steps:

1. Enter the field names for the output area in these cells:

B:A4:	**First Name**
B:B4:	**Last Name**
B:C4:	**"Salary**
B:D4:	**"Job Code**

This is all that is required to set up the output area as shown here:

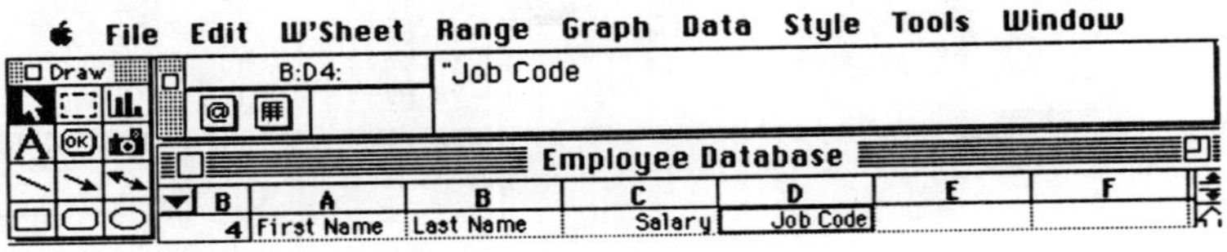

Now you are ready to extract the matching records.

2. Choose Query from the Data menu and select the range B:A4..B:D4 in the Output Range text box.

This tells 1-2-3 where the output area is located.

You have to tell 1-2-3 only the range containing the field names. 1-2-3 erases any data from below the field names to the bottom of the sheet before it extracts matching records, so you do not want to put data below the field names in the output range.

You can also select a range containing the field names and an appropriate number of rows beneath it. If you choose the latter approach, the output area you choose must be large enough to contain all of the selected records, or you will get an error message, but 1-2-3 will not erase any data below the selected range.

3. Select the Extract button.
4. Move to sheet B to view the copied records, which look like this:

12

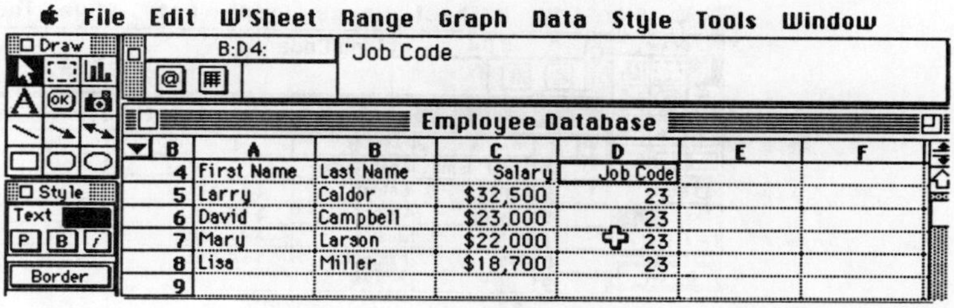

Applications: *You can use the Extract database query operation to generate exception reports. Use the criteria to select the records you want to appear in the report, and then after you extract the matching records, you only need to add the report heading above the output range to allow yourself to focus on the exceptions rather than all the detail.*

A Few More Examples

You entered more than one set of criteria as you looked at some of the ways to enter criteria in worksheet cells. You can try an extract with the two other sets of criteria, using just a few easy steps. Follow these steps to use the criteria that select records in which the salary is greater than $25,000, and then use records in which the last name begins with"Camp":

1. Choose Query in the Data menu and select the range B:C1..B:C2 in the Criteria Range text box.

This is where you stored the criterion to select records by the Salary field. 1-2-3 continues to use the same input area and the same output area as your previous query.

2. Select the Extract button to write the records to the extract area, as shown here:

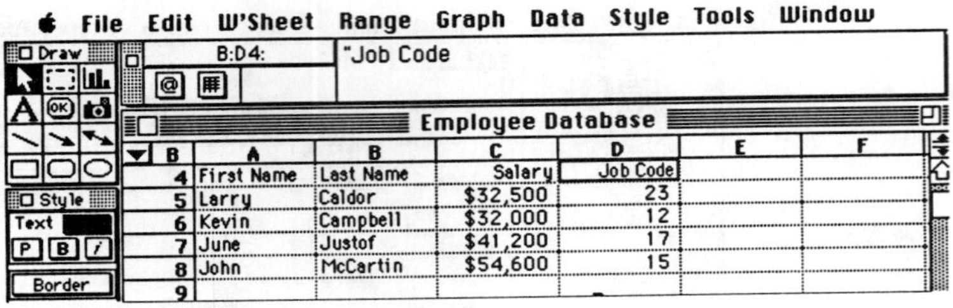

3. Choose Query in the Data menu and select the range B:E1..B:E2 in the Criteria Range text box.

This uses the criteria you entered earlier to select last names that begin with "Camp."

4. Select the Extract button to produce the data shown here:

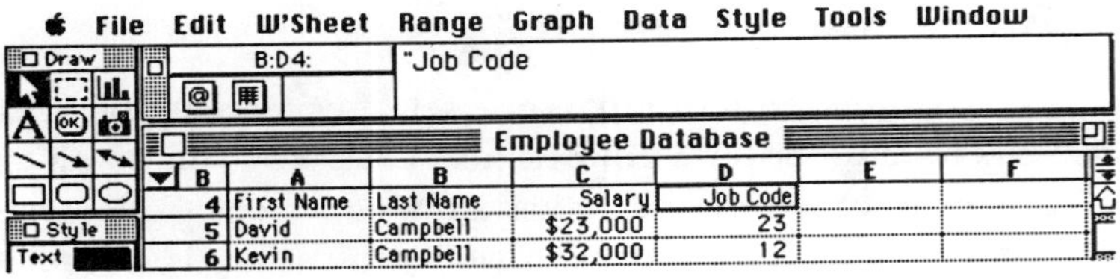

Querying the Database with Forms

An alternative to using entries directly in the worksheet is to query it with forms. To query a database using a form, you enter the criteria in a form and tell 1-2-3 to find the records that match your entries. Since you now know how to enter criteria for the Query command in the Data menu, entering criteria to query a database with a form will be easy.

Creating Criteria in a Form

The criteria you enter to query a database using a form is just like the criteria you earlier entered on a worksheet except instead of entering the field names in one cell and the criteria in another, you enter the matching text, value, or formula next to the field name in a form. Try this using the same criteria by following these steps:

1. Choose the View Form command from the Data menu, select Employee Data in the list box and the View button to display the form you created earlier.
2. Select the Query button to display a form for querying the database.

This query has a name, Untitled, which, since nothing is entered in the boxes, matches every record in the database. You can create additional queries that will match only selected records.

3. Choose the Form Options command from the Data menu and select Name Query.
4. Type **Job Code is 23** in the text box, select the Save As button and the Use button to rename the query.
5. Select the box after Job Code, type **23** in the box, and finalize your entry to create the query shown in Figure 12-9.
6. Select the Find button to browse through the forms for database records that have a job code of 23.
7. Select the Next button four times to see the next four records with a job code of 23.

Since the database has only four records with a job code of 23, when you select the Next button the fourth time, 1-2-3 beeps to indicate that there are no more records. At this point, you can modify the query, modify records, or return to the worksheet.

8. Select the Query button to display a form for querying the database.
9. Choose the Form Options command from the Data menu and choose Name Query.
10. Select Untitled in the list box, type **Salary >25000** in the text box, select the Save As button and the Use button to copy the Untitled query to one called Salary >25000.
11. Select the box after Salary, type **>25000**, and finalize the entry.

Figure 12-9. *Query form completed to find records with a job code of 23*

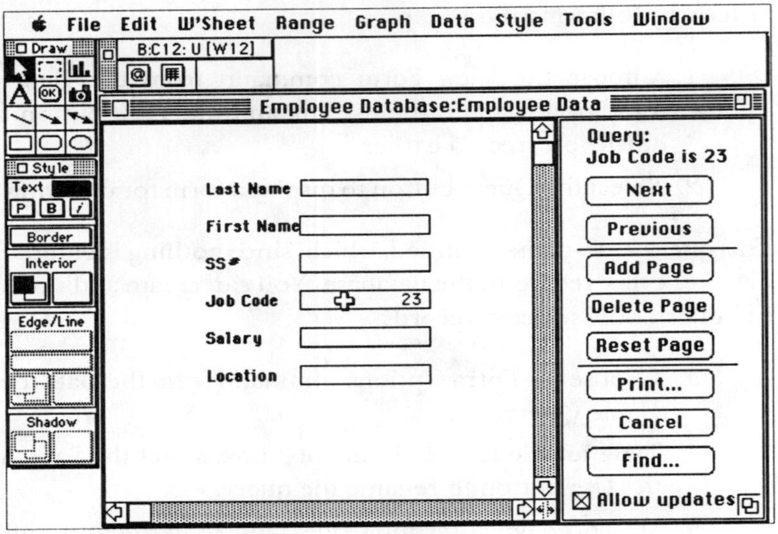

12. Select the Find button and then select the Next button until you see all of the matching database records.
13. Select the Query button, choose the Form Options command fromm the Data menu, and choose Name Query.
14. Select Untitled in the list box, type **Last Name = Camp*** in the text box, select the Save As button and the Use button to copy the Untitled query to one called Salary >25000.
15. Move to the box after Last Name, type **Camp***, and finalize the entry.
16. Select the Find button and select the Next button until you see all of the matching database records.
17. Choose the Form Options command from the Data menu, and choose Name Query, select Untitled in the list box, and select the Use button to use the Untitled query, which includes all database records because all of the boxes in the query form are empty.

18. Select the form's close box to close the form's window.

The advantage of named queries is how quickly you can use them again. Try using the queries you have created following these steps:

1. Choose the View Form command from the Data menu, select Employee Data in the list box, and select the View button to display the form with the queries you have added.
2. Choose the Form Options command from the Data menu and choose Name Query.
3. Select Job Code is 23 in the list box, the Use button, and the Find button.

1-2-3 automatically uses this query without having to reenter the data because the named query also remembered the criteria to use.

4. Select the Next button until you have reviewed all of the matching records.
5. Choose the Form Options command from the Data menu and choose Name Query, select Salary >25000 in the list box, the Use button and the Find button to reuse the query that finds records with salaries greater than $25000.
6. Select the Next button until you have reviewed all of the matching records.
7. Choose the Form Options command from the Data menu and choose Name Query, select Untitled in the list box, the Use button and the Find button to use the query that matches all database records.
8. Select the form's close box to close the Form window.

Special Features

Now that you have completed the basics of data management, you may want to take a look at some of 1-2-3's data-management features. These include referencing the database with a range name and using powerful database functions.

Naming the Database

Using a name rather than a range address to refer to the database can provide flexibility and formulas that are easier to understand. Using a name means you can refer to your employee data by the name Employee rather than A1..F11. You can assign names with the Name command in the Range menu and selecting Create from the Range pop-up menu, or pressing ⌘-R, which you learned about in Chapter 4,"@Functions and Other Formula Options." Try it now with the employee database:

1. Select the range A:A1..A:F11, select Create in the Range pop-up menu in the console, type **Employee** in the Create Range Name text box, and select the OK button.

You can now reference the range A1..F11 by the name Employee. When you use this range name in formulas, as you will shortly, 1-2-3 automatically uses the database even if the database has changed size or location.

Using the Database Functions

The *database functions* are @functions designed to work exclusively with databases. Like other @functions, they are prerecorded formulas that can perform calculations for you. Unlike other @functions, they operate on a database and require that you establish criteria to designate the records that are to be included in the calculations they perform. Using these @functions requires the same preliminary work as using the Query command in the Data menu. Table 12-1 provides a list of the database functions.

All of the database functions except @DQUERY have the same format for their arguments, as follows:

@DFUNCTION(*database,field in database,criteria location*)

Table 12-1. *Database Functions*

Function	Description
@DAVG	Averages a field of matching records
@DCOUNT	Counts the nonblank entries in a field of matching records
@DGET	Returns the value of a field of the one matching record
@DMAX	Returns the highest value of a field from the matching records
@DMIN	Returns the lowest value of a field from the matching records
@DQUERY	Returns the value of an external database function
@DSTD	Calculates the standard deviation of a field for matching records
@DSTDS	Calculates the sample standard deviation of a field for matching records
@DSUM	Totals a field for matching records
@DVAR	Computes the variance of a field for matching records
@DVARS	Computes the sample variance of a field for matching records

The first argument is the location of the database. The range address or name should include the field names as well as the data. The second argument is the field name, in quotes, that you want used in the calculations. You can also select the field by providing its *offset,* which is the number of columns the field is from the left side of the database table. The offset is always one less than what you would expect with the ordinary way of counting. The first column has an offset of zero and each column to the right has its offset increased by one. The last argument is the range name or address specifying the location of the criteria. You define the criteria in the same way you define criteria for the Query command in the Data menu. Putting a few of these functions to work will clarify exactly how you use them.

Applications: *Use the database functions to create a management summary report by creating criteria that the functions can use for different groups that you want to summarize. For example, if you are totaling inventory by location, you would have criteria that matched each location for different @DSUM functions.*

@DAVG

The @DAVG function computes the average for a field in a selected group of database records. You can use this function to determine the average salary for employees with a job code of 23. You can use the same criteria you entered for the data query operations. Just follow these steps:

1. Move to B:H1, type **Average Salary for Job Code 23:**, and move to B:K1 to finalize your entry.
2. Type **@DAVG(Employee,"Salary",A1.A2)** and finalize your entry.

Notice that the database reference uses the range name, Employee, which includes the field names, all records, and all fields. The field name is Salary; this field contains the values you want to average. The formula uses the criteria in A1..A2 on the current sheet (sheet B) to select the records whose salary entries are averaged. The results are shown here:

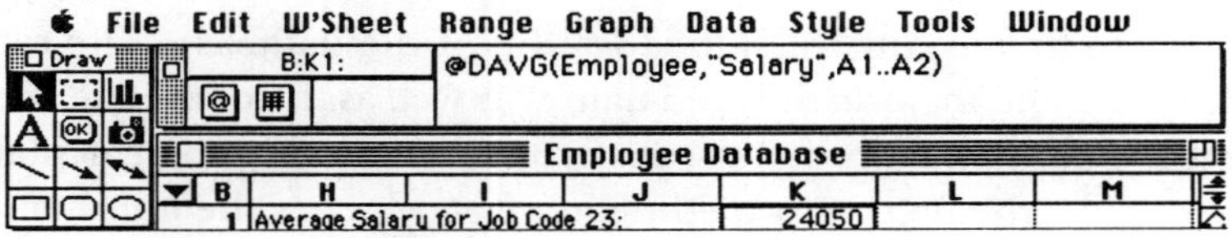

@DSUM

The @DSUM function follows the same pattern as the @DAVG function. If you want to total the salaries for all records with a job code of 23, you can use the same criteria. Follow these steps:

1. Move to B:H2, type **Total Salaries for Job Code 23:**, and move to B:K2 to finalize your entry.
2. Type **@DSUM(Employee,"Salary",A1.A2)** and finalize your entry.

The result of this calculation is 96200, which is the total of the salaries for employees with a job code of 23.

@DCOUNT

The @DCOUNT function selectively counts the number of nonblank entries in records that match your criteria. You can try this function to count the number of employees with a job code of 23. Follow these steps to enter the function:

1. Move to B:H3, type **Number of Employees in Job Code 23:**, and move to B:K3 to finalize your entry.
2. Type **@DCOUNT(Employee,"Job Code",A1.A2)** and finalize your entry.

The count operation is performed on the Job Code field, although you could have selected any field that contains an entry. The result is 4—the same result you would get if you manually counted records for employees with a job code of 23.

Using @DMIN

The @DMIN function searches for the minimum value in the column specified. Only records that match your criteria are eligible for this minimum comparison. You can use this function to determine the lowest salary paid to an individual in location 2 or the lowest salary paid to someone with a job code of 23. Follow these steps to use the @DMIN function:

1. Move to B:H4, type **Minimum Salary for Job Code 23:**, and move to B:K4 to finalize your entry.

2. Type **@DMIN(Employee,"Salary",A1.A2)** and finalize your entry to produce these results:

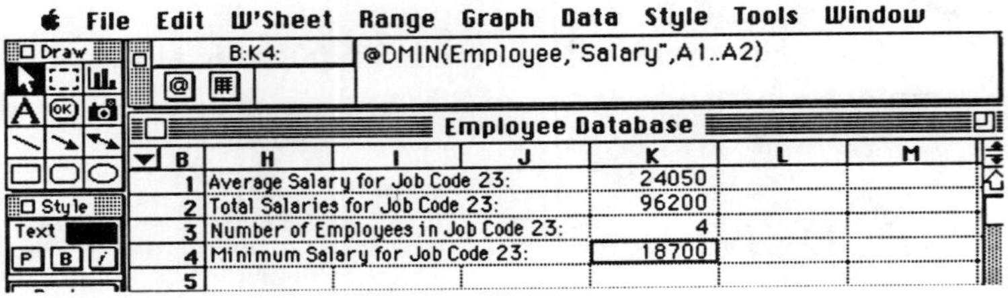

Review

In this chapter, you learned how to create, sort, and query databases in 1-2-3. The topics you covered include the following:

- You can use 1-2-3 to create and use databases. You can store a database in any location, but you want to keep other data away from it so the database can grow. The first row of the database contains the field names, with one in each cell. The rows beneath the field names contain the database records.
- You can enter a database directly into a worksheet or you can create a form and use the form to enter the database. The form is created with the New Form command in the Data menu. Once a form is displayed, you can modify it by selecting Form Options in the Data menu and selecting Customize Form. This makes the 1-2-3 commands that you use to enhance your worksheet available to enhance your form.
- You can resequence the records in a 1-2-3 database with the Sort command in the Data menu. You include only the database records as the range to sort, not the field names. Primary, second, third, and extra keys control the sequence of the records.

- 1-2-3's Query command in the Data menu finds records in a database that match conditions, or criteria, you create. You can select matching records with the Find button or copy them to a new area on the worksheet if you set up an output area and use Extract. Only records that match your criteria are selected or copied.
- Before you query a database, you must enter the criteria a record must meet to be selected. You can use exact-match criteria for text or value data. With text data you can also use the ? and * wildcard characters to represent one or many characters. Logical formulas are another option. They describe acceptable entries for fields containing either text or value data.
- You can create queries with a form that let you review one at a time the records that match criteria. The criteria you enter to query using a form are entered after selecting the Query button and typing the entries the matching records must match before selecting the Find button.
- The database functions are @functions that work with the records in a 1-2-3 database and the criteria you have established to select records of interest. You can obtain a total, average, minimum, maximum, and other statistical computations on a selected group of records with these functions.

Keys and Commands

The commands you learned in this chapter enable you to sort and query a database and to repeat a query by simply pressing a function key. These commands and keys are

Entry	Action
Data Form Options Customize Form	Changes the form from being used as a form so you can make changes to it
Data Form Options Name Query	Assigns a name to a query in a form and makes that query the one currently used
Data New Form	Creates a database form using a database you select

Data Query	Finds matching records in a database and even copies them to another location
Data Sort	Sorts a database according to the keys you select
Data View Form	Makes a database form current or renames it
shift-enter	Clears the entries in a database so you can enter a new record

13

Advanced Techniques

1-2-3 has several advanced features that you will want to add to your toolkit of 1-2-3 skills. One of these features is Backsolve, which finds the value in one cell that produces the result that you specify. This lets you work backward through a problem.

1-2-3 also lets you add drawings to a worksheet. These drawings can be simple lines, shapes and text, or images you have created with other applications. You can also use this feature to further enhance the graphs you have created and placed on your worksheet.

By now you are probably an expert at the basic features for opening and closing your worksheets. These commands are the workhorses of the commands in the File menu because they play a central role in every worksheet session. A number of other document-management commands are used less commonly but provide powerful options that you will want to incorporate into your set of skills. These include dividing worksheets into multiple worksheets and combining them. You can also share data between 1-2-3 and other applications. Together, these commands provide ways to increase productivity by letting you reuse existing data rather than reenter it.

In this chapter, you learn to develop and solve a problem with Backsolve. Also, you learn to add drawings to your worksheet. Then you learn to extract part of a worksheet to another worksheet. This feature lets you create a new worksheet that starts off with account names or end-of-period totals, for example. You learn to combine worksheets, which lets you combine an entire or a range of data with the current worksheet. Finally, you explore the procedures for transferring data from 1-2-3 into other programs and transferring data from other programs into 1-2-3, including transferring data between 1-2-3 for the Macintosh and 1-2-3 for DOS.

Backsolve

You use Backsolve when you need to know the value of one cell that returns the results you want in another cell. Backsolve is like a spreadsheet version of the game Jeopardy, where you provide the answer and have 1-2-3 find the initial value that will return the result you want.

Setting Up a Problem for Backsolve

You must create the worksheet Backsolve will use before trying to invoke it. The creation process includes deciding the cell that contains the value Backsolve will change, creating the formulas that use that cell to calculate another result.

As an example of a problem that you can work with Backsolve, suppose you want profits of $100,000 but you do not know how many units you must sell to achieve that profit level. Rather than working backward through the income calculations, you can have 1-2-3 find the number of units to sell. To set up a worksheet to use with Backsolve like the one shown in Figure 13-1, follow these steps:

1. Make the following entries:

A1:	**Unit Sales**	C1:	**100000**
A2:	**Unit Price**	C2:	**5**
A3:	**Sales**	C3:	**+C1*C2**
A4:	**Cost of Goods Sold**	C4:	**+2.83*C1+150000**
A5:	**Gross Profit**	C5:	**+C3-C4**

A6:	**Operating Expenses**	C6:	**400000**
A7:	**Operating Income**	C7:	**+C5-C6**
A8:	**Taxes**	C8:	**+C7*.4**
A9:	**Net Income**	C9:	**+C7-C8**

The formulas in column C calculate the sales and costs. For costs, there is a 2.83 cost for each unit produced plus $150,000 of fixed production costs (costs that do not change with volume) and $400,000 operating expenses. The taxes reduce the operating income by 40%.

2. **Choose Global Settings from the Worksheet menu, select Currency in the Format pop-up menu, type 0 in the text box, and select the OK button.**
3. **Move to column C, select Column Width in the Worksheet menu, type 10 in the text box, and select the OK button or drag the right edge of column C one character to the right.**
4. **Select C1, select Format in the Range menu, Comma in the list box, and the OK button.**

Figure 13-1. *Worksheet setup for Backsolve*

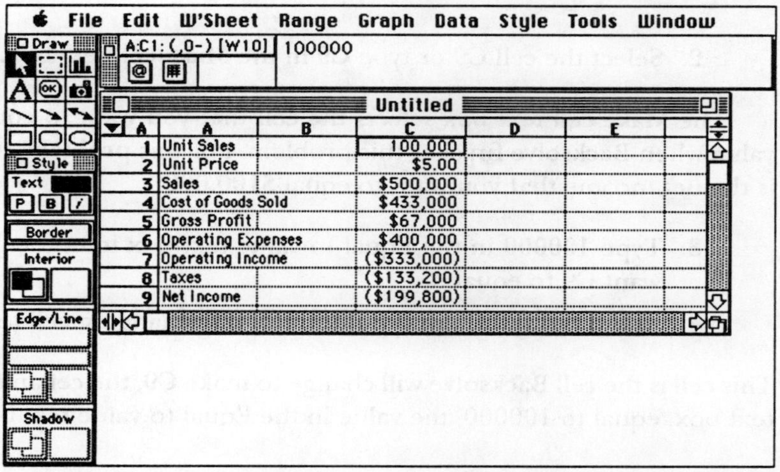

5. Select C2, choose $1,234.12 in the Range menu to format this cell as currency with two decimal digits.

At this point, your entries look like the ones in Figure 13-1 and you are ready to use Backsolve.

Solving a Problem

Once you enter the information Backsolve will use to solve the problem, you are ready to use the Backsolve command in the Tools menu. To try this with the problem you have created, follow these steps:

1. Choose Backsolve from the Tools menu to display this dialog box:

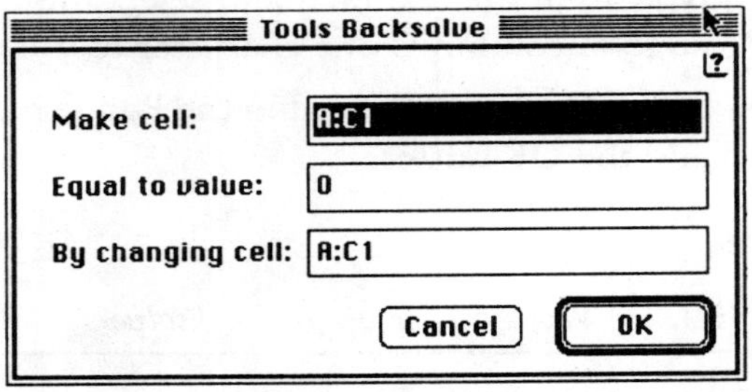

2. Select the cell C9 or type **C9** in the Make cell text box.

The Make cell text box selects the cell that you want to equal a specific value when Backsolve finishes this problem. For this problem, it is C9 which is the net income that you want to equal $100,000.

3. Type **100000** in the Equal to value text box to enter the value you want C9 to equal.
4. Select the cell C1 or type **C1** in the By changing cell text box.

This cell is the cell Backsolve will change to make C9, the cell in the Make cell text box, equal to 100000, the value in the Equal to value text box.

5. Select the OK button.

1-2-3 solves the problem and displays the new value in C1 with all of the formulas adjusted to use this new value as shown in Figure 13-2.

6. Choose Save in the File menu, type **Backsolve** in the Save As text box, and select the Save button to save the worksheet.

Drawing on a Worksheet

1-2-3 lets you draw on the worksheet. The Draw palette includes tools that let you draw lines, arrows, ovals, and rectangles. You can also add text boxes which are text that is separate from worksheet entries and are treated like graphical objects. These graphical objects can also use the Style palette and

Figure 13-2. *Solution from Backsolve*

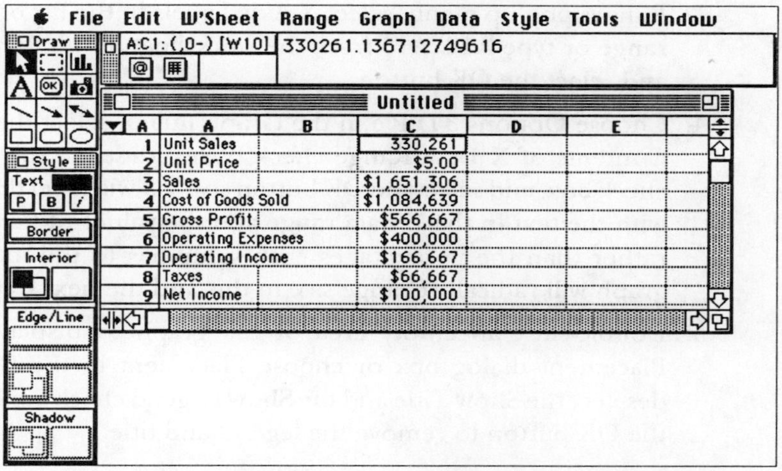

the Style commands that you learned about in Chapter 6, "Changing the Appearance of Worksheet Entries," to change the color of the object, line style or other feature shown in the Style palette or Style menu.

1. Make the following entries:

A12:	**Cost of Goods Sold**	C12:	**@ROUND(C4,0)**
A13:	**Net Income**	C13:	**@ROUND(C9,0)**
A14:	**Operating Expenses**	C14:	**@ROUND(C6,0)**
A15:	**Taxes**	C15:	**@ROUND(C8,0)**

The @ROUND function which you saw in Chapter 4, "@Functions and Other Formula Options," rounds a number to have a specific number of digits after the decimal point. The first argument this function expects is the number to round and the second number is the number of digits you want after the decimal point.

2. Select the range C12..C15 as the worksheet data you want in the graph, choose New Graph in the Graph menu, and select the 3-D pie graph, which is the last one on the third row.
3. Choose Ranges in the Graph menu, select Individually in the Assign Ranges pop-up menu, select X-Axis Labels in the list box, select the range or type **A12..A15** from the worksheet in the Range text box, and select the OK button.
4. Choose Options 3-D Pie in the Graph menu, select the Values and Contents of X Data Range check boxes, deselect the Percentages check box, and select the OK button so 1-2-3 will label the pie wedges with the text in the X data range and the values of the pie wedges, rather than the percentages each value has to the total (your pie graph will radically change size in this and the next step).
5. Double-click an empty area of the graph to display the Graph Placement dialog box or choose Placement in the Graph menu, deselect the Show Title and the Show Legend check boxes, and select the OK button to remove the legend and title.

If you accidentally get the wrong dialog box, select the Cancel button and try again.

6. Double-click the graph's frame to display the Style Frame dialog box or choose Frame in the Style menu, select None in the Edge pop-up menu and select the OK button to remove the graph's frame.

After making the graph's changes, you will need to move it, so it is not on top of the worksheet entries you want to show, and enlarge it, so you can see all the graph's text.

7. Move the pointer to the upper-left handle and drag this handle to A10.
8. Move the pointer to the lower-right handle and drag it to F19 so your graph looks like Figure 13-3.

Applications: *Use drawing to focus attention on important information. Lines and arrows can direct a reader's attention to the important information quickly.*

Figure 13-3. *Data for the first quarter*

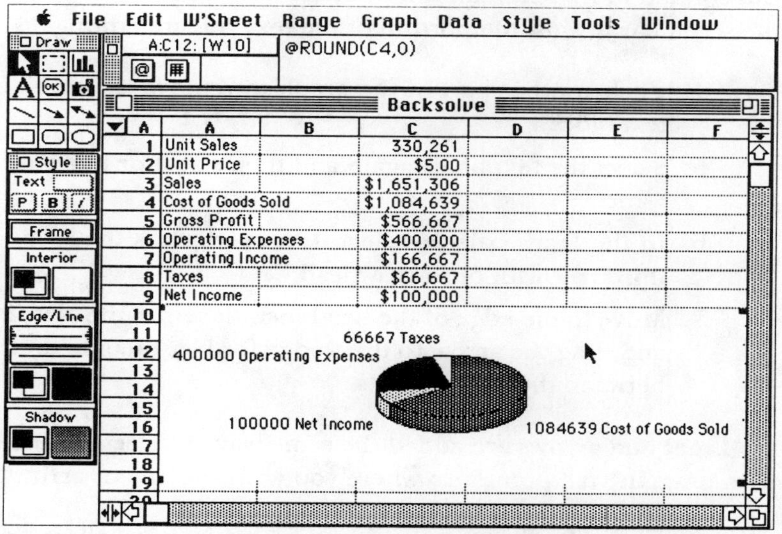

Now that you have text and a graph on your worksheet, you can add drawings to the worksheet. You can add drawings to worksheet entries or to graphs. Try these steps to add some drawings to your worksheet:

1. Select Text, which is the A icon in the Draw palette.
2. Draw a box by moving to the left edge of the graph below 100000 Net Income and dragging the box's outline to the bottom of the graph to the right of 100000 Net Income.

1-2-3 displays a *text block* that you can use to enter the text that this text block contains. A text block is separate from worksheet entries so you can size and move the text block just as you would size and move the graph.

3. Type **Net Income is just 6% of Sales** in the text block.

If your text block is not wide enough to fit the text on one line, 1-2-3 will wrap it onto other lines. You can later change the size and position of the text block just as you change the size and position of a graph, since a text block is a graphic added to a worksheet rather than a worksheet entry. A text block can contain more text than can fit in the size you have selected. You can use the scroll bar to shift the portion of the text you are editing.

4. Click another part of the graph to remove the scroll bar from the text block.
5. Select the text block again and then size it or move it to where you want.
6. In the Draw palette, select Arrow, which is the second one in the third row with one arrowhead.
7. Move to the edge of the text block closest to the Net Income wedge and drag the arrow to the wedge for Net Income to draw an arrow between these two points.

Lines and arrows are added the same way by selecting one location and then dragging the pointer to where you want the line or arrow to end.

8. In the Draw palette, select the oval icon, which is the oval in the lower-right corner of the Draw palette.

9. Move to below and to the left of the grid line around 100000 in C9 and drag the box's outline to above and to the right of C9.

1-2-3 draws an oval to fit the size of the box you have selected. This is also how you add rectangles and rounded rectangles, which are available in the bottom row of the Draw palette. The problem with this oval is that it now hides the entry in C9. Since this object is still selected, you can use the Style palette to change the oval's appearance, including using a thicker line and using the pattern None, which allows underlying worksheet entries to show through.

10. In the Style palette, select the Pattern button (the right one underneath Interior) and the None pattern, which is the first one in the second row.
11. In the Style palette, select the Edge button, immediately underneath Edge/Line and the second line thickness option, so your worksheet entries look like Figure 13-4.

Figure 13-4. *Worksheet after adding drawings*

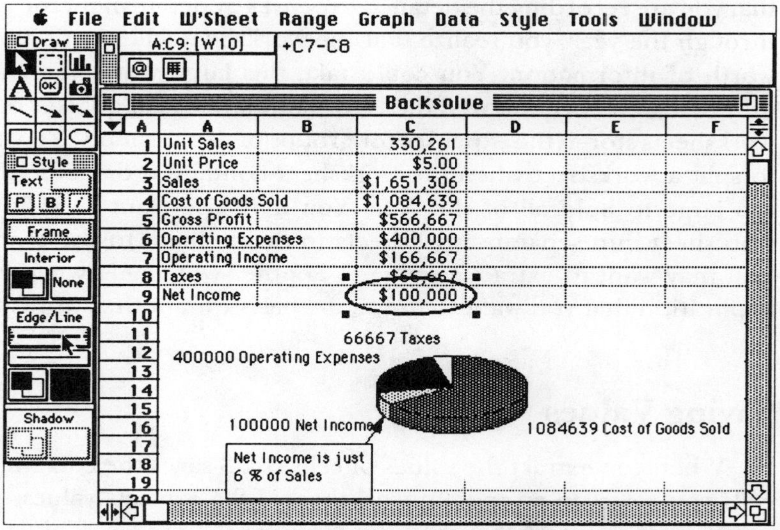

If your oval is too small, you can change its size by dragging one of the four handles to a new location.

12. Choose Save from the File menu to save the updated worksheet.

Saving a Section of the Worksheet

You can save a range in a worksheet to another worksheet. You have complete control over the amount of data that is saved to a worksheet. Saving part of a worksheet to another one with the Extract To command in the File menu lets you split the data between the different worksheets you want to create. When you extract data to a worksheet, you can save just the values in the selected range, or if you prefer, you can save the formulas. You will get the chance to try both so you can become familiar with some of the potential problems encountered when you save formulas.

You may wonder why you would want to save a portion of a current worksheet to a separate worksheet. You may want to do this when you are working on very large applications and are running out of memory. Suppose that you are recording the detailed expenses by department for 1992. Halfway through the year, you realize that the worksheet will not fit an entire year's worth of information. You could take this large worksheet and split it so different worksheets stored the information for each quarter or so different worksheets stored the expenses for groups of departments. You may also want to split a worksheet when the worksheet contains a database that is getting too large to hold all of the data. You may also want to split a multisheet worksheet into separate worksheets to divide them to use them separately. You may want to extract a range to another worksheet when you have one application that you want to use as the basis for another worksheet.

Saving Values

When you extract the values of cells, 1-2-3 saves the current values of the cells you select in a separate worksheet. 1-2-3 extracts values, text, and the results of formulas rather than the formulas themselves. This is a convenient way to put the result of calculations in a new worksheet. The extracted data is placed in the new worksheet beginning in cell A:A1. The data in the extracted worksheet retains the same size and shape as in the current worksheet, although each cell's addresses are determined by its offset from the beginning of the range.

You can try extracting entries to another worksheet with the Backsolve worksheet. Although these entries are not enough data to cause a condition of insufficient memory, the concept and potential actions required are exactly the same as you would need with much larger worksheets. Follow these steps to extract the values of a range:

1. Select the range A3..C7 as the range to extract.
2. Choose Extract To from the File menu.

This dialog box has most of the same options as the Save command in the File menu. 1-2-3 provides a default name unless you enter another one in the Save Selected Range As text box. The Convert Formulas To Values check box determines whether formulas in the selected range are saved as formulas or as their values.

3. Type **Sales Values** in the Save Selected Range As text box, select the Convert Formulas To Values check box, and select the Extract button.

The current values of the selected cells are written to the new worksheet, Sales Values.

4. Choose Open from the File menu, select Sales Values in the list box, and select the Open button to display this worksheet:

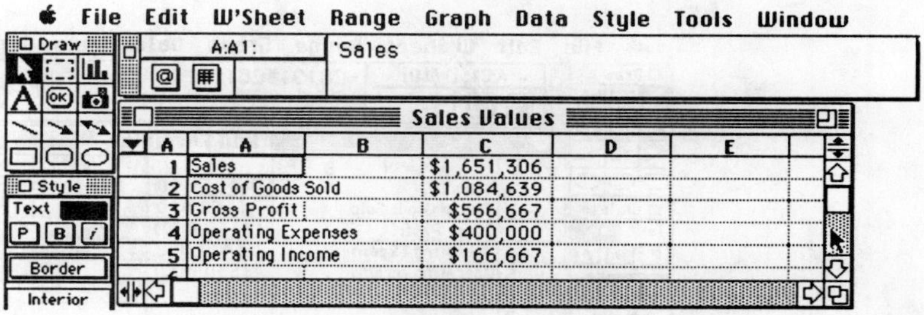

5. Move to the cells in column C.

As you move to each cell you can see how they no longer contain formulas but contain values instead. For example, C2 contains the value $1,084,639 rather than the formula 2.83*C1+150000.

6. Click the close box to close the Sales Values worksheet.

Saving Formulas

Saving formulas is just as easy as saving values, but before you save formulas when you extract the worksheet data, you must consider whether you are copying the entries the formulas use. If you save the formulas without the data they need, the formulas may return erroneous results. You extract entries and the formulas when you are extracting the entries the formula uses. Follow these steps to extract formulas:

1. Select A3..C7 as the range to extract.
2. Choose Extract To from the File menu, type **Bad Formulas** in the Save Selected Range As text box, and select the Extract button.

1-2-3 extracts values, text, and the formulas. 1-2-3 adjusts any references in formulas in the new worksheet just as if you had copied the selected entries to a new worksheet.

3. Choose Open from the File menu, select Bad Formulas from the list box, and select the Open button.
4. Move to C1 to see the worksheet as shown here:

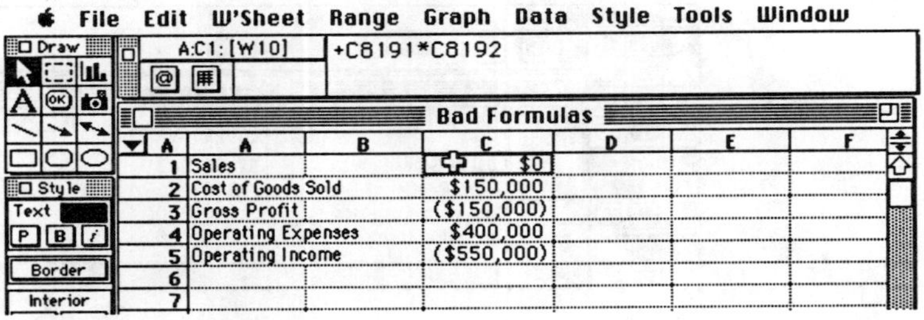

Notice that the formulas are adjusted for the new worksheet. Since you did not include the values the formulas use in the range to extract, these formulas are meaningless in the new worksheet. In this case, extracting values meets your needs better.

5. Click the close box to close the Bad Formulas worksheet.
6. Select the range A1..C7 as the range to extract.
7. Choose Extract To from the File menu, type **Good Formulas** in the Save Selected Range As text box, and select the Extract button.
8. Choose Open from the File menu, select Good Formulas in the list box, and select the Open button to display this worksheet:

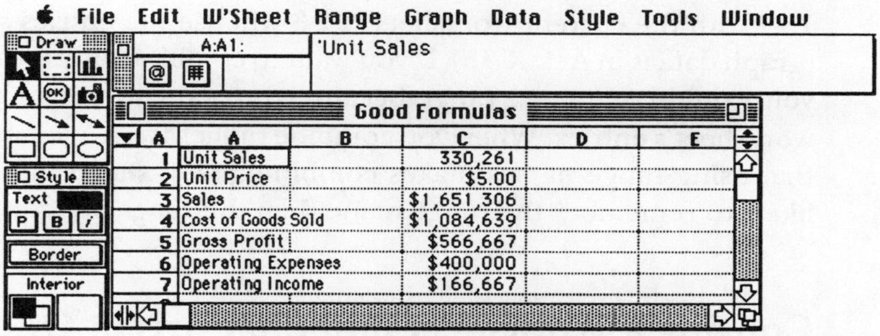

Notice that the formulas are useful because you included the values the formula uses. You extract formulas when you want to include the formulas in the new worksheet and you are including the data the formulas use in the range to extract.

9. Click the close box to close the Good Formulas worksheet.

Combining Data from Other Worksheets with Your Worksheet

1-2-3 lets you combine worksheets in three ways: you can replace the entries in one worksheet with entries in another, add values from one worksheet to another, or subtract values from one worksheet to another. You will have the opportunity to try the three ways of combining data. You can use this command to total subsidiary worksheets or to subtract a division's contribution from the total. The File Combine From command provides the perfect solution for adding and subtracting values from other worksheets; using this command does not destroy the formulas in the current worksheet as you bring the values from other worksheets.

You have two options when combining a worksheet with the current one—to combine everything in the worksheet or to combine a range from the worksheet. The option you choose depends on whether the worksheet contains other information that you do not want to combine. When you combine an entire worksheet, everything in the worksheet you select is combined with the current worksheet. For example, if you want to combine the data in Figure 13-4 with the current worksheet, 1-2-3 will use the entries stored in A1..C15 (graph data is in A12..C15). If you want to combine only the entries in A1..C3, you would combine a range because you want to use only a subset of the worksheet's entries. When you combine ranges from worksheets, you will find that using range names makes combining worksheets easier; you are more likely to remember the range name than the range address.

Copying a Worksheet into the Current One

One of the easiest combinations you can use is replacing the entries in the current worksheet with the entries in another worksheet. To try this feature, you will want to name a range to replace and create a new worksheet to use with the data from the named range. Follow these steps to modify the Backsolve worksheet and then create a new worksheet to replace current entries as you combine them:

1. Select the range A1..C3, choose Create in the Range pop-up menu, type **Product A** in the Create Range Name text box, and select the OK button.

2. Select the range C1..C3, choose Create from the Range pop-up menu, type **Prod A Numbers** in the Create Range Name text box, and select the OK button.

Later you will see how 1-2-3 handles text, values, and formulas when you combine a range.

3. Choose Save from the File menu to save the worksheet with the range names you have created.
4. Click the close box or press ⌘-W to close the Backsolve worksheet.
5. Choose New from the File menu to open a new worksheet.
6. Move to C2, type **"Product A**, and then move to A3 to be the first cell where you want to combine the Backsolve worksheet with this one.

The active cell when you combine worksheets is very important. The active cell determines the cell in the current worksheet that is combined with the first cell from the incoming worksheet (if you are combining an entire worksheet) or the first cell in the range (if you are combining a range).

7. Choose Combine From in the File menu, select Backsolve from the list of worksheets, and select the Combine button.

1-2-3 replaces the current worksheet's entries with the contents of the Backsolve worksheet. Since A3 was the active cell, 1-2-3 starts making the replacements in this cell and shifts the remaining entries from the Backsolve worksheet. The worksheet's graphics are not combined. Besides combining an entire worksheet, you can also combine a range.

8. Choose Undo in the Edit menu to remove the replaced entries.
9. Choose Combine From in the File menu, select Backsolve in the list box, select Range in the Include pop-up menu, type **Product A** in the Range to Combine text box, select the OK button and then the Combine button.
10. Move to C5 to display the worksheet and its formulas as shown here:

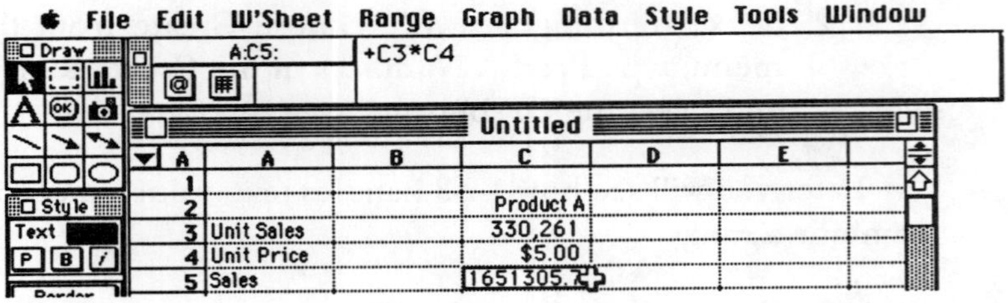

1-2-3 replaces the current worksheet's entries with the contents of the Product A range in the Backsolve worksheet. Since A3 was the active cell, 1-2-3 starts making the replacements in this cell and displaces the entries from the Product A range from this point. Using the Combine From command when you replace entries has the same effect as copying the entries to the Clipboard and then pasting them in the new worksheet. This combination brings in text, values, and formulas from the incoming worksheet.

11. Select the range C3..C5 and choose Clear from the Edit menu.

Adding a Worksheet to the Current Worksheet

The Adding option of the Combine From command in the File menu adds the values of the incoming worksheet to the values in the current worksheet. Which values are added is determined by the active cell's position and the placement of the values within the incoming worksheet. When you add values, 1-2-3 ignores text in the incoming worksheet, and any formulas in the current worksheet are not changed. Any formulas in the incoming worksheet are added as values at the time you add the two worksheets. Follow these steps to try adding worksheets:

1. Move to C3 to be where the data is combined.
2. Choose Combine From in the File menu, select Backsolve in the list box, select Range in the Include pop-up menu, type **Product A** in the Range to Combine text box, select the OK button, and select Adding in the Combine By pop-up menu.

3. Select the Combine button to add the range named Product A to the current worksheet starting at C3 as shown here:

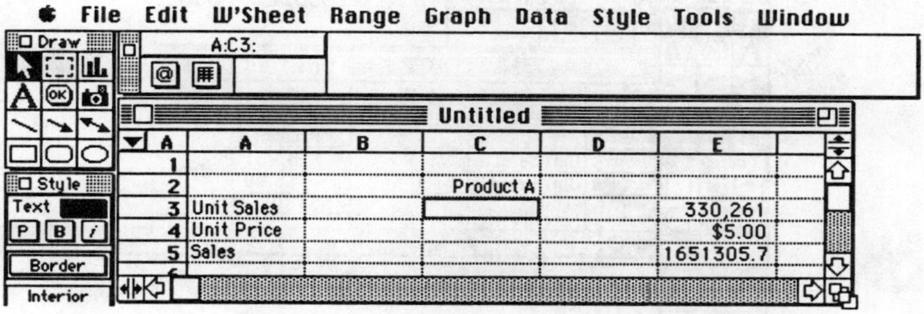

Since the text in A1..A3 is included in the range Product A, you should have selected the cell A3 since 1-2-3 ignores these text entries when it adds the worksheets. Making the active cell A3 would have caused the first value in the named range to match with C3.

4. Choose Undo in the Edit menu to remove the added range and return the worksheet to the way it was before you added the named range.
5. Move to A3.
6. Choose Combine From in the File menu, select Backsolve in the list box, select Range in the Include pop-up menu, type **Product A** in the Range to Combine text box, select the OK button, select Adding in the Combine By pop-up menu, and select the Combine button to add the worksheets.
7. Move to C5 to see the worksheet as shown in Figure 13-5.

The entry in C5 is a value, rather than the formula that produced the value. Adding and subtracting worksheets converts formulas to their values. These values are added or subtracted, rather than the formulas. Try this again to see if it really adds. This time, instead of using the Product A range name, we will use Prod A Numbers. Since the first cell in this named range contains the first value to add, the active cell should be C3 instead of A3.

Figure 13-5. *Adding data to the worksheet with Combine From in the File menu*

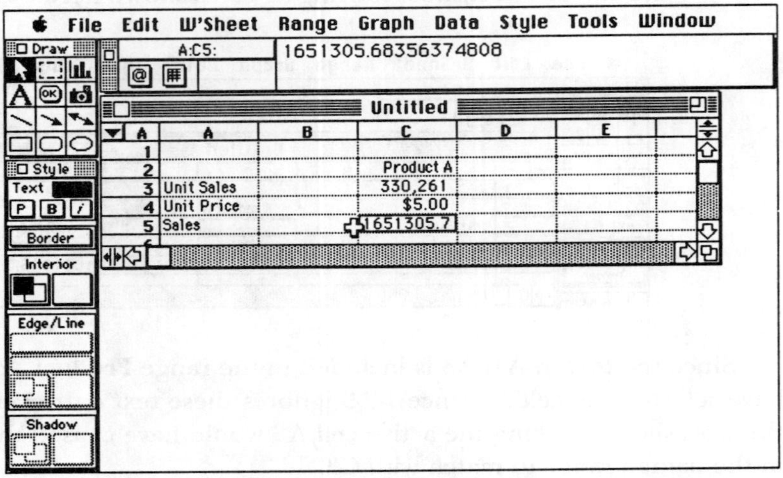

8. Move to C3, choose Combine From in the File menu, select Back-solve in the list box, select Range in the Include pop-up menu, type **Prod A Numbers** in the Range to Combine text box, select the OK button, select Adding in the Combine By pop-up menu, and select the Combine button.
9. Move to C5 to see the doubled values as shown here:

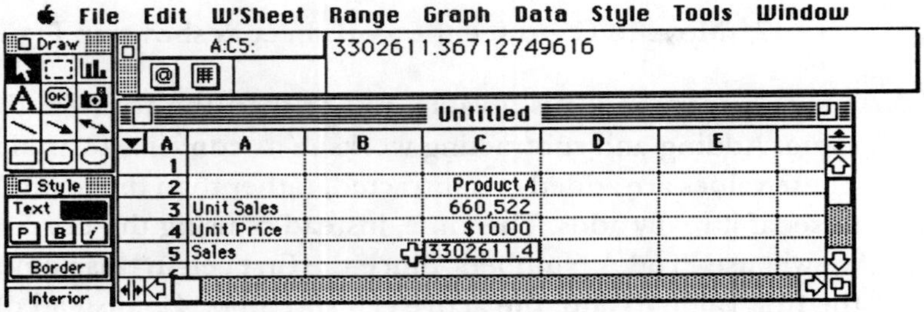

You can see that each of the numbers in the current worksheet doubled as the numbers on the worksheet were added to the current worksheet.

Applications: *Use the Adding option of Combine From to consolidate data from several products, branches, or geographic locations.*

Subtracting from the Current Worksheet

The subtraction option of the Combine From command in the File menu is the exact opposite of the addition option. It subtracts the values stored on disk from the current worksheet cells. This option depends on the active cell's location and the offset within the worksheet that controls which numbers will be subtracted from which entries. You can try this by subtracting the values you have stored in the Backsolve worksheet from the current worksheet:

1. Move to C3, choose Combine From in the File menu, select Backsolve in the list box, select Range in the Include pop-up menu, type **Prod A Numbers** in the Range to Combine text box, select the OK button, select Subtracting in the Combine By pop-up menu, and select the Combine button.

The worksheet now looks like the one in Figure 13-5. Each of the entries returned to its original value from the first addition combination as the subtract operation was completed.

2. Click the close box to close the worksheet and select No to omit saving this worksheet.

Applications: *Use the Subtracting option in Combine From to evaluate what would happen to expenses and profits if you closed a branch or discontinued a product.*

Transferring Data Between Applications

Sharing data between applications can provide a significant savings in data-entry time. If you have account names, employee numbers, inventory items, or other lists of data in a document for one application and need the same information in another application, why retype it when you can transfer the data directly from the document? If you transfer the data, you are assured of data consistency between the two applications.

You may want to take data from another application and bring it into 1-2-3. 1-2-3, like most Macintosh applications, can put data onto the Clipboard and take data from the Clipboard and put it into one of its documents, a worksheet. You can also bring into 1-2-3 text documents and export worksheet data as text documents. You can try the different import and export options with 1-2-3.

Sharing Data Between 1-2-3 and Other Applications

In Chapter 9, "Making 1-2-3 Do Your Work," you learned how to copy and move data with the Clipboard within the worksheet. The Clipboard remembers not only the contents of the Clipboard data in 1-2-3, but also as you switch to other applications. This means you can put data onto the Clipboard in one application and paste it into another. Most Macintosh applications have some of the same commands including the Copy, Cut, and Paste commands in their Edit menu to share data with the Clipboard. To try transferring text and graphics with 1-2-3 and another application, follow these steps:

1. Choose Open in the File menu, select Backsolve in the list box, and select the Open button.
2. Select the range A1..C9 and choose Copy from the Edit menu (or press ⌘-C) to copy these entries to the Clipboard.
3. Choose Quit in the File menu to leave 1-2-3.
4. Double-click TeachText (it may be in a folder like Accessories or the main disk folder, which you will have to open first).

If you do not have TeachText, open another word processor.

5. Choose Paste in the Edit menu to copy the worksheet entries into the TeachText document as shown here:

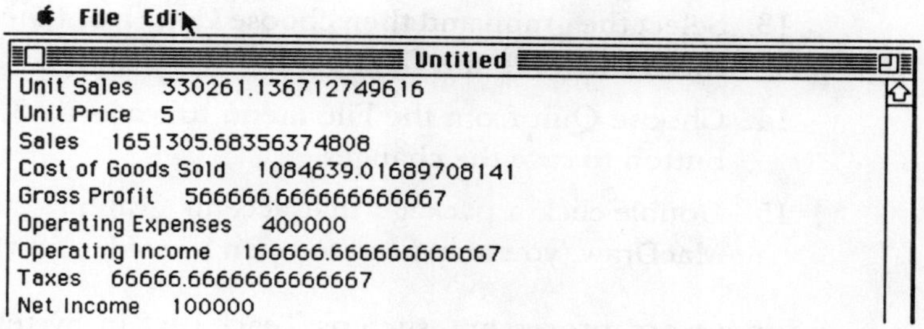

6. Press (return) twice and type the following entries, pressing (return) after each one.

   During the next year, the following improvements are planned:

   Redesigning 15 products to reduce moveable parts and reduce assembly time

   Expand distribution to include wholesale outlets

7. Select the three lines you have just typed by dragging the mouse over them.
8. Choose Copy from the Edit menu to copy this text to the Clipboard.
9. Choose Save in the File menu, type Transfer Data in the Save As text box, and select the Save button to save the TeachText document.

These instructions apply to most Macintosh word processors.

10. Choose Quit in the File menu to leave TeachText.
11. Select the Lotus 1-2-3 folder and double-click Backsolve (assuming Backsolve is in the Lotus 1-2-3 folder) to open the Backsolve worksheet in 1-2-3.
12. Select D1 and choose Paste in the Edit menu to copy the text you have copied from TeachText as shown here:

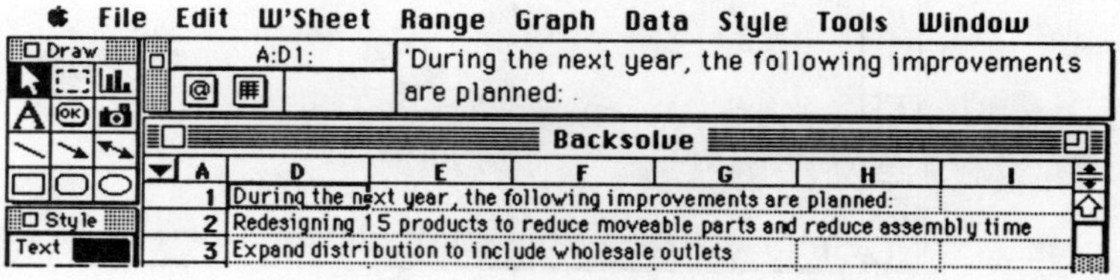

13. Select the graph and then choose Copy from the Edit menu to copy these entries to the Clipboard.
14. Choose Quit from the File menu to leave 1-2-3, and select the Yes button to save the changes.
15. Double-click a package that accepts graphics such as MacPaint or MacDraw (you may need to open its folder first).

Some word processors, such as TeachText in System 7 and Microsoft Word, can also incorporate graphics. Other programs may also accept graphic images so you can try and find out which of your applications will accept graphics from the Clipboard.

16. Choose Paste from the Edit menu to paste the graph into this application as in Figure 13-6.

Figure 13-6. *Graph copied to another application using the Clipboard*

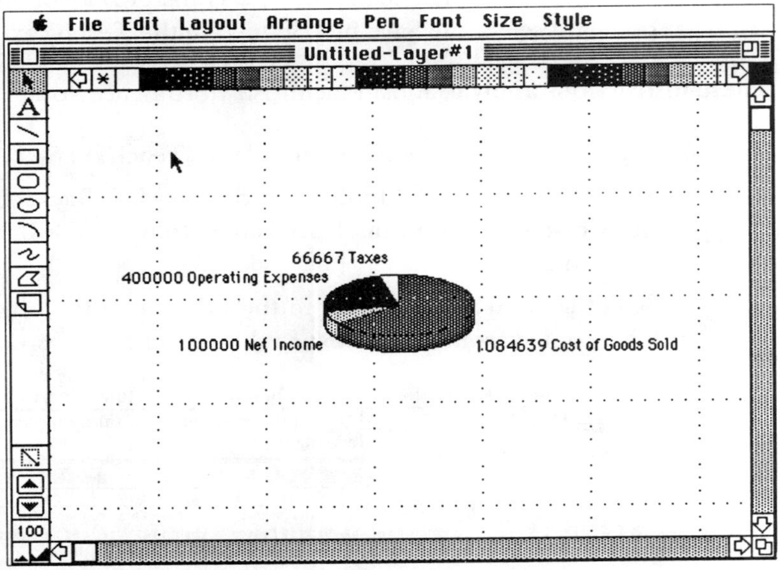

The application you paste the graphics to will determine how the pasted graphics appears so your graph may look different than Figure 13-6.

17. Choose Quit in the File menu to leave the application and select the No button to omit saving the document.

If you have created graphics in another package, you can also copy them to the Clipboard and then paste them from the Clipboard into a worksheet.

Sharing Worksheets Between 1-2-3 for the Macintosh and 1-2-3 for DOS

1-2-3 for the Macintosh and 1-2-3 for DOS can also share data. This allows you to transfer your data from one machine to another. The steps to bring

Translating from 1-2-3 for DOS to 1-2-3 for the Macintosh

Follow these steps to translate a 1-2-3 for DOS worksheet that you have copied to a 3 1/2-inch disk formatted by DOS:

1. Double-click Apple File Exchange after opening its folder.
2. In the left list box, select the folder where you want the translated worksheet placed.
3. Put your DOS formatted 3 1/2-inch disk in the drive.
4. Select the worksheet to translate in the right list box.
5. Select the Translate button.
6. Choose Quit in the File menu to leave Apple File Exchange.
7. Activate the Lotus 1-2-3 folder and select Lotus 1-2-3.
8. Choose Open in the File menu, select All Types in the Show pop-up menu, select the worksheet in the list box, and select the Open button.

your 1-2-3 for DOS worksheets to 1-2-3 for the Macintosh are listed in the box, "Translating from 1-2-3 for DOS to 1-2-3 for the Macintosh."

If you want to transfer a worksheet from the Macintosh to 1-2-3 for DOS, you need to save the worksheet in a format that 1-2-3 for DOS will accept and then use the Apple File Exchange application to copy this document from the Macintosh to an IBM 3 1/2-inch disk. To export data from 1-2-3 for the Macintosh to 1-2-3 on a DOS-based machine, you must follow several steps.

1. Select the Lotus 1-2-3 folder and double-click Backsolve (this assumes Backsolve is in the Lotus 1-2-3 folder) to open the Backsolve worksheet in 1-2-3.
2. Choose Save As in the File menu, type **123 DOS** in the Save As text box, select 123 DOS (.wk1) in the File Type pop-up menu, and select the Save button.

1-2-3 for the Macintosh adds .WK1, which is the extension that releases 2.01, 2.2, and 2.3 of 1-2-3 for DOS use.

3. Choose Quit in the File menu to leave 1-2-3.
4. Double-click Apple File Exchange (it may be in a folder like Accessories or MacLink Plus, which you will have to open first) to open a window like the one shown in Figure 13-7.
5. Put your DOS formatted 3 1/2-inch disk in the drive.

If you have a SuperDrive in your Macintosh and the disk has two holes in it, you can format the disk as 1.44MB for your IBM PC. If the drive in your Mac is not a SuperDrive, it formats the disk as 720K. This disk must be formatted with DOS, rather than with the Macintosh.

6. Select the Lotus 1-2-3 folder and the 123 DOS.WK1 document in the left list box (this assumes your worksheets are stored in the Lotus 1-2-3 folder, if the worksheet documents are in another location, you will need to select the folders leading to the document before you select 123 DOS.WK1).
7. Select the Translate button.

Figure 13-7. *Apple File Exchange*

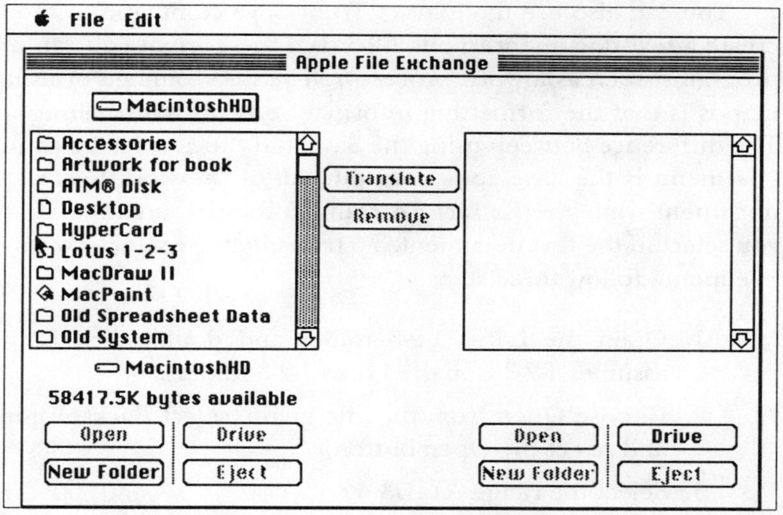

The Apple File Exchange converts and copies the worksheet to the DOS disk. The worksheet's name may be changed to fit within DOS restrictions. This includes removing spaces and other invalid characters and truncating the name after eight characters.

8. Repeat steps 7 and 8 for each worksheet you want to translate.

If all of your worksheets that you want to translate are in a folder, you can select the folder in step 7. Then the Apple File Exchange will create a subdirectory on the DOS disk that contains the translated worksheets.

9. Choose Quit in the File menu to leave Apple File Exchange.

Applications: *If you check with friends and business associates, you may find that they have hundreds of 1-2-3 for DOS worksheets. They may let you use them as the basis for your Macintosh applications to give you a quick start on making new Macintosh applications. If you want to use worksheets created by other Macintosh applications, you can do this by using the Open command and then selecting the document (1-2-3 can translate many worksheets directly).*

Extracting to a Text File

You can also use the Extract To or Save command in the File menu to create a text document to put 1-2-3 data in a format you can use with other programs, such as a word processor. The disadvantage of using these commands is that the formatting information is not saved along with the data. The difference between using the Save and the Extract To commands in the File menu is the Save command puts all of the worksheet data into a text document while the Extract To command only puts the data from a range you select in the text document. To try using the Extract To command in the File menu, follow these steps:

1. Open the Lotus 1-2-3 folder and double-click Lotus 1-2-3 (this assumes 1-2-3 is in the Lotus 1-2-3 folder).
2. Choose Open from the File menu, select Backsolve in the list box and select the Open button.
3. Select the range A1..D3.
4. Choose Extract To from the File menu, select Text in the File Type pop-up menu, type **Text** in the Save Selected Range As text box, and select the Extract button.
5. Choose Quit in the File menu to leave 1-2-3.
6. Select the folder containing TeachText (or another word processor) and double-click it.
7. Click the close box to close the empty document.
8. Choose Open from the File menu, select the hard disk name in the pop-up menu above the list box, select the Lotus 1-2-3 folder in the list box, select Text in the list box, and select the Open button to display the results shown here:

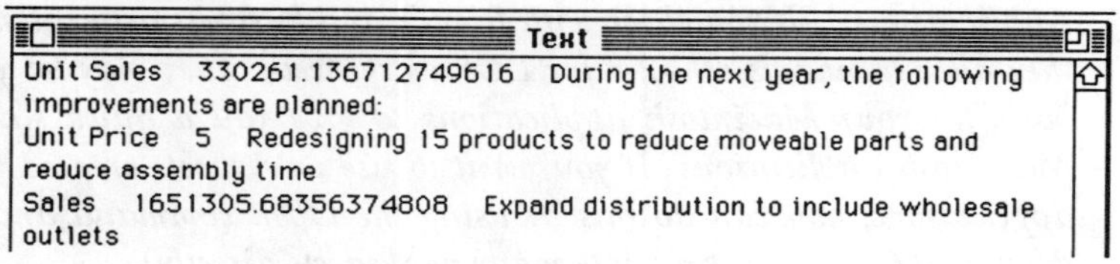

9. Choose Quit in the File menu to leave TeachText.

You could have used the Save command in the File menu to put all of the worksheet entries in a text document. If you had done so, the only difference in the steps you would perform is you would not select a range before you selected Save command in the File menu.

Bringing Text Files into a Worksheet

If you have data in a text document, you can bring it into 1-2-3 for the Macintosh by importing it. Regardless of how you create the document, bringing in a text document into 1-2-3 has two options: putting each line of text into a single cell or dividing a line of information into separate cells. You can only use the second option if you are importing columns of numbers. You can try this using the text document you created in the previous section. Since the Text document you have created contains more information than a column of numbers, you will want to bring each line in as a single cell into the worksheet. To try this, follow these steps:

1. Select the Lotus 1-2-3 folder and double-click Lotus 1-2-3.
2. Choose Import From in the File menu, select Text in the list box, and select the Import button to create these results:

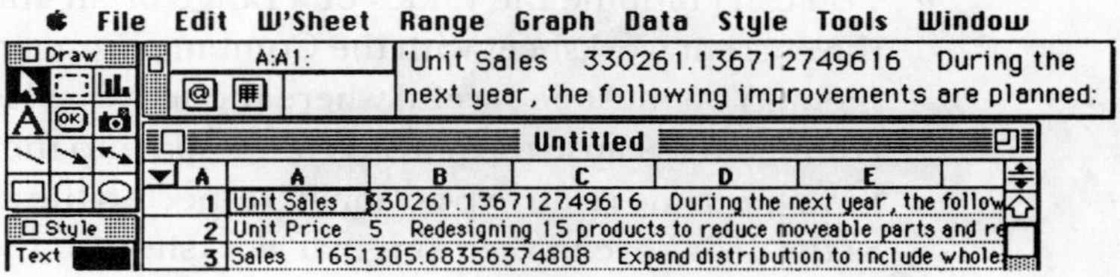

You can also open text documents using the Open command in the File menu. To do this, choose Open in the File menu, select Text in the Show pop-up menu, select the text document in the list box, and select the Open button. You will then have another dialog box to select the Import into a single column radio button and the OK button to open a new worksheet with the text document.

Review

In this chapter you learned how to use the Backsolve feature, add drawings to a worksheet, save sections of a worksheet, combine worksheets, and transfer data between applications. The topics you covered include the following:

- The Backsolve command from the Tools menu works backward through a worksheet to adjust one cell so another cell contains a desired result.
- You can use the Draw palette to add enhancements, such as lines, arrows, text, and shapes to the worksheet. These shapes can be subsequently modified using the commands in the Style menu and Style palette. These objects can be positioned and sized just as you would move or size a graph on the worksheet.
- You can extract a portion of a worksheet to another worksheet with the Extract To command in the File menu. This command copies either values (formulas are converted to their values in the new worksheet) or formulas (formulas remain intact). You should extract formulas only if the cells the formulas reference are part of the range extracted to the new worksheet. Once a worksheet is extracted, you can open it and use it just as you do other worksheets.
- You can combine the values of a range or an entire worksheet into the current worksheet with the Combine From command in the File menu. You must be careful where the active cell is when you use this command because the entries combined into the current worksheet have the same relative position in respect to the active cell's position as the cells have in their original worksheet to the upper-left corner of the range or worksheet. You can combine worksheets by replacing entries, adding them, or subtracting them.
- 1-2-3 can share data with other applications. You can use the Clipboard to copy data to and from worksheets and other Macintosh applications. The data you share can be text, numbers, formulas, or graphics.

- You can share your worksheets with IBM-compatible computers using the Apple File Exchange utility, which copies documents between the Macintosh and a DOS formatted disk.
- 1-2-3 can create and import (bring in) text documents from another computer program if the other computer program can produce a text document. You have learned how to import the data into a column of long text entries for each line in the document.

Keys and Commands

The commands and features you learned accessed more advanced features of 1-2-3. These commands and keys are

Entry	Action
Edit Copy	Copies selected data or graph object to the Clipboard
Edit Paste	Pastes data from the Clipboard into the current application
File Combine From	Adds, replaces, or subtracts range or worksheet data from another worksheet to the current worksheet
File Extract To	Copies a range to a new worksheet or text document
File Import From	Brings data from a text document into 1-2-3
Tools Backsolve	Finds the value of a cell that makes another cell equal a specific value

14

Macros

A *macro* is a list of instructions that performs a series of tasks upon a single request. Many 1-2-3 users are intimidated by macros. They may have heard about the failures that others have experienced when attempting to use them. However, if you use the step-by-step approach presented in this chapter, you have no need for concern. There is no reason why you cannot be just as successful with macros as you are with 1-2-3's commands in the pull-down menus.

In their simplest form, macros are nothing more than a way to automate the selections you have been making from 1-2-3's menus. Such macros are referred to as *keyboard-alternative macros.* In their most complex form, macros provide an entire programming language with the special 1-2-3 command-language instructions. Attempting to use the most sophisticated form of macros without mastering the keyboard variety is a little like practicing diving before you have learned to swim—you could find yourself well over your head and doomed to failure.

This chapter focuses on keyboard-alternative macros and introduces them in a logical sequence to help you avoid problems. It presents a step-by-step approach for recording selections in the Macro Transcript window to ensure your success. The Macro Transcript window is a record of the steps you take in 1-2-3 as macro instructions. You learn how 1-2-3 for the Macintosh records menu selections, keystrokes, and mouse selections in the Macro Transcript window for replay or later copying to worksheet cells. You also learn 1-2-3's rules for naming macros and how you can execute the macro instructions stored on the worksheet. You create several ready-to-use macros that will be your foundation for creating macros that fit your particular needs.

Keyboard-Alternative Macros

Keyboard-alternative macros are nothing more than a column of text entries that have a range name assigned to them. The contents of the text entries are macro instructions you want 1-2-3 to execute for you. After you copy the macro instructions to the worksheet from the Macro Transcript window or enter them directly in a column of worksheet cells, you name the first cell in the range.

When you save the worksheet on which you created a macro, you save the macro for later use. You can use a macro on any sheet or worksheet. This means that you can create a macro on one sheet and use it on another sheet. You can also perform on the current worksheet a macro that is stored in another open worksheet. This allows you to create a library of macros in a worksheet that you can use with all your other worksheets.

Keyboard-alternative macros provide a wealth of time-saving features. You can use them to automate printing, formatting, and any other 1-2-3 task. After you have learned the basics, you will want to examine the tasks you execute repeatedly. The more frequently a task is performed, the greater the potential reward of automating it with a macro. Some users find that data-management tasks such as sorting and extracting are the most important to automate; other users feel that printing and formatting have the highest priority because they use these commands most frequently. Although the macros in the remainder of the chapter have widespread applications, only you can decide which tasks offer you the greatest payback when automated.

Applications: Printing is a frequent application of macros, especially if you have several reports in a worksheet. Macros for each report can print the report with any specific changes to the print settings such as header and footer. This information is separate for each report.

Macro Building Blocks

The secret to creating macros that run correctly the first time you try them is having a structured approach that you use consistently for each macro you create. At first glance, the steps recommended here might seem unnecessarily time consuming; it might seem easier to type the macro instructions directly in a column of worksheet cells and run the macro. However, you will find that the Macro Transcript window's building-block approach guarantees immediate success and thereby avoids using time later to fix errors.

The first step for successful macros is to lay out a road map of where you want to go with the macro. This is nothing more than a mental plan or a few notes jotted down about what you want the macro to accomplish. Next, you can use the Macro Transcript window to record the macro instructions, and then use the Clipboard to copy the macro on the worksheet. You will know that the macro works correctly, since you will have tested it as the Macro Transcript window recorded it. Once the instructions are stored on the worksheet, you need to name them. Documenting the workings of the macro is an often overlooked step, but it can guarantee continued trouble-free execution and ease of future modification. Complete this step for every macro. Only then will you be ready to try your new macro. You can examine each of these steps more closely in the sections that follow.

Planning the Macro's Actions Before You Begin

You need to plan the actions a macro will take before trying the commands, keystrokes, and mouse selections. If you do not at least make a mental road map of what you want to accomplish, you will probably end up making many changes to the actions captured in the Macro Transcript window before you can use them. You can even jot a few notes on paper if it helps keep you on track for completing all aspects of the task. Proceeding to enter a macro without a plan is like going to the store without a list of what you need. As soon as you finish shopping, you remember what you forgot. You do not want to wait until your macro is recorded to begin thinking about what else it should do. The planning may be as simple as deciding that a macro will enter row headings or insert a row.

Using the Macro Transcript Window

You can use 1-2-3's Macro Transcript window to capture the keystrokes, menu selections and mouse selections (collectively called *actions*) for your keyboard alternative macros, rather than typing the macro instructions into worksheet cells yourself. This approach offers a couple of major advantages. First, you can try out your plan for a macro and have 1-2-3 record your entries. If you make a few mistakes, you do not need to start over; you can edit the entries in the Macro Transcript window with the same techniques you use for changing any entry. You can play back these instructions even before copying the entries to the worksheet. Second, you do not need to remember the macro keywords that 1-2-3 uses for keystrokes, commands, and other special 1-2-3 features. All you do is press the proper keys, move the mouse, and choose commands–1-2-3 records the actions correctly as macro instructions. To make recording macros easy for you, 1-2-3 automatically records all the actions you make. You do not need to tell 1-2-3 to start recording because 1-2-3 has been recording your actions since you started the 1-2-3 session. The Macro Transcript window contains all of your actions since you started 1-2-3 or since you told 1-2-3 to empty the Macro Transcript window. 1-2-3 records your actions as you open, alter, close, and switch between worksheets.

To use the Macro Transcript window to record a macro, you must follow several steps. First, you clear the current contents of the Macro Transcript window so you do not include your earlier recorded actions with the actions you want to record. Then you perform the actions you want 1-2-3 to record. Finally, you copy the instructions to the worksheet. You can try out this procedure with a macro that enters some headings in a column; any time you need the headings entered into a worksheet, you can use the macro you will create rather than retype the entries.

Activating the Macro Transcript Window

Since 1-2-3 records every action you make, you should clear the entries in the Macro Transcript window before you record the actions that you want in a macro. Perform this step at the beginning of the macro-recording process. Since the active cell can make a difference in how the macro performs, move to the cell where you want to begin recording the macro instructions before you clear the Macro Transcript window. To display and activate the Macro Transcript window and then clear the window's contents so you are ready to record a macro, follow these steps:

1. Choose Macro from the Tools menu and choose Show Transcript to display a Macro Transcript window that looks like this:

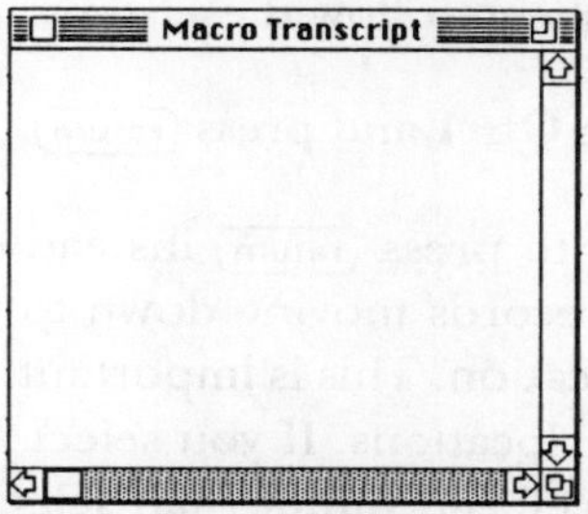

You may see entries already in this window. The entries are macro instructions for the actions you have made since you began this 1-2-3 session. As you record your macro, you will see 1-2-3 add instructions to the window.

2. Choose Arrange in the Window menu and then choose Vertical Tile to display the worksheet window and the Macro Transcript window side by side.

This allows you to watch 1-2-3 record macro instructions in the Macro Transcript window as you make entries in the worksheet. You do not need to see the Macro Transcript window to record macros, but having it visible as you record your first macros makes creating them easier.

3. Select A:A3 in the worksheet to move to the cell where you want to start recording the macro.

4. Choose Macro from the Tools menu and choose Clear Transcript to remove {Window-Arrange "vertical-tile"} and any other macro instructions in the Macro Transcript window.

The Macro Transcript window is now empty and ready to store a new set of macro instructions. Removing any old macro instructions prevents you from being confused about which of the macro instructions that appear in the window belong to the macro you want to create.

Recording a Macro

Once you clear the Macro Transcript window, you are ready to record the macro. To record the macro, perform the steps that you want recorded, and they will automatically appear in the Macro Transcript window. For the current worksheet, follow these steps:

1. Type **Qtr 1** and press (return).

You want to press (return) instead of clicking A4, since when you press (return), 1-2-3 records moving down to the next cell below, regardless of the active cell's location. This is important, since you may want to use this macro again in other locations. If you select A4 with the mouse, 1-2-3 records you selecting the cell A4, rather than selecting the next cell below. You can see from the Macro Transcript window that 1-2-3 is recording that you are making a cell entry and that you are moving down one cell. You will learn about these macro instructions later.

2. Type **Qtr 2** and press (return).
3. Type **Qtr 3** and press (return).
4. Type **Qtr 4** and press (return).
5. Type **Total** and press (return) so the Macro Transcript window and worksheet window look Figure 14-1.

Recording Macro Instructions

1-2-3 has a number of special *macro instructions* which record the actions you make. You have seen two of them with the macro you have just recorded. Most of them are recorded in the Macro Transcript window as you use the

Figure 14-1. *Worksheet and Macro Transcript windows after recording a macro*

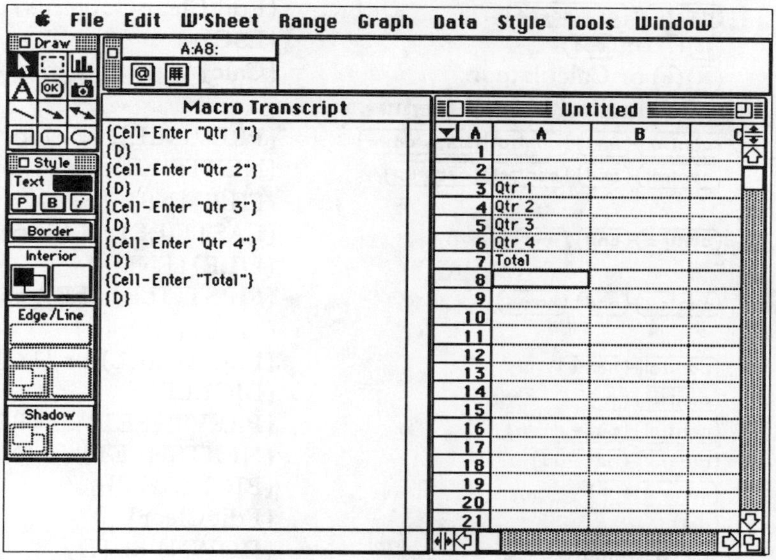

keystrokes, menu commands, and mouse selections. 1-2-3 has other macro instructions that are not recorded because they add macro performance features that do not have menu, keyboard, or mouse equivalents. These advanced programming capabilities are beyond the scope of this chapter.

To use macros, you will want to be familiar with how 1-2-3 records macro instructions. These macro instructions for keystrokes are shown in Table 14-1 and those for some of the menu commands you have learned in this book are shown in Table 14-2. Some of the commands change settings, so they use the {Set} command. For example, if you use the Global Settings command in the Worksheet menu to change the worksheet's global column width to 12, you will see the {Set "worksheet-column-width";12} macro instruction for changing the global column width as well as the {Set} macro instructions for the other sixteen settings you can change with this command.

Notice that all the macro instructions are enclosed in curly braces: { }. You will find it easy to remember most of these words; they are the same

Table 14-1. *Macro Instructions for Keystrokes*

Keystroke	Macro Instruction
delete/backspace	{Edit-Clear-Contents}
⌘-. or esc	{ESC}
⌘-= or Calculate in @Function pop-up menu	{Calc}
control-end control-page down	{PREVFILE}, {PF}, or {FILE}{PS}
control-end control-page up	{NEXTFILE}, {NF}, or {FILE}{NS}
control-end end	{LASTFILE}, {LF}, or {FILE}{END}
control-end home	{FIRSTFILE},{FF}, or {FILE}{HOME}
control-home	{FIRSTCELL} or {FC}
control-←	{BIGLEFT}
control-page down	{PREVSHEET} or {PS}
control-page up	{NEXTSHEET} or {NS}
control-→	{BIGRIGHT}
del	{Edit-Clear}
↓ or return	{DOWN} or {D}
end	{END}
end control-home	{LASTCELL} or {LC}
enter	~
F6 (Window) or ⌘-option-X	{Window}
home	{HOME}
← or shift-tab	{LEFT} or {L}
option-F6 or ⌘-option-Z	{Zoom}
page down	{PGDN}
page up	{PGUP}
→ or tab	{RIGHT} or {R}
↑ or shift-return	{UP} or {U}

words you probably connect with the keys or command—for example, {Range-Format} represents the Format command in the Range menu. 1-2-3 does not care if the macro instructions are in upper- or lowercase, although the examples in this chapter will follow how they appear in the Macro Transcript window. If you make any editing changes to the macro instructions be sure

Table 14-2. *Macro Instructions for Menu Commands*

Menu and Command	**Macro Instruction**
Data Fill	{Data-Fill *range;start;step;stop;interval*}
Data New Form	{Data-Form-New}
Data Query	{Data-Query-*query operation input range; output range; criteria*}
Data Sort	{Data-Sort *range;1st key;order;2nd key; order;...*}
Data View Form	{Data-Form-View *name*} {Data-Form-Delete *name*} or {Data-Form-Rename *old_name;new _name*}
Edit Clear	{Edit-Clear}
Edit Clear Contents	{Edit-Clear-Contents}
Edit Clear Styles	{Edit-Clear-Styles}
Edit Copy	{Edit-Copy}
Edit Cut	{Edit-Cut}
Edit Find	{Edit-Find}
Edit Move Cells	{Edit-Move-Cells *2nd_range;1st_range*}
Edit Paste	{Edit-Paste}
Edit Quick Copy	{Edit-Quick-Copy *2nd_range;1st_range*}
File Close	{File-Close} or {Window-Close}
File Combine From	{File-Combine *combine_option;document;; range*}
File Extract To	{File-Extract *document*;"worksheet"; ;"replace";;"formulas" | "values"}
File Import From	{File-Import "text";*document*}
File New	{File-New}
File Open	{File-Open *document*}
File Print	{File-Print?}
File Print Selection	{File-Print-Selection?}
File Quit	{File-Quit}
File Save	{File-Save *document*;;;"replace"}
File Save As	{File-Save *document*;;;"replace"}
Graph New Graph	{Graph-New *graph type*}
Graph View	{Graph-View *name*}

14

Table 14-2. Macro Instructions for Menu Commands (continued)

Range Convert To Value	{Range-Value *2nd_range;1st_range*}
Range Format	{Range-Format *format;decimals;;;;;range*}
Range Name Create	{Range-Name-Create *range name;range*}
Range Name Delete	{Range-Name-Delete *range name*}
Range Transpose	{Range-Transpose *2nd_range*;"rows-to-columns" *1st_range*}
Style Align	{Style-Align *alignment*}
Style Border	{Style-Border *side*;"on" | "off"}
Style Font	{Style-Font-All *typeface,size,bold,italic, underline,outline,shadow,condensed, extended*}
Tools Backsolve	{Tools-Backsolve *make cell;value;change cell*}
Window Arrange	{Window-Arrange *arrangement*}
Window *Worksheet name*	{Window-Activate *document*;" ";0}
Worksheet Column Width	{Column-Width *width*} or {Column-Width-Reset}
Worksheet Delete	{Delete-Columns} or {Delete-Rows} or {Delete-Sheets}
Worksheet Hide | Show	{Show-Columns} or {Hide-Columns}
Worksheet Insert	{Insert-Columns} or {Insert-Rows} or {Insert-Sheets}
Worksheet Page Break Column	{Page-Break-Column "yes" | "no"}
Worksheet Page Break Row	{Page-Break-Row "yes" | "no"}
Worksheet Row Height	{Row-Height *height*} or {Row-Height-Reset}
Worksheet Titles	{Worksheet-Titles *direction*}

to include the braces. Without the braces, 1-2-3 will not recognize the entry as a special key. Keystroke combinations that are substitutions for commands, such as ⌘-T for the Font command in the Style menu, are recorded just as if you used the menu.

Some of the macro instructions for menu commands also have arguments, which provide information that the macro instruction needs to perform. These are just like the arguments for @functions. They are described in italics in Table 14-2. Most of the arguments are enclosed in quotes. The ones with | indicate that you must select one of the available choices. Not all arguments are required so some of the macro instructions in Table 14-2 include several semicolons together without anything between them. The entries you might put between the semicolons would be for a command's option that you have not learned about.

Application: *When you need a macro instruction for a menu command in your own macros, perform the macro instruction and copy it from the Macro Transcript window to the worksheet. This prevents misspellings and ensures that you have all the information the macro instruction needs.*

Selecting Cells in a Macro

When you are creating a macro, the cell you select is represented with keywords. If you move using the arrow keys, 1-2-3 records macro instructions such as {U} and {R}. These macro instructions can also be spelled out as in {UP} and {RIGHT} and can represent moving multiple cells by adding a number as in {UP 3} or {RIGHT 20}. When you select a range by holding down the (shift) key, 1-2-3 records the macro instruction {Select-*key*} where *key* is the macro instruction for the key you pressed to expand the range as in {Select-Left}. When you select a cell or range with the mouse, 1-2-3 records the macro instruction {Select-Range *range*} where range represents the cell or range address of the cells you select. 1-2-3 will not spell out the arrow keys or use repeat numbers but you can when you edit a macro.

Whether you use the mouse or keyboard to make selections depends on what you plan to do with the macro. For example, in a macro that formats a column of entries starting with the active cell when you execute the macro, you want to use the keyboard so the recorded macro instructions will adjust themselves to any location. On the other hand, when you are creating a macro to sort a database for you and the database seldom changes size, the specific cell addresses that the mouse picks up are very useful, since you always want 1-2-3 to use the same database location. You always have the option of changing how the macro selects cells between using specific addresses and using generic directions by editing the macro.

When you edit a cell, 1-2-3 will record in the Macro Transcript window the macro instruction for the final entry as if you had made that entry in the first place. For example, if you edit the entry ABC Company to be XYZ Company, 1-2-3 will record {Cell-Enter "XYZ Company"} in the Macro Transcript window.

Copying the Macro Instructions to the Worksheet

Once you execute the steps for the macro, you are ready to transfer the macro instructions from 1-2-3's Macro Transcript window to a worksheet. After the macro instructions are copied to the worksheet, you can name the range, and the macro is ready to run. For the row headings macro, follow these steps to copy the macro instructions you have recorded in the Macro Transcript window to your worksheet:

1. Click the Macro Transcript window or choose Macro from the Tools menu and choose Show Transcript to make the Macro Transcript window active.
2. Choose Select All Text from the Edit menu to select the macro instructions that you want to copy.

If you want, you can be more selective about the macro instructions to copy by dragging the pointer from one end of the instructions you want to copy to the other with the mouse or (shift) and the arrow keys. You can also edit the macro instructions if you want to make changes just as you would edit a cell's entry.

3. Choose Copy from the Edit menu to copy the macro instructions to the Clipboard.
4. Select cell A:H1 in the worksheet to make the worksheet window active and select the cell where the macro will start.
5. Choose Paste from the Edit menu to copy the macro instructions from the Clipboard to the worksheet.
6. Click the Zoom box to display the copied macro instructions, which look like Figure 14-2.

Figure 14-2. *Macro added to the worksheet*

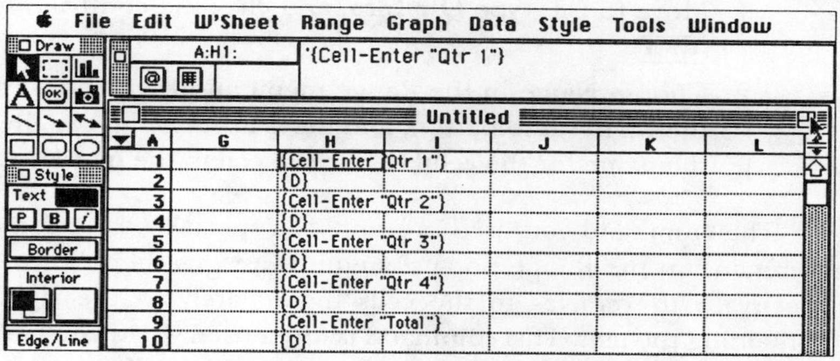

Now your worksheet contains a copy of the macro instructions that were recorded in the Macro Transcript window. All you have to do to make these macro instructions a macro is name the cell containing the first macro instruction.

Naming the Macro

Now that you have copied the macro instructions, you are ready to name the macro. You can use the Create command in the Range pop-up menu to apply the name to the top cell in the macro. You can also enter the name in a cell to the left of the top macro cell, and then use Name command in the Range menu, choose Label Create, and Right to apply the name to the cell. You need to name only the top cell in a macro because 1-2-3 continues executing macro instructions in a column of macro instructions until it reaches a cell that does not contain text or an advanced macro instruction that tells 1-2-3 to stop executing a macro.

Like other range names, macro names cannot use more than 15 characters. You can use any acceptable range name for the macro. A special type of macro name is a backslash and a letter as in \P, which can be executed by pressing (control)-(option)-*letter*. This special type of macro name lets you create 26 unique, quickly executable macros on one worksheet. (1-2-3 does not distinguish between upper- and lowercase letters in a macro name.)

Name the macro you have created by following these steps:

1. Move to G1, type **Qtr Info**, and click the confirm button or press (enter).
2. Choose Name in the Range menu and then choose Label Create, the Right radio button, and the OK button to use the text in G1 as the name for the cell H1, the top cell in the macro.

The command you used in step 2 is a specialized version of the Create command in the Range pop-up menu. It assigns the text in the range you specify to the entries in the cells immediately to the right of the cells containing the text. This command is often used when you have several cells to name that have their names in text in adjacent cells.

Documenting the Macro

You will want to develop a few easy documentation rules for yourself so your documentation is always stored in the same place. A good strategy is to place the macro name in the cell immediately to the left of the top cell in the macro. For example, for the macro you have created, you have entered **Qtr Info** in G1.

The second piece of information documentation provides is a description of the macro's instructions. A good area to use for documenting the macro is the column to the right of the actual macro instructions. Entering a brief description of every instruction can make the purpose of the macro much clearer when you go back to examine it at a later time.

Saving a worksheet after you name and document it saves both the macro and the worksheet data so the macro is available when you use the worksheet. Follow these steps to document the macro you have created and save it along with the other worksheet data:

1. Make the following entries:

J1: **Enter Qtr 1 in active cell**	J6: **Move down one cell**
J2: **Move down one cell**	J7: **Enter Qtr 4 in active cell**
J3: **Enter Qtr 2 in active cell**	J8: **Move down one cell**
J4: **Move down one cell**	J9: **Enter Total in active cell**
J5: **Enter Qtr 3 in active cell**	J10: **Move down one cell**

Now your macro looks like Figure 14-3.

2. Choose Save in the File menu, type **My Macro** in the Save As text box, and select the Save button to save the worksheet with the macro it contains.

Executing the Macro

Once you have entered and named a macro, you can use it whenever you wish. Whenever you have a macro that requires the active cell to be a specific cell, you must select that cell before you execute the macro. You do not need to select the first cell of the macro to execute it. After you select the cell you want to be active, you can execute the macro by choosing Macro in the Tools menu and then choosing Run Macro. 1-2-3 will display a dialog box containing range names that you can select and then select the OK button. Once you select the OK button, 1-2-3 performs the macro instructions starting at the first cell in the named range and continuing until 1-2-3 reaches a cell that does not contain text. Another option for macros is to add them to the Tools menu just as you add specific formats and fonts to the Range and Style menus. Macros are added by choosing Macro in the Tools menu, choosing Add To Menu, selecting the macro name and the Add To Menu button. If you name your macro with a backslash and a letter, you have the third option of pressing (control)-(option) and the letter to start the macro.

14

Figure 14-3. *Macro after documentation*

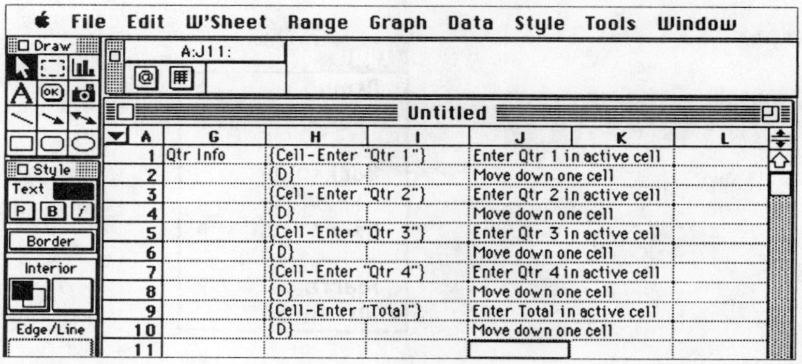

Follow these instructions to try two ways of executing your new macro:

1. Select C1 as the cell you want initially to be the active cell when this macro is run.
2. Choose Macro from the Tools menu and choose Run Macro.
3. Select Qtr Info in the list box and the OK button to execute the macro as shown here:

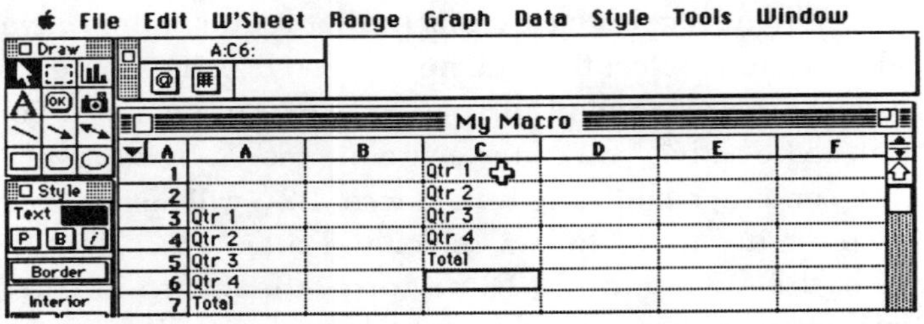

4. Choose Macro from the Tools menu and choose Add To Menu.
5. Select Qtr Info in the list box, the Show In Menu button, and the Done button to add this macro to the Tools menu.
6. Select E2 so when you execute the Qtr Info macro again, it will start in this cell.
7. Select the Tools menu to display the pull-down menu with the added macro as shown here:

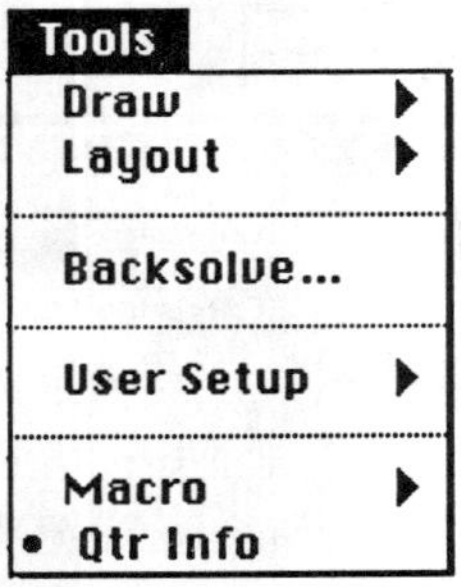

8. Choose Qtr Info from the Tools menu to execute the macro again.
9. Click the close box and select the Yes button to close the worksheet and save the changes made to it.

The macro name you have added to the Tools menu will appear whenever a worksheet that contains the macro is open. If you want to remove this macro from the Tools menu when this worksheet is open, choose Macro from the Tools menu and choose Add To Menu. Next, Select Qtr Info in the list box, the Remove From Menu button, and the Done button to remove this macro from the Tools menu.

Special Macro Topics

1-2-3 has many macro options—so many, in fact, that complete books are written on the subject. This chapter cannot cover all possible options, but it can present a few of particular interest that go beyond the simpler keyboard alternatives, to show you how you create macro buttons, use macro libraries, create automatic macros, and debug macros to fix errors.

Creating Macro Buttons

Macro buttons are graphical buttons added to a worksheet that has a macro assigned to it—when you select the button, you execute the macro. You can use macro buttons to make macros easier to execute. They can explicitly offer the features of the macro without having to check if the worksheet contains any macros. Macro buttons are added to a worksheet like the drawings that you added in the last chapter.

You can create macro buttons to insert and delete blank rows in a worksheet. Macros like this are useful for databases if you want some blank rows between field names and records. Since blank rows can cause problems for the Query command in the Data menu, you can have one macro to add them when you need them and another macro to remove them.

Follow these steps to create two macro buttons—one that will insert two blank rows and another that will remove them:

1. Choose Open in the File menu, Employee Database in the list box and the Open button to open the database that you used in Chapter 12 to learn about the database features. Move to A:A1.

If you do not have this database available, make the following entries to have the beginnings of the database.

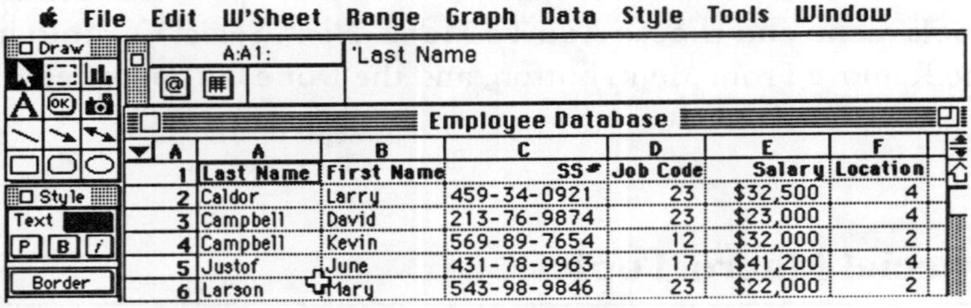

2. Select A1..A2, choose Insert from the Worksheet menu, select the Row radio button, deselect Insert Selected Range, and select the OK button.

This adds two rows and also puts the macro instruction you need to add two rows in the Macro Transcript window.

3. Click the Macro Transcript window or choose Macro from the Transcript window, and then choose Show Transcript.

You can see in the Macro Transcript window that 1-2-3 continues recording your actions even as you switch between worksheets.

4. Select {Insert-Rows ;2;"no"} that is at the bottom of the information stored in this window.
5. Choose Copy from the Edit menu to put a copy of this macro instruction into the Clipboard.
6. Click the worksheet to switch to that window and then click the button in the Draw palette which looks like .

7. Drag the pointer from the upper-right corner of A1 to the lower-right corner of B2 to define the size and placement of the macro button on the worksheet.

When you finish drawing the box, 1-2-3 displays the Button dialog box. This dialog box contains a text box for the button's name, a text box for the macro's text or instructions and radio buttons to tell 1-2-3 whether the macro instructions are stored in a worksheet range or entered as part of the button.

8. Type **Insert**, which is also the text that appears in the macro button on the worksheet, in the Button Name text box.
9. Type **{Select-Range A:A4..A:A5}** in the Macro Text box and then press ⌘-V or F4 to copy the Clipboard's contents to this box (the Paste command in the Edit menu is not available) to enter the macro instructions the macro button will perform.
10. Select the OK button to finish defining the macro button and add it to the worksheet.
11. Click the button in the Draw palette again to add another macro button to the worksheet.
12. Drag the pointer from the upper-right corner of C1 to the lower-right corner of D2 for where you want the second macro button on the worksheet.
13. Type **Delete** for the macro button's name in the Button Name text box.
14. Select the Range radio button, type **A:H1** in the Range text box, and select the OK button.

The Range radio button tells 1-2-3 that the macro instructions for this macro button are on the worksheet, rather than entered into the dialog box. You could have typed a range name or an address. Since you have told 1-2-3 that the macro this button performs starts in A:H1, you need to put some macro instructions there.

15. Move to A:H1, type **{Select-Range A:A4..A:A5}**, and finalize the entry as the Delete macro button's first instruction.

14

16. Select A:H2 and choose Paste in the Edit menu to copy the macro instruction {Insert-Rows ;2;"no"} to A:H2.
17. Edit A:H2 so it changes from {Insert-Rows ;2;"no"} to the macro instruction {Delete-Rows ;"no"}.

Since the Delete command in the Worksheet menu does not have the quantity box, the {Delete-Rows} macro instruction does not include the 2 and the second semicolon. Normally you would have added documentation to the macro in H1..H2 but for now try these macro buttons to see how they work.

18. Scroll the worksheet to display the cell A1.
19. Click the Insert macro button so the beginning of the database looks like this:

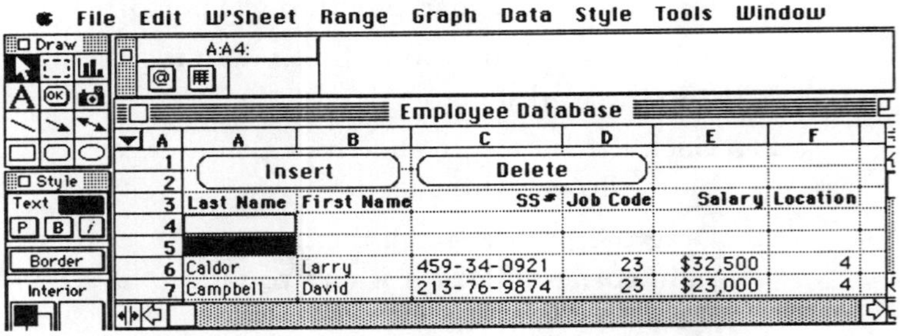

When you have a macro that inserts and deletes rows, you must be sure that it does not insert or delete any macro instructions. If you put the macro where rows are deleted or inserted, deleting the rows may also delete some of the macro instructions and inserting the rows will stop a macro's execution before all the instructions are performed.

20. Click the Delete macro button to remove the two rows you have added.
21. Choose Save As in the File menu, type **Database Macro** in the Save As text box and select the Save button to save this worksheet with a new name.
22. Click the close box to close this worksheet.

Applications: *Use buttons on a worksheet to provide quick access to the macros you have created specifically for the worksheet. Some of the buttons you will want to create for your own worksheets include ones for macros that query a database, use its database form, and print reports.*

Creating a Macro Library

14

If you have a macro you want to use in several worksheets, you don't have to put the macro in every worksheet that uses the macro; you can create a macro library. A *macro library* is any worksheet that contains macros that you use on other worksheets. When you execute a macro, the macro is run using the current worksheet, even if the macro is stored in another open worksheet.

You can use the Qtr Info macro you created earlier in other worksheets, thus using the My Macro worksheet as a macro library. To do so, follow these steps:

1. Choose Open from the File menu, select My Macro in the list box, and select the Open button to open the My Macro worksheet you created earlier.
2. Choose New from the File menu to open another worksheet.
3. Move to B2.
4. Choose Qtr Info from the Tools menu so the new worksheet looks like this:

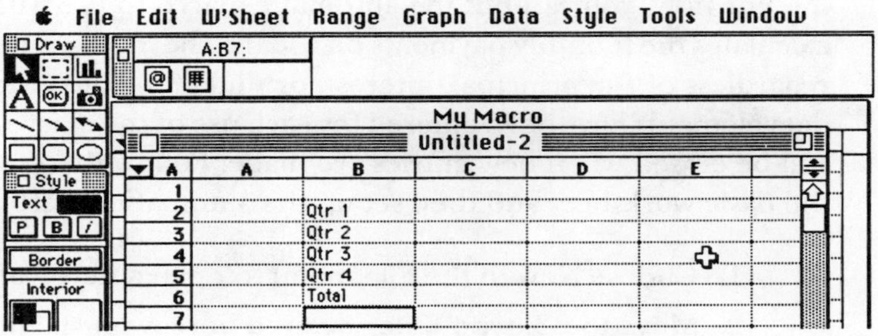

5. Click the close box and select No to remove the new worksheet without saving it.
6. Click the close box of the My Macro worksheet to close it.

If you want a macro library to always be open when you use 1-2-3, name the worksheet containing the macro library Auto123. When you start 1-2-3, it will open a worksheet called Auto123 if it exists in the default folder.

Creating Automatic Macros

1-2-3 has a unique feature that lets you create an *automatic macro.* Every time a worksheet containing an automatic macro is opened, 1-2-3 immediately executes this macro as long as the Run \0 Macro When Opening Document check box is selected in the User Setup Preferences dialog box. There are numerous applications for such macros, although they are usually used with the more advanced 1-2-3 macro features.

The only difference between an automatic macro and other macros is the name that you assign to the automatic macro. An automatic macro must have a name of \0 (backslash zero).

Applications: *Automatic macros are frequently used to create worksheets completely controlled by a macro. For example, a macro might guide a user of a payroll worksheet through the entries that need to be made each time, all the way through the printing of the report and saving the modified data. Once the worksheet is opened with a macro like this, the only entries the user makes will be the ones the macro prompts for.*

For now, you can put the automatic macro to use with a worksheet that calculates the monthly payments on a loan. The macro is designed to function regardless of the principal, interest, or time. So that you can easily tell what data elements have been entered for each use of the macro, the old data fields will be erased when new entries are made. Follow these directions to set up the basic worksheet and then set up the automatic macro:

1. Choose New in the File menu to open a new worksheet.
2. Move to B3, type **Enter desired borrowings:**, and move to B6.
3. Type **Enter interest rate:** and move to B9.

4. Type **Enter term in years:** and move to B12.
5. Type **** Your Payments Will Be **** and move to E3.
6. Select Outside from the Border button in the Style palette to add a border to the four sides of the cell as you learned to do in Chapter 6, "Changing the Appearance of Worksheet Entries."
7. Repeat step 6 after moving to E6, E9, and E12 to add a border around these four cells.
8. Type **@PMT(E3,E6/12,E9*12)** in E12 and finalize the entry.

The formula currently equals ERR but that will change when you enter values in E3, E6, and E9. When you put the principal in E3, the interest rate in E6 and the number of years in E9, this formula will calculate the loan's monthly payment.

9. Choose $1,234.12 from the Range menu to format this cell as Currency with two decimal places.
10. Choose Display Options from the Window menu, deselect the Grid lines, and select the OK button.
11. Choose Save in the File menu, type **Payment** in the Save As text box, and select the Save button to save the worksheet.

Now your worksheet looks like Figure 14-4.

You have already completed quite a bit of work, but you have yet to enter the automatic macro. Follow these instructions to create the macro by recording most of the macro's actions and then modifying them:

1. Choose Macro from the Tools menu and then choose Clear Transcript to remove any previous instructions. Move to E3.
2. Choose Clear Contents in the Edit menu to remove any entry without removing the border around the cell.

This step insures that when you execute the macro based on the actions 1-2-3 is recording right now, 1-2-3 will remove the previous entry in this cell.

3. Repeat step 2 after moving to E6 and E9.
4. Select E3, type **60000** and select E6.

Figure 14-4. *Calculating a payment amount*

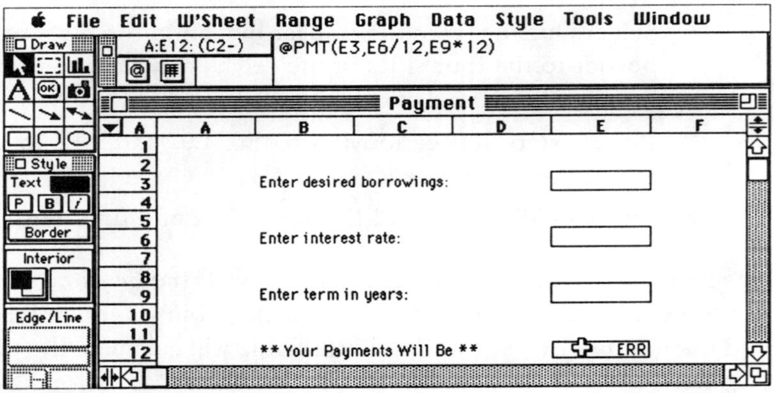

5. Type **.1** and select E9.
6. Type **30** and select E12.
7. Click the Macro Transcript window or choose Macro from the Tools menu and choose Show Transcript to make the Macro Transcript window active.
8. Choose Select All Text from the Edit menu to select the macro instructions that you want to copy.
9. Choose Copy from the Edit menu to copy the macro instructions to the Clipboard.
10. Select cell B21 in the worksheet to make the worksheet window active and select the cell where the macro will start.
11. Choose Paste from the Edit menu to copy the macro instructions from the Clipboard to the worksheet.

At this point, you need to change the macro instructions that enter $60,000, .1, and 30 into macro instructions that let you enter different numbers each time this macro is run. The {Get-Number} macro instruction will fulfill this purpose. This macro instruction displays a prompt for a number and then stores the number in a cell you designate. This macro instruction has the additional advantage of using text you have entered in a cell as the prompt to enter the number. At this point, the macro instructions copied to the worksheet look like Figure 14-5. If you have made extra entries such as correcting entries or moving to different cells, your entries will be in different locations and you will want to move the macro instructions from their current location to where they appear in Figure 14-5.

12. Select B28, type **{Get-Number B3;E3;;}** and move to B30.

This macro instruction tells 1-2-3 to display the text stored in B3 as a prompt for the macro user to enter a number, and then tells 1-2-3 to store the number in E3. If you wanted to use other text as the prompt for this macro instruction, you would enter the text in the macro instruction in quotes, as in {Get-Number "Enter Loan Amount";E3;;}.

13. Type **{Get-Number B6;E6;;}** in B30 and move to B32.
14. Type **{Get-Number B9;E9;;}** and finalize the entry.
15. Type **'\0** in A21 and finalize the entry.

Figure 14-5. *Macro instructions for an automatic macro copied to the worksheet*

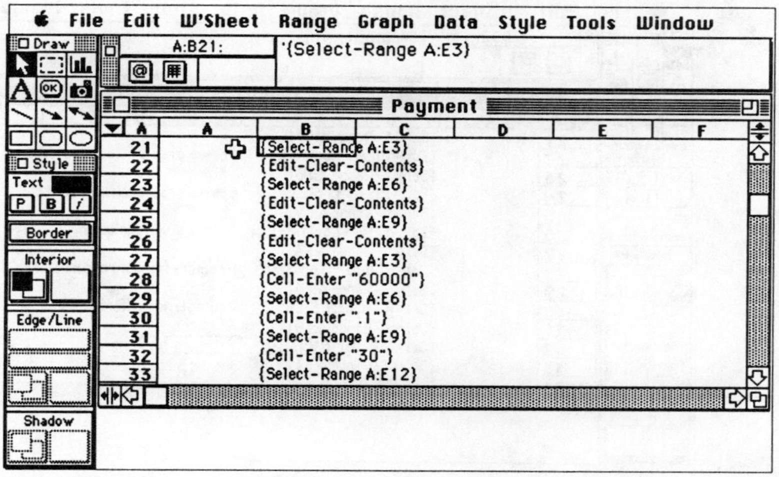

The apostrophe prevents 1-2-3 from filling A21 with 0s.

16. Select B21, choose Create from the Range pop-up menu, type **\0** in the Create Range Name text box, and select the OK button.
17. Make the following documentation entries:

D22:	**Erases previous borrowing amount**
D24:	**Erases previous interest rate**
D26:	**Erases previous term**
D28:	**Prompts for borrowing amount**
D30:	**Prompts for interest rate**
D32:	**Prompts for term**

Your completed automatic macro looks like Figure 14-6.

18. Move to A1 so when the worksheet is later opened, the entries in column B are in sight.
19. Choose Save in the File menu to save the worksheet again.

Figure 14-6. *Automatic macro using the {Get-Number} macro instruction*

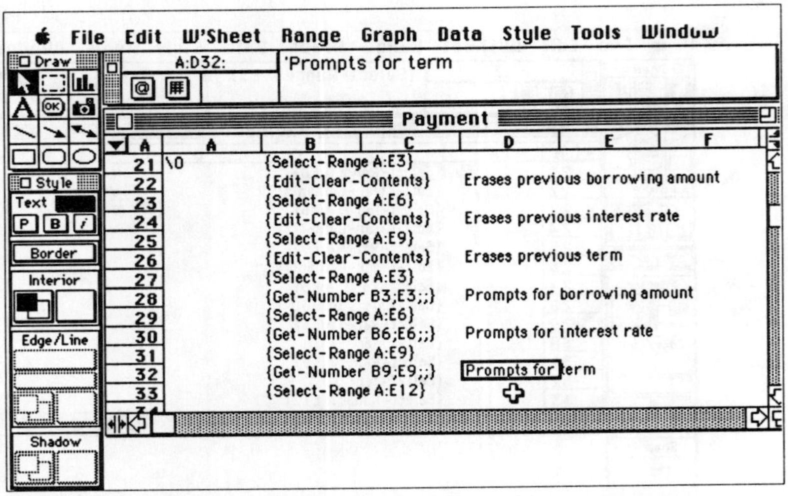

20. Click the close box to close the worksheet.
21. Choose Open in the File menu, select **Payment** in the list box, and select the Open button to open the worksheet.

The dialog box created by the first {Get-Number} instruction looks like this:

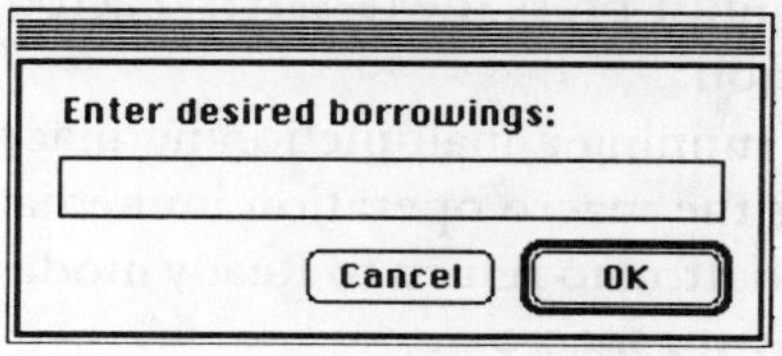

If the macro does not begin executing immediately, choose User Setup in the Tools menu, choose Preferences and then select the Run \0 Macro When Opening Document and the OK button. Then close and open the worksheet again.

22. Enter **75000**, **10%**, and **15** in response to the three prompts, selecting OK after completing each one.

If you get an error message, you probably have a typing mistake in the macro instructions and you should compare your macro with the one shown in Figure 14-6.

23. Click the close box and select the No button to remove the worksheet without saving the new data.

Debugging Macros

When a macro contains an error, you must *debug* it, which means to fix any errors. The debugging process involves testing and correcting macros to ensure that you are obtaining the desired results. One of the most common mistakes you may make is when you edit or type in the macro instructions a macro performs and you forget a character, such as {Insert-Row} instead of {Insert-Rows}.

1-2-3's Step mode lets you execute a macro one keystroke at a time. This allows you to follow its progress and spot the area of difficulty if problems are encountered. To activate Step mode, choose Macro in the Tools menu and choose Debug. Since this is a toggle process, repeating this disables Step mode. When Step mode is operational, you see the Step indicator in the status window. When Step mode is on, any macro you invoke is executed one step at a time. You must press the (spacebar) each time you are ready for the next macro instruction.

If you are running a malfunctioning macro, you can press (⌘)-(.) to stop it. This cancels the macro operation immediately and presents an alert box. Select the OK button to return to Ready mode so you can make the necessary corrections to your macro.

Follow these instructions to try a macro in Step mode:

1. Choose Macro from the Tools menu and choose Debug.
2. Choose Open in the File menu, select Payment in the list box, and select the Open button.
3. Press the (spacebar) to execute the first macro instruction, which selects A:E3.
4. Press the (spacebar) again to execute the second macro instruction, which removes the prior entry in A:E3 with the Clear Contents command in the Edit menu.
5. Continue pressing the (spacebar) until you see the dialog box to supply the amount to borrow.
6. Supply an amount to borrow, select the OK button, and continue pressing the (spacebar) until you see the dialog box to supply the interest rate.
7. Supply an interest rate, select the OK button, and continue pressing the (spacebar) until you see the dialog box to supply the number of years.
8. Supply a number of years, select the OK button, and continue pressing the (spacebar) until the macro is done.
9. Choose Macro in the Tools menu and choose Debug.
10. Click the close box and select the No button to close the worksheet window without saving it.

Review

In this chapter, you have learned some basics about creating macros. As you move your 1-2-3 skills beyond the scope of this book, you will find that macros provide even more features than the few that were introduced. The macro features you learned about in this chapter include the following:

- 1-2-3's keyboard-alternative macros allow you to perform repetitive tasks with ease. You can type the macro instructions in a cell, or record them in 1-2-3's Macro Transcript window and copy them to the worksheet. Once a macro is named, you can execute it.
- Macros are saved with the worksheet that contains them. However, they execute on the worksheet with the active cell.
- If you edit a recorded macro or want to type macro instructions into cells, you must use 1-2-3's keywords for keystrokes, cell selections, and menu commands. These macro instructions are entered in curly braces. For some menu command macro instructions, you must also supply other information, such as the number of rows to insert.
- You enter macros in a group of text entries in contiguous cells in a column of the worksheet.
- You name macros the same way you name ranges. Macro names follow the same rules as range names. You can use either the Create command in the Range menu, the Name command in the Range menu and then choose Create, or the Name command in the Range menu and then choose Label Create.
- To execute a macro, choose Macro from the Tools menu and choose Run Macro. Select the macro you want to run from the list and select the OK button. You can also run a macro by choosing Macro in the Tools menu, Add to Menu, the macro's name, and the Show In Menu button. If you have named a macro with a backslash and a letter, as in \S, you can also execute a macro by pressing CONTROL-OPTION-*letter*.
- You can create a macro that executes every time the worksheet containing the macro is opened by naming the macro \0. 1-2-3 runs

14

these macros when the Run \0 Macro When Opening Document check box is selected in the User Setup Preferences dialog box.

Keys and Commands

The keys and commands you have learned to use in this chapter provide aids to help you create and use macros. These keys and commands are

Entry	**Action**
control-option-*letter*	Executes a macro named with \ and the *letter*
Range Name Label Create Right	Names cells immediately to the right of selected text entries
Tools Macro Add To Menu	Adds a macro's name to the Tools menu when the worksheet containing the macro is open, so you can execute the macro by selecting it from the menu
Tools Macro Clear Transcript	Removes previously recorded macro instructions from Macro Transcript window
Tools Macro Debug	Toggles Step mode to execute a macro a step at a time
Tools Macro Run Macro	Executes a selected macro
Tools Macro Show Transcript	Displays the Macro Transcript window
Tools User Setup Preferences	Run \0 Macro When Opening Document check box determines if 1-2-3 tries to execute a macro called \0 when a worksheet is opened

A

Installing 1-2-3 for the Macintosh

This appendix tells you how to install 1-2-3 for the Macintosh. If your copy of 1-2-3 for the Macintosh has already been installed, you do not need to read this appendix. If your copy of 1-2-3 is still covered in shrink wrap, you need to install the package. In that case, you will find this appendix a valuable reference for the steps that you must take. If you are not familiar with the Macintosh, read Appendix B, "Using the Macintosh," which covers some of the Macintosh basics that you will want to use with 1-2-3 for the Macintosh.

System Requirements for 1-2-3 for the Macintosh

1-2-3 for the Macintosh is designed to run on an Apple Macintosh with System 6.0.4 or later or A/UX operating system 2.0.1 or later. 1-2-3 for the Macintosh requires that you have a minimum of 2 megabytes (MB) of main memory if you are using System 6 without the MultiFinder or 3 megabytes of main memory if you are using System 7 or System 6 and the MultiFinder. If you have more than the minimum, you can run more applications and have them work more quickly. 1-2-3 must also be run from a hard disk with at least 6.5MB of available space when you install 1-2-3 (it will shrink to 3.9MB after installation). 1-2-3 also has a guided tour, which requires 4.5MB of hard disk space to install, it but shrinks to 3MB afterward.

Installing 1-2-3

Installing 1-2-3 for the Macintosh copies files to the hard disk and registers your software. When you purchase 1-2-3, you receive several disks that you will use as you install it. These instructions assume the Macintosh's System is already installed. If this is not the case, install the System software before you install 1-2-3.

Follow these steps for installation:

1. Start your system. This may involve turning it on or pressing the power-on key on the keyboard.
2. Put Disk 1: Program in your floppy-disk drive, and choose Select All from the Edit menu to select all of the files on this disk.
3. Drag the file icons from the 1-2-3 Program 1 window to on top of your hard-disk window or icon.
4. Select the close box in the upper-left corner of the window and then drag the icon of the disk to the Trash to eject it.
5. Repeat steps 2 through 4 for Disk 2 and Disk 3.
6. Switch to your hard disk's window. If your hard-disk window is not open, click the hard-disk icon.
7. Double-click Lotus 1-2-3.dd.1 to open this document.

This document, the Lotus 1-2-3.dd.2, and Lotus 1-2-3.dd.3 documents will be expanded and the files that are created are put in a Lotus 1-2-3 folder.

8. Drag DDMiniExpand™ in the hard-disk window to the Trash.

9. Double-click Lotus 1-2-3 to open this folder, and double-click Lotus 1-2-3 in the Lotus 1-2-3 folder to open the application.
10. 1-2-3 prompts you to register your name and the organization's name. In the first box, enter your name. In the second box, enter your organization name. If you do not have a organization name to supply, reenter your name. Then select the OK button. 1-2-3 starts and you are ready to use 1-2-3's features.

Installing Adobe Type Manager

1-2-3 for the Macintosh also includes the Adobe Type Manager (ATM), which provides additional fonts and font enhancements to make your worksheets look better on screen and in printed output. You can install and run 1-2-3 without ATM, but if you want to install ATM, follow these steps:

1. Put Disk 6: Adobe Type Manager and Fonts in your floppy-disk drive, and choose Select All from the Edit menu to select all of the files on this disk.
2. Drag the file from the ATM Disk window to on top of your hard-disk window or icon.
3. Click the close box in the upper-left corner of the window, and drag the icon of the disk to the Trash to eject it.
4. Switch to your hard disk's window. If your hard-disk window is not open, click the hard-disk icon.
5. Double-click ATM® Disk.dd to open this document.

This document will be expanded, and the files that are created will be put in an ATM® Disk folder.

6. Drag DDMiniExpand™, in the hard-disk window, to the Trash.
7. Copy the ~ATM™, ~ATM 68000 (Macintosh Classic, SE, or Portable) or ~ATM 68020/030 (Macintosh IIsi, LC, or SE/30), and the thirteen outline fonts (they have A icons in a suitcase or A with lines) to the System Folder. In System 7, you can put these files in the

Extensions folder in the System folder. In System 6, they must be in the System folder.

8. Copy the Font Porter and the documents in the Bitmapped Fonts folder to the System folder.

Bitmapped fonts provide fonts that are quicker to use. If you do not want the Font Porter to load the fonts when you start your computer, you will need to use the Font/DA Mover or another program to load the bitmapped fonts.

9. Choose Control panel in the menu and select ~ATM™.
10. You are prompted to personalize your copy of ATM by typing your name and organization. In the first box, enter your name. In the second box, enter your organization name. If you do not have a organization name to supply, reenter your name.
11. Select the OK button and restart your computer.

Installing 1-2-3's Guided Tour

1-2-3 includes a guided tour that you can install to help you learn the basics of using 1-2-3 for the Macintosh. You may want to install this guided tour. You may even want to install it initially and remove it later when you need more disk space. This guided tour, unlike the program files, can be copied freely for evaluation purposes. To install the guided tour, follow these steps for installation:

1. Put Disk 4 in your floppy-disk drive and choose Select All from the Edit menu to select all of the files on this disk.
2. Drag the file from the 1-2-3 Tour 1 window to on top of your hard-disk window or icon.
3. Select the close box in the upper-left corner of the window, and then drag the icon of the disk to the Trash to eject it.
4. Repeat steps 1 through 3 using Disk 5 instead of Disk 4.

5. Switch to your hard disk's window. If your hard-disk window is not open, click the hard-disk icon.
6. Double-click 1-2-3 Tour.dd.1 to open this document.

This file and 1-2-3 Tour.dd.2 will be expanded, and the files that are created will be put in a 1-2-3 Tour folder (it may take a few minutes).

7. Drag DDMiniExpand™ in the hard-disk window to the Trash.

At this point the 1-2-3 tour is installed, so you can start the tour by double-clicking the 1-2-3 Tour folder and double-clicking Guided Tour of 1-2-3.

B

Using the Macintosh

The Macintosh makes working with applications easy. The Macintosh features an easy-to-use interface that uses graphics and the mouse to make most of your actions intuitive. If 1-2-3 for the Macintosh is your first Macintosh application, read this appendix to learn about some basic Macintosh features you will want to use.

The Macintosh organizes where it puts its data by putting data into *documents*. Documents can either contain your data or an application, called an *application document.* You can organize your documents into *folders* just as you organize your papers into folders. These folders and any other documents that are not put into a folder are stored on disks.

The Macintosh is used with a mouse. Using a mouse allows you to select the objects you want to use. Some of the terms related to a mouse and their meanings are listed in Table B-1. Hold the mouse with the cable away from you and your palm on the top of the mouse opposite the side with the button.

Table B-1. *Mouse Terms*

Mouse Term	Meaning
Click	Point to the object and press the mouse button once
Double-click	Point to the object and press the mouse button twice in rapid succession
Drag	Point to one location, hold the mouse button as you move the mouse to another location, and release the button

Starting the Macintosh

The interface between you and your computer is the operating system. Since you are using 1-2-3 for the Macintosh, you are using System 6 or System 7. When you turn on your computer, you are adding the System to your computer's memory. Once the System is read, a display appears that shows your desktop when you last shut down your system. Figure B-1 shows an example of a desktop that appears after turning on your system. This desktop has several components which are labeled in Figure B-1. If you are using System 7, you will notice several differences, such as having Label, Help (the question mark), and the Application menu (the last icon in the menu bar in System 6 with MultiFinder and System 7) in the menu bar.

Each disk, folder, or document can be put in a separate *window*. A window contains a title bar, zoom box, size box, close box, and the contents of the disk, folder or document. When a document window is open it is opened as part of an application.

Shutting Down the Macintosh

When you finish using the Macintosh, you will want to quit your applications and shut down the Macintosh instead of just flipping the off switch. Quitting applications ensures that you do not lose data that you intended to

Figure B-1. *Sample Macintosh desktop*

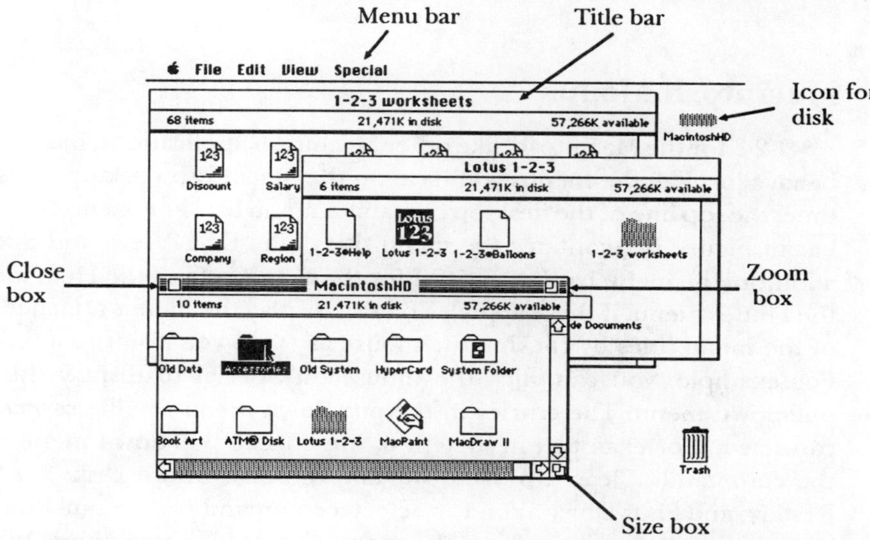

B

save. Shutting down the Macintosh directs the Macintosh to perform any necessary housecleaning. Before you shut down the Macintosh, you should quit any open applications.

To shut down the Macintosh, choose Shut Down from the Special menu. To do this, point to Special in the menu bar and press the mouse button as you drag the mouse and its pointer so Shut Down is highlighted. Depending on your hardware, you will see a message that you may safely turn the computer off or the machine will turn itself off.

The Macintosh Desktop

Once you see the Macintosh desktop, you can open, manipulate, and close the windows that appear on the desktop and open, use and close documents. You can customize the size of each window and where each window appears.

You can change how folders and documents are displayed in a window. The Macintosh remembers the location and state of the windows.

Macintosh Menus

1-2-3 for the Macintosh, like other Macintosh applications, has menus that behave just like the menus you have on the Macintosh desktop. Most of the time, the top line of the desktop contains a menu bar. For example, the menu bar in Figure B-1 contains the menu titles File, Edit, View, and Special. In addition, the menu bar has an icon for the menu (and the Help menu and the Finder menu, if these apply). You can display the menus attached to each of the menu titles by clicking the mouse as when you point to a menu title. For example, you can click the mouse on Special to display the Special pull-down menu. The entries in the pull-down menu are the *commands* you can select. For example, in System 6, the Special pull-down menu contains the commands Clean Up Window, Empty Trash, Erase Disk, Set Startup, Restart, and Shut Down. You can select a command from a pull-down menu by dragging the pointer from the menu title to the command. When you release the mouse, you select the highlighted command. Chapter 5, "Menus, Dialog Boxes, and Palettes," describes menus.

Opening and Closing Windows

Windows can contain the contents of disks, folders, or documents. You can select which windows appear on your desktop by opening and closing them. You can open a window by selecting the icon to open by clicking on the icon once, which will turn it dark. Use the Open command in the File menu or double click the icon you want to open. For example, you can open a hard-disk window with the Open command in the File menu or by double-clicking the drive icon. This also works for the Trash, which allows you to see the contents of the Trash. The Trash is where you drag files and folders to delete them.

Once a window is open, it is added to the top of a desktop. If you have opened an application, the menu titles in the menu bar will change to the application's menu titles. If you are using System 6 without MultiFinder turned on, opening an application window hides other windows from the desktop. With System 7 or MultiFinder in System 6, you may see windows behind the document window for the application that is on the top. Even when MultiFinder is not turned on, some applications let you work with multiple documents, as long as you open them from within the application. For example, in 1-2-3 you can open many Lotus 1-2-3 documents, as long as you open them within 1-2-3.

For documents, you can open an application document or a document that was specifically designed for an application. When you open a document for a specific application, the application is opened as well. For example, you can open 1-2-3 by opening Lotus 1-2-3, the application document, or by opening a Lotus 1-2-3 document.

When you finish with a window, you'll want to close the window to free the desktop for other windows you may want to use. To close a window, click the close box in the upper-left corner or choose Close from the File menu. To quit an application as well as close any document windows the application has open, select Quit in the File menu. In an application, you will probably see prompts that you need to respond to about saving your data. Once you quit an application, the previously open window becomes open again.

Switching to a Window

You can select which window is at the top of the desktop, or which will be the *active window,* by selecting it. To select a window, click any part of it. Since you have many options for sizing and moving your windows, you may need to move an open window out of the way to get to the one that is behind it. You can tell which window is the active window of several because it has visible scroll bars and boxes, size box, close box, zoom box, and stripes on the title bar.

Positioning and Sizing Windows

You can put your windows anywhere on the desktop and make the windows any size you want. To size a window, drag the size box in the lower-right corner to where you want the new lower-right corner of the window to be. Some other windows, like windows for the desktop accessories, cannot change sizes so they do not have a size box. You can only change the lower-right corner of the window, so you may want to size a window and then move it to where you want it.

To move a window, drag anywhere on the title bar of the window to move the temporary outline to where you want the window. You can even move the window so it is partially off of the desktop.

You can also easily make a window larger by clicking the zoom box in the upper-right corner. Clicking the zoom box enlarges a window to its maximum size. Clicking it a second time reduces the window to its previous size.

Changing the Display of a Disk or Folder Window

Disk windows and folder windows contain several options for how the contents are displayed. You can change the way the contents of a window are displayed to show icons or small icons of the window's contents or to sort the window's contents by name, date, size, kind, or label (System 7 only). To set how the window's contents are displayed, select one of the commands in the View menu. For example, you can change your hard disk's window to display the contents by file name so the window looks something like this:

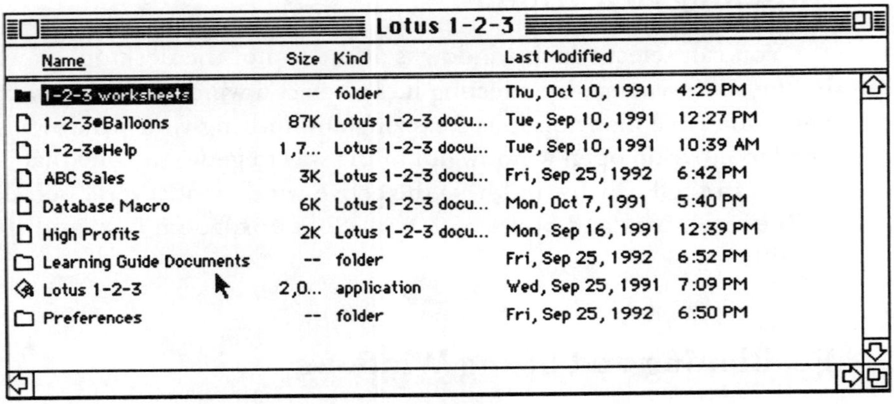

Working with Documents and Folders

From the desktop, you can use a variety of features that control the documents and folders you have on your disk. You can copy, move, rename, and delete documents and folders. You can also create new folders and initialize disks to prepare them to store your documents and folders.

Many of the desktop management features described below work with a selected document or folder. You can select a document or folder by clicking it—it goes dark or is highlighted. If you want to select multiple documents and folders, press the (shift) key as you click the items you want to add to the current selection. When you select a folder, you are also selecting the contents of the folder. This means that if you delete a folder, you are also deleting any documents and folders in the selected folder.

Deleting Documents and Folders

B

When you no longer need a document or folder, you will want to delete it so it no longer fills unnecessary space on the disk. To delete a document or folder, select it and drag it to the Trash, the icon in the lower-right corner of the desktop, until the Trash can is highlighted. If the selected document is an application or if the folder contains an application, you must confirm that you want to remove it by clicking the OK button when prompted. The Trash icon is now bulging, indicating that the Trash has contents. The Trash will keep these documents and folders until it is emptied. In System 6, the Trash is emptied when you select Empty Trash from the Special menu, shut down or turn off your computer, start a program, or eject a disk that contains some documents and folders that were placed in the Trash. In System 7, the Trash is only emptied when you select Empty Trash from the Special menu. Also in System 7, when you select Empty Trash from the Special menu, you must select the OK button from the confirmation dialog box displayed.

If you decide that you want to recover a document or folder that you have placed in the Trash, you can recover it as long as the Trash has not been emptied. To recover a document or folder from the Trash, open the Trash icon to display a window for the Trash's contents and drag the document or folder from the Trash to another location.

Moving and Copying Documents and Folders

You can copy and move a document or folder to make a duplicate of it in another location. You may want to copy a document or folder to a disk to make a backup copy of an important worksheet or to move a document from one folder to another. To copy or move a document or folder, follow these steps:

1. Open the window containing the document or folder to copy and make sure you can still see the window or icon of the disk or folder where you want to place the copy.
2. Select the document or folder to copy.
3. Drag the document or folder to the window or icon where you want the document or folder added, so the outline of the document or folder is in the window or the icon's name is highlighted, and release the button.

If the folder or disk containing the original is on the *same* disk as where you dragged the document or folder, 1-2-3 moves the document or folder. If the folder or disk containing the original is on a *different* disk than the folder or disk where you dragged the document or folder from, 1-2-3 copies the document or folder. If you want to copy a document or folder from one location to another on the same disk, press the (option) key as you drag the document or folder to the second window.

You can also make a copy of a document or folder in the same location as the original by choosing Duplicate in the File menu. The duplicate will have the same name as the original, preceded by "Copy of". This is another option for copying documents or folders to another location on the same disk.

Renaming Documents and Folders

The Macintosh puts very few restrictions for what you use for document, folder, and disk names. You can modify or enter a new name for a document, folder, and disk. To rename a document, folder, or disk, select the icon for the document, folder, or disk and type the new name. With System 7, you must wait until the box around the current name appears before you make any changes.

Creating Folders

To create a folder, open the window you want to contain the folder and choose New Folder in the File menu. An empty folder called Empty Folder is created, which you can rename by typing the new name. Once the folder is created, you can add documents and other folders to it.

Ejecting Floppy Disks

When ejecting a floppy disk, you need to tell 1-2-3 to remove the disk from the desktop rather than merely ejecting the disk. To remove a floppy disk from the desktop, select it and drag it to the Trash until the Trash icon is highlighted. The disk will be ejected (*not* erased) so you can put another disk in the drive. If you use the Eject command in the File menu, you still have the disk icon on the desktop although it is shaded to indicate that it is removed. Using Eject to remove floppy disks from the disk drive is a bad idea because later the Macintosh may prompt you to reinsert the disk and it may no longer be readily available.

Initializing a Floppy Disk

Before you can save data to a floppy disk, the disk must be *initialized.* Initializing a disk prepares it to store data. When you initialize a disk, any data that was on it before is lost. To initialize a disk, follow these steps:

1. Put a floppy disk in the disk drive.

You will see a dialog box that lets you select whether to eject or initialize the disk. The way the disk is initialized depends on your selection and the capacity of the disk. High capacity disks, which have two notches opposite the disk cover, can be initialized as 1.4 MB on a SuperDrive or as 800K or 400K. Regular disks, which only have one notch, can be initialized as 400K (one-sided) or 800K (two-sided).

2. Click the Initialize (for 1.4MB disks), One-Sided, or Two-Sided button to initialize the disk.
3. Click the Erase button to confirm that you will erase any information on the disk.
4. Type a name for the floppy disk and click the OK button.

After the disk is initialized, you will see the icon and name for the floppy disk added to the desktop. If you want to reinitialize a disk and erase its current contents, choose Erase Disk in the Special menu and then repeat steps 2 through 4.

The Macintosh does not recognize IBM formatted disks and an IBM PC will not read the disks that you initialize on a Macintosh. The exception is when you use the Apple File Exchange or another utility to transfer information between your Macintosh and IBM formatted disks as described in Chapter 13, "Advanced Techniques."

Index

A

B

C

E

F

K

L

M

N

O

P

Q

R

S

T

U

V

W

X

Y

Z